Lecture Notes in Computer Science 9963

Commenced Publication in 1973
Founding and Former Series Editors:
Gerhard Goos, Juris Hartmanis, and Jan van Leeuwen

More information about this series at http://www.springer.com/series/7410

Giovanni Livraga · Vicenç Torra
Alessandro Aldini · Fabio Martinelli
Neeraj Suri (Eds.)

Data Privacy Management and Security Assurance

11th International Workshop, DPM 2016
and 5th International Workshop, QASA 2016
Heraklion, Crete, Greece, September 26–27, 2016
Proceedings

 Springer

Editors
Giovanni Livraga
Università degli Studi di Milano
Crema
Italy

Vicenç Torra
University of Skövde
Skovde
Sweden

Alessandro Aldini
University of Urbino
Urbino
Italy

Fabio Martinelli
IIT National Research Council CNR
Pisa
Italy

Neeraj Suri
Technische Universität Darmstadt
Darmstadt
Germany

ISSN 0302-9743   ISSN 1611-3349 (electronic)
Lecture Notes in Computer Science
ISBN 978-3-319-47071-9   ISBN 978-3-319-47072-6 (eBook)
DOI 10.1007/978-3-319-47072-6

Library of Congress Control Number: 2016952826

LNCS Sublibrary: SL4 – Security and Cryptology

Printed on acid-free paper

This Springer imprint is published by Springer Nature
The registered company is Springer International Publishing AG
The registered company address is: Gewerbestrasse 11, 6330 Cham, Switzerland

Foreword from the DPM 2016 Program Chairs

This volume contains the proceedings of the 11th International Workshop on Data Privacy Management (DPM 2016), held in Heraklion, Crete, Greece, on September 26–27, 2016, in conjunction with the 21st European Symposium On Research In Computer Security (ESORICS 2016). The DPM series started in 2005 when the first workshop took place in Tokyo (Japan). Since then, the event has been held every year in different venues: Atlanta, USA (2006), Istanbul, Turkey (2007), Saint Malo, France (2009), Athens, Greece (2010), Leuven, Belgium (2011), Pisa, Italy (2012), Egham, UK (2013), Wroclaw, Poland (2014), and Vienna, Austria (2015).

The aim of DPM is to promote and stimulate international collaboration and research exchange in areas related to the management of privacy-sensitive information. This is a very critical and important issue for organizations and end-users. It poses several challenging problems, such as translation of high-level business goals into system-level privacy policies, administration of sensitive identifiers, data integration and privacy engineering, among others.

In response to the call for papers of this edition, 24 submissions were received and each of them was evaluated on the basis of significance, novelty, and technical quality. The Program Committee, comprising 39 members, performed an excellent task and with the help of additional reviewers all submissions went through a careful anonymous review process (three or more reviews per submission). The Program Committee's work was carried out electronically, yielding intensive discussions. Of the submitted papers, the Program Committee accepted nine full papers (resulting in an acceptance rate of 37.5 %) and four short papers for presentation at the workshop.

The success of DPM 2016 depends on the volunteering effort of many individuals, and there is a long list of people who deserve special thanks. We would like to thank all the members of the Program Committee and all the external reviewers, for all their hard work in evaluating the papers in a short time window, and for their active participation in the discussion and selection process. We would like to express our gratitude to the ESORICS 2016 organizers for their support in the organization of the workshop. Our gratitude goes to Pierangela Samarati, Steering Committee chair of the ESORICS Symposium, for all her arrangements that made possible the satellite events, and Javier Lopez, the workshops chair of ESORICS 2016. We would also like to thank the keynote speakers for accepting our invitation and for their enlightening talks.

Last but certainly not least, our thanks goes to all the authors who submitted papers and to all the attendees of the workshop. We hope you find the program of DPM 2016 interesting, stimulating, and inspiring for your future research.

September 2016

Giovanni Livraga
Vicenç Torra

11th International Workshop on Data Privacy Management – DPM 2016

Program Chairs

Giovanni Livraga	Università degli Studi di Milano, Italy
Vicenç Torra	University of Skövde, Sweden

Steering Committee

Josep Domingo-Ferrer	Universitat Rovira i Virgili, Spain
Joaquin Garcia-Alfaro	Telecom SudParis, France
Guillermo Navarro-Arribas	Autonomous University of Barcelona, Spain
Vicenç Torra	University of Skövde, Sweden

Program Committee

Ken Barker	University of Calgary, Canada
Michele Bezzi	SAP, France
Jordi Casas-Roma	Universitat Oberta de Catalunya, Spain
Jordi Castellà-Roca	Universitat Rovira i Virgili, Spain
Jorge Cuéllar	Siemens AG, Germany
Frédéric Cuppens	Telecom Bretagne, France
Nora Cuppens	Telecom Bretagne, France
Sabrina De Capitani di Vimercati	Università degli Studi di Milano, Italy
Josep Domingo-Ferrer	Universitat Rovira i Virgili, Spain
Vladimir Estivill-Castro	Griffith University, Australia
Carmen Fernandez-Gago	University of Málaga, Spain
Simone Fischer-Hübner	Karlstad University, Sweden
Sara Foresti	Università degli Studi di Milano, Italy
Steve Furnell	Plymouth University, UK
Sébastien Gambs	University of Rennes, France
Joaquin Garcia-Alfaro	Telecom SudParis, France
Stefanos Gritzalis	University of the Aegean, Greece
Javier Herranz	Universitat Politècnica de Catalunya, Spain
Jordi Herrera-Joancomarti	Universitat Autònoma de Barcelona, Spain
Marc Juarez	Katholieke Universiteit Leuven, Belgium
Sokratis Katsikas	Giøvik University College, Norway
Florian Kerschbaum	SAP, Germany
Hiroaki Kikuchi	Tokai University, Japan

Jiguo Li	Hohai University, China
Traian Marius-Truta	Northern Kentucky University, USA
Fabio Martinelli	IIT-CNR, Italy
Chris Mitchell	Royal Holloway, UK
Atsuko Miyaji	JAIST, Japan
Anna Monreale	University of Pisa, Italy
Melek Önen	EURECOM, France
Gerardo Pelosi	Politecnico di Milano, Italy
Cristina Pérez-Solà	Universitat Autonoma de Barcelona, Spain
Silvio Ranise	FBK Security and Trust Unit, Italy
Pierangela Samarati	Università degli Studi di Milano, Italy
Andreas Schaad	Huawei, Germany
Matthias Templ	Vienna University of Technology, Austria
Yasuyuki Tsukada	NTT Communication Science Labs, Japan
Edgar Weippl	SBA Research/TU Wien, Austria
Lena Wiese	University of Göttingen, Germany

External Reviewers

Giovanni Agosta
Daniel Ricardo Dos Santos
Andreas Fischer
Benny Fuhry
Paolo Guarda
Christos Kalloniatis
Javier Parra-Arnau
Jordi Ribes-González
Fatemeh Shirazi

Maria Sideri
Hari Siswantoro
Chunhua Su
Thao Tran
Aggeliki Tsohou
Tim Waage
Benjamin Weggenmann
Artsiom Yautsiukhin

Foreword from the QASA 2016 Program Chairs

This proceedings volume contains the papers presented at QASA 2016: the 5th International Workshop in Quantitative Aspects in Security Assurance, held during September 26–27, 2016 in Heraklion, as an affiliated event of ESORICS 2016, and in cooperation with DPM.

The QASA workshop series responds to the increasing demand for techniques to deal with quantitative aspects of security assurance at several levels of the development life-cycle of systems and services, from requirements elicitation to run-time operation and maintenance. The aim of QASA is to bring together researchers and practitioners interested in these research topics with a particular emphasis on the techniques for service-oriented architectures. The scope of the workshop is intended to be broad, including aspects as dependability, privacy, risk, and trust.

QASA 2016 received eight submissions, each one reviewed by at least three Program Committee members. The committee decided to accept three full papers and one short one for the proceedings.

The presentations and the discussions during the workshop showed that the area of quantitative security, in its many facets, is an active and interesting field of research.

We would like to thank the authors of submitted papers, the members of the Program Committee, the external reviewers, and the sponsors, namely, the EU projects NeCS and the IFIP WG 11.14 (NESSoS) on Secure Engineering. We are also grateful for the use of the EasyChair platform, which offered an effective and clear way of managing the entire review process as well as the proceedings production. Finally, we are also grateful to the ESORICS 2016 organization team for providing the venue for QASA2016.

September 2016

Alessandro Aldini
Fabio Martinelli
Neeraj Suri

5th International Workshop on Quantitative Aspects in Security Assurance – QASA 2016

Workshop Chairs

Alessandro Aldini	University of Urbino, Italy
Fabio Martinelli	IIT-CNR, Italy
Neeraj Suri	TU Darmstadt, Germany

Program Committee

Habtamu Abie	Norsk Regnesentral, Norway
Marijke Coetzee	University of Johannesburg, South Africa
Jorge Cuellar	Siemens, Germany
Joaquin Garcia-Alfaro	Telecom SudParis, France
Sotiris Ioannidis	Forth, Greece
Michaela Iorga	NIST, USA
Mohamed Kaaniche	LAAS-CNRS, France
Giovanni Livraga	University of Milan, Italy
Javier Lopez	University of Malaga, Spain
Jesus Luna	CSA, Germany
Ilaria Matteucci	CNR-IIT Pisa, Italy
Martin Ochoa	Singapore University of Technology, Singapore
Juha Röning	University of Oulu, Finland
Einar Snekkenes	Gjøvik University College, Norway
Ruben Trapero	TU Darmstadt, Germany

Contents

Security and Secure Applications

DPM Short Papers

Quantitative Aspects in Security Assurance

Metrics for Transparency

Dayana Spagnuelo, Cesare Bartolini, and Gabriele Lenzini(✉)

Interdisciplinary Centre for Security Reliability and Trust (SnT),
University of Luxembourg, Luxembourg, Luxembourg
{dayana.spagnuelo,cesare.bartolini,gabriele.lenzini}@uni.lu

Abstract. Transparency is a novel non-functional requirement for software systems. It is acclaimed to improve the quality of service since it gives users access to information concerning the system's processes, clarifying who is responsible if something goes wrong. Thus, it is believed to support people's right to a secure and private processing of their personal data. We define eight quality metrics for transparency and we demonstrate the usage and the effectiveness of the metrics by assessing transparency on the Microsoft HealthVault, an on-line platform for users to collect, store, and share medical records.

Keywords: Transparency · Metrics · Non-functional requirements · Requirements engineering · Quality factors

1 Introduction

Transparency is defined as a quality that enables users to get informed of what will happen or what happened to their data [3,22]. When users of an IT system have an interest in being informed on how the system manages data, and in particular their personal data, transparency ensures an open policy about the system's functioning and processing information. Transparency is a non-functional requirement (NFR) that is believed to increase the quality of a service.

Transparency is also key in achieving privacy and personal data protection. It cannot *per se* guarantee confidentiality, but it can promote to have clear and transparent privacy policies or the availability of mechanisms that users can use to verify whether a system works as intended or as declared or to find who is accountable otherwise. This very perspective of having clear and transparent data protection policies is one of the founding principles of the new European General Data Protection Regulation (GDPR).

Transparency can be suitably expressed as a requirement in Requirements Engineering (RE). RE offers techniques and tools to specify, model, represent, implement, measure, and track functional and non-functional requirements of a system. The so-called non-functional requirements (NFRs), rather than describing *what* a system does, specify *how* the system performs in terms of costs, performance, reliability, maintainability, portability, robustness, usability and the

D. Spagnuelo—Supported by FNR/AFR project 7842804 TYPAMED.

© Springer International Publishing AG 2016
G. Livraga et al. (Eds.): DPM and QASA 2016, LNCS 9963, pp. 3–18, 2016.
DOI: 10.1007/978-3-319-47072-6_1

like [6]. Transparency falls into this category. As a NFR, it can be modelled and expressed in formal terms, but it has so many facets that modelling transparency requires approaches that differ somewhat from those already available for other NFRs. This is why we believe that resorting to RE practices may help model transparency and, in principle, it would be possible to introduce transparency as a requirement in the Systems Development Life Cycle (SDLC). Extending RE methodologies in order to encompass transparency as a new requirement is an activity that can be performed at several different levels, each requiring different processes [21]. Here, we focus on requirement *modelling* and *validation*.

Modelling transparency requires representing it in some formalism. A preliminary model of transparency has been presented in [22]. Validation means to measure whether and up to which degree a system provides transparency. This is usually the task of software metrics. In the control of software quality, they introduce a more formal and less subjective [15] assessment. We need metrics to describe and measure transparency.

We propose eight metrics that measure the degree of transparency of a system.

Outline. Section 2 qualifies transparency in IT and surveys the related literature. Section 3 outlines the methodology that we use to classify and define metrics for the main factors of transparency. Section 4 defines and comments the mathematical functions that we can use to measure each of the selected factors. Section 5 applies the proposed metrics to an actual system. Section 6 concludes the paper and suggests future research.

2   Related Work

We have already determined in [22] that transparency means mainly to provide 1. *information* (e.g., data or evidence) on how a user's personal data will be handled or has been handled by the system; and 2. *mechanisms* (e.g., apps, plug-in) to assist the users in retrieving and presenting that information. In [22] we present 41 requirements that define transparency, but without suggesting how one can validate their implementation.

To this aim non-functional metrics [18] can help but not all NFRs can be expressed in terms that allows them to be easily measured [12,24]. The definition of metrics for validating software quality is an activity which has been the subject of attention. In particular, a standard [15] defines a methodology for defining metrics. We follow that methodology here.

What features metrics should have in order to provide useful results is clearly explained in [16], while the correctness of software metrics for specific NFRs can be validated using formal methods [20]: maintainability [7], re-usability [4] or reliability [1], safety and redundancy [11] have all been subject of formal analysis.

Unfortunately these metrics are not defining transparency. Metrics for transparency can be found in software design for control applications. Here an algorithm is considered transparent if "it is easy and clear to see what the controller does in the moment and what it will do in the next steps" [11]. However, these metrics are not applicable in our context, because they are intended to measure inputs, outputs, and the graphical representation of an algorithm.

A possible quest for metrics for transparency may look at the factors that have been proposed to qualify transparency. For instance [23], while studying requirements for trust and other trust-terms, describe transparency as an attribute that requires the *observability* of several types of *data* concerning the users. In our work [22], these trust-terms correspond to the attribute *instrument*. No metrics is discussed, but both the works indicate the terms to be considered when defining a criterion to measure transparency.

Metrics for transparency exist in eGovernment [25], where transparency is discussed as a way of assessing accountability and qualified for efficiency, effectiveness and accessibility of the volume of information that public administrators provide to users. A potential metric for transparency is defined as "the percentage of processes on which there is information available for users". A metric for efficiency is defined in terms of the time a user spends to use a service and in terms of the time spent by the organisation to produce the service. Effectiveness is regarded as "the closeness to user needs and expectations", and the authors suggest that it can be measured considering the presence (or absence) of complaints. These are all valid suggestions for metrics, despite none of them is expressed formally.

3   Methodology

We adopt the methodology presented in the IEEE standard 1061 [15]. It consists of five steps that should be followed to define software metrics: 1. establish requirements, 2. identify metrics, 3. implement the metrics, 4. analyse them, and finally 5. validate them. Step 1 has been carried out in [22]. Steps 2 to 5 are considered here.

Transparency is a multi-faceted concept, and assigning direct metrics for it would end up in a very coarse assessment. Instead, following the suggestion of the IEEE standard, we first identify the quality *factors* and quality *sub-factors* that contribute to establishing transparency. Then, building on top of previous NFR literature, we search for suitable qualities that define the factors and the sub-factors identified. Eventually, we propose and assign metrics for those qualities. As an assistance for this task, we first build a questionnaire whose goal is to clarify how to decide when a quality is to be considered satisfied.

The search for quality factors that help define transparency does not present any difficulty. As stated in Sect. 2, implementing transparency means to provide information and mechanisms. These are the *instruments* required to achieve transparency. The search for quality sub-factors required a review of the literature for software qualities and NFRs [5,6,19,25]. Four major sub-factors appear relevant: informativeness, understandability, accessibility, and validity. The first three refine the "providing information" factor, whereas the last two refine the "providing mechanisms" factor. Accessibility related to both factors.

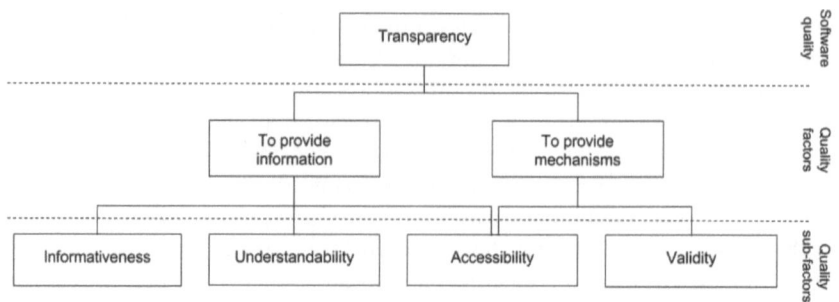

Fig. 1. Transparency and its factors and sub-factors

Informativeness concerns the ability of conveying a good quality of information, and helps understand the excellence of the information provided. *Understandability* represents the ability of "achieving a comprehensible meaning". It is also connected to the provision of information once it explores the linguistic quality of an instrument. *Accessibility*, here in the sense of "being easy to obtain", is a quality that refers to both categories of instruments. Since the instrument expresses the act of providing something, it must be easy for a user to obtain it, regardless of whether this something is information or mechanisms. *Validity*, here in the sense of "being precise and producing the correct result", is linked with the provision of mechanisms, and defines how sound the mechanism is in doing its job. Figure 1 summarises the selected factors and sub-factors.

The questionnaire that we used to find out how to assess whether each quality is satisfied or not is reported in Table 1. We defined the questions on the basis of the definitions and descriptions found while exploring the literature. To maintain a high level of granularity, where necessary, questions are partitioned into sub-questions.

Not all of the questions correspond to some metric. Questions whose answer may vary depending on the user's perceptions, such as question 3, have been disregarded. Instead, questions that admit objective answers (the grey boxes in Table 1) have been assigned metrics to measure the corresponding factors and sub-factors. The metrics are discussed in details in the next section.

4   Metrics

The eight metrics that we propose are: *accuracy* (questions 1 and 1.1); *currentness* (question 2 and 2.1); *conciseness* (question 5); *detailing* (question 6); *readability* (question 7); *availability* (questions 9 and 9.1); *portability* (questions 10 and 10.1–10.3); and *effectiveness* (questions 11 and 11.2).

4.1   The Eight Metrics

Table 2 shows the metrics associated with the transparency sub-factors. All the metrics are normalised, ranging from 0 (worst value) to 1 (best value).

Table 1. Qualities questionnaire. The questions in grey cells have led to metrics

Factor	Question	Sub-question
Informativeness	1. Is the system providing accurate information?	1.1. Is the system providing consistent and flawless information?
	2. Is the system providing up-to-date information?	2.1. Is the system providing timely information?
	3. Is the information consistent to what the user experiences?	
	4. Is the system providing unbiased information?	
Understandability	5. Is the system providing the minimum possible information for the understanding of the matter?	
	6. Is the system providing enough details on the information for the understanding of the matter?	
	7. Is the system helping the user to understand the information provided?	
	8. Is the system providing clear and neat information?	8.1. Is the system providing information using the terminology appropriate to the area?
		8.2. Is the system providing information that does not use jargon?
Accessibility	9. Is the system making the instrument available?	9.1. Is the system providing an instrument that can be used whenever needed?
	10. Is the system providing portable information?	10.1. Is the system providing information that can be used in different environments?
		10.2. Is the system providing information that can be extracted in different formats?
		10.3. Is the system providing information that can be accessed through different means?
Validity	11. Is the system providing correct and precise mechanism?	11.1. Is the system providing ways to verify a mechanism?
		11.2. Is the system providing a mechanism that reaches the goal for which it has been provided?
		11.3. Is the system providing the source code of the mechanism?

Accuracy. This metric measures how much the information provided matches the real process of the system. The metric demands statements extracted from the information to be observed in the real system. To measure accuracy, we must

Table 2. Metrics associated to quality sub-factors

Sub-factor	Metric Name		Sub-factor	Metric Name
Informativeness	Accuracy		Accessibility	Availability
	Currentness			Portability
Understandability	Conciseness		Validity	Effectiveness
	Detailing			
	Readability			

first define what is considered a statement. Statements are going to depend on the nature of the information, but we suggest that at least claims and affirmations about what the system is or does should be considered. A representation of the system's process (for example, a model such as a business diagram) might also be considered, as it may help in the assessment of accuracy.

Each statement should be linked (mapped) to some part of the process. If it is not possible to link the statement, either because it is not present, or because it is dubious, then the information should not be considered accurate. The result is the proportion of accurate statements. If LS is the number of statements that can be linked to some parts of the process, and NLS is the number of statements which do not correspond to a specific part of the process, then accuracy $\mathcal{A}c$ can be expressed as shown in Eq. (1).

$$\mathcal{A}c = \frac{LS}{LS + NLS} \tag{1}$$

Currentness. Currentness depends on the time that passes between something happening in the system and the system providing information about it. More specifically, if Δt is the interval of time that the system has taken to inform about the change, and Δt_u is a time unit that measures the reasonable interval time (i.e., the ideal time) for updating that piece of information, the currentness is measured as shown in Eq. (2).

$$\mathcal{C}u = \begin{cases} 1, & \text{if } \Delta t \leq \Delta t_u \\ 2^{-\lfloor \frac{\Delta t - \Delta t_u}{\Delta t_u} \rfloor}, & \text{if } \Delta t > \Delta t_u. \end{cases} \tag{2}$$

In other words, anything that takes less time than what would be deemed ideally reasonable for that information has $\mathcal{C}u = 1$.

It should be noted that while some pieces of information should be updated in a matter of minutes or hours (e.g., information on security breaches), for others a longer time would be acceptable (e.g., results of a research with patients). The time unit Δt_u is highly dependent on the nature of the system and of the type of information that must be updated, and must be carefully chosen for each case. A poorly chosen unit will result in inaccurate currentness values.

The floor function in the exponential simplifies the metric by providing discrete values (e.g., anything in the time range $\Delta t_u \leq \Delta t < 2\Delta t_u$ has the same currentness value). Let us consider an example in which an information is extremely relevant, for example because it concerns a security breach, and the time unit Δt_u is defined as one minute. If the system takes one hour ($\Delta t_u = 60$) for updating the information, then the currentness is $Cu = 2^{-60} \simeq 0$. On the other hand, if the acceptable range is 30 min, then this duration can be used as the time unit, and the currentness is $Cu = 2^{-\lfloor \frac{60-30}{30} \rfloor} = 2^{-1} = 0.5$.

Conciseness. The conciseness metric measures how straightforward an information is. We measure the conciseness of an information in terms of the average number of words per sentence. The scales of this metric are based on recommendations for the English language. While [8] suggests that the average length of sentences should be between 15 and 20, it is stated in [13] that an average of 5 to 8 words per sentence can be read by people with moderate learning disabilities, and that by using common words it is possible to help all users to understand a sentence with around 25 words. For this reason, we use a Gaussian curve $N(\mu, \sigma^2)$, with a mean $\mu = 20$ and a standard deviation $\sigma = 5$, as expressed in Eq. (3). However, we normalise this function so that its maximum value is one. The resulting formula for measuring the conciseness is shown in Eq. (4). Here ASL denotes the average number of words per sentence, and it is calculated as N_W/N_S, where N_W is the total number of words, and N_S is the total number of sentences.

$$N(\mu, \sigma^2) = \frac{c^{-\frac{1}{2\sigma^2}(x-\mu)^2}}{\sigma\sqrt{2\pi}} \tag{3}$$

$$Co = \sigma\sqrt{2\pi}N(\mu, \sigma^2) = e^{-\frac{1}{50}(ASL-20)^2} \tag{4}$$

We understand that conciseness is not only about short sentences, and that semantics analysis should be considered too. What is presented here, however, is an easy-to-calculate approximation for syntactic straightforwardness.

Detailing. This metric describes a strategy for measuring whether an information provided is detailed enough for the general understanding of its subject. Detailing is measured by checking if the main crucial details are present in the instrument "information" that the system provides. The crucial details will vary from instrument to instrument, but we suggest that, at least, basic questions should be answered, such as: what? who? why? when? to whom? which? and so on. The information provided has to be cross-checked with the questions, and the result is a matrix of details provided versus important details. The metric $\mathcal{D}$ is the proportion of important details provided.

The detailing matrix should be constructed in such a way that only the questions pertinent to a given piece of information are counted towards the proportion. For example, assuming the system must inform the users on how their data are stored and who has access to them, questions like "why [is the data accessed]?" and "when [was the data stored]?" are not pertinent.

If n_I is the number of pieces of information provided, and m_Q is the total number of detailing questions, the detailing matrix has a size of $n_I \times m_Q$. For each piece of information $i = 1 \ldots n_I$, there will be a number P_i^D of questions pertinent to the detailing metric, and a number $NP_i^D = m_Q - P_i^D$ of non-pertinent questions. The non-pertinent questions are not relevant and therefore do not count towards the metrics. On the other hand, the pertinent questions can be partitioned into a number d_i of questions for which the details are provided, and a number u_i of questions for which details are not provided, such that $d_i + u_i = P_i^D$. Under these premises, the detailing metrics $\mathcal{D}$ can be expressed as shown in Eq. (5).

$$\mathcal{D} = \frac{\sum_{i=1}^{n_I} d_i}{\sum_{i=1}^{n_I} P_i^D} = 1 - \frac{\sum_{i=1}^{n_I} u_i}{\sum_{i=1}^{n_I} P_i^D} \tag{5}$$

A highly-detailed system ($\mathcal{D} = 1$) will possibly answer all pertinent questions for each piece of information.

Readability. This metric measures how easy it is for a user to read and understand a specific text. There are several well-established formulas available for this purpose. Each formula has its advantages and there are no general recommendations or standards stating which one should be used in each case. To select the formula, we searched the literature to understand how to measure readability in the medical domain (the domain used for our requirements). The most used formulas are the Flesch-Kincaid grade level (FKGL), the Simple Measure Of Gobbledygook (SMOG), and the Flesch Reading Ease (FRES) [9,14,17,26]. FKGL and FRES are variants of the same method, and both use the average sentence length and the average word length as an input. SMOG is calculated using the number of long words (three syllables or more). We chose to use FRES for being the only one that provides the results in easiness grades.

As already introduced in *conciseness* metric, the average sentence length is measured as $ASL = N_W/N_S$, where N_W is the total number of words and N_S is the total number of sentences. Similarly, the average number of syllables per word is $ASW = N_{SY}/N_W$, where N_{SY} is the total number of syllables. The *FRES* can be expressed as shown in Eq. (6). In theory, the higher boundary of the *FRES* is 121.22, which is achieved by applying it to a sentence with one word of one syllable, like "yes" or "no". There is no theoretical lower boundary, but by applying the formula to long sentences with long words it is possible to reach huge negative scores. However, such extremes are non-realistic in the documentation of a system. The common interpretation of *FRES* considers scores from 0 to 100 only [10]. As a measure of the readability metric $\mathcal{R}$, we consider the bounded and normalised *FRES*, as shown in Eq. (7).

$$FRES = 206.835 - (1.015 \times ASL) - (84.6 \times ASW) \tag{6}$$

$$\mathcal{R} = \begin{cases} 0, & \text{if } FRES < 0 \\ \frac{FRES}{100}, & \text{if } 0 \le FRES \le 100 \\ 1, & \text{if } FRES > 100 \end{cases} \tag{7}$$

Availability. This metric measures how easy it is for a user to access the instrument, if accessible at all. To measure the availability $\mathcal{A}v$, we first define N_{int} as the number of interactions the user needs to perform to reach the desired instrument. An interaction is considered as any action the user must perform, such as typing, clicks, taps, slides, etc. Availability applies to any sort of information or mechanisms the system provides, and we define its metric as follows:

$$\mathcal{A}v = \begin{cases} 1 - \frac{(1-\omega)}{k} N_{\text{int}}, & \text{if } 0 \leq N_{\text{int}} \leq k \\ \omega e^{(1 - \frac{N_{\text{int}}}{k})}, & \text{if } N_{\text{int}} > k \end{cases} \tag{8}$$

Here k is the maximum number of interactions that are considered acceptable for reaching access, while $\omega \in [0,1]$ is the grade that we give when accessing the instrument takes exactly k steps. Equation (8) degrades linearly from the maximum value 1, obtained when no steps are required to get access to the instrument, till value ω, obtained when k steps are required to get access to the instrument. From that point on, the degradation is exponential in the number of steps.

Portability. This metric measures how easy it is for an information to be transferred and used in different systems. To measure portability, we reused the popular classification provided by the 5 star open data [2], which is a scheme for rating the degree of structuredness of data on the web. It is a model that uses an incremental scale from 1 to 5. To measure how portable an information is, we need to verify whether the properties described in each scale are implemented. We adapted the scale and normalised it to our context as shown in Eq. (9).

$$\mathcal{P} = \begin{cases} 0, & \text{if no information available} \\ 0.2, & \text{if available in any open format} \\ 0.4, & \text{if available as a structured data} \\ 0.6, & \text{if available in a non-proprietary format} \\ 0.8, & \text{if uses URI} \\ 1, & \text{if based on linked data} \end{cases} \tag{9}$$

Effectiveness. This metric measures how satisfactory the mechanism provided is. The strategy is very similar to the one presented in Eq. (5). Effectiveness is measured by checking whether the goal of the mechanisms is being reached. The goal varies according to the requirements, but we suggest that the output of the mechanism addresses at least basic questions, such as: what? who? why? when?

If n_I is the number of pieces of information provided as the output, and m_Q is the total number of questions, the effectiveness matrix has a size of $n_I \times m_Q$. For each piece of information $i = 1 \dots n_I$, there will be a number P_i^E of questions pertinent to the effectiveness metric, and a number $NP_i^E = m_Q - P_i^E$ of non-pertinent questions. The pertinent questions can be partitioned into a number

e_i of questions whose goal is reached, and a number v_i of questions whose goal is not reached, such that $e_i + v_i = P_i^E$. Under these premises, the efficiency metrics $\mathcal{E}$ can be expressed as shown in Eq. (10).

$$\mathcal{E} = \frac{\sum_{i=1}^{n_I} e_i}{\sum_{i=1}^{n_I} P_i^E} = 1 - \frac{\sum_{i=1}^{n_I} v_i}{\sum_{i=1}^{n_I} P_i^E} \qquad (10)$$

4.2   Synthesis

Although normalised and aligned on the same ranges, the metrics proposed are heterogeneous and cannot easily be combined into a mathematical expression that can clearly measure transparency as a whole. Instead, we adopt a benchmarking strategy, where each of the proposed metrics serves to assess the performance of one or more of the factors that determine the transparency quality.

The benchmark can be represented as a radar chart (an example is shown in Fig. 2). The blue area represents the best possible measurement for the factor "providing information", while the orange area shows the best outcomes for the factor "providing mechanisms". The metric "availability" appears twice in the chart because it is applicable to both factors.

The metrics we present are potentially applicable to any transparency requirement. In the context of our previous work [22], for example, our eight metrics apply to each of the 41 requirements according to what instrument the requirement is about. That means that for a complete assessment of transparency we may need to apply these metrics to each requirement. The interpretation of these results, regardless of the context in which transparency is desired, should provide insights on the factors and requirements that have room for improvement, and guide the way to a better transparency.

5   Use Case

Microsoft HealthVault[1] is an integrated online platform that allows users to gather, store and share health information. The information in HealthVault can be: provided by the user, in which case the system acts as the means for the user to fill in his/her personal and medical data, or to upload files with any kind of medical record in it; provided by compatible health applications, since the system can use information provided by external mobile or web applications whenever authorised by the user; or provided by compatible health devices, as the system can also use information collected by specific compatible health devices, such blood pressure monitors, weight scales, and others. To evaluate the applicability of our metrics in Microsoft HealthVault we choose two transparency requirements: 1. "S must provide P with disclosure of policies, regulations or terms concerning data sharing, processing and the use of data"; and 2. "S must provide P with accountability mechanisms" [22]; where S stands for "the system" and P for "the patient", or (in our example) "the user".

---

[1] https://www.healthvault.com/lu/en.

To implement the first functionality, HealthVault provides a dedicated section called "Microsoft Privacy Statement" concerning the personal and medical data. To test for *accuracy* we selected only the section of the privacy statement that directly addresses the peculiarities of HealthVault that are not common to other Microsoft products. That section contains information on signing in, on the account and records, on sharing health data, on reporting to health care providers in the US, on access and control, and on email communications. We chose the main statement for each of those topics: 1. "You can use more than one credential with HealthVault to help ensure continued access"; 2. "You can add or remove data to a health record you manage at any time"; 3. "As a custodian, you can share data in a health record with another person by sending an email invitation through HealthVault. You can specify what type of access they have (including custodian access), how long they have access, and whether they can modify the data in the record"; 4. "In the United States, we enable participating providers to obtain reports about whether the information they send to a record is used"; 5. "You can review, edit or delete your HealthVault account data, or close your HealthVault account at any time"; and 6. "You can unsubscribe from these emails [communications] at any time".

Statements 2, 3, 5 and 6 could be easily verified, as for each of those the system contains areas available to the users. There is also a specific area for managing the credentials, but the only option offered is to use the Microsoft credentials (at least in the version of the system available in Europe), which invalidates statement 1. Statement 4 could not be verified as it is only valid in the United States, and so it is not considered in the calculation. As a result we have $\mathcal{A}c = 0.8$.

Microsoft HealthVault provides no information on how long they take to update the privacy statement once something has changed in the policy. Although they inform when was the last time the statements changed and what exactly has changed, we do not have enough information to calculate *currentness* metric. Thus currentness metric is not measurable without access to the internal system.

The privacy statements from HealthVault score very high in *conciseness*. In average, sentences are 17.71 words long, slightly less than the mean considered in the metric. This value, applied to Eq. (4), provides a conciseness value of $\mathcal{C}o \simeq 0.90$. Although HealthVault has a good score for conciseness, the *FRES* formula only results in 36.02 when applied to the privacy statements. This value indicates that the text is reasonably difficult to understand; applied to Eq. (7), it provides a readability $\mathcal{R} \simeq 0.36$.

The *detailing* metric can be calculated considering the purpose for which the information has been made available. In this case, the users must be informed of the policies and regulations for data sharing, processing and usage of the data. So the privacy statement should ideally help the users understand: whether the data is shared, with whom, and for what purpose; whether the data is processed and for what purpose; how is the data used and for what purpose. Relevantly for this requirement, the privacy statement provides information separated into the

Table 3. Detailing matrix: desirable details compared with the delivered details. Greyed-out cells represent the non-pertinent questions.

	Delivered Details					
Desired Details	DWC	UPD	SPD	CST	IPI	MHS
Is data shared? With whom? For what purpose?			✓			
Is data processed? For what purpose?	✓	✓				
How is data used? For what purpose?				✓	✓	✓

following categories: Personal Data We Collect (DWC); How We Use Personal Data (UPD); Reasons We Share Personal Data (SPD); Cookies and Similar Technologies (CST); Other Important Privacy Information (IPI); and Microsoft Health Services (MHS). We use a three letters identifier to simplify Table 3. The detailing metric reaches the maximum score $\mathcal{D} = 1$, as all the desired details are provided by the privacy statement.

To measure *availability*, we first need to define the maximum number of acceptable interactions k, and the grade ω we attribute for k. For this example, we chose $k = 3$ and set its grade $\omega = 0.7$. To access these data, users simply need to access the "Privacy & Cookies" section available through the main page of the system. As the user needs only one interaction to reach the desired content, the availability metric reaches the score: $\mathcal{A}v = 0.9$.

Regarding the *portability* of the privacy statement section, HealthVault scores the value $\mathcal{P} = 0.8$. Applying Eq. (9), we have the following: the information is provided in HTML, an open format; since it is presented as HTML, it is also structured, and available in a non-proprietary format; the information is available on the web and can be accessed through a Uniform Resource Locator (URL), which is a subset of a Uniform Resource Identifier (URI). Although the statement contains several links to other data that provide a better understanding, these do not provide access to external data sources and cannot be considered linked data.

The second requirement "S must provide P with accountability mechanisms" is implemented by Microsoft HealthVault by providing a way for users to consult the history of accesses and changes made on their data up to one year ago. They can see the changes made by one specific person or application, or even see the history of granted access rights. These functions are centralised in a section called "Record History" that can be accessed with one click from the main page, provided the user is already logged in the system. Considering the same parameters $k = 3$ and $\omega = 0.7$, Microsoft HealthVault reaches again the score $\mathcal{A}v = 0.9$ in the *availability* metric with regard to this requirement.

Finally, in our example, we claim that HealthVault provides accountability mechanisms by making a "Record History" available to their users. For a mechanism to be effective in helping a user hold a person accountable for an action, it requires some means to check what actions happened in the system with regard to the user's data; who did the action; when the action happened;

Table 4. Effectiveness matrix: desired goals compared with the real outputs. Grey cells represent the non pertinent questions.

Desired Goals	Delivered Outputs					
	Date	Action	Type	Changed by	App	Summary
What action?		✓	✓		✓	✓
Who did it?				✓	✓	
When did it happen?	✓					
For what purpose?						

and the purpose of the action. As seen in Table 4, HealthVault reaches three out of the four desired goals in accountability tools. Thus, the *effectiveness* metric scores $\mathcal{E} = 0.75$.

A summary of the results is presented in Fig. 2. The results for the first requirement (information-based) are shown in blue together with those for the second one (mechanism-based), which are in orange. The assessment of Microsoft HealthVault is presented in Fig. 2a, whereas Fig. 2b displays what the ideal scenario would be. Currentness is the only metric that is not applicable, and therefore it is presented with no value in the chart.

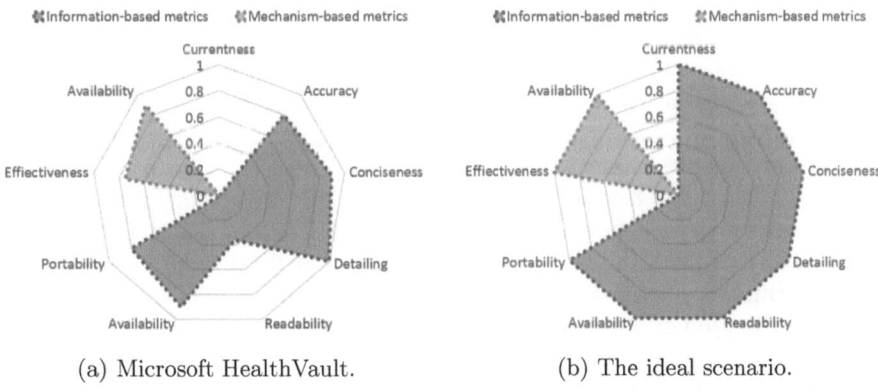

(a) Microsoft HealthVault.   (b) The ideal scenario.

Fig. 2. Synthesis of the transparency measurement. (Color figure online)

6   Discussion and Conclusion

Non-functional requirements are a useful instrument to compare systems that offer similar functionalities. They help assess which systems perform better, or which ones more faithfully embed specific user requirements. For this reason, modern SDLC methodologies tend to integrate NFRs in the system design.

Transparency is a new NFR that is recently becoming crucial as a promoter of the quality of a service and as a guarantee of respect of users' rights. Since we live in a digitalised world where mobile devices are ubiquitous and cloud computing is in our public and private daily activities, end users have the right to know whether the personal information they entrust to their devices and online services are managed securely and privately. Providing such information to end users is of paramount importance: what a device, an application, a service actually do, what they access, and for what purpose. Transparency comes into play by enabling users to endow devices and services (and their manufacturers and providers) with a motivated trust. Besides, as it can be used to express commitment to users and clarify accountability, transparency may also become a significant competition factor.

Designing for transparency, however, can be problematic. On the one side, the relevant information should be provided without exposing the system's security to wanton risk. On the other side, users might lack the technical skills to understand the content of the information, or to isolate meaningful material from an informative flooding. Thus, the information should be carefully selected and presented in a concise and intelligible form. Alternatively, users can be assisted by tools that convert a completely inscrutable streams of bytes into a human-friendly fashion.

Transparency is not a monolithic concept. It is rather a complex quality partitioned into several requirements. However, there are a few factors that all those requirements have in common. They all have to provide information (e.g., about a policy, a process) or the tools to get that information. These factors offer different perspectives under which transparency can be viewed.

In this work, we prove that *transparency* of a system is not just a high-level concept but a quality that can be measured. We introduced a few metrics to separately assess some of the most significant factors of transparency. This provides a meaningful way of benchmarking transparency and comparing systems. Our set of metrics is not complete, and each metric may not be the most accurate possible. But we demonstrate that the metrics are applicable to obtain a reasonable estimation of a system's transparency with respect to a specific desired requirement.

Further research directions are possible. An interesting work for the future is to apply the proposed metrics to systems in different domains, and analyse the differences in the results. In this way, it would be possible to classify the various sub-factors of transparency according to their importance in specific domains. Another planned research direction is to evaluate the transparency metrics to a new use case, but having access to the internal documentation and SDLC (i.e., with the assistance of the provider). Such an analysis could unveil some details (which could be measured on their own) about the asymmetry of information between the provider and the user. The problem of asymmetry of information is well-known but, to the best of our knowledge, has never been explored from an analytic perspective. Finally, another possible evolution would be to adjust the model presented in our research to allow its integration into a

SDLC, for example by modifying the software development workflow to address the transparency requirement. In order to extend a software design methodology (and tools) in such a way, it is necessary to analyse the interaction and possible collisions between transparency and other NFRs.

References

1. Bauer, E., Adams, R.: Reliability and Availability of Cloud Computing, 1st edn. Wiley-IEEE Press, Hoboken (2012)
2. Berners-Lee, T.: Linked data. https://www.w3.org/DesignIssues/LinkedData.html. Accessed May 2016
3. Berthold, S., Fischer-Hübner, S., Martucci, L., Pulls, T.: Crime and punishment in the cloud - accountability, transparency, and privacy. In: Pre-Proceeding of International Workshop on Trustworthiness, Accountability and Forensics in the Cloud in conjunction with the 7th IFIP WG 11.11 International Conference on Trust Management (2013)
4. Caldiera, G., Basili, V.R.: Identifying and qualifying reusable software components. Computer **24**(2), 61–70 (1991)
5. Cappelli, C.: Uma abordagem para transparência em processos organizacionais utilizando aspectos. Ph.D. thesis, PUC-Rio (2009)
6. Chung, L., Nixon, B.A., Yu, E., Mylopoulos, J.: Non-Functional Requirements in Software Engineering. International Series in Software Engineering, vol. 5. Springer, New York (2000)
7. Coleman, D., Ash, D., Lowther, B., Oman, P.: Using metrics to evaluate software system maintainability. Computer **27**(8), 44–49 (1994)
8. Cutts, M.: Oxford Guide to Plain English. Oxford University Press, Oxford (2007)
9. Eloy, J.A., Li, S., Kasabwala, K., Agarwal, N., Hansberry, D.R., Baredes, S., Setzen, M.: Readability assessment of patient education materials on major otolaryngology association websites. Otolaryngol. Head Neck Surg. **147**(5), 848–854 (2012)
10. Flesch, R.F.: How to Write Plain English. Barnes & Noble (1981)
11. Frey, G., Litz, L.: A measure for transparency in net based control algorithms. In: IEEE International Conference on Systems, Man, and Cybernetics, vol. 3, pp. 887–892 (1999)
12. Glinz, M.: On non-functional requirements. In: Proceeding of the 15th International Requirements Engineering Conference (RE), pp. 21–26. IEEE (2007)
13. GOV.UK: UK Government Digital Service Style Guide. https://www.gov.uk/guidance/content-design/writing-for-gov-uk#short-sentences. Accessed May 2016
14. Greywoode, J., Bluman, E., Spiegel, J., Boon, M.: Readability analysis of patient information on the american academy of otolaryngology-head and neck surgery website. Otolaryngol. Head Neck Surg. **141**(5), 555–558 (2009)
15. IEEE Computer Society: IEEE standard for a software quality metrics methodology. IEEE Standard, pp. 1061–1998. IEEE Computer Society (1998)
16. Kaner, C., Bond, W.P.: Software engineering metrics: what do they measure and how do we know? In: Proceeding of the 10th International Symposium on Software Metrics. IEEE (2004). http://kaner.com/pdfs/metrics2004.pdf
17. Kasabwala, K., Agarwal, N., Hansberry, D.R., Baredes, S., Eloy, J.A.: Readability assessment of patient education materials from the American academy of otolaryngology-Head and neck surgery foundation. Otolaryngol. Head Neck Surg. **147**(3), 466–471 (2012)

18. Keller, S., Kahn, L., Panara, R.: Specifying Software Quality Requirements with Metrics. IEEE Computer Society Press, Los Alamitos (1990)
19. Leite, JCSdP, Cappelli, C.: Business and information. Softw. Transparency **2**, 127–139 (2010)
20. Schneidewind, N.F.: Methodology for validating software metrics. IEEE Trans. Softw. **18**(5), 410–422 (1992)
21. Sommerville, I.: Software Engineering, 10th edn. Addison-Wesley Longman Inc., Boston (2016)
22. Spagnuelo, Dayana, Lenzini, Gabriele: Patient-centred transparency requirements for medical data sharing systems. New Advances in Information Systems and Technologies. AISC, vol. 444, pp. 1073–1083. Springer, Heidelberg (2016). doi:10.1007/978-3-319-31232-3_102
23. Sullivan, K., Clarke, J., Mulcahy, B.P.: Trust-terms ontology for defining security requirements and metrics. In: Proceeding of the 4 European Conference on Software Architecture: Companion Volume, ECSA 2010, pp. 175–180. ACM, New York (2010)
24. Berntsson Svensson, Richard, Gorschek, Tony, Regnell, Björn: Quality requirements in practice: an interview study in requirements engineering for embedded systems. In: Glinz, Martin, Heymans, Patrick (eds.) REFSQ 2009. LNCS, vol. 5512, pp. 218–232. Springer, Heidelberg (2009). doi:10.1007/978-3-642-02050-6_19
25. Viscusi, G., Batini, C., Mecella, M.: Quality assessment. Information systems for eGovernment: A Quality-of-Service Perspective, pp. 127–144. Springer, Heidelberg (2010)
26. Zarcadoolas, C.: The simplicity complex: exploring simplified health messages in a complex world. Health Promot. Int. **26**(3), 338–350 (2011)

Understanding Bifurcation of Slow Versus Fast Cyber-Attackers

Maarten van Wieren[1(✉)], Christian Doerr[2], Vivian Jacobs[1],
and Wolter Pieters[2]

[1] Deloitte Nederland, Amsterdam, The Netherlands
mvanwieren@deloitte.nl
[2] Delft University of Technology, Delft, The Netherlands

Abstract. Anecdotally, the distinction between fast "Smash-and-Grab" cyber-attacks on the one hand and slow attacks or "Advanced Persistent Threats" on the other hand is well known. In this article, we provide an explanation for this phenomenon as the outcome of an optimization from the perspective of the attacker. To this end, we model attacks as an interaction between an attacker and a defender and infer the two types of behavior observed based on justifiable assumptions on key variables such as detection thresholds. On the basis of our analysis, it follows that bi-modal detection capabilities are optimal.

Keywords: Cyber-attack · Economic models · APT · Smash-and-Grab · Information security · Behavioral optimization · Bifurcation

1 Introduction

The exponential rise of connectivity thanks to ICT has made many ways of value creation more efficient. The associated web of connectivity, commonly referred to as "cyberspace", has different scaling properties than our physical world [3] leading to the reduction of typical timescales for interactions, eliminating the need for middlemen and ensuring far more efficiently operating markets (see for instance Van Ark, Inklaar, and McGuckin [13]). As an undesired, but natural side-effect, we have also seen a rise of more "parasitic" forms of value creation in this cyber space. These are agents that make use of its scaling benefits at the expense of other agents' value, e.g. through cyber-attacks. This concerns cyberspace activity linked to commonly known criminal activities such as acts of espionage, fraud, scams, vandalism and terrorism.

Although attribution of cyber-attack to threat actors is still a hard problem [12], it has become apparent that cyber-attacks can be broadly categorized into two groups. On the one hand, there are "Smash-and-Grab"(S&G) type attacks where the threat actor for instance employs malware linked to known vulnerabilities. On the other hand, there are the so-called "Advanced Persistent Threat" (APT) type of attacks, where the threat actor employs the tactic to avoid detection by the defender for as long as possible while slowly realizing their goals. Well known examples are Stuxnet, Duqu, Flame and Red October, which in some cases evaded detection for years [15].

G. Livraga et al. (Eds.): DPM and QASA 2016, LNCS 9963, pp. 19–33, 2016.
DOI: 10.1007/978-3-319-47072-6_2

However, the rationale for the existence of those two groups of fast versus slow attackers is still poorly understood. This paper describes a model for analyzing optimal attack strategies for cyber-attackers depending on detection capabilities of defenders. Attackers having an incentive not to be detected, adopt a type of behavior aimed at remaining unnoticed by the defender's detection capabilities, this means acting slowly. Since acting faster increases the probability of being detected, attackers cannot at the same time act fast and remain undetected, and therefore need to make a choice between these two approaches. In some cases, it is rational to act slow in order to avoid being detected, while in other cases a quick attack makes sense. However, this intuitive argument alone does not explain why attackers may want to choose either fast (S&G) or slow (APT) strategies, since intermediate attack speeds should then also appear. The model explains the observed bifurcation of attack behavior, distinguishing slow and fast cyber-attacks, by showing that intermediate attack speeds are associated to a smaller return on investment for the attacker.

Based on the model, a defense strategy is suggested that implements a stochastic optimization of the parameters under control of the defender. The formulation is kept abstract on purpose, in order to ensure a broad applicability of the model to organizations that differ in their cyber risk capabilities and management, while nonetheless giving insight in the relevant metrics to consider in the first place and the general, organization-independent behavior of attackers and defenders. In practice, to test the bifurcation hypothesis and optimize the defense capabilities for a specific organization, more work is required. Detection parameters should be determined based on the details of the defender's analytics, activity level has to be defined and the loss has to be measured for different activity levels. A relatively simple attacker model like the one presented here, could help to interpret the measurements and put the right capabilities into place.

The remainder of this article is structured as follows. Section 2 describes related work, and Sect. 3 defines the main concepts used throughout the remainder of the article. Section 4 introduces a basic defender detection model. Section 5 relates the defender model to attacker behavior and Sects. 6 and 7 provide analysis of the behavior with respect to this model. Section 8 describes the associated perspective of the defender and Sect. 9 provides conclusions and discussion.

2   Related Work

This paper fits in a tradition of economic modeling of behavior of attackers and defenders, in order to predict or explain real-world phenomena (e.g. Gordon and Loeb [6]). In this paper, we frame the optimization question in terms of the optimal choices for a defender, under the assumption that the population of attackers will also optimize their behavior. This is essentially a minimax optimization in a two-step game, in which the defender moves first [4]. For illustrating the explanation of the bifurcation phenomenon this is sufficient. When assuming that attackers know that defenders take the bifurcation into account in their strategies, more advanced game-theoretic models are of use. We will come back to this in the discussion.

More specifically, this paper focuses on the time dimension of the behavior of attackers. In this context, several related questions have been addressed, mostly focusing on the optimal timing of attacks. The FlipIt game [8,10,14] investigates timing decisions of attacker and defender moves in order to maximize control over a shared resource, with minimal cost. The basic game only considers a single attack type. Pieters and Davarynejad [11] present a model for deriving attack frequencies from optimal timing decisions of attackers, with different attack vectors and a fixed income for the attacker per unit of time. Axelrod and Iliev [2] discuss the optimal timing of the use of exploits in cyber conflict, taking into account that using an exploit now may make it unavailable for later use. In contrast to this related work, the present paper focuses on the speed of attacks, in order to explain the observed separation between fast and slow strategies. As far as we are aware, this aspect has not been investigated yet.

In our work, key defender parameters are related to detection thresholds. Similar considerations have been studied by others in game-theoretic settings involving multiple attacker types [5]. However, in our current work, the attacker types (fast and slow) are what is explained by the analysis, rather than a starting point. More generally, we are not aiming at developing attacker personas or profiles [1], nor on using those in a security analysis [9], but rather on explaining different styles of attacker behavior that follow from optimization.

3   Definitions

The optimal way to organize defense capabilities for the various assets in an organization depends on the precise incentives of the cyber attackers targeting specific assets via various attack vectors. Before describing the model in more detail, in this section we discuss various types of assets, attacker motives, and attack vectors, that may assist defenders in their considerations. The rest of the paper should be seen as separately applicable to each of the concepts discussed here.

Cyber-attacks are defined here as an attempt by a threat actor to abuse Information Assets of some defending party. Information Assets are defined as the set of information that holds value to the defender, either direct (i.e. abuse directly reduces value of the defender) or indirect (i.e. where abuse leads to loss of value for third parties associated to the defender). Indirect losses may of course materialize in further direct losses through fines and/or claims. Value can take multiple forms, the most commonly ascribed values are: economic, financial, well-being, human lives, culture, nature, political, etc. For the purpose of this article and without prejudice to other forms of value, we have foremost financial value in mind.

Information Assets may be characterized through the well-known Confidentiality - Integrity - Availability triad. Confidentiality means an Information Asset may contain information asymmetry that leads to the potential to create value and/or to the potential to destroy value. Integrity means an Information Asset may contain records of reference that if the reference is changed it destroys value for the defender. Availability means an Information Asset may be (partially) lost so that, even if it is only temporarily, it destroys value for the defender. Information Assets may fall into all three categories or combinations.

Abuse of Information Assets typically arrives in three forms: cyber-espionage, cyber-fraud and cyber-destruction. Cyber-espionage concerns breaking information asymmetry (confidentiality), where usually it has more value to the attacker if this remains unknown to the defender. Typical motives for the attacker include: market competition, geo-politics, national-defense and insider trading. Cyber-fraud concerns breaking the integrity of the Information Assets. Here it depends on the motive if the attacker is even able to keep the cyber-fraud hidden to the defender after the attack. Some motives for cyber-fraud include: payments and transactions fraud, cover-ups of criminal acts, terrorism, war, accreditation and smuggling. Finally, cyber-destruction means making an Information Asset (temporarily) unavailable. Some motives for cyber-destruction include: hacktivism, terrorism, war, extortion and competition.

Of course combinations of these three forms into a composite attack is also possible. This means there is an initial attack followed by another type of attack. One example of this is where intelligence gets stolen to assist in a follow-up attack. Another example is a DDoS attack to momentarily distract the defender from another attack. In particular, the most dangerous type of attacks concerns abuse of the integrity of (security) controls as a pre-cursor for any other type of attack. Clearly, such a composite attack would classify as a sophisticated attack given that it requires a wide range of capabilities from the attacker. On the other hand, "unsophisticated" attackers that employ a more limited set of (known) techniques to exploit (known) vulnerabilities, may still cause significant levels of abuse since they can operate more agile thus quickly and on a larger scale.

We define two layers of defense in the security architecture description. The first layer concerns the technical/physical boundary between the public and the private domains of any network. If an internet connection exists, then vulnerabilities are likely to be identifiable. The second layer concerns the boundary between the private domain and the Information Asset at risk. All (technical) protection measures that are in place to prevent any form of abuse of Information Assets is part of the second protection layer. With respect to these defense layers, three channels can be identified for cyber-attacks. The first attack channel makes use of critical vulnerabilities in the first defense layer to gain access. The second attack channel works through insiders (knowingly or unknowingly, effectively circumventing the first protection layer with the knowing or unknowing help of insiders within the firm, granting them instant access across the first layer of defense. The third attack channel is through third parties, effectively circumventing the first two protection layers. This is the case for instance with a DDoS attack or if data gets abused in the "cloud" (which is in effect a third party's computer). Combinations of attack channels is of course again possible and associated to more sophisticated attackers.

When considering a defense strategy, defenders must know what Information Assets to protect, which attacker types these Information Assets attract, and which potential attack channels may be used. Some attacks like cyber-espionage and cyber-fraud on intangibles are only likely to occur as slow attacks. In contrast, cyber-fraud on tangibles as well as cyber-destruction attacks will likely end in a fast phase. Defenders thus will want to be capable to deal with slow as well as fast attacks, which must be dealt with by developing bi-modal detection capabilities: one slower regime with as low granularity as possible against slow attacks and one fast regime with higher granularity against fast attacks. We will come back to this in Sect. 8.

4 Modeling Detection and Response

In this section we set up a model for the defender's detection capability. Attackers will adapt their behavior in line with their goal(s). We assume that they can adapt their activity level, i.e., the number of attack-related moves against or in the defender's system per unit time. We assume that attackers get closer to their goal(s) by abusing Information Assets, and define the (average) rate of abuse of an Information Asset by the attacker as proportional to its activity level. This means that attackers in absence of defense simply have an incentive to act as quickly as possible to realize their goal(s).

The defender has the capability to detect and respond to an (attempted) attack. With the typical detection setup described below there is a certain monotonically increasing probability per activity level of the attacker that an attack will be detected. This also means that there is a typical time it takes the defender to neutralize the attack. Initially, we set the detection capability to be fixed, later we will consider that it may be varied by the defender.

Detection depends on identifying suspect activity with respect to normal activity. For this purpose, the defender will continuously sample a given scope containing a number of continuously changing elements $0 \ll S \in \mathbb{N}$ to test for suspect behavior.[1] For this test, a selection threshold $\theta_0 > 0$ is set that is defined through the expected number of elements S_0 that will be considered suspicious based on detection granularity $a_0 > 0$ without being associated to a specific attack (false positives):

$$S_0 = Se^{-\frac{\theta_0}{a_0}}. \tag{1}$$

This indicates that increasing the threshold θ_0 will reduce the number of suspicious elements, while lower detection granularity a_0 reflects an improving capacity of the defender to pick out suspect behavior. Lower detection granularity a_0 would thus reduce the number of false positives.

---

[1] A typical example is an analytics capability scanning through a large number of log files generated periodically by the system, checking them against predefined (mis)use cases or rules.

Depending on the activity level a of the attacker,[2] some small fraction of the scope is associated to a specific attack. The number of elements $S_a > 0$ that are actually detected as suspect elements depends on the threshold:

$$S_a = Se^{-\frac{\theta_0}{a}}. \tag{2}$$

Thus, the total number of suspicious elements is the sum of the false and true positives, $S_0 + S_a$. Suppose the defender randomly picks a suspect element, then the conditional probability that investigation of this element will lead to detection of the attack is defined as:

$$P_D = \frac{S_a}{S_0 + S_a} = \frac{1}{1 + e^{\theta_0(\frac{1}{a} - \frac{1}{a_0})}}. \tag{3}$$

Now suppose the scope is refreshed on regular intervals of duration T_r and let $p \in \mathbb{N}$ denote the investigative power of the defender, determining how many of such suspect elements can be investigated in time $T_r > 0$. Then, in case $p \ll S_a + S_0$, the rate (probability per unit time) of detection may be approximated by:

$$r_D = \frac{1 - (1 - P_D)^p}{T_r}. \tag{4}$$

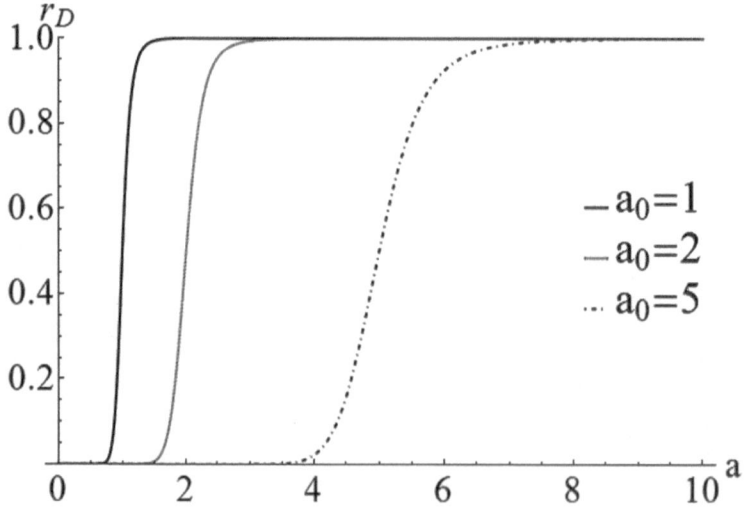

Fig. 1. Detection rate r_D as a function of attacker activity a for $T_r = p = 1$, $\theta_0/a_0 = 15$ and for various values of a_0, where a_0 determines the a-value for which detection has a crossover from a low to a high rate.

---

[2] The activity level parameterizes in an abstract and general way the number of actions performed during the attack per unit time. A concrete value depends on the details of the attack and the system. E.g., it may be the rate of data exfiltration from the defender's network.

Table 1. Model parameters and their meaning.

a_0	Detection granularity
θ_0	Detection threshold
T_r	Time interval between refreshes
p	Investigative power

In Fig. 1 some sample graphs are displayed for the detection rate as a function of the activity, with $T_r = 1$ and $p = 1$.

An interpretation guide to the various degrees of freedom of our detection model is given in Table 1.

The expected time before the attack will be detected is then given by

$$T_D = \frac{1}{r_D} = \frac{T_r}{1 - (1 - P_D)^p}. \tag{5}$$

After detection, it will take some additional time $T_N > 0$ before the attack will actually be neutralized through the response function so that the total expected maximum duration of an attack is

$$T_{A,\max} = T_D + T_N. \tag{6}$$

We can be more concrete by estimating the typical values and ranges for the parameters in the model based on a realistic situation. A typical refresh time is of the order of hours to days, so $T_r = 1$ (day). Based on our experience in the field, the fraction of false positives may vary between 10^{-7} 10^{-3}, depending on the maturity of the defender's analytics. This implies a range for θ_0/a_0 of 7 to 16 for a typical and mature defender, respectively. Furthermore, the investigative power p for a typical and mature defense system will lie between 1 and 1000 respectively. For instance, the number of employees judging suspicious elements can be a proxy for the investigative power p of the organization at hand.

5   Optimizing Attacker Strategy

Consider the return on investment for a collective of attackers with varying activity levels. For a given pair of fixed defender-attacker, we assume that the rate at which the attacker accumulates benefits is equal to the rate at which the defender accumulates losses[3]

$$r_{\text{abuse}} = C \cdot a, \tag{7}$$

---

[3] This assumption takes into account loss occurring within any time interval after an attack. Not only incidents with a direct financial loss result in value loss for an organization. Also indirect impact in the form of lost investments and future income, as well as the consequences of (so far) unnoticed attacks usually lead to value loss for the defender in the long term.

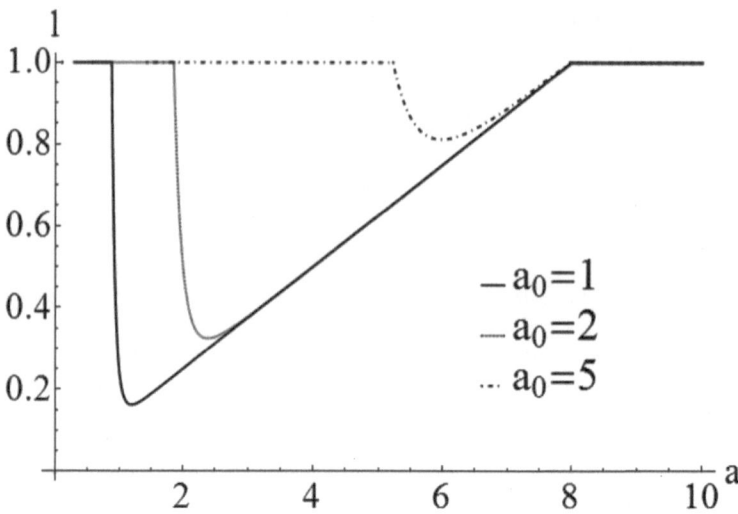

Fig. 2. Loss fraction l as a function of a for various values of the parameter a_0, and for $C = p = T_r = 1$, $T_N = 0$, $L_{\max} = 8$, and $\theta_0/a_0 = 15$. The minimum $a_{\min}$ is apparent. Clearly, lowering a_0 results in a decrease of the minimum $a_{\min}$, while at the same time lowering the loss fraction $l(a_{\min})$.

where $C > 0$ is some constant that does not depend on the defender's detection and response function. The expected total loss cannot exceed a certain limit given a finite size of the Information Asset being abused. It is therefore bounded from above by the total exposed value $L_{\max}$ and is given by

$$L(a) = \min(r_{\text{abuse}} \cdot T_{A,\max}, L_{\max}). \tag{8}$$

Assuming an undetected attacker leaves the system when the maximal value $L_{\max}$ is extracted, the maximal attack time is $L_{\max}/C\,a$. Figure 2 displays the expected fraction of value loss $l = L/L_{\max}$ for the same parameter values as used in the graph for the detection rate in Sect. 4.

Disregarding the trivial case when the loss fraction is equal to 1 for all a (not sufficiently low a_0), it has a non-trivial minimum as a function of attacker activity at some $a_{\min}$ so that

$$l(a) \geq l(a_{\min}) \qquad \forall\, a > 0. \tag{9}$$

The minimum $a_{\min}$ can be determined analytically for $p = 1$, in which case it is given by

$$a_{\min} = \frac{\theta_0}{1 + X}, \tag{10}$$

where X is the principal solution of $Xe^X = (T_r + T_N)e^{\theta_0/a_0 - 1}/T_r$, also known as the Lambert-W function. For $p \neq 1$, $a_{\min}$ can be proven to exist given continuity and boundedness of $l(a)$. In this case, $a_{\min}$ can be computed numerically.

For a given type of Information Asset, the loss for the defender will in first approximation be linearly proportional to the (gross) gains for the attacker $\tilde{G}(a)$, which we define by

$$\tilde{G}(a) = G_0 \cdot L(a). \tag{11}$$

Here, the proportionality factor G_0 is usually of the order $10^{-2} - 10^{-1}$. The existence of a minimum in the loss fraction combined with the fact that defender loss is proportional to attacker gain, implies that for attackers to optimize gains, they have an incentive to act either more slowly or more quickly (the derivative is either positive or negative, depending on which side of the minimum the attackers find themselves). In fact, given that a singular minimum $a_{\min}$ exists (a_0 low enough), it also follows that for every activity level $a_{\mathrm{slow}} < a_{\min}$ there is at least one value $a_{\mathrm{fast}} > a_{\min}$ such that

$$l(a_{\mathrm{slow}}) = l(a_{\mathrm{fast}}). \tag{12}$$

From this it already follows that attackers (also depending on their exact properties) will tend to split into two categories: slow and fast attackers. This is a bifurcation phenomenon and heuristically represents the two main strategies that attackers may follow with respect to detection by the defender: stealth (not get detected) or speed (act quicker than defenses). This may be a rational strategic choice by the attacker related to the details of their objectives and capabilities as portrayed in Sect. 2. However, even without such rational decision making, this will be the result of a selection mechanism where successful attackers amplify strategies that have worked best in the past.

6   Economic Considerations Attacker

For better understanding of attacker behavior, we need to consider the net gains for the attacker by including the costs and limitations associated to an attack. For this purpose we observe the two extremes of very slow and very fast attacks.

For very slow attacks, the time required to accumulate gain becomes prohibitively long given that attackers need to invest an increasing amount of time. During this time they will have a fixed level of expenses (living cost as well as the cost of invested capital at risk due to uncertain returns). This implies that costs are proportional to the time required for the attack so we include $c_0\,T_A(a)$ as a cost term (we assume zero interest returns on the invested capital).

For very fast attacks, it will be increasingly costly for the attacker to arrange the required infrastructure and capabilities. This effect can be summed up as the law of diminishing returns. A given increase in activity level will cost an exponentially increasing amount of investment for the required capabilities

$$J(a) = J_0 e^{\frac{a}{\theta_J}}. \tag{13}$$

Here, J_0 is a (small) fixed investment cost and θ_J is the capability investment threshold.

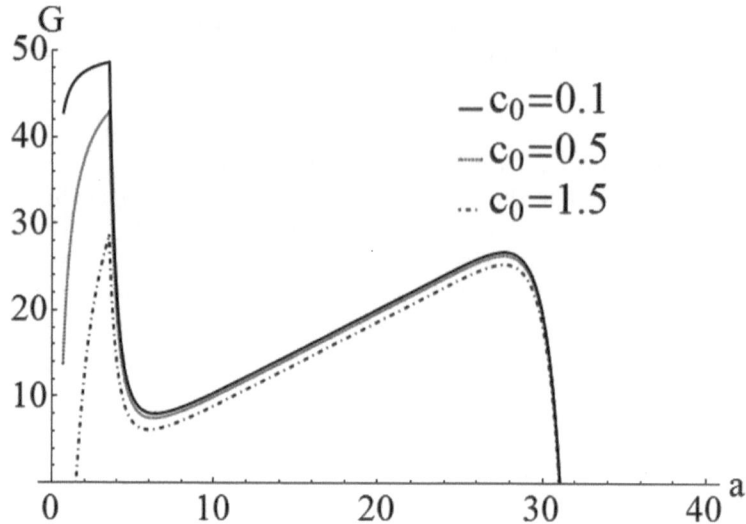

Fig. 3. Net gain function G as a function of a for various values of the operation cost c_0, and for $C = p = T_r = G_0 = \theta_J = 1$, $T_N = 0$, $L_{\max} = 50$, $J_0 = 10^{-12}$, and $\theta_0/a_0 = 6$.

Combining the gross gain with the time-dependent cost and the up-front investment for the capabilities, we define the net gain as

$$G(a) = G_0 \cdot L(a) - C_0 \cdot T_A(a) - J(a). \tag{14}$$

This net gain function is plotted for some parameter values in Fig. 3.

The net gain has two local maxima, corresponding to a slow and fast optimal activity level with respect to net gain. Which one of these is the global maximum depends on the choice of parameter values. In Fig. 3 we see that the highest gain is obtained by slower attackers. In between these two local maxima there is a minimum in the gain function, meaning the bifurcation mechanism is still intact.

7   Attacker Behavior Analysis

We now revisit the types of cyber-attack we defined earlier (cyber-espionage, cyber-fraud and cyber-destruction) and will relate these to the analysis made in the previous section and will see what considerations attackers will have to move either fast or slow. Here, we define fast attackers as having an activity $a > a_{\min}$, while slow attackers have an activity $a < a_{\min}$.

In case of cyber-espionage, there is typically a clear incentive that the attack does not get uncovered after the fact. This means there is a penalty involved for detection that changes the gain function to have only a single optimum. This means that there is an incentive to move slowly, consistent to what is for example being observed with APT's. (This obviously does not mean that all such attacks go undetected.) In case that it doesn't matter to the attacker if the defender knows about the attack however, then fast attacks for the purpose of cyber-espionage are still perfectly rational and this has indeed recently been observed.

In case of cyber-fraud, it will depend on the details whether slow or fast attacks are attractive. If the fraud concerns tangibles (for instance money trans-actions), then it can safely be assumed by the attacker that it will be uncovered after the abuse has succeeded given the many controls in place on the defender side. In this case it becomes attractive to move fast as is commonly observed. If the fraud on the other hand concerns intangibles, e.g. hiding criminal acts, then the goal is to remain undetected after the fact. Other types of attack may also benefit from cyber-fraud attacks on intangibles, e.g. through placement of back doors or covering tracks.

In case of cyber-destruction, it is clear that the abuse will get detected after the fact, so in principle there is no real incentive to move slowly. Even more strongly, these attackers have the incentive to move quickly to facilitate a broad reach before the unavoidable detection will lead the defender to block further attempts.

Of course, attackers do not need to choose a fixed strategy i.e. activity level. For all fast attacks, a preparatory attack (for instance to weaken controls of the defender) is an option. These are the composite attacks referred to in Sect. 3. The incentive for such preparatory attacks is to remain undetected at least until the fast attack ensues. This means that the preparatory attack will benefit from slow movement. Conversely, fast attacks like DDoS attacks have also been used in composite attacks to serve as distraction for the defender. Such composite attacks however require a significant level of sophistication that is fortunately still relatively rare. For less sophisticated attackers, the smash-and-grab tactics still make perfect sense.

Finally, another consideration that may favor fast attacks as compared to slow attacks is that fast attacks allow for a larger number of targets in a given time-span than is possible for slow attacks. This larger sample of defenders means the fast attacker likely encounters multiple distinct realizations of detection capa-bilities. This implies that diversification effects will tend to dampen the volatility in results that fast attackers will experience, thus leading to a more stable (crimi-nal) return on investment. In terms of natural selection principles acting to favor one attacker over the other, this helps the persistence of fast attackers.

8   The Defender's Dilemma

Typical defenders have to make choices on what capability to invest in to obtain sufficient and optimal security. Given the gain function for attackers described above, which has two local maxima, the defender's hypothesis is that the attacker population is split into slow and fast attackers. With respect to each population, two optimal defense configurations exist for each population that minimize their impact. Here we observe the considerations from the perspective of the defender related to this optimization.

Consider the capabilities associated to the model introduced in Sects. 4 and 5. There are four degrees of freedom that can be controlled by the defender: the detection threshold θ_0, the detection granularity a_0, the power p and the time to refresh the scope T_r. From the model as well as logic, it follows that the defender should typically aim to reduce the detection threshold, limit and refresh time, while increasing the detection power.

Optimizing the value of these parameters will also lower $a_{\min}$ as can for example be seen in Fig. 2, reflecting that it requires ever lower attacker activity levels to remain undetected sufficiently long to benefit as attacker. Although this effect may be small on short time-scales, attackers will tend to also adapt to changing properties in the environment created by the defender (and making the attacker move slower is of course still a good thing since it will take longer for the same loss to accumulate).

However, the impact for each parameter is not the same for slow or fast attackers as can be seen in Fig. 4. The impact of lowering the detection granularity a_0 is foremost lowering the optimal activity rate for slow attackers, while there is hardly any impact for fast attackers, thus forcing attackers to act fast. The same holds true for improving the detection threshold θ_0 and power p. In contrast, lowering the time to refresh the detection scope T_r and time to neu-

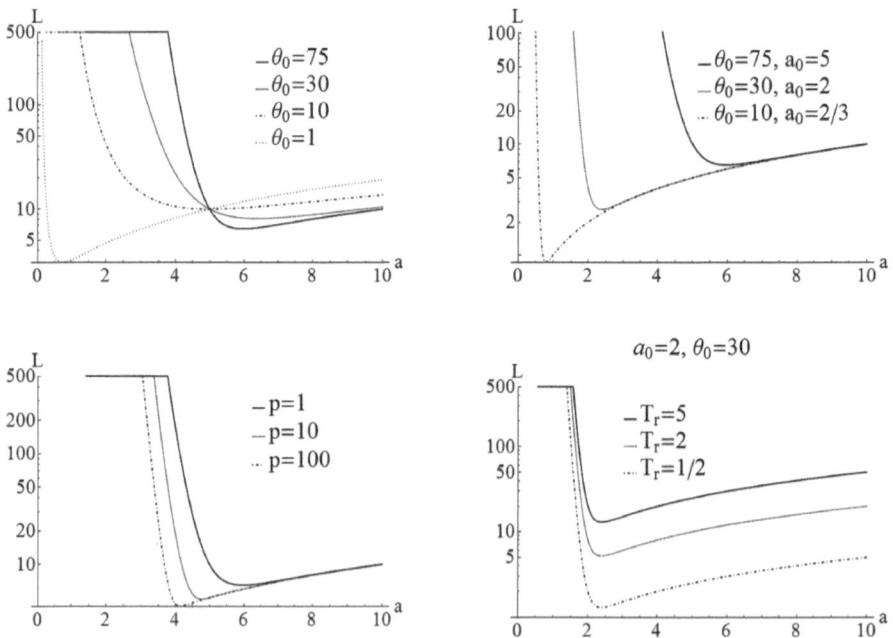

Fig. 4. Effects of parameter variation on the loss function. When parameter values are not explicitly mentioned we have taken the values $p = T_r = C = \theta_J = 1$, $T_N = 0$, $A_0 = 5$, $L_{\max} = 500$ and $\theta_0 = 15$. The panels in this figure illustrate the effects discussed in Sect. 8 and represented in Table 2.

Table 2. Effects of parameter optimization on fast and slow attacks. In each row all unmentioned parameters are kept fixed. The term "reduces" indicates that the defender's loss $L(a)$ decreases for fast or slow attacks, i.e., high or low values of a, respectively.

Effect on loss	Slow attack	Fast attack
Decrease a_0	Reduces	No
Decrease θ_0	Reduces	Increases
Decrease T_r	Reduces very little	Reduces
Decrease T_N	Reduces very little	Reduces
Increase p	Depends	Reduces slightly

tralize the attack T_N are only effective to reduce the impact from fast attacks. However, given that a decrease of the time to refresh T_r will likely reduce the detection power p, this may in effect work counterproductively with respect to countering slow attacks. The abovementioned effects of optimizing the four parameters on fast and slow attackers are summarized in Table 2.

From this follows a defender's dilemma when investing in capabilities. As follows from the analysis in Sect. 7, most defenders will need to defend against slow and fast attacks alike and will thus have to make tough choices on how to optimize with respect to both types of attack. The dilemma here is: do we make sure we detect even very slow attackers at the expense of reacting to fast attackers, or do we make sure that fast attackers are dealt with quickly and hope that no attacker arrives that is too slow? The way to deal with this dilemma, is to have the defense capabilities act in two regimes simultaneously. We refer to this as bi-modal detection where part of detection resources should be spent on acting quickly with higher granularity (i.e. lower resolution), while another part of the resources should be spent on carefully checking all elements derived with low threshold θ_0 and feeding the results back into reducing the detection granularity a_0 further and further (i.e. increasing resolution). By creating a linear combination of these two regimes in this way, the resulting optimum will be better for the same number of resources as when only optimizing a single configuration (i.e. set of parameters).

9   Conclusion and Discussion

This paper describes a model aimed at analysis of the interaction between attackers avoiding detection and defenders attempting to detect and neutralize attacks. We have seen that there are two natural optima for attackers: moving fast and moving slow. This coincides with observed properties of real world attackers. As far as we are aware, this is the first analytical model showing this bifurcation in time of attacker behavior under minimal and logical assumptions.

In Sect. 8 we recommend creating a bi-modal detection capability. Such a bi-modal detection would benefit from a quantitative analysis of the performance of detection modes against the framework set out in Sects. 4, 5, 6 and 7. This is left for future research.

In the present paper, we have assumed that attackers will naturally tend to optimize their behavior for a given defense configuration. In reality however, the defenders as well as the attackers may choose to adapt their strategies. For instance, we have not considered the possibility of multiple attacks by the same attacker. This could also be of interest when to each attack an initial cost is associated [7]. In our case, this cost depends on the quality of the protection capability. An example of such a strategy could be attackers attempting to exhaust the defensive detection capability with many fake fast attacks for the purpose of hiding the actual slow attack. Defenders could adapt again to such strategies, and investigating this interaction in a game-theoretic model would be interesting as well for future research.

Acknowledgements. The research leading to these results has received funding from the European Union's Seventh Framework Programme (FP7/2007–2013) under grant agreement ICT-318003 (TRESPASS). This publication reflects only the authors' views and the Union is not liable for any use that may be made of the information contained herein.

References

1. Atzeni, A., Cameroni, C., Faily, S., Lyle, J., Fléchais, I.: Here's Johnny: A methodology for developing attacker personas. In: Sixth International Conference on Availability, Reliability and Security (ARES), pp. 722–727. IEEE (2011)
2. Axelrod, R., Iliev, R.: Timing of cyber conflict. Proc. Nat. Acad. Sci. **111**(4), 1298–1303 (2014)
3. Barabási, A.L., Albert, R., Jeong, H.: Scale-free characteristics of random networks: the topology of the world-wide web. Physica A Stat. Mech. Appl. **281**(1), 69–77 (2000)
4. Cox Jr, L.A.T.: Game theory and risk analysis. Risk Anal. **29**(8), 1062–1068 (2009)
5. Dritsoula, L., Loiseau, P., Musacchio, J.: Computing the nash equilibria of intruder classification games. In: Grosklags, J., Walrand, J. (eds.) GameSec 2012. LNCS, vol. 7638, pp. 78–97. Springer, Heidelberg (2012)
6. Gordon, L.A., Loeb, M.P.: The economics of information security investment. ACM Trans. Inf. Syst. Secur. (TISSEC) **5**(4), 438–457 (2002)
7. Herley, C.: The plight of the targeted attacker in a world of scale. In: WEIS (2010)
8. Laszka, A., Horvath, G., Felegyhazi, M., Buttyán, L.: FlipThem: Modeling targeted attacks with FlipIt for multiple resources. In: Poovendran, R., Saad, W. (eds.) GameSec 2014. LNCS, vol. 8840, pp. 175–194. Springer, Heidelberg (2014). doi:10.1007/978-3-319-12601-2_10
9. Lenin, A., Willemson, J., Sari, D.P.: Attacker profiling in quantitative security assessment based on attack trees. In: Bernsmed, K., Fischer-Hübner, S. (eds.) NordSec 2014. LNCS, vol. 8788, pp. 199–212. Springer, Heidelberg (2014)
10. Nochenson, A., Grosklags, J., et al.: A behavioral investigation of the FlipIt game. In: Proceedings of the 12th Workshop on the Economics of Information Security (WEIS) (2013)

11. Pieters, W., Davarynejad, M.: Calculating adversarial risk from attack trees: control strength and probabilistic attackers. In: Garcia-Alfaro, J., Herrera-Joancomartí, J., Lupu, E., Posegga, J., Aldini, A., Martinelli, F., Suri, N. (eds.) DPM/SETOP/QASA 2014. LNCS, vol. 8872, pp. 201–215. Springer, Heidelberg (2015)
12. Rid, T., Buchanan, B.: Attributing cyber attacks. J. Strateg. Stud. **38**(1–2), 4–37 (2015)
13. Van Ark, B., Inklaar, R., McGuckin, R.H.: Changing gear: productivity, ICT and-service industries in Europe and the United States. The Industrial Dynamics ofthe New Digital Economy, Edward Elgar, pp. 56–99 (2003)
14. Van Dijk, M., Juels, A., Oprea, A., Rivest, R.L.: FlipIt: the game of "stealthy takeover". J. Cryptology **26**(4), 655–713 (2013)
15. Virvilis, N., Gritzalis, D.: The big four - what we did wrong in advanced persistent threat detection? In: Eighth International Conference on Availability, Reliability and Security (ARES), pp. 248–254. IEEE (2013)

Decomposing Global Quantitative Properties into Local Ones

Ilaria Matteucci[1] and Francesco Santini[2(⊠)]

[1] Istituto di Informatica e Telematica, IIT-CNR, Pisa, Italy
ilaria.matteucci@iit.cnr.it
[2] Dipartimento di Matematica e Informatica, Università di Perugia, Perugia, Italy
francesco.santini@dmi.unipg.it

Abstract. In this paper we address the problem of identifying what local properties the sub-components of a system have to satisfy in order to guarantee a (security) property on the behaviour of the whole system. We associate each action with a value. Hence, we end up with quantitative properties on them, which are specified through a modal logic equipped with a parametric algebraic structure (i.e., a c-semiring). The aim is to have a value related to the satisfaction of a formula. Starting from the behaviour of a general distributed system (or *context*), we propose a formal approach to decompose a global quantitative property into the local quantitative properties to be satisfied by its sub-contexts.

1 Introduction

Understanding, reasoning, and designing distributed systems can be problematic. As such systems grow in size and decentralisation degree, their development demands for rigorous formal approaches. An example is the verification of security properties, as which actions a component is allowed to perform at a given moment, depending upon what actions a different component has executed.

For instance, let us consider the classical *Chinese-Wall* security-policy regulating the access to two sets of resources A and B, and a system that is a composition of two unknown components, both able to access to A and B. The global system satisfies the Chinese-Wall property if and only if the two components coordinate their actions in such a way that the system accesses to only one of the two sets; thus, if it is accesses to A, it cannot then access to B (and vice-versa). The goal of the paper is to describe a formal machinery that allows us to opportunely find out the properties that must be locally satisfied by each of the unknown components over their composition, to guarantee a given property (i.e., in this case, the Chinese-Wall policy).

Furthermore, we consider quantitative aspects in order to add to the picture costs, execution times, rates and, in general, other non-functional aspects. Therefore, the relevant question is not only whether a system verifies a boolean property (as a security feature), but also how much enforcing it impacts on other desiderata. This "how much" corresponds to a generic cost needed to verify that

G. Livraga et al. (Eds.): DPM and QASA 2016, LNCS 9963, pp. 34–50, 2016.
DOI: 10.1007/978-3-319-47072-6_3

property, for instance by considering the cost of all the actions required to satisfy it. In particular, the ultimate aim of this work is to identify the quantitative constraints each system subcomponents has to satisfy in order to allow the whole system to behave as expected (i.e., verifying a boolean property), and, at the same time, with a cost better than a user-defined threshold t.

In the following, Sect. 2 presents the necessary background-notions about *c-semirings* [2,3], the algebraic structure we use to parametrise different cost/preference metrics: anything that can be cast to a semiring is still usable in the same framework. In Sect. 3, we introduce the notion of *quantitative contexts*, i.e., contexts whose actions are associated with a c-semiring value. Contexts have been introduced in [11] with the purpose to formally specify and analyse generic distributed-systems.

Sections 4 and 5 represent the core of this work: there (i) we recall and enhance a quantitative Hennessy-Milner logic (i.e., c-HM logic) [15] to define quantitative properties on n-ary context and (ii) we provide all the necessary formal tools for decomposing quantitative properties satisfied by an *n*-ary context into n local ones, each of them satisfied by a unary (quantitative) context. Each context represents a different component of a distributed system.

In Sect. 6 we sketch an example of a well-known security model, i.e., the Chinese-Wall, rephrased with security-levels and then decomposed. In this way we can observe *(i)* whether the specified policy is classically respected, and *(ii)* whether the contribution of each distributed component (in terms of the security-level of its actions) is enough to guarantee a minimum global-security. Finally, Sect. 7 reports the related work, and Sect. 8 presents conclusions and future work.

2   C-semirings

We introduce c-semirings, the core of the presented computational framework.

Definition 1 (Semiring [9]). *A commutative semiring is a five-tuple* $\mathbb{K} = \langle K, +, \times, \bot, \top \rangle$ *such that* K *is a set,* $\top, \bot \in K$, *and* $+, \times : K \times K \to K$ *are binary operators making the triples* $\langle K, +, \bot \rangle$ *and* $\langle K, \times, \top \rangle$ *commutative monoids (semigroups with identity), satisfying*

- *(distributivity)* $\forall a, b, c \in K.a \times (b + c) = (a \times b) + (a \times c)$.
- *(annihilator)* $\forall a \in A.a \times \bot = \bot$.

Definition 2 (Absorptive semirings). *Let* $\mathbb{S}$ *be a commutative semiring. An absorptive semiring verifies the absorptiveness property:* $\forall a, b \in K.a + (a \times b) = a$, *which is equivalent to* $\forall a \in S.a + \top = \top$.

Absorptive semirings are referred as *simple*, and their $+$ operator is necessarily idempotent [9]. Semirings where $+$ is idempotent are *tropical*, or *diods*.

Definition 3 (C-semiring [3]). *C-semirings are commutative and absorptive semirings. Therefore, c-semirings are tropical semirings where* $\top$ *is an absorbing element for* $+$.

The idempotency of $+$ leads to the definition of a partial ordering $\leq_K$ over the set K (K is a poset). It is defined as $a \leq_K b$ if and only if $a + b = b$, and $+$ finds their *least upper bound* in K. This intuitively means that b is "better" than a. Therefore, we can use $+$ as an optimisation operator and always choose the best available solution.

Some more properties can be derived on c-semirings [3]: *(i)* both $+$ and $\times$ are monotone over $\leq_K$, *(ii)* $\times$ is intensive (i.e., $a \times b \leq_K a$), *(iii)* $\times$ is closed (i.e., $a \times b \in K$), and *(iv)* $\langle K, \leq_K \rangle$ is a complete lattice. $\perp$ and $\top$ are respectively the bottom and top elements of such lattice. When also $\times$ is idempotent, *(i)* $+$ distributes over $\times$, *(ii)* $\times$ is the *greater lower bound* (glb, or $\sqcap$) of the lattice, and *(iii)* $\langle K, \leq_K \rangle$ is a distributive lattice. $\sum$ denotes the set-wise extension of $+$.

Some c-semiring instances are: *boolean* $\langle \{F, T\}, \vee, \wedge, F, T \rangle$[1], *fuzzy* $\langle [0, 1],$ $\max, \min, 0, 1 \rangle$, *bottleneck* $\langle \mathbb{R}^+ \cup \{+\infty\}, \max, \min, 0, \infty \rangle$, *probabilistic* $\langle [0, 1], \max,$ $\hat{\times}, 0, 1 \rangle$ (or Viterbi semiring), *weighted* $\langle \mathbb{R}^+ \cup \{+\infty\}, min, \hat{+}, +\infty, 0 \rangle$. Capped operators stand for their arithmetic equivalent.

Although c-semirings have been historically used as monotonic structures where to aggregate costs (and find best solutions), the need of removing values has raised in local consistency algorithms and non-monotonic algebras using constraints (*e.g.*, [2]). A solution comes from *residuation theory* [6], a standard tool on tropical arithmetic that allows for obtaining a division operator via an approximate solution to the equation $b \times x = a$.

Definition 4 (Division [2]**).** *Let $\mathbb{K}$ be a tropical semiring. Then, $\mathbb{K}$ is residuated if the set $\{x \in K \mid b \times x \leq a\}$ admits a maximum for all elements $a, b \in K$, denoted $a \div b$.*

Since a complete[2] tropical-semiring is also residuated, all the classical instances of c-semiring presented above are residuated, i.e., each element in K admits an "inverse", which is unique in case $\leq_K$ is a total order. For instance, the unique "inverse" $a \div b$ in the weighted semiring is defined as follows:

$$a \div b = \min\{x \mid b \hat{+} x \geq a\} = \begin{cases} 0 & \text{if } b \geq a \\ a \hat{-} b & \text{if } a > b \end{cases}$$

Definition 5 (Unique invertibility [2]**).** *Let $\mathbb{K}$ be an absorptive, invertible semiring. Then, $\mathbb{K}$ is uniquely invertible iff it is cancellative, i.e., $\forall a, b, c \in A.(a \times c = b \times c) \wedge (c \neq 0) \Rightarrow a = b$.*

Since all the previous examples of c-semirings (*e.g.*, weighted or fuzzy) are cancellative, they are uniquely invertible as well. Furthermore, it is also possible to consider several optimisation criteria at the same time: the Cartesian product of c-semirings is still a c-semiring. Clearly, in this case the ordering induced by $+$ is partial, *e.g.*, when we have $\langle k_1, k_2 \rangle$ and $\langle k_3, k_4 \rangle$, and $k_1 \leq k_3$ while $k_2 \geq k_4$.

---

[1] Boolean c-semirings can be used to model crisp problems.
[2] $\mathbb{K}$ is complete if it is closed with respect to infinite sums, and the distributivity law holds also for an infinite number of summands [2].

3   Quantitative Contexts

The notion of *context* has been introduced in [11] as an expression describing the partial implementation of a system, $C(X_1, \ldots, X_n)$, where C denotes the known part, and $X_1, \ldots, X_n$ are free variables representing the unknown ones.

In this section, we enhance the definitions of *context* given in [11] by adding the notion of a weight associated with tuple of actions. This allows us to quantitatively specify and analyse the behaviour of a distributed system with some unknowns part, which have nevertheless to participate to the satisfaction of a quantitative global-property on the whole system.

Definition 6 (Quantitative context). *A* quantitative context-system *is a structure* $\mathcal{C} = (\langle C_n^m \rangle_{n,m}, Act, \mathbb{K}, \langle \to_{n,m}^K \rangle_{n,m})$ *where* $\langle C_n^m \rangle_{n,m}$ *is a set of n-to-m tuple of n-to-m quantitative contexts;* $\mathbb{K} = \langle K, +, \times, \bot, \top \rangle$ *is a c-semiring;* Act *is a set of actions;* $Act_0 = Act \cup \{0\}$ *where* $0 \notin Act$ *is a distinguished no-action symbol,* Act_0^n *is the set of tuples of n actions in* Act_0, *and* $\to_{n,m}^K \subseteq C_n^m \times ((Act_0^n, K) \times (Act_0^m, K)) \times C_n^m$ *is the* quantitative transduction-relation *for the n-to-m contexts satisfying* $(C, (\tilde{a}, k), (\tilde{0}, h), D) \in \to_{n,m}^K$ *if and only if* $C = D$ *and* $\tilde{a} = \tilde{0}$ *for all contexts* $C, D \in C_n^m$ $(h, k \in K)$, *and* $\langle \to_{n,m}^K \rangle_{n,m}$ *are n-to-m tuple of quantitative transduction-relation.*

For $(C, (\tilde{a}, k), (\tilde{b}, h), C') \in \to_{n,m}^K$ we usually write $C \xrightarrow[(\tilde{a},k)]{(\tilde{b},h)} C'$, leaving the indices of $\to$ to be determined by the context. The informal interpretation is that the context C takes in input the set of actions $\tilde{a}$ performed with a weight k, and it returns as output $\tilde{b}$ weighted by h, finally becoming C'. If $\tilde{a}$ is 0 (i.e., no action) then the context produces an output without consuming any internal action; if $\tilde{b}$ is 0 then there is not any observable transition and we omit the vector of outputs; if both $\tilde{a}$ and $\tilde{b}$ are equal to 0, then both the internal process and the external observer are not involved in the transduction.

We compose contexts by means of two operations: *composition* and *product*.

Definition 7 (Composition). *Let* $\mathcal{C} = (\langle C_n^m \rangle_{n,m}, Act, \mathbb{K}, \langle \to_{n,m}^K \rangle_{n,m})$ *be a quantitative context-system. A* composition *on* $\mathcal{C}$ *is a dyadic operation* $\circ$ *on contexts such that, whenever* $C \in C_n^m$ *and* $D \in C_m^r$, *then* $D \circ C \in C_n^r$ *according to the following rule:*

$$\frac{C \xrightarrow[(\tilde{a},k)]{(\tilde{b},h)} C' \quad D \xrightarrow[(\tilde{b},h)]{(\tilde{c},w)} D'}{D \circ C \xrightarrow[(\tilde{a},k)]{(\tilde{c},w)} D' \circ C'}$$

where $\tilde{a} = \langle a_1, \ldots, a_n \rangle$, $\tilde{b} = \langle b_1, \ldots, b_m \rangle$ *and* $\tilde{c} = \langle c_1, \ldots, c_r \rangle$ *are vectors of actions, while* k, h, w *represent the weight associated to the vector af actions* $\tilde{a}$, $\tilde{b}$, *and* $\tilde{c}$ *respectively.*

The basic idea is that two contexts can be composed if the output of the first one (cfr. D) is exactly the same in terms of *(i)* the tuple of performed actions, *(ii)* its associated weight, with respect to the input of the second context (cfr. C). In this way, the two contexts combine their actions in such a way that the transduction of the composed context takes the input of D and its weight as input, and it returns the output of C and its weight as output.

To compose n independent processes through the same context $C \in C_n^m$ we define an *independent combination*, referred as the *product* operator of n contexts $D_1 \times \ldots \times D_n$, where $D_i \in C_{m_i}^1$, $i = 1, \ldots, n$ and D_i is an expansion of the i'th subcomponent of C such that the cardinality m is exactly equal to the sum of each cardinality m_i associated with contexts D_i.

Definition 8 (Product). *Let* $\mathcal{C} = (\langle C_n^m \rangle_{n,m}, Act, \mathbb{K}, \langle \rightarrow_{n,m}^K \rangle_{n,m})$ *be a context system. A* product *on* $\mathcal{C}$ *is a context operation* $\times$*, such that whenever* $C \in C_n^m$ *and* $D \in C_r^s$ *then* $C \times D \in C_{n+r}^{m+s}$*. Furthermore the transduction for a context* $C \times D$ *are fully characterized by the following rule:*

$$\frac{C \xrightarrow[(\tilde{a},k)]{(\tilde{b},h)} C' \quad D \xrightarrow[(\tilde{c},w)]{(\tilde{d},s)} D'}{C \times D \xrightarrow[(\tilde{a}\tilde{c},k \times w)]{(\tilde{b}\tilde{d},h \times s)} C' \times D'}$$

where juxtaposition of vectors $\tilde{a} = \langle a_1, \ldots, a_n \rangle$ *and* $\tilde{c} = \langle c_1, \ldots, c_r \rangle$ *is the vector* $\tilde{a}\tilde{c} = \langle a_1, \ldots, a_n, c_1, \ldots, c_r \rangle$*, and juxtaposition of vectors* $\tilde{b} = \langle b_1, \ldots, b_m \rangle$ *and* $\tilde{d} = \langle d_1, \ldots, d_s \rangle$ *is the vector* $\tilde{b}\tilde{d} = \langle b_1, \ldots, b_m, d_1, \ldots, d_s \rangle$*. Note that the weight of the juxtaposition of two action vectors is just the* $\times$ *of their weights.*

For sake of readability, in the following we will write the combined process $C(D_1, \ldots, D_n)$ as a shorthand for $C \circ (D_1 \times \ldots \times D_n)$.

Note that, since we consider *asynchronous* contexts, it is not required that all the components $D_1, \ldots, D_n$ contribute in a transition of the combined process $C(D_1, \ldots, D_n)$, i.e., some D_i can perform a 0 action.

4   Quantifying Properties in a Distributed Environment

In this section, we mainly focus on how we can express quantitative properties/constraints on distributed systems. To this aim, we propose a variant of a quantitative Hennessy-Milner logic, the c-HM logic firstly proposed in [15]; thus, we can specify a property on a tuple of actions, extending it to c-HM^n.

4.1   Multi-action C-semiring Hennessy-Milner Logic (c-HM^n)

We start by defining the transition system on which c-HM^n is defined:

Definition 9 (MLTS). *A (finite) Multi-Labelled Transition-System (MLTS) is a five-tuple* $MLTS = (S, L^n, \mathbb{K}, T)$*, where (i)* S *is the countable (finite) state-space, (ii)* L^n *is a finite set of transition labels, where each label is a vector of labels in* L*: the label* $\langle a_1, \ldots, a_n \rangle \in L^n$ *and for all* $i = 1, \ldots, n$*,* $a_i \in L$*. (iii)* $\mathbb{K} = \langle K, \leq, \times, \div, 1, \bot, \top \rangle$ *is an IReM used for the definition of transition weights, and (iv)* $T : (S \times L^n \times S) \longrightarrow \mathbb{K}$ *is the transition weight-function.*

Table 1. The semantic interpretation of c-HM. We have $\sum(\emptyset) = \bot$ and $\bigsqcap(\emptyset) = \top$.

$$
\begin{aligned}
[\![k]\!](C) &= k \in K \ \forall C \in C_n^m \\
[\![\phi_1 \sqcup \phi_2]\!](C) &= [\![\phi_1]\!](C) \sqcup [\![\phi_2]\!](C) \\
[\![\phi_1 \times \phi_2]\!](C) &= [\![\phi_1]\!](C) \times [\![\phi_2]\!](C) \\
[\![\phi_1 \sqcap \phi_2]\!](C) &= [\![\phi_1]\!](C) \sqcap [\![\phi_2]\!](C) \\
[\![\langle \tilde{a} \rangle \phi]\!](C) &= \bigsqcup_R (k_a \times [\![\phi]\!](C')) \\
[\![[\tilde{a}]\phi]\!](C) &= \bigsqcap_R (k_a \times [\![\phi]\!](C'))
\end{aligned}
$$

where $R = \{C' \in C_0^m \mid (C, (\tilde{a}, k_a), (0, \top), C') \in T\}$

Definition 10 syntactically defines the correct formulas given over an MLTS.

Definition 10 (Syntax). *Given an MLTS $M = \langle S, L^n, \mathbb{K}, T \rangle$, and let $\tilde{a} \in L^n$, the syntax of a formula $\phi \in \Phi_M$ is as follows, where $k \in K$:*

$$\phi ::= k \mid \phi_1 \sqcup \phi_2 \mid \phi_1 \times \phi_2 \mid \phi_1 \sqcap \phi_2 \mid \langle \tilde{a} \rangle \phi \mid [\tilde{a}]\phi$$

The operators $\sqcup$ and $\sqcap$ (respectively the lub and glb derived from $\geq$ in $\mathbb{K}$), and $\times$ (still in the definition of $\mathbb{K}$) are used in place of classical logic operators $\vee$ and $\wedge$, in order to compose the truth values of two formulas together. Truth values are all the $k \in K$. In particular, while *false* corresponds to $\bot$, we can have different degrees of *true*, where "full truth" is $\top$. As a reminder, when the $\times$ operator is idempotent, then $\times$ and $\sqcap$ coincide (Sect. 2). Finally, we have the two classical modal operators, i.e., "possibly" ($\langle\ \rangle$), and "necessarily" ($[\cdot]$).

The semantics of a formula ϕ is interpreted on a system of quantitative contexts, given on top of an MLTS $M = (C_n^m, Act_0^n \times Act_0^m, \mathbb{K}, \rightarrow_{n,m}^K)$. The aim is to check the specification defined by ϕ over the behaviour of a weighted transition system M that defines the behaviour of a quantitative context. While in [11] the semantics of a formula computes the states $U \subseteq C_n^m$ that satisfy that formula, our semantics $[\![\ ]\!]_M : (\Phi_M \times C_n^m) \longrightarrow K$ (see Table 1) computes a truth value for the same U. In particular, in the following we deal with n-ary contexts (C_0^n), hence the set of labels is $L^n = Act_0^n$. Note that we consider finite contexts C_n^m, i.e., they are defined over a finite MLTS, they are not recursive, and the contexts composed with them are closed and finite as well.

In Table 1 and in the following (when clear from the context), we omit M from $[\![\ ]\!]_M$ for the sake of readability. The semantics is parametrised over a context $C \in C_n^m$, which is used to consider only the transitions that can be fired at a given step (labelled with a vector of actions $\tilde{a}$).

In Definition 11 we rephrase the notion of satisfiability of a c-HM^n formula ϕ on a context C by taking into account a threshold t (t-satisfiability):

Definition 11 ($\models_t$). *A context $C \in C_n^m$ satisfies a c-HM^n formula ϕ with a threshold-value t, i.e., $C \models_t \phi$, if and only if the interpretation of ϕ on C is better/equal than t. Formally: $C \models_t \phi \Leftrightarrow t \leq [\![\phi]\!]_C$.*

This means that C is a model for a formula ϕ, with respect to a certain value t, if and only if the weight corresponding to the interpretation of ϕ on C is better or equal to t in the partial order $\leq$ defined in $\mathbb{K}$.

Remark 1. Note that, if C does not satisfy a formula ϕ then $[\![\phi]\!]_C = \bot$. Consequently, the only t such that $C \models_t \phi$ is $t = \bot$. If $[\![\phi]\!]_C \neq \bot$, then ϕ is satisfiable with a certain threshold $t \neq \bot$.

5   Decomposition of Properties

In this section we provide a machinery for decomposing quantitative properties satisfied by a context C_0^n, which can be written as the product of n C_0^1 contexts, into local quantitative properties, each of them satisfied by such a unary context.[3] Indeed, let $C(X_1, \ldots, X_n)$ be a distributed system, in which $X_1, \ldots, X_n$ are system sub-components. We are interested in identifying which are the local properties, expressed by a logic formula c-HM^1, each X_i, $i = 1, \ldots, n$ has to quantitatively satisfy that $C(X_1, \ldots, X_n)$ quantitatively satisfies a global property expressed by a n-ary logic formula in c-HM^n. This satisfaction is given with respect to a threshold value t concerning a quantitative requirement on the evaluation of ϕ, which is required to be better than $t \in K$. Formally, this can be expressed as

$$\forall X_i, \ i = 1, \ldots, n \quad C(X_1, \ldots, X_n) \models_t \phi. \tag{1}$$

Due to the expressive power of c-HM^n (see Sect. 4.1), we mainly consider *safety properties*, e.g., properties expressing that if something goes wrong it can be detected in a finite number of steps.

In order to solve the problem in Eq. 1, we provide formal tools to simplify this problem by splitting ϕ into local properties to be projected on each unknown X_i i.e., the problem in Eq. 1 is reduced to a set of problems $X_i \models_{t_i} \phi_i$, $\forall i \in I$, where $X_i \in C_0^1$ and ϕ_i and t_i are the output of the decomposition procedure. In words, we decompose ϕ' over the unknown parts. Similarly to [11], we define a *n-tuple formula* as a unary c-HM^n formula represented as a vector of n components $\langle \phi_1, \ldots, \phi_n \rangle$, where each $\phi_1, \ldots, \phi_n$ is a closed and unary formula in c-HM^1. $\langle \phi_1, \ldots, \phi_n \rangle$ is unary because we let its evaluation correspond to $[\![\phi_1 \times \ldots \times \phi_n]\!]$.

Definition 12 (Tuple-formulas). $\langle \phi_1, \ldots, \phi_n \rangle$ *is an n-tuple formula where each ϕ_i, $i = 1, \ldots, n$ is a unary formula such that, for the context $X_1 \times \ldots \times X_n$:*

$$[\![\langle \phi_1, \ldots, \phi_n \rangle]\!](X_1 \times \ldots \times X_n) = [\![\langle \phi_1 \rangle]\!](X_1) \times \ldots \times [\![\langle \phi_n \rangle]\!](X_n)$$

For a tuple formula ϕ, we say that ϕ is *quantitatively weakly valid* if it is satisfied by all the possible n-product contexts $X_1 \times \ldots \times X_n$, within a given quantitative context-system.

Hereafter we focus on the decomposition of a formula ϕ into the components of a tuple-formula. To do this, we first introduce the notion of equality between

---

[3] It is worth noting that this follows the notion of *weakly validity* introduced in [11].

two formulas i.e., $\phi_1 = \phi_2$, in such a way that the result is $\top$ if they are both evaluated to the same $k \in K$, $\bot$ otherwise. Formally,

$$[\![\phi_1 = \phi_2]\!](C) = \begin{cases} \top \ if \ [\![\phi_1]\!](C) = [\![\phi_2]\!](C). \\ \bot \ otherwise. \end{cases} \tag{2}$$

Hence, the decomposition we need can be formally stated as the search for a single tuple formula $\langle \phi_1, \ldots, \phi_n \rangle$ such that $\langle \phi_1, \ldots, \phi_n \rangle = \phi$ is a tautology, i.e., $[\![\langle \phi_1, \ldots, \phi_n \rangle = \phi]\!](C) = \top$ for any C. Therefore, we can state $\langle \phi_1, \ldots, \phi_n \rangle$ is quantitatively weakly valid. Note that, according to the definition of $=$, this is equivalent to state that $[\![\langle \phi_1, \ldots, \phi_n \rangle]\!](C) = [\![\phi]\!](C)$ for any C. Hereafter, when we use this notation we omit (C) for the sake of brevity.

Usually there does not exist a single tuple formula that decomposes ϕ. Let ϕ be finite, there exists a finite collection of tuple formulas $\langle \phi_1^i, \ldots, \phi_n^i \rangle_{i \in I}$, for n finite collections of unary closed formulas $\langle \phi_j^i \rangle_{i \in I}$ (I is a finite indexes set) s.t.

$$\sum_{i \in I} \langle \phi_1^i, \ldots, \phi_n^i \rangle = \phi \tag{3}$$

is a tautology (see Eq. 2). For the sake of clarity and simplicity, we curb to consider the decomposition of ϕ into 2-tuple formulas, that is $\sum_{i \in I} \langle \phi_1^i, \phi_2^i \rangle$.

Definition 13 (Saturation). *A summation tuple-formula $\sum_{i \in I} \langle \phi_1^i, \phi_2^i \rangle$ is said to be* saturated *with respect to any binary product context $C_1 \times C_2$ if*

$$[\![\sum_{i \in I} \langle \phi_1^i, \phi_2^i \rangle]\!](C_1 \times C_2) \ is \ equivalent \ to \ \exists \ i \in I \ s.t. \ [\![\phi_1^i]\!](C_1) \ and \ [\![\phi_2^i]\!](C_2)$$

The basic idea of this definition is to identify all the possible binary product-formulas that have to be included in a summation product-formula ψ, with the purpose to guarantee ψ is a tautology.

In general, not all the summation tuple-formulas are saturated; however, they can be saturated by adopting the following construction.

Definition 14 (Saturation construction). *Let Φ be a tuple-formula $\sum_{i \in I} \langle \phi_1^i, \phi_2^i \rangle$. Then we define two tuple-formulas $\mathcal{L}(\Phi)$ and $\mathcal{R}(\Phi)$ as follows:*

$$\mathcal{L}(F) = \sum_{J \subseteq I} \left\langle \sum_{j \in J} \phi_1^j, \prod_{j \in J} \phi_2^j \right\rangle, \quad \mathcal{R}(F) = \sum_{J \subseteq I} \left\langle \prod_{j \in J} \phi_1^j, \sum_{j \in J} \phi_2^j \right\rangle$$

where $\sum_\emptyset = \bot$ and $\prod_\emptyset = \top$.

Example 1. Let us consider $\phi = \langle 5, 3 \rangle + \langle 6, 4 \rangle$ in the weighted semiring. This is not saturated because it is possible to find two unary contexts C_1 and C_2 whose product satisfies ϕ, but none of them satisfies (see Eq. 2) neither $\langle 5, 3 \rangle$ nor $\langle 6, 4 \rangle$. For instance, according to the semantics of $+$, $[\![\langle 5, 3 \rangle + \langle 6, 4 \rangle]\!](C_1 \times C_2)$ can be

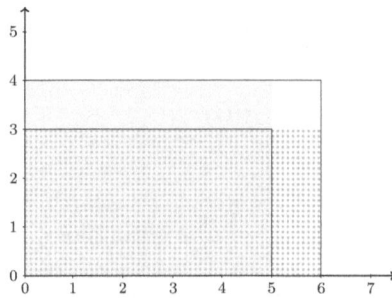

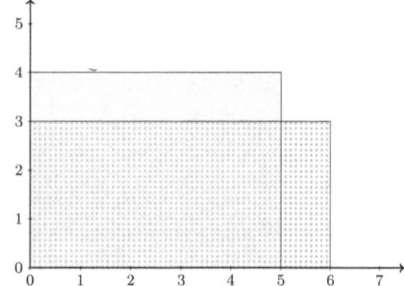

Fig. 1. Saturation of a totally ordered summation formula $\langle 5,3 \rangle + \langle 6,4 \rangle$.

Fig. 2. Saturation of a partially ordered sum. formula $\langle 5,4 \rangle + \langle 6,3 \rangle$.

rewritten as $[\![\langle 5,3 \rangle]\!](C_1 \times C_2) + [\![\langle 6,4 \rangle]\!](C_1 \times C_2)$. For the semantics of a binary product formula, $[\![\langle 5,3 \rangle]\!](C_1 \times C_2) = [\![5]\!](C_1) \times [\![3]\!](C_2)$ or $[\![\langle 6,4 \rangle]\!](C_1 \times C_2) = [\![6]\!](C_1) \times [\![4]\!](C_2)$. Let us consider $[\![5]\!](C_1)$ and $[\![4]\!](C_2)$, then $[\![\phi]\!](C_1 \times C_2) = 9$ (the product satisfies ϕ). However, the binary product formula $\langle 5,4 \rangle$ is not in the original summation formula.

Formula ϕ represents the intersection of two rectangles represented by the couple $\langle 5,3 \rangle$ and $\langle 6,4 \rangle$: the grey and dotted area in Fig. 1 (i.e., $\langle 5,3 \rangle$). All the rectangles completely included in the grey-and-dotted intersections in Fig. 1 imply ϕ in all the possible contexts of any context system: in this case, $\langle 5,4 \rangle$ and $\langle 6,3 \rangle$. Let us now compute the saturation of ϕ, $\mathcal{R}(\mathcal{L}(\phi))$: $\mathcal{R}(\mathcal{L}(\langle 5,3 \rangle + \langle 6,4 \rangle)) = \langle \top, \bot \rangle + \langle \bot, \top \rangle + \langle 5,3 \rangle + \langle 6,4 \rangle + \langle (5+6), (3 \sqcap 4) \rangle + \langle (5 \sqcap 6), (3+4) \rangle = \langle \top, \bot \rangle + \langle \bot, \top \rangle + \langle 5,3 \rangle + \langle 6,4 \rangle + \langle 5,4 \rangle + \langle 6,3 \rangle$. As hinted by Fig. 1, the two rectangles $\langle 5,3 \rangle$ and $\langle 6,4 \rangle$ appear in such saturation.

Note that $\langle 5,3 \rangle$ and $\langle 6,4 \rangle$ are totally ordered: one dominates both dimensions of the other. Whether we consider partially ordered summation formulas, such as $\langle 5,4 \rangle + \langle 6,3 \rangle$ depicted in Fig. 2, the saturation just includes the decomposition of $\bot$ in accordance with $\bot \leq k$ for every $k \in \mathbb{K}$. This also depends on the fact that, if the semantic interpretation of $\langle 5,4 \rangle$ and $\langle 6,3 \rangle$ is the same, then there is no other value in the middle whose decomposition should be considered.

The composition of $\mathcal{L}(F)$ and $\mathcal{R}(F)$ allows the desired saturation:

Theorem 1 (Saturation). *Let Φ be a summation-tuple formula, then $\Phi = \mathcal{L}(\Phi)$ and $\Phi = \mathcal{R}(\Phi)$ are qualitatively weakly valid and $\mathcal{R}(\mathcal{L}(\Phi))$ is saturated.*

Proof. We need to prove that $[\![\Phi]\!] = [\![\mathcal{L}(\Phi)]\!]$ and $[\![\Phi]\!] = [\![\mathcal{R}(\Phi)]\!]$. Let us consider the case $\mathcal{L}(\Phi)$.

$$[\![\mathcal{L}(\Phi)]\!] = [\![\bigsqcup_{J \subseteq I} \left\langle \bigsqcup_{j \in J} \phi_1^j, \bigsqcap_{j \in J} \phi_2^j \right\rangle]\!] = \bigsqcup_{J \subseteq I} [\![\left\langle \bigsqcup_{j \in J} \phi_1^j, \bigsqcap_{j \in J} \phi_2^j \right\rangle]\!] = \bigsqcup_{J \subseteq I} ([\![\bigsqcup_{j \in J} \phi_1^j]\!] \times [\![\bigsqcap_{j \in J} \phi_2^j]\!])$$

$$[\![\mathcal{R}(\Phi)]\!] = [\![\bigsqcup_{J \subseteq I} \left\langle \bigsqcap_{j \in J} \phi_1^j, \bigsqcup_{j \in J} \phi_2^j \right\rangle]\!] = \bigsqcup_{J \subseteq I} [\![\left\langle \bigsqcap_{j \in J} \phi_1^j, \bigsqcup_{j \in J} \phi_2^j \right\rangle]\!] = \bigsqcup_{J \subseteq I} ([\![\bigsqcap_{j \in J} \phi_1^j]\!] \times [\![\bigsqcup_{j \in J} \phi_2^j]\!])$$

By construction, anyway we select a specific $j \in (J \subseteq I)$, we have

$$[\![\sum_{j \in J} \phi_1^j]\!] \times [\![\prod_{j \in J} \phi_2^j]\!] = k = [\![\Phi]\!].$$ $\square$

The equivalences in Table 2 are a means for decomposing quantitative properties. We now prove their validity in Theorem 2.

Theorem 2 (Weak validity). *The equivalences in Table 2 are all quantitatively weakly valid.*

Proof. The intuition is that, when $k = \bot$, according to rule *(i)* in Table 2, we simply decompose it as $\{\langle \bot, \top \rangle, \langle \top, \bot \rangle\}$. For $k = \top$, the single value of decomposition is equal to $\{\langle \top, \top \rangle\}$. These two results completely recall the original work in [11]. Still following [11], the more difficult equivalence is the *(v)* one. Let us consider $C_1 \times C_2 \models_t [ab](\bigsqcup i \in I \phi_1^i \times \phi_2^i)$ holds. This means that $C_1 \times C_2 \xrightarrow{(ab, k_a \times k_b)} C_1' \times C_2'$ and $C_1' \times C_2' \models_{t'} \bigsqcup i \in I \phi_1^i \times \phi_2^i$. Being $\bigsqcup i \in I \phi_1^i \times \phi_2^i$ saturated, this means that $\exists i \in I$ such that $C_1' \models_{t_1'} \phi_1^i$ and $C_2' \models_{t_2'} \phi_2^i$. According to the semantics definition of context product, $C_1 \times C_2 \xrightarrow{(ab, k_a \times k_b)} C_1' \times C_2'$ means that $C_1 \xrightarrow{(a, k_a)} C_1'$ and $C_2 \xrightarrow{(b, k_b)} C_2'$. Hence, $C_1 \models_{t_1} [a]\phi_1^i$ and $C_2 \models_{t_2} [b]\phi_2^i$. Then $C_1 \times C_2 \models_t \bigsqcup_{i \in I} \langle [a]\phi_1^i, [b]\phi_2^i \rangle^4$. The other weakly equivalences are simpler to prove, and the reasoning behind is similar.

Remark 1. [Decomposing k] The decomposition of k in Table 2 is finite and it is the maximal one. This depends on the semantics of a formula k. Indeed, k is a tautology because its semantics interpretation is always the same for any context system. Following the intuition of saturation, we would like to decompose k in all the possible product-formulas whose interpretation is k, i.e., $k = \sum_{i,j \in I} \langle k_i, k_j \rangle$ such that $k_i \times k_j = k$. However, this decomposition is infinite if the domain of the c-semiring is infinite. Nevertheless, if we consider finite c-semirings with a finite set K, it is possible to prove that it collapses to using the decomposition provided by *(i)* in Table 2. Furthermore, even though we consider a c-semiring with an infinite set of preferences, the two decompositions are equivalent:

$$\langle k, \top \rangle + \langle \top, k \rangle = \sum_{i,j \in I} \langle k_i, k_j \rangle \quad s.t. \ k_i \times k_j = k$$

This is because $[\![k]\!](C) = k$ for every context C.

Theorem 3 (Decomposition existence). *Let $\phi \in c\text{-}HM^2$ be a finite formula and I a finite set of indexes. It always exists a saturated decomposition of ϕ, i.e., $\sum_{i \in I} \langle \phi_1^i, \phi_2^i \rangle$, such that $\phi = \sum_{i \in I} \langle \phi_1^i, \phi_2^i \rangle$ is a quantitatively weakly valid formula.*

---

[4] At this level, we are not interested in values t, t_1, t_2 and so on, hence we do not calculate their exact value as the product of k_a and k_b.

Table 2. Quantitative equivalences for the decomposition of properties.

$$(i) \qquad\qquad k = \langle k, \top \rangle + \langle \top, k \rangle$$
$$(ii)\ \langle \phi_1, \psi_1 \rangle \times \langle \phi_2, \psi_2 \rangle = \langle \phi_1 \times \phi_2, \psi_1 \times \psi_2 \rangle$$
$$(iii)\ \langle \phi_1, \psi_1 \rangle \sqcap \langle \phi_2, \psi_2 \rangle = \langle \phi_1 \sqcap \phi_2, \psi_1 \sqcap \psi_2 \rangle$$
$$(iv) \qquad \langle\langle a, b \rangle\rangle\langle \phi, \psi \rangle = \langle\langle a \rangle \phi, \langle b \rangle \psi \rangle$$
$$(v) \qquad [\langle a, b \rangle] \sum_i \langle \phi^i, \psi^i \rangle = \sum_i \langle [a] \phi^i, [b] \psi^i \rangle$$

where in (v) $\sum_i \langle \phi^i, \psi^i \rangle$ is assumed to be saturated.

Proof. The proof is obtained by induction on the structure of ϕ.

Base case: $\phi = k$ According to Table 2, $k = \langle k, \top \rangle \sqcup \langle \top, k \rangle$. As we have already said in Remark 1, this decomposition is saturated because, according to Table 1 all the elements of the domains of a c-semiring are tautologies. Hence, adding all the couples of elements whose semantics is equal to k is redundant.

Inductive step

– $\phi = \phi_1 \times \phi_2$: By inductive hypothesis, there exists a saturated decomposition for both ϕ_1 and ϕ_2. Hence, $\phi = \phi_1 \times \phi_2 = (\bigsqcup_{i \in I} \langle \phi^i_{1,1}, \phi^i_{1,2} \rangle) \times (\bigsqcup_{j \in I} \langle \phi^j_{2,1}, \phi^j_{2,2} \rangle)$.
The $\times$ operation is distributive on the $\sqcup$ one, thus, $(\bigsqcup_{i \in I} \langle \phi^i_{1,1}, \phi^i_{1,2} \rangle) \times$
$(\bigsqcup_{j \in I} \langle \phi^j_{2,1}, \phi^j_{2,2} \rangle) = \bigsqcup_{i,j \in I} \langle \phi^i_{1,1}, \phi^i_{1,2} \rangle \times \langle \phi^j_{2,1}, \phi^j_{2,2} \rangle$. It is worth noting that we
have considered the same set of indexes for both the decomposition but this does not influence the validity of the proof because this is only a matter of notation. According to rule (ii) Table 2, $\bigsqcup_{i,j \in I} \langle \phi^i_{1,1}, \phi^i_{1,2} \rangle \times \langle \phi^j_{2,1}, \phi^j_{2,2} \rangle =$
$\bigsqcup_{i,j \in I} \langle \phi^i_{1,1} \times \phi^j_{2,1}, \phi^i_{1,2} \times \phi^j_{2,2} \rangle$. This is a possible decomposition of $\phi_1 \times \phi_2$; to
be saturated we have to prove that for any couple of contexts C_1 and C_2, there exist $i, j \in I$ such that

$$[\![\bigsqcup_{i,j \in I} \langle \phi^i_{1,1} \times \phi^j_{2,1}, \phi^i_{1,2} \times \phi^j_{2,2} \rangle]\!](C_1 \times C_2) = [\![\langle \phi^i_{1,1} \times \phi^j_{2,1} \rangle]\!](C_1) \times [\![\langle \phi^i_{1,2} \times \phi^j_{2,2} \rangle]\!](C_2).$$

$$[\![\bigsqcup_{i,j \in I} \langle \phi^i_{1,1} \times \phi^j_{2,1}, \phi^i_{1,2} \times \phi^j_{2,2} \rangle]\!](C_1 \times C_2) = \bigsqcup_{i,j \in I} [\![\langle \phi^i_{1,1} \times \phi^j_{2,1}, \phi^i_{1,2} \times \phi^j_{2,2} \rangle]\!](C_1 \times C_2) =$$

$$\bigsqcup_{i,j \in I} [\![\langle \phi^i_{1,1} \times \phi^j_{2,1} \rangle]\!](C_1) \times [\![\langle \phi^i_{1,2} \times \phi^j_{2,2} \rangle]\!](C_2) =$$

$$\bigsqcup_{i,j \in I} [\![\phi^i_{1,1}]\!](C_1) \times [\![\phi^j_{2,1}]\!](C_1) \times [\![\phi^i_{1,2}]\!](C_2) \times [\![\phi^j_{2,2}]\!](C_2) =$$

$$\bigsqcup_{i \in I} [\![\phi^i_{1,1}]\!](C_1) \times [\![\phi^i_{1,2}]\!](C_2) \times \bigsqcup_{j \in I} [\![\phi^j_{2,1}]\!](C_1) \times [\![\phi^j_{2,2}]\!](C_2).$$

Being the decomposition of ϕ_1 and ϕ_2 saturated by inductive hypothesis, there exists at least $i \in I$ such that $\bigsqcup_{i \in I} [\![\phi_{1,1}^i]\!](C_1) \times [\![\phi_{1,2}^i]\!](C_2) = [\![\phi_{1,1}^i]\!](C_1) \times [\![\phi_{1,2}^i]\!](C_2)$ and there exists $j \in I$ such that $\bigsqcup_{j \in I} [\![\phi_{2,1}^j]\!](C_1) \times [\![\phi_{2,2}^j]\!](C_2) = [\![\phi_{2,1}^j]\!](C_1) \times [\![\phi_{2,2}^j]\!](C_2)$. Hence, there exists $i, h \in I$ such that $\bigsqcup_{i \in I} [\![\phi_{1,1}^i]\!](C_1) \times [\![\phi_{1,2}^i]\!](C_2) \times \bigsqcup_{j \in I} [\![\phi_{2,1}^j]\!](C_1) \times [\![\phi_{2,2}^j]\!](C_2) = [\![\phi_{1,1}^i]\!](C_1) \times [\![\phi_{1,2}^i]\!](C_2) \times [\![\phi_{2,1}^j]\!](C_1) \times [\![\phi_{2,2}^j]\!](C_2) = [\![\langle \phi_{1,1}^i, \phi_{2,1}^j \rangle]\!](C_1) \times [\![\langle \phi_{1,2}^i, \phi_{2,2}^j \rangle]\!](C_2)$. It is worth noting that it is possible to rename the set of indexes in order to have an index, $e.g.$, $w = \langle i, j \rangle$, which allows us to conclude the proof of $\phi = \phi_1 \times \phi_2$. The proof of $\phi = \phi_1 \sqcap \phi_2$ follows the same reasoning.

$- \phi = \langle a, b \rangle \phi_1$: by inductive hypothesis, ϕ_1 has a saturated decomposition, $\phi_1 = \bigsqcup_{i \in I} \langle \phi_{1,1}^i, \phi_{1,2}^i \rangle$. Hence, $\phi = \langle a, b \rangle \bigsqcup_{i \in I} \langle \phi_{1,1}^i, \phi_{1,2}^i \rangle$. It means that

$$[\![\phi]\!](C) = \bigsqcup_{C \xrightarrow{(\langle a,b, \rangle, k_{\langle a,b, \rangle})} C'} k_{\langle a,b \rangle} \times [\![\phi_1]\!](C') =$$

$$\bigsqcup_{C \xrightarrow{(\langle a,b, \rangle, k_{\langle a,b, \rangle})} C'} k_{\langle a,b \rangle} \times [\![\bigsqcup_{i \in I} \langle \phi_{1,1}^i, \phi_{1,2}^i \rangle]\!](C') =$$

$$\bigsqcup_{C \xrightarrow{(\langle a,b, \rangle, k_{\langle a,b, \rangle})} C'} k_{\langle a,b \rangle} \times \bigsqcup_{i \in I} [\![\langle \phi_{1,1}^i, \phi_{1,2}^i \rangle]\!](C').$$

Since we are considering a product context $C = C_1 \times C_2$, then, according to the semantics of the product operator, we have $k_{\langle a,b \rangle} = k_a \times k_b$ (if C_1 performs a and C_2 performs b). Hence,

$$\bigsqcup_{C \xrightarrow{(\langle a,b, \rangle, k_{\langle a,b, \rangle})} C'} k_{\langle a,b \rangle} \times \bigsqcup_{i \in I} [\![\langle \phi_{1,1}^i, \phi_{1,2}^i \rangle]\!](C') =$$

$$\bigsqcup_{C_1 \times C_2 \xrightarrow{(\langle a,b, \rangle, k_{\langle a,b, \rangle})} C_1' \times C_2'} k_a \times k_b \times \bigsqcup_{i \in I} [\![\langle \phi_{1,1}^i, \phi_{1,2}^i \rangle]\!](C_1' \times C_2') =$$

$$\bigsqcup_{C_1 \times C_2 \xrightarrow{(\langle a,b, \rangle, k_{\langle a,b, \rangle})} C_1' \times C_2'} \bigsqcup_{i \in I} k_a \times k_b \times [\![\langle \phi_{1,1}^i, \phi_{1,2}^i \rangle]\!](C_1' \times C_2') =$$

$$\bigsqcup_{i \in I} \bigsqcup_{C_1 \times C_2 \xrightarrow{(\langle a,b, \rangle, k_{\langle a,b, \rangle})} C_1' \times C_2'} k_a \times k_b \times [\![\langle \phi_{1,1}^i, \phi_{1,2}^i \rangle]\!](C_1' \times C_2') =$$

$$\bigsqcup_{i \in I} [\![\langle a, b \rangle \langle \phi_{1,1}^i, \phi_{1,2}^i \rangle]\!](C_1 \times C_2).$$

According to rule iv Table 2,

$$\bigsqcup_{i\in I} [\![\langle a,b\rangle\langle \phi_{1,1}^i, \phi_{1,2}^i\rangle]\!](C_1 \times C_2) = \bigsqcup_{i\in I} [\![\langle\langle a\rangle\phi_{1,1}^i, \langle b\rangle\phi_{1,2}^i\rangle]\!](C_1 \times C_2).$$

This is a decomposition of ϕ. To prove it is saturated, we have two cases:
(i) $C_1 \times C_2$ does not perform $\langle a,b\rangle$. This means that $[\![\langle\langle a\rangle\phi_{1,1}^i]\!](C_1) = \bot$ and $[\![\langle\langle b\rangle\phi_{1,2}^i]\!](C_2) = \bot$ for any $i \in I$. Hence, $\bigsqcup_{i\in I} [\![\langle\langle a\rangle\phi_{1,1}^i, \langle b\rangle\phi_{1,2}^i\rangle]\!](C_1 \times C_2) = \bot$.
And vice-versa, whether $\bigsqcup_{i\in I} [\![\langle\langle a\rangle\phi_{1,1}^i, \langle b\rangle\phi_{1,2}^i\rangle]\!](C_1 \times C_2) = \bot$, according to the definition of interpretation of product formula there is at least one of the two contexts that evaluates the formula to $\bot$.
(ii) For all the contexts $C_1 \times C_2$ such that $[\![\phi]\!](C_1 \times C_2) \neq \bot$ then $C_1 \times C_2 \xrightarrow{(\langle a,b\rangle),k_{\langle a,b,\rangle})} C_1' \times C_2'$. This means that $[\![\bigsqcup_{i\in I}\langle \phi_{1,1}^i, \phi_{1,2}^i\rangle]\!](C_1' \times C_2') \neq \bot$.
Being saturated, there exists $i \in I$ such that $[\![\bigsqcup_{i\in I}\langle \phi_{1,1}^i, \phi_{1,2}^i\rangle]\!](C_1' \times C_2') = [\![\phi_{1,1}^i]\!](C_1') \times [\![\phi_{1,2}^i]\!](C_2')$. Hence,

$$\bigsqcup_{C_1\times C_2 \xrightarrow{(\langle a,b,\rangle),k_{\langle a,b,\rangle})} C_1'\times C_2'} k_{\langle a,b\rangle} \times [\![\bigsqcup_{i\in I}\langle \phi_{1,1}^i, \phi_{1,2}^i\rangle]\!](C_1' \times C_2') =$$

$$\bigsqcup_{C_1\times C_2 \xrightarrow{(\langle a,b,\rangle),k_{\langle a,b,\rangle})} C_1'\times C_2'} k_{\langle a,b\rangle} \times [\![\phi_{1,1}^i]\!](C_1') \times [\![\phi_{1,2}^i]\!](C_2') =$$

$$\bigsqcup_{C_1\times C_2 \xrightarrow{(\langle a,b,\rangle),k_{\langle a,b,\rangle})} C_1'\times C_2'} k_a \times k_b \times [\![\phi_{1,1}^i]\!](C_1') \times [\![\phi_{1,2}^i]\!](C_2') =$$

$$(\bigsqcup_{C_1 \xrightarrow{(a,k_a)} C_1'} k_a \times [\![\phi_{1,1}^i]\!](C_1')) \times (\bigsqcup_{C_2 \xrightarrow{(b,k_b)} C_2'} k_b \times [\![\phi_{1,2}^i]\!](C_2')) =$$

$$[\![\langle a\rangle\phi_{1,1}^i]\!](C_1) \times [\![\langle b\rangle\phi_{1,2}^i]\!](C_2).$$

The proof of $\phi = [a,b]\phi_1$ follows a similar reasoning. $\square$

Note that, the result of Theorem 3 is equivalent to say that the interpretation of both ϕ and $\sum_{i\in I}\langle \phi_1^i, \phi_2^i\rangle$ is the same for any product of a couple of unary contexts in any context system: $[\![\phi]\!] = [\![\sum_{i\in I}\langle \phi_1^i, \phi_2^i\rangle]\!]$.

6   Quantitative Chinese-Wall Policy

A possible application of the proposed framework is to security. By identifying the necessary and sufficient conditions of each system subcomponent, it is possible to guarantee security by analysing those subcomponents that may attack the system.

We extend the well-known Chinese-Wall access-policy with side-quantities associated with access actions (as advanced in Sect. 1). In the following we suppose to use $\langle \mathbb{R}^+ \cup \{+\infty\}, min, \hat{+}, +\infty, 0\rangle$ as the reference (weighted) semiring. We refer to it as *Quantitative Chinese-Wall Policy*, where a policy is expressed by $\phi = \phi_1 + \phi_2$ and ϕ_1, ϕ_2 represent two distinct strategies to access to two different sets of resources (A and B, e.g., files or data). Each (boxed) access action is associated with a different weight, which can be interpreted as a monetary cost demanded to exploit such resource, or a cost in terms of capabilities to be spent in order to access. The two formulas are $\phi_1 = [access\_A]5 \times [access\_B]3$ and $\phi_2 = [access\_B]6 \times [access\_A]4$.

This behaves as the classical Chinese-Wall if the threshold is $t = 3$, or $t = 4$: in the first case, one can access to B with strategy ϕ_1, while with $t = 4$ one can access to either B (ϕ_1) or to A using strategy ϕ_2. With $8 > t \geq 5$, both strategies can be adopted to access to both resources, still exclusively (either A or B); hence, it corresponds to a "relaxed" version of Chinese Wall. Finally, with $t \geq 8$, it is possible to contemporary access to both resources with ϕ_1; with $t \geq 10$ even with both strategies, thus completely breaking the classical Chinese-Wall Policy. Thus, to be sure to respect the classical or relaxed policy, one has to select t worse than the cost of the best strategy (here, worse than 8).

Let us decompose the Quantitative Chinese-Wall Policy into local constraints on X_1 and X_2. Hence, we have to decompose ϕ according to quantitative equivalences *(i)* and *(v)* in Table 2.

$$\phi_1 = ([access\_A](\langle 5, \top\rangle + \langle \top, 5\rangle) \times ([access\_B](\langle 3, \top\rangle + \langle \top, 3\rangle))$$
$$= ((\langle [access\_A]5, \top\rangle + \langle \top, [access\_A]5\rangle) \times ((\langle [access\_B]3, \top\rangle + \langle \top, [access\_B]3\rangle))$$
$$\phi_2 = ([access\_B](\langle 6, \top\rangle + \langle \top, 6\rangle) \times ([access\_A](\langle 4, \top\rangle + \langle \top, 4\rangle))$$
$$= ((\langle [access\_B]6, \top\rangle + \langle \top, [access\_B]6\rangle) \times ((\langle [access\_A]4, \top\rangle + \langle \top, [access\_A]4\rangle))$$

We now prove that $X_1 \times X_2 \models_t \phi$, where t is a threshold cost. Fixing $t = 5$ then, $X_1 \times X_2 \models_t \phi$ may be not satisfy ϕ for one of these two reasons:

1. $X_1 \times X_2 \models_t \phi$ with $t \leq 5$. This happens when, for instance $X_1 = (access\_A, 1).0$ and $X_2 = (access\_B, 1).0$ then $X_1 \times X_2 = ((access\_A, access\_B), 1).0$. According to the decomposition both the actions at the same time may not be performed, hence the formula is not satisfied even though the whole evaluation of the formula is better than 5.
2. The Chinese-Wall Policy is respected, but the security level of the product does not satisfy the required threshold yet, and ϕ is not 5-satisfied. This is the case in which both X_1 and X_2 perform a valid sequence of actions, e.g., one $access\_A$ each, but the level of one of these actions is worse than 5. For instance, one access to A happens with a weak password (e.g., level 6).

7   Related Work

The most direct comparison is with [11]: this paper promotes a quantitative view of such work, presenting semirings as a general framework where to decompose weighted properties. We show that most of the notions given in [11], in particular decomposition (Sect. 5) are still valid even if considering different metrics. We discuss related work about these two main aspects. Some examples of a quantitative temporal logic are [1,7,10]. In [7] the authors present $QLTL$, a quantitative analogue of LTL and presents algorithms for model checking it over quantitative versions of Kripke structures and Markov chains. Thus, weights are in the interval of Real numbers $[0,1]$. In [1] the authors combine robustness scores with the satisfaction probability to optimise some control parameters of a stochastic model: the goal is to best maximise robustness of the desired specifications. However, even this approach is focused on (continuous-time) Markov Chains, and not on semiring algebraic-structures. One more example is the weighted CTL logic in [10], which adopts weight intervals instead of a single score.

In [10] the authors associate each transition in *weighted modal transition systems* with an interval of weights, implementing a sort of "loose" specification. The presence of both negative and positive preferences in [10] can be achieved by using bipolar-semiring structures [4]. In addition, the interval idea suggests a re-phrasal our framework into a *Soft Constraint Satisfaction Problem (SCSP)* [3,4], where weights correspond to explicit constraints on transitions. Hence, finding a solution on a SCSP leads to satisfying all the intervals.

Some works about decomposition are mostly related to adaptation and negotiation protocols that allow multiple agents to cooperate and reach a goal by agreeing on which part of the goal they respectively satisfy. In our approach we propose a general decomposition framework that is valid regardless the behaviour of the involved agents. We obtain all possible decomposition (the saturated one) while the protocols proposed in the literature obtain a possible decomposition suitable for the involved parties. In the following of this section we briefly introduce some of them. In [8] and [19] the authors analyse a selected list of design patterns for managing the coordination in the literature of self-organising systems. The work in [14] deals with *Security Adaptation Contracts (SACs)* consisting of a high-level specification of the mapping between the signature and the security policies of services, plus some temporal logic restrictions and secrecy properties to be satisfied. In [17] the authors focus on automated adaptation of an agent's functionality by means of an agent factory. An agent factory is an external service that adapts agents, on the basis of a well-structured description of the software agent. Structuring an agent makes it possible to reason about an agent's functionality on the basis of its blueprint, which includes information about its configuration. In [12], Li et al. present an approach for securing distributed adaptation. A plan is synthesized and executed, allowing the different parties to apply a set of data transformations in a distributed fashion. In particular, the authors synthesise "security boxes" that wrap services. Security boxes are pre-designed, but interchangeable at run time. In [18], the *AVISPA* tool is run first to obtain the protocol of the composition, and second to verify that it preserves the desired security properties.

8   Conclusion and Future Work

We have presented a verification framework where to study quantitative properties, i.e., properties with an associated value. This value can be interpreted as how much costly the verification of a property is in terms of non-functional aspects as, *e.g.*, time and cost to execute an action. Hence, it is possible to set a threshold t representing the last sustainable cost, and check if the total value is better than t. In particular, the main goal of the framework is the decomposition of a property into simpler ones, which needs to be locally satisfied by the subcomponents (i.e., quantitative contexts) of a system.

We can extend such a framework in several ways. A possible direction is the identification of comparative monitoring strategies able to guarantee the security of a system. Such strategies will be based on the partial ordering of a semiring and be compared in order to synthesise the best one (whether it exists). Furthermore, we can distinguish between centralised and decentralised ways of monitoring [16] different locations of a distributed system (or run-time [5] from static). The aim is to find the best strategies and compare them to understand which properties are better enforced in a centralised way, and which one in a decentralised way. Finally, we would like to manage infinite contexts by extending our logic to deal with fix-points, taking the inspiration from [13].

References

1. Bartocci, E., Bortolussi, L., Nenzi, L., Sanguinetti, G.: On the robustness of temporal properties for stochastic models. In: 2nd International Workshop on Hybrid Systems and Biology, EPTCS, vol. 125, pp. 3 19 (2013)
2. Bistarelli, S., Gadducci, F.: Enhancing constraints manipulation in semiring-based formalisms. In: ECAI, pp. 63–67 (2006)
3. Bistarelli, S., Montanari, U., Rossi, F.: Semiring-based constraint satisfaction and optimization. J. ACM **44**(2), 201–236 (1997)
4. Bistarelli, S., Santini, F.: Two trust networks in one: using bipolar structures to fuse trust and distrust. In: 2014 Twelfth Annual International Conference on Privacy, Security and Trust, pp. 383–390. IEEE (2014)
5. Bistarelli, S., Santini, F., Martinelli, F., Matteucci, I.: Automated adaptation via quantitative partial model checking. In: Proceedings of the 31st Annual ACM Symposium on Applied Computing, pp. 1993–1996. ACM (2016)
6. Blyth, T.S., Janowitz, M.F.: Residuation Theory, vol. 102. Pergamon press, Oxford (1972)
7. Faella, M., Legay, A., Stoelinga, M.: Model checking quantitative linear time logic. ENTCS **220**(3), 61–77 (2008)
8. Gardelli, L., Viroli, M., Omicini, A.: Design patterns for self-organising systems. In: Burkhard, H.-D., Lindemann, G., Verbrugge, R., Varga, L.Z. (eds.) CEEMAS 2007. LNCS, vol. 4696, pp. 123–132. Springer, Heidelberg (2007)
9. Golan, J.: Semirings and Affine Equations Over Them: Theory and Applications. Kluwer Academic Pub., Dordrecht (2003)
10. Juhl, L., Larsen, K.G., Srba, J.: Modal transition systems with weight intervals. J. Log. Algebr. Program. **81**(4), 408–421 (2012)

11. Larsen, K.G., Xinxin, L.: Compositionality through an operational semantics of contexts. J. Logic Comput. **1**(6), 761–795 (1991)
12. Li, J., Yarvis, M., Reiher, P.: Securing distributed adaptation. Comput. Netw. **38**(3), 347–371 (2002)
13. Lluch-Lafuente, A., Montanari, U.: Quantitative mu-calculus and CTL defined over constraint semirings. TCS **346**(1), 135–160 (2005)
14. Martín, J.A., Martinelli, F., Pimentel, E.: Synthesis of secure adaptors. J. Log. Algebr. Program. **81**(2), 99–126 (2012)
15. Martinelli, F., Matteucci, I., Santini, F.: Semiring-based specification approaches for quantitative security. In: Proceedings Thirteenth Workshop on Quantitative Aspects of Programming Languages and Systems, QAPL, EPTCS, vol. 194, pp. 95–109 (2015)
16. Martinelli, F., Matteucci, I., Santini, F.: There are two sides to every question. In: Bodei, C., Ferrari, G.-L., Priami, C. (eds.) Programming Languages with Applications to Biology and Security. LNCS, vol. 9465, pp. 304–318. Springer, Heidelberg (2015). doi:10.1007/978-3-319-25527-9_20
17. Splunter, S., Wijngaards, N.J.E., Brazier, F.M.T.: Structuring agents for adaptation. In: Alonso, E., Kudenko, D., Kazakov, D. (eds.) AAMAS 2001-2002. LNCS, vol. 2636, pp. 174–186. Springer, Heidelberg (2003). doi:10.1007/3-540-44826-8_11
18. Viganò, L.: Automated security protocol analysis with the AVISPA tool. ENTCS **155**, 69–86 (2006)
19. De Wolf, T., Holvoet, T.: Design patterns for decentralised coordination in self-organising emergent systems. In: Brueckner, S.A., Hassas, S., Jelasity, M., Yamins, D. (eds.) ESOA 2006. LNCS, vol. 4335, pp. 28–49. Springer, Heidelberg (2007)

Efficient SAT-Based Pre-image Enumeration for Quantitative Information Flow in Programs

Alexander Weigl[(⊠)]

Karlsruhe Institute of Technology,
Am Fasanengarten 5, 76131 Karlsruhe, Germany
weigl@kit.edu

Abstract. Quantitative Information Flow Analysis (QIF) measures the loss of an attacker's uncertainty about the confidential information (pre-image) inside a software system after observing the system outputs (image). In this paper, we supplement the SAT-based QIF analysis for deterministic and terminating C programs, by introducing three algorithms for counting the pre-images and images, which utilizes advantages of incremental SAT solvers. Our tool SHARPPI is competitive to MQL, QUAIL and CHIMP. An implementation is provided under http://formal.iti.kit.edu/sharpPI.

1 Introduction

Under Quantitative Information Flow Analysis (QIF) we subsume techniques and approaches to measure information flow in software systems. The information flow is an influence between two program variables and is usually described with entropy, which is a measure for the uncertainty about an information. The typical application for QIF is associated with an attacker, who tries to reduce its uncertainty over secrets, e.g. passwords or pin numbers, of a system by viewing the observable information. The desired property of a system is the absence of information flow between the secret and observable information, hence the attacker is not able to learn anything about the secret information. This *non-interference* property is not always achievable in practice. For example, the usual login on web pages leaks a bit information over the users and passwords with every login attempt. QIF's motivation is to provide a metric for the assessment and comparison of information flows between different implementations. A smallest possible information flow to the observable information is desired (information leakage), because it leaves behind the highest uncertainty about the secret information for the attacker.

This work bases on [5], which introduces an approach for calculating the min entropy of information flow in C programs. The authors use CBMC [6] to

---

A. Weigl—This work was supported by the DFG (German Research Foundation) in Priority Programme Reliably Secure Software Systems (RS3) – DFG Priority Programme 1496. Thanks to Vladimir Klebanov for feedback during the creation of this paper and Laurent Simon for a dessert in Lisbon.

© Springer International Publishing AG 2016
G. Livraga et al. (Eds.): DPM and QASA 2016, LNCS 9963, pp. 51–58, 2016.
DOI: 10.1007/978-3-319-47072-6_4

generate a formula in conjunctive normal form of a program and apply model counting on the propositional formula to enumerate all possible observable information. This SAT-based approach has some advantages. Every performance gain in #SAT or SAT solver is directly applicable. We support real (bounded) C programs, but the input language is changeable, as long there is a translation into a CNF formula.

Contributions. We supplement the SAT-based approach from [5] with three different algorithms UNGUIDED, BUCKET-WISE and SYNC (Sect. 2) for counting the secret state (pre-image) and corresponding observable output (image) for the calculation of the Shannon entropy. We compare the our algorithms to other QIF analysis tools with a part of the case study in [1] (Sect. 3). An implementation is provided.

Foundations. We give a brief overview to foundations of QIF analysis. A detailed overview is in [5]. We investigate the degree of influence during the program execution between the secret information (*high*) at the start state and the observable information (*low*) at the final state. For measuring, we model this this influence as a function π, that maps from high value $\mathcal{H}$ to the low output value $\mathcal{O}$:

$$\pi \colon \mathcal{H} \to \mathcal{O}.$$

With this model, we omit the local variables, which have a fix value at the start state given by the program semantics, whereas the high variables have an arbitrary value (for the attacker unknown). For clarification, $\mathcal{H}$ is the domain, $\mathcal{O}$ the codomain of the function π, the images $o \in \mathcal{O}$ are the output values and the pre-images $\pi^{-1}(o) \subseteq \mathcal{H}$, defined as $\pi^{-1}(o) = \{h \in \mathcal{H} \mid \pi(h) = h\}$. For deterministic programs the pre-images are disjoint. For convenience, we silently lift multiple high or low variables to tuples.

We use CBMC for the translation of a program into a corresponding propositional formula φ over a signature Σ in conjunctive normal form (CNF). The formula φ represents a program, s.t. every model of φ is a valid program trace. Each variable is encoded by a set propositional variables. We are interested into the signature $\mathbb{H} \subseteq \Sigma$ that encodes the high variable, and $\mathbb{O} \subseteq \Sigma$ the low variable. By projection on these both signatures, we obtain the function π. $\varphi|_\Delta$ denotes the projection of φ to the signature $\Delta \subseteq \Sigma$. The projection $\varphi|_\Delta$ is the strongest Δ-formula, that is entailed by φ if interpreted over Σ. The projection of a model m is obtained by dropping every variable $v \notin \Delta$. A model m of φ contains the encoded values for high and low variables, that we retrieve by projection $m|_{\mathbb{H}}$, resp. $m|_{\mathbb{O}}$.

Under the assumption of termination, determinism and with uniform distribution of the input values, we the conditional Shannon entropy [5,7].

Definition 1 (Cond. Shannon Entropy for Deterministic Programs).

$$H(\mathbf{X}|\mathbf{Y}) = \frac{1}{\#(X)} \sum_{y \in \mathcal{Y}} \#(\pi^{-1}(y)) \log \#(\pi^{-1}(y))$$

The conditional Shannon entropy only depends on the sizes of the pre-images and images and is invariant on the their order. In the remaining sections of this paper, we always reference to this conditional version of the Shannon entropy.

2   Counting Algorithms for (Pre-)Images

We introduce the three algorithms UNGUIDED, BUCKET-WISE and SYNC with different ways of counting, which are special instance of the model counting problem with projection #SAT-p. We need to count with projection to the signature of either the high input variable $\mathbb{H} \subseteq \Sigma$ or the low output variable $\mathbb{O} \subseteq \Sigma$. We want to utilize the working principals of the incremental SAT solver to achieve an efficient counting of the images and the pre-images.

The algorithms produce a histogram $Hist \colon \mathcal{O} \to \mathbb{N}$ (Fig. 1), which associates every possible output of π to the size of its pre-image: $Hist(o) = \#(\pi^{-1}(o))$. We denote o's place in an histogram as its *bucket*.

Input and Output of the Algorithms. The algorithms have three input parameters: a propositional formula φ over signature Σ in conjunctive normal form (CNF), the signature of the high input variable $\mathbb{H} \subseteq \Sigma$ and the signature $\mathbb{O} \subseteq \Sigma$ of the low output variable.

The result of the algorithms is the precise histogram *Hist*. Furthermore, the algorithms BUCKET-WISE and SYNC are able to decide whether all inputs values of a pre-image are counted, represented by the function $closed \colon \mathcal{O} \to \{true, false\}$. If $closed(o)$ is true, then the bucket $Hist(o)$ is final. Histogram *Hist* is initialized with zeros, resp. *closed* with *false* entries.

Used Functions. The algorithms are based upon the decision problem (SAT) for satisfiability of propositional formula φ. $SAT(\varphi)$ denotes a call to the SAT solver with a CNF formula. The returned value is either a model m or $\bot$ to signal unsatisfiability. We can supply an assumption a, denoted as $SAT(a \Rightarrow \varphi)$. An assumption is a partial assignment of variables, which constrains the SAT solver to find a model that ensures the assumption's assignments.

Our counting algorithms work by adding blocking clauses to exclude already found values of input or output variables. For the construction of blocking clauses, we define the function $block(\varphi, m, \Delta)$, which takes a CNF formula φ, a model m and a signature Δ. The function returns a new CNF formula φ', s. t. the projected model $m|_\Delta$ is not a part of any model of φ'.

Implementation. An efficient implementation of the algorithms UNGUIDED, BUCKET-WISE and SYNC requires an incremental SAT solver, which offers two operations: (a) appending of new clauses to CNF formula and (b) finding a satisfying assignment under an assumption. An incremental SAT solver reuses information from previous runs. Hence, subsequent calls to solver take less time. In the concrete implementation, we reuse the SAT solver instance and block a model by adding the blocking clause to the instance. This detail is omitted in shown version of the algorithms to attain a better readability.

Brief Overview of the Algorithm. We give here a brief overview of the algorithms, cf. Fig. 1. The Algorithm UNGUIDED iterates over all models in the order determined by the SAT solver. The occurrence of corresponding pairs of input and output values may be chaotic or random (Fig. 1a). The Algorithm BUCKET-WISE counts a pre-image for a particular image, before it starts with a further pre-image (Fig. 1b). In each iteration, the Algorithm SYNC searches for one new input value for every image, until all input values are found (Fig. 1c). The experiments and discussion takes place in Sect. 3.

Unguided Counting. The Algorithm UNGUIDED is the logical extension of the algorithm given in [5, Fig. 2]. The choice of the next model is left to the (incremental) SAT solver, which we give the most degrees of freedom to reuse the most information from the previous runs.

In comparison to [5], both implementations iterate over the sets of models $models(\varphi|_\Delta)$, but our implementation does not collect the models. Instead, we extract the output value $m|_{\mathbb{O}}$, and increase the corresponding bucket in the histogram $Hist(m|_{\mathbb{O}})$ for each found model. Due to the determinism of program, there is no other output value for the last found input value $m|_{\mathbb{H}}$. Hence, we block the input value from further occurence to prevent a double counting. The function call $block(\varphi, m, \mathbb{H})$ returns a clause set that prohibits the assignment of input values in the further calls of the SAT solver. The algorithm does not provide information if a bucket is closed (Fig. 2).

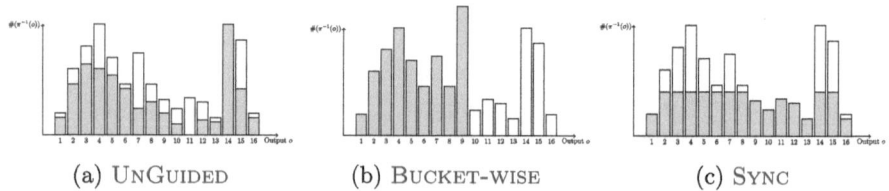

(a) UNGUIDED   (b) BUCKET-WISE   (c) SYNC

Fig. 1. Graphical representation of the effects of different algorithms on distribution of the size of the input partitions during counting. The gray bar represents the counted elements of the bucket, whereas the white bar symbolizes the true, but unknown, part.

Input: A propositional formula φ over Σ, a signature $\mathbb{O} \subseteq \Sigma$ representing the output variable, and $\mathbb{H} \subseteq \Sigma$ for the input variable
Output: Histogram $\forall o \in \mathcal{O}: Hist(o) = \#(\pi^{-1}(o))$
1 **begin**
2   **while** $m := \text{SAT}(\varphi)$ **do**
3         $Hist(m|_{\mathbb{O}}) := Hist(m|_{\mathbb{O}}) + 1$
4         $\varphi := block(\varphi, m, \mathbb{H})$
5   **end**
6 **end**

Fig. 2. Algorithm UNGUIDED iterates unstructured over every model.

Input: A propositional formula φ over Σ, a signature $\mathbb{O} \subseteq \Sigma$ representing the output variable, and $\mathbb{H} \subseteq \Sigma$ for the input variable

Output: Histogram $\forall o \in \mathcal{O}$: $Hist(o) = \#(\pi^{-1}(o))$

```
1  begin
2  |   while m := SAT(φ) do
3  |   |   o ← m|_O
4  |   |   do
5  |   |   |   Hist(m|_H) := Hist(m|_H) + 1
6  |   |   |   φ := block(φ, m, ℍ)
7  |   |   while m := SAT(o ⇒ φ)
8  |   |   closed(o) := true
9  |   |   φ := block(φ, m, O)
10 |   end
11 end
```

Fig. 3. Bucket-wise counting (BUCKET-WISE) tries to fill a bucket, before it descends a new bucket.

Input: A propositional formula φ over Σ, a signature $\mathbb{O} \subseteq \Sigma$ representing the output variable, and $\mathbb{H} \subseteq \Sigma$ for the input variable

Output: Histogram $\forall o \in \mathcal{O}$: $Hist(o) = \#(\pi^{-1}(o))$ and $closed: \mathcal{O} \to \mathbb{B}$

```
1  begin
2  |   O := {m|_O | m ∈ models(φ)}
3  |   finished := false
4  |   while ¬finished do
5  |   |   finished := true
6  |   |   for o ∈ O ∧ ¬closed(o) do
7  |   |   |   if m := SAT(o ⇒ φ) then
8  |   |   |   |   Hist(m|_O) := Hist(m|_O) + 1
9  |   |   |   |   φ := block(φ, m, ℍ)
10 |   |   |   |   finished := false
11 |   |   |   else
12 |   |   |   |   closed(o) := true;
13 |   |   |   end
14 |   |   end
15 |   end
16 end
```

Fig. 4. Algorithm SYNC, synchronized counting of every bucket, by finding (1) all reachable output values and (2) iterating over all output values and increasing its bucket, until all pairs of input and output values are reached.

Bucket-wise Counting. The idea behind the Algorithm BUCKET-WISE (Fig. 3) is to fix an output value $o \in \mathcal{O}$ and exhaustively count all input values in the corresponding pre-image. We guide the SAT solver through the iteration over the models by setting assumptions. We hope the focus on one pre-image increases the performance of the SAT solver, because the SAT solver *only* needs to find another input value, after it has discovered a similar input and output value relation.

The Algorithm BUCKET-WISE starts with $SAT(\varphi)$ to find the first relation between an input value and output value of function π. In the next step, we fix the output value $o = m|_{\mathbb{O}}$ and use o as the assumption in further SAT applications $SAT(o \Rightarrow \varphi)$ until the φ is unsatisfiable under this assumption, so the pre-image is counted exhaustively and the bucket is closed. The Line 9 in Fig. 3 blocks an exhaustively explored output value o. Blocking the output value o is not required, because all possible input values of o have been blocked. We block o to give more explicit information to the SAT solver. We repeat this procedure, until all output values are blocked and φ becomes unsatisfiable.

Synchronized Counting. An uniform distribution of input values over the images is the best case for an attacker. This idea motivates the Algorithm SYNC to maintain an uniform distribution as long as possible, as the lower bound of the Shannon entropy.

The Algorithm SYNC (Fig. 4) starts with calculation of the reachable output values in the π's codomain. The main part is a fix point algorithm, which stops if φ becomes unsat during the counting iff all pre-images are counted. The inner for-loop iterates over all output values O, that might have an undiscovered corresponding input value. If a model m is found, then we increase the corresponding bucket and block the input value; the fix point isn't reached. If no model is found, the bucket is closed.

The concrete implementation integrates the search for the reachable output values (Line 2) and assigns each blocking clause of an output value a fresh label literal for selecting the desired output value.

3   Experiment and Discussion

This experiment serves for the comparison of our tool SHARPPI with other state-of-the-art tool for QIF analysis. We use the "all houses" scenario inside the "Smart Grid" case study [1]. The Fig. 5 gives the program in C. This scenario describes an attacker, who wants to gain knowledge about occupied houses of a city block, which contains N houses, evenly split up in three different sizes. Every house size has a specific consumption. The attacker is able to observe the *global consumption* of the block, which is sum of every consumption of every occupied house. In the following we consider the case B, with the 1 unit for small, 3 units for medium and 5 units for large consumption.

```
int allhouses(bool presence[N]){
    int low = 0;
    for(int i = 0; i < N; i++) {
        if (presence[i]) {
            if      (i< N/3)      { low = low + SMALL; }
            else if (i< 2*(N/3)) { low = low + MEDIUM;}
            else                 { low = low + LARGE; }
        }}
    return low;}
```

Fig. 5. "All houses" case study from [1] given as C program. N is the number of all houses.

Houses N	UnGuided	Bucket-wise	Sync	MQL9	MQL15	QUAIL	CHIMP
12	0.91	0.35	0.48	0.10	191.04	72.65	156.03
13	3.21	0.80	1.36	0.11	195.20	t/o	t/o
14	12.00	1.80	4.34	0.11	194.16		
15	49.36	4.51	10.20	0.14	192.91		
16	206.52	12.08	30.87	0.16	191.08		
17	t/o	34.00	139.63	0.18	190.48		
18		98.54	t/o	0.19	190.86		

Fig. 6. Comparison of the algorithm to other tools. CPU time in seconds for "all houses" from Smart Grid case study of [1].

We compare MQL[1] [3], QUAIL[2] [2] and CHIMP[3] [4] with our tool SHARPPI. These tools calculate a precise Shannon entropy. We leave out tools which only returns an estimation of the information flow.

Figure 6 shows the runtime in seconds, measured on Intel Core(TM) i7 CPU 860 with 2.80 GHz and 8 GB RAM. The timeout is set to five minutes and the integer width of MQL to 9 resp. 15 bits. SHARPPI uses the MINISAT. We select the timeout and the city block size N to a range, that shows differences between the tools.

Discussion. In direct comparison is MQL the fastest tool with an a priori set integer width of 9 bits. With 15 bits, MQL becomes slower with larger integer width, which determines mainly its run-time in this case study. QUAIL and CHIMP separate magnitudes to the MQL or SHARPPI.

The Algorithm BUCKET-WISE is the fastest counting algorithm presented in this paper. We observe the reusing of a found models brings a performance gain (cf. BUCKET-WISE) and SYNC to UnGuided, especially if it was found in the last call (BUCKET-WISE). One explanation could be the behavior of the decision stack in incremental SAT solver. An assumption is pushed as the first assignments on this stack. The decision and learned clauses are based on these assignments. If we use the same assumption in the next SAT solver call, the decision stack and all derived decisions are reusable.

4   Related Work

MQL [3] uses MOPED, a symbolic model checker, to calculate a boolean representation of a given program as an arithmetic decision diagram (ADD). The ADD encodes the function π, that maps the secret values to the observable values. Counting of the images and pre-images are reduced to operations on ADDs.

---

[1] https://sites.google.com/site/mopedqleak/, Access: 2016-07-15.

[2] https://project.inria.fr/quail/, Version: 2.0.

[3] http://www.cs.bham.ac.uk/research/projects/infotools/chimp/, Version: 2.1.

QUAIL [2] uses Markov Decision Procedure (MDP), that are built by depth-first search for the final states on the given program. The specification of secret and observable variables are fixed during execution and like our information flow model, the authors assumes completely defined start state. Finally, for the calculation of the entropy the MDP is striped down to discrete-time Markov chains (DTMC). CHIMP [4] builds directly an DTMC of the program in a similar fashion as QUAIL, but with a different information flow model, allowing partial assigned start state. MQL, QUAIL and CHIMP support probabilistic programs with their own input language.

5   Conclusion

We presented three different algorithms UNGUIDED, BUCKET-WISE and SYNC for the counting of images and pre-images of deterministic C programs encoded as CNF formulas, which utilizes the advantages of incremental SAT solvers. Algorithm BUCKET-WISE is by far fastest algorithm of our three introduced algorithms. In comparison with other tools, SHARPPI performs well against MQL, QUAIL and CHIMP for deterministic programs. We provide an implementation of all introduced algorithms in our tool SHARPPI.

References

1. Biondi, F., Legay, A., Quilbeuf, J.: Comparative analysis of leakage tools on scalable case studies. In: Fischer, B., Geldenhuys, J. (eds.) SPIN 2015. LNCS, vol. 9232, pp. 263–281. Springer, Heidelberg (2015)
2. Biondi, F., Legay, A., Traonouez, L.-M., Wąsowski, A.: QUAIL: a quantitative security analyzer for imperative code. In: Sharygina, N., Veith, H. (eds.) CAV 2013. LNCS, vol. 8044, pp. 702–707. Springer, Heidelberg (2013)
3. Chadha, R., Mathur, U., Schwoon, S.: Computing information flow using symbolic model-checking. In: Raman, V., Suresh, S.P., (eds.) 34th International Conference on Foundation of Software Technology and Theoretical Computer Science (FSTTCS), vol. 29 of Leibniz International Proceedings in Informatics (LIPIcs), pp. 505–516, Dagstuhl, Germany, Schloss Dagstuhl-Leibniz-Zentrum fuer Informatik (2014)
4. Chothia, T., Kawamoto, Y., Novakovic, C., Parker, D.: Probabilistic point-to-point information leakage. In: Proceedings of the 26th IEEE Computer Security Foundations Symposium (CSF 2013), pp. 193–205. IEEE Computer Society, June 2013
5. Klebanov, V., Manthey, N., Muise, C.: SAT-based analysis and quantification of information flow in programs. In: Joshi, K., Siegle, M., Stoelinga, M., D'Argenio, P.R. (eds.) QEST 2013. LNCS, vol. 8054, pp. 177–192. Springer, Heidelberg (2013)
6. Kroening, D., Tautschnig, M.: CBMC – C bounded model checker. In: Ábrahám, E., Havelund, K. (eds.) TACAS 2014 (ETAPS). LNCS, vol. 8413, pp. 389–391. Springer, Heidelberg (2014)
7. Smith, G.: On the foundations of quantitative information flow. In: de Alfaro, L. (ed.) FOSSACS 2009. LNCS, vol. 5504, pp. 288–302. Springer, Heidelberg (2009)

Privacy Protection

Controlled Management
of Confidentiality-Preserving
Relational Interactions

Joachim Biskup$^{(\boxtimes)}$, Ralf Menzel, and Jaouad Zarouali

Technische Universität Dortmund, Dortmund, Germany
{joachim.biskup,ralf.menzel,jaouad.zarouali}@cs.tu-dortmund.de

Abstract. This article builds on given fundamental concepts and a prototype implementation for history-aware and policy-driven inference control by means of a confidentiality-preserving security server, which mediates interactions between a relational database and a semi-honest (human) user. Within this already broad-ranging framework, we enhance the prototype towards efficient and effective user administration and monitoring by introducing and verifying two interactive and semi-automatic functionalities. The first one serves for the administration of global settings and the initial state of each user's internal surrogate. Reacting on a submitted interaction request, the second functionality handles the security server's dynamic selection of an admissible confinement method and its actual application, together with a corresponding state transition of the requesting user's surrogate. These functionalities employ extendible descriptors of surrogate states, interaction requests, database instances and confinement methods, respectively, as a kind of security labels.

Keywords: Availability · Client-server architecture · Censor · Confidentiality · Controlled interaction execution · Confinement method · Descriptor · Extendability · History · Inference control · Policy · Query · Relational database · Security automaton · Security ordering · Surrogate · Update

1 Introduction

Sharing information by means of a logic-oriented relational database [1] might raise the need to confine the information content of interaction data returned to a user by *inference control* [13]. Materialized views, answers to queries, notifications to update or revision requests as well as data refreshments should not enable the user to acquire knowledge in violation of declared *confidentiality*

This work has been partially supported by the Deutsche Forschungsgemeinschaft (German Research Council) under grant BI-311/12-2 and grant SFB 876/A5.

G. Livraga et al. (Eds.): DPM and QASA 2016, LNCS 9963, pp. 61–77, 2016.
DOI: 10.1007/978-3-319-47072-6_5

requirements, even under rational reasoning exploiting a priori knowledge and the full interaction history [15].

Previous fundamental work on and an ongoing prototype implementation of *Controlled Interaction Execution*, CIE, surveyed in [3] based on [4–10] and various further reports, offer a rich variety of confinement methods, called *censors*, for sequences of dedicated kinds of interactions, with quite diverse and sophisticated application requirements. Each *individual* censor has been formally proved to enforce any suitable user-specific confidentiality policy under any suitable assumptions about the respective user's a priori knowledge, where both of these items have to be declared by a security officer as additional input besides the interaction requests submitted by the user. Here, the intuitive meaning of a *confidentiality policy* demands that for each sentence of the policy the following holds: based on the controlled reactions returned by the censor, the respective user will always believe in the *possibility* that the sentence does *not* hold in the actual (but hidden) instance of the database.

Within this broad-ranging CIE framework, in this article we mainly address the following problems not dealt with in previous work:

- How to express the diversity of application requirements for all censors developed so far and preferably also in future in a *uniform* and efficient way such that all censors can be correctly managed by a single extendible tool?
- How to *notify* the user about the applicability or non-applicability of a censor for a requested interaction without violating confidentiality?
- How to ensure that *mixed* usages of several censors with different application requirements for one user do not lead to a violation of confidentiality?

To the best of our knowledge, other approaches to inference control for relational databases, e.g., establishing k-anonymity [11], do no show a similar degree of diversity and thus the first problem has not arisen at all so far. Regarding the second problem, the previous focus on a single censor has led to consider the preservation of confidentiality by controlled reactions on a user's *functional* interaction requests, rather than to study a user's explicit or implicit *control* requests to employ a specific censor. The third problem is closely related to the well-known vulnerability of returning several views on the same data, even if each of them is individually confidentiality-preserving, see [14].

To deal with the problems stated above, we have designed two interactive and semi-automatic *functionalities*. The first one serves for the *administration* of global settings and the initial state of a specific user's internal surrogate. Reacting on a submitted interaction request, the second functionality handles the *dynamic selection* of an admissible confinement method and its actual application, together with a corresponding transition of the surrogate's state of the requesting user. These functionalities employ extendible *descriptors* of surrogate states, of interaction requests, of database instances and of censors, as a kind of multi-dimensional security labels of varying size (similarly to but in a more expressive way than mandatory access control [2]).

Essentially, whenever due, a decision on applying a specific censor for a given request submitted by a principally authorized user is efficiently supported by

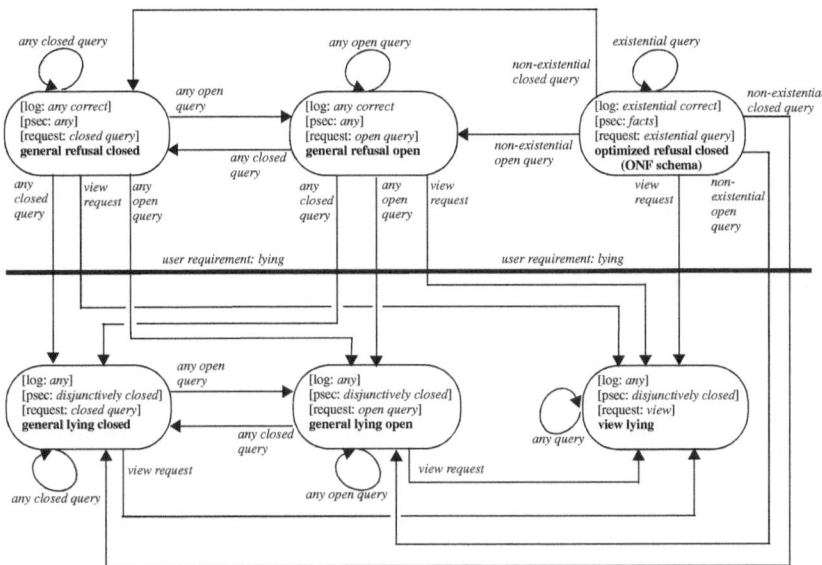

Fig. 1. A simplified fragment of the conceptual security automaton capturing the possible selections (nodes) and transitions (edges) of a user's currently chosen censor.

comparing the current descriptors related to the user's surrogate with those assigned to the censor regarding a predefined but extendible partial *security ordering*. That ordering has been defined to comprehensively capture all features needed for effective inference control. In particular, the ordering is employed to specify the *confidentiality-preserving transitions* of the *state* of a surrogate. As an important component, this state contains the *currently chosen censor*. Accordingly, the specification of the state transitions also implies the possible censor selections. Conceptually, these possibilities can be captured by the graph of a kind of a *security automaton* [2,12], an instance of which is thought to be generated for each user represented by his/her internal surrogate.

In the following we briefly and simplifying exemplify our goals and achievements, focusing on query answering and data publishing only.

The following censors (out of a larger collection) are supposed to be available:

– *general refusal* for any *closed* (yes/no-)query [4],
– *general refusal* for any *open* ("give me all x such that ..."-)query [6],
– *optimized refusal* for an existential, closed (yes/no-)query and restricted a priori knowledge about a relational schema in *Object Normal Form* [7],
– *general lying* for any *closed* (yes/no-)query [4],
– *general lying* for any *open* ("give me all x such that ..."-)query [6],
– *lying* for a materialized *view* (data publishing) [10].

Figure 1 shows the simplified fragment of the conceptual security automaton covering these censors. For each censor, there is a node (depicted as an oval) which is identified by the censor's name (in boldface) and bears a three-dimensional descriptor whose components[1] are referenced by *log, psec* and *request*, respectively. The *log*-component expresses a precondition on a requesting user's current knowledge gathered from the a priori knowledge and previously returned reactions; the *psec*-component specifies which forms of a confidentiality requirement can be enforced; and the *request*-component indicates which kinds of a request can be controlled. Moreover, there are edges labeled with the designation of a class of requests. An edge from the node identified by *censor₁* to the node identified by *censor₂* with label *class* specifies the following:

> If the currently chosen censor for the user's surrogate is *censor₁* and the user then issues a request expressed in the language designated by *class*, then *censor₂* may be assigned to the user's surrogate to process the request, provided the conditions declared for censor *censor₂* are satisfied by the user's surrogate state.

Initially, the administration functionality assigns some suitable censor to a user's surrogate as the *currently chosen* one. Afterward, the dynamic-selection functionality governs the behavior. As a default, an assignment is maintained as long as the issued requests can be controlled by the currently chosen censor. If the *class* of a request does not match the *request*-component of the currently chosen censor's descriptor, and/or triggered by interactively expressed user requirements, another censor is selected according to the possibilities captured by the conceptual security automaton, or some exception handling is due.

Now, consider a user *Mary* who herself requires to start with refusals but would also accept lying later on. Her a priori knowledge is assumed to be correct but it contains some elements outside of the class of existentially quantified atomic sentences. Moreover, her confidentiality requirements are closed under disjunctions. Further, the assumed a priori knowledge is checked to be not violating confidentiality right from the beginning. Finally, for reasons of efficiency, mostly closed queries are anticipated. Accordingly, Mary's surrogate gets a descriptor comprising the components [*prior* : *any correct*] and thus also [*log* : *any correct*] as well as [*psec* : *disjunctively closed*]. Hence, initially the censor **general refusal closed** would be the currently chosen censor. Notably, the censor **optimized refusal closed** could not be selected for Mary as her initial currently chosen censor. Notifying Mary about this fact would be harmless, basically because she could derive it by herself without any interaction.

While Mary is issuing closed queries, her currently chosen censor would remain unchanged, unless she explicitly requires to switch to lying. This might happen after some time, together with a request of an open query, since for open queries lying performs better than refusal. The switch to the censor **general lying open** is possible, since her confidentiality requirements are disjunctively closed. Finally, given the reaction data received so far, Mary might request a materialized view. Mary's currently chosen censor is then transferred to the censor **view lying**. Since this happens for the first time, this censor generates a

---

[1] The components will be more precisely redefined in Sect. 4.

confidentiality-preserving view specifically tailored for Mary, in particular considering previously received information as part of her a priori knowledge. Afterward, any further query request by Mary is evaluated using this view rather than the stored database instance. But any further view request by Mary would be denied, since otherwise she would see several views whose combination could be harmful. And she would be notified accordingly, since she is assumed to know the denial anyway.

In the remainder of this article, to provide the necessary background about controlled interaction execution, first we briefly summarize the fundamentals in Sect. 2 and also outline the basics of our prototype implementation in Sect. 3. Then we start with our original contributions. In Sect. 4, we present the essentials of descriptors and of the security ordering, and we describe how they are exploited in the innovative administration functionality. Section 5 continues the description by introducing the innovative dynamic-selection functionality. In Sect. 6 we report some details on how the prototype enhanced by the new functionalities actually behaves for the example introduced above. Moreover, in Sect. 7 we sketch a formal verification of the claimed achievements. Finally, we conclude in Sect. 8, in particular listing several open issues.

2   Fundamentals of Controlled Interaction Execution

As shown in Fig. 2, Controlled Interaction Execution, CIE, provides a shielding security mechanism that mediates interaction messages between a user (employing some client software on a hardware device) and an isolated database (managed by a database management system on possibly different hardware) in order to confine the information content of reactions returned to the user according to both global and user-specific security settings.

The *database* is structured in an (intensional) *schema*, in particular comprising the declaration of relation names, attributes, their domains and integrity constraints, and an (extensional) *instance*, formed by data in form of sets of tuples (logically seen as ground facts) complying with the schema. In principle, from a pure functional point of view, the database offers the usual kinds of *interactions* with a user, including query evaluation, update processing, refreshment production, transaction management and view materialization. At the external interface of the database, each interaction consists of some *request* message(s) submitted by a user and the *reaction* message(s) returned by the database server.

Basically, the shielding *security mechanism* intercepts these messages in order to interpret and modify them according to the initially configured *security settings*. The current state of these settings directs the user-specific interpretation of an incoming request by some dynamically selected *censor*, which prepares a suitably modified reaction to be finally returned to the submitter of the request. Additionally, the state of the security settings is appropriately updated to reflect the progress of the interaction history and the gain of knowledge obtainable by the user. While the security settings abstractly *specify* the current confidentiality and availability requirements for each of the users, the task of the selected censor is to actually *enforce* these requirements for the current request.

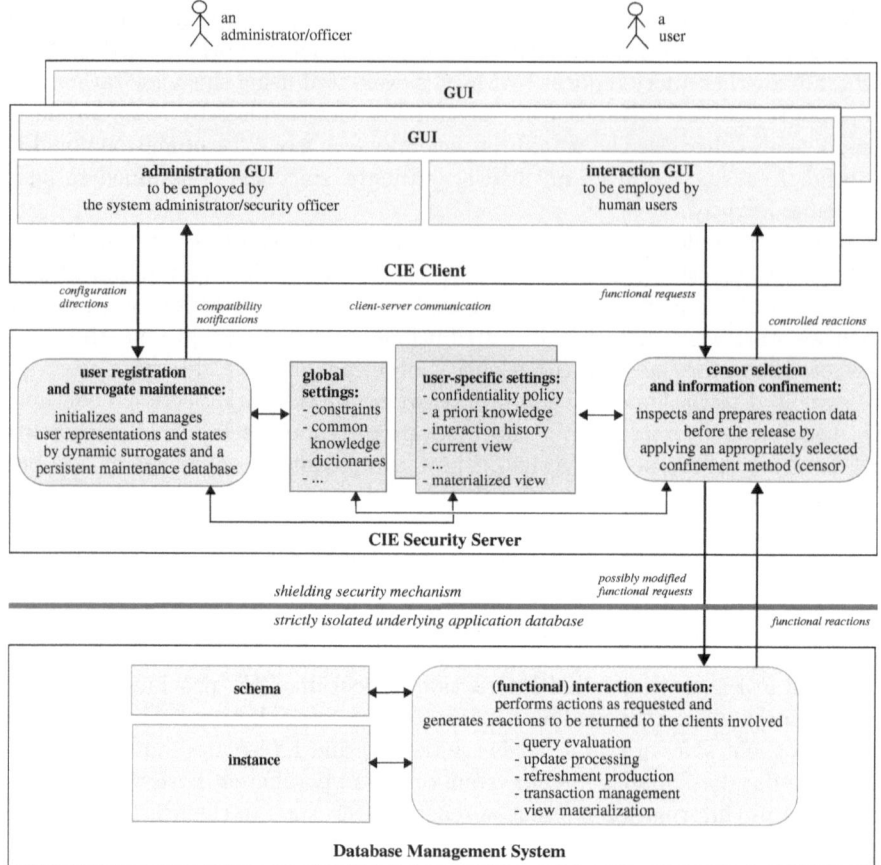

Fig. 2. Conceptual design of Controlled Interaction Execution, CIE.

Initially, for each individual user, a system administrator or security officer has to identify those domain-independent/safe closed (yes/no) queries that he/she considers as too sensitive. In this context, the term "sensitive" means that the user should never be able to observe directly or to infer by reasoning that the (hidden) stored instance generates a positive answer. But the user might well know a negative answer. In other words, the user should always believe in the possibility that the negative answer could be the correct one. To capture this somehow asymmetric condition, such a sentence is called a *potential secret*, and the set of all these sentences forms the user-specific *confidentiality policy*.

As far as needed, an *enforcing censor* minimally distorts a functionally correct reaction message. First of all, the censors differ in the kind of a distortion: by explicitly *weakening* the correct message, with the special case of explicitly *refusing* to return an informative message, or by *lying* in some form, or by suitably *combining* weakening and lying. Furthermore, the censor might be effective only for dedicated, syntactically defined classes of the following items: *confidentiality policies*, *a priori knowledge* including schema properties like integrity constraints, *queries* and *update parameters*, and the history *logs* comprising a priori knowledge as well as answers to previous queries and other notifications. Effectiveness might also depend on other parameters, e.g., whether or not the user is aware of the policy, or which censors have been employed previously.

3   Outline of the CIE Prototype

Our prototype implementation of Controlled Interaction Execution constitutes a mediating frontend to any SQL-complying relational *database management system* (bottom part of Fig. 2), with dedicated wrappers for the Oracle and the Apache Derby DBMS. The prototype also uses the external services of a *theorem prover*, either via a TPTP-complying wrapper for any suitable prover or with a direct wrapper for Prover9 [16]. Implemented in Java as a *client-server system*, the code[2] of the prototype consists of the following three parts:

- for the CIE-client processes, one for each active (human) user (see upper part of Fig. 2),
- for the CIE-security-server process (see middle part of Fig. 2), and
- for loosely coupled, asynchronous CIE-communication between a process of the CIE-client and the process of the CIE-security-server (see messages between upper part and middle part of Fig. 2).

The conceptually ongoing (but suspendable) execution of the CIE-security-server starts by two activities: it first initializes the *maintenance database*, which in particular will persistently keep the states of all registered users later on and is already filled with the state of a pre-registered root user; and it then creates a single instance of the class `Server` that subsequently continuously waits for establishing a connection to some process executing the CIE-client.

Whenever someone starts an execution of the CIE-client, the created client process seeks for a connection to the single server process, which, by means of the maintenance database, then (i) checks identification, authenticity and authorizations of the (human) user acting via the client process, (ii) initializes an instance of the class `Surrogate` for that user, and (iii) establishes a virtual connection between the client process and the surrogate for further communications with the help of an instance of the class `ComLink`. Depending on the user data submitted and the role derived, the further activities of the client process are structured by either the *administration GUI* or the *interaction GUI*.

If a client process is acting on behalf of the *root user*, it can employ the full administration functionality, as detailed in Sect. 4, which includes the declaration of *global settings* and the registration of new users granting them the role of either an *security officer* or an *applicator*. Furthermore, such a process can also employ the additional parts of the administration functionality to declare *user-specific*

---

[2] The names used in this article might differ from those found in the actual code.

settings, as can any process acting on behalf of a security officer. If a client process is acting on behalf of a registered user in the role of an applicator, it can perform interactions with the database, exploiting the full functionality of dynamic censor selection and employment, as detailed in Sect. 5.

As a basis for the latter functionality, there is a dedicated subclass of the abstract class `Censor` for each kind of a censor provided by the underlying fundamental work. Among others, the censor selection depends on the state of the pertinent surrogate and the grammatical analysis and classification of the interaction request as performed by the package `parser`.

4   Global Settings and Initial Client States

The CIE prototype exploits extendible *descriptors* that characterize the users' surrogate states, their interaction requests, the database schema with its actual instance, and the implemented censors, respectively. A *component* [*dom* : *value*] of a descriptor is given by the name *dom* of a predefined *domain* of interest and the pertinent *value*. The dynamic employment of the CIE prototype is mainly steered and supervised by means of decisions that are based on comparing descriptors. For example, let a joint descriptor δ_1 of the underlying database, the surrogate state and a request express the properties of a wanted activity, and further let another descriptor δ_2 of a censor formalize the requirements of the facilities needed for the activity, then the comparison should indicate whether or not the wanted activity can be executed on the needed facilities.

To enable algorithmic decisions whenever possible and meaningful, for each domain *dom* a suitable partial ordering $\preceq_{dom}$ on the set of its possible values has been defined, as far as needed also introducing a unique artificial upper bound $\top_{dom}$ as a kind of "don't care"-value. Depending on the concrete meaning of the domain, $v_1 \preceq_{dom} v_2$ might intuitively express that (the feature denoted by) v_1 is "stronger", "more specific", "more restrictive", or "also satisfying" (the feature denoted by) v_2. For some domains, however, we have to use equality as a degenerated partial ordering. These domain-specific orderings induce a partial *security ordering* on descriptors as follows: a descriptor δ_1 *matches* (is dominated by, complies with, ...) a descriptor δ_2,

$\delta_1 \preceq \delta_2$:iff for each domain *dom* occurring in δ_2:

$$dom \text{ also occurs in } \delta_1 \text{ and } \delta_1(dom) \preceq_{dom} \delta_2(dom).$$

In terms of the example, a *matching* $\delta_1 \preceq \delta_2$ intuitively means that all requirements of the facilities formalized by δ_2 are satisfied by the properties of the wanted activity expressed by δ_1, and thus the security server should allow the wanted activity. Though most decisions for steering and supervising are automated based on matchings, some aspects of the behavior of the security server are still determined interactively by the security officer or the user.

Clearly, before starting to employ the security server, all needed descriptors have to be generated and suitably initialized. As a basis for several purposes, the package `parser` provides means to classify a *formula* of the underlying logic alone or in connection with an *operator* like QUE(ry), V(iew)UP(date) or VIE(w) as belonging to a certain *sublanguage*, where the ordering on the captured sublanguages is defined by set inclusion. The descriptor of an *interaction request* is simply obtained in this way, assigning the values found to the domains *operator* and *subclass*, respectively.

Regarding the *censors*, an implementation of a further censor including its descriptor is added as a new subclass of the abstract class **Censor**. Accordingly, the system administrator has to derive the pertinent descriptor from the fundamental conceptual work, in particular identifying the precondition on the current knowledge for the domains *back*(groundknowledge)*subclass*, *logsubclass* and *logstatus*, the kind of an accepted request for the domains *operator* and *subclass*, and the form and the properties of a handled confidentiality policy for the domains *psecsubclass*, *disjclosed* and *awareness*, mainly in terms of a sublanguage. Examples of further domains and their values are the following ones: a normal form condition on the underlying database schema – as *3NF*, *BCNF* or *ONF* with $ONF \preceq_{dbschema} BCNF \preceq_{dbschema} 3NF$ – for the domain *dbschema*; the strength of the underlying database instance – being either *complete* (under closed-world assumption) or *incomplete* with $complete \preceq_{dbinstance} incomplete$ – for the domain *dbinstance*; and the user's assumed awareness of the policy instance – either *unknown* or *known* with $known \preceq_{awareness} unknown$ – for the domain *awareness*.

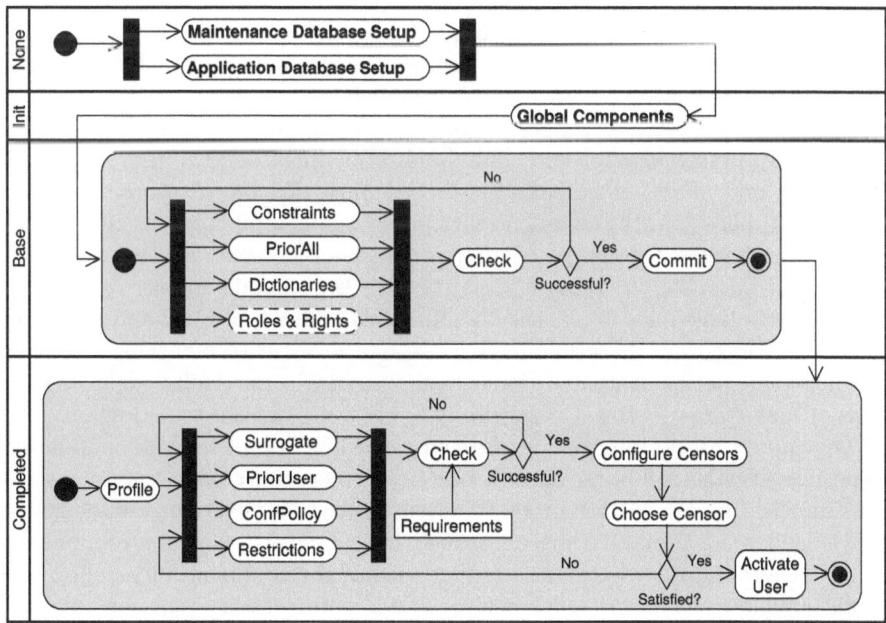

Fig. 3. Outline of the administration functionality: setting activities depicted as being performed in parallel can be executed in any order but are preferred to be executed as shown from top to bottom.

Regarding the *database schema* with its actual *instance* and a particular user's *surrogate* state, the new *administration functionality* has been provided. As shown in Fig. 3, while executing this functionality, the security server runs through four subsequent server states, where a transition to the next server state requires committing the actions of the present server state. The initial server state NONE only serves to guarantee that the application database and the maintenance have been set up properly. In the second server state INIT the values of some global domains are set, e.g., for the domain *dbmodel* either confirming that the underlying database system is a classical *relational* one indeed or indicating that it should be treated as managing only simple *propositions* (such that semantics can be based on propositional logic rather than first-order logic).

In the third server state Base, the security officer can specify settings in form of data associated with all those domains that are common to all prospective users and are therefore inherited by all surrogate states. If a setting demands to treat a set of sentences of the logic, instead of explicitly inputting the pertinent components of the descriptor, the security officer declares the associated data and the system *automatically* determines the pertinent descriptor values for the relevant domains, e.g., the respective sublanguage. In particular, the states of the following domains can be set: for the domain *dbconstraint* a set of sentences, expressing integrity constraints on the underlying database instance in particular those declared in the schema; for the domain *priorall* a set of sentences expressing common background knowledge about the application, assumed to be shared by all users; for a domain of the kind *dictionary$_i$* a list of constants to be used to generate answers to open queries or published views (see [6, 10]). Furthermore, roles and the associated access rights can be defined.

Similarly, the fourth server state COMPLETED supports the security officer in determining the settings for each individual user, including the user's personal data, roles and access rights, the (assumed) more specific a priori knowledge about the application, the confidentiality policy to be applied for executing later requests, and some further restrictions on his/her behavior or achievements. Notably, to initialize the state associated with the domain *logsubclass* and its value, the available data about the domains *dbconstraint*, *priorall* and *prioruser* is merged. Moreover, the user him/herself, or the security officer on behalf of him/her, can specify some additional *requirements*, in particular regarding the kinds of *distortions* – refusal, weakening, lying, etc. – he/she would agree to.

The inputs are automatically checked regarding useful or even mandatory properties like the following ones: syntactic correctness, conformity to restrictions imposed by the DBMS or the theorem prover, satisfaction of background knowledge by the actual database instance, logical consistency, non-redundancy of the background knowledge, non-redundancy of the confidentiality policy, and conflict-freeness of background knowledge and confidentiality requirements.

If some failure occurs or the security officer interactively wants to change or augment the settings, the inputs can iteratively be modified until a *successful* combination has been reached. Subsequently, the pertinent descriptor δ for the user is employed to determine all *admissible censors* just by searching for censor descriptors matching δ, and one of the admissible censors is *chosen* as the initial one. If the security officer is *satisfied* with the result, a new user *surrogate* is created and linked with the descriptor δ, the associated states of domains, and the initial currently chosen censor.

5   Dynamic Censor Selection

Once the global settings have been committed and a user has been activated as described in the preceding section, the following descriptors with components for at least the listed domains are initialized, and subsequently for each interaction suitably maintained and updated as far as applicable and appropriate:

- for the underlying database: *dbmodel, dbschema, dbinstance*;
- for the restrictions and the requirements imposed on the user's surrogate: *operator, subclass*, and *distortion*, respectively;
- for the knowledge and the policy declared for the user's surrogate: *backsubclass, logsubclass, logstatus, psecsubclass, disjclosed, awareness*.

Moreover, for each particular interaction another descriptor with components for at least the listed domains is created:

- for a submitted user request: *operator, subclass*.

Furthermore, each of the censors installed for the security server has a descriptor with components for all these domains.

At the beginning, the security server checks whether or not the interaction request is *permitted* by relating the values for the domains *operator* and *subclass* regarding the request to the values for the domains *operator* and *subclass* regarding the restrictions.

If the request is permitted, first of all the currently chosen censor, as associated with the user's surrogate, is inspected whether or not it is *applicable* for the request. Applicability has been defined as the strongest relationship between a user's situation and a censor:

- A censor is *acceptable*, if the values for the global domains and for the restriction and requirement domains of the user's situation match the respective values of the censor, i.e., (at least) the values for the domains *dbmodel, dbschema, dbinstance* as well as *operator, subclass* and *distortion* of the user's situation are dominated by the respective values of the censor.
- An acceptable censor is *admissible*, if additionally the values for the knowledge and the policy domains of the user's situation match the respective values of the censor, i.e., (at least) the values for the domains *backsubclass, logsubclass, logstatus, psecsubclass, disjclosed* and *awareness* of the user's situation are dominated by the respective values of the censor.
- An admissible censor is *applicable*, if additionally the values for the interaction domains for the user's situation match the respective values of the censor, i.e., (at least) the values for the domains *operator* and *subclass* of the user's situation are dominated by the respective values of the censor.

If the currently chosen censor is *applicable* indeed, possibly after an interactive confirmation by the user, the requested interaction is executed by *starting* its controlled execution by that censor. On the one hand, the result of this execution is returned to the user; on the other hand, the result is also employed to *update* the state of the user's surrogate accordingly.

If the check on *permission* fails, the user gets a suitable notification, and he can then continue by submitting another interaction request. If the check on *applicability* fails, suitable and mainly automatic but partly also interactive activities are triggered. Basically, these activities first of all aim at *calculating* all censors that are applicable in the user's situation and then, if there are any, choosing one of them as the new current censor. However, in some cases some restriction or some requirement can be changed or the state of the user's situation can be modified, possibly only after some iteration, under the strict precaution that the preservation of confidentiality will not be threatened.

In case of a failed check, whether on permission or applicability, a particular precaution is also due for the content of denying notifications returned to the user, in order to avoid meta-inferences based on a notified failure, which might contain pieces of information related to answers to implicit queries, e.g., whether the currently logged knowledge is actually true in the (hidden) instance. Like for treating functional update requests [3,8], dealing with harmful situations might turn out to require some quite sophisticated protocols, which first of all should aim at making a harmful situation indistinguishable from a harmless one. The details of such case-by-case considerations are beyond the scope of this article.

Figure 4 shows the overall functionality of dynamic censor selection and employment, depicting the main control flow **Perform Interaction** together with the auxiliary control flow **Choose Censor**. The latter one is only executed if the applicability check fails, as well as in the last step of the administration functionality. To prepare for the planned further functionality of an automatic runtime *optimizer*, the auxiliary control flow already contains the so far empty activity of estimating the computational costs of employing each of the applicable censors.

6   Example of Settings and Censor Selections

We now outline the actual behavior of our prototype for our introductory example in a more formal but still sketchy form along the behavior in time.

As a prerequisite, we assume that the underlying database management system already stores the database instance of Table 1. Moreover, Fig. 5 visualizes the set-inclusion ordering of the sublanguages occurring in the example. We also postulate that the censors shown in Table 2 have been installed during the configuration of the security server, together with their descriptors. Further assuming that the security officer already committed the actions performed in the server states NONE and INIT during the administration functionality, in particular setting [*dbmodel* : *relational*], [*dbschema* : ⊤] and [*dbinstance* : *complete*], in Table 3 we then describe his actions in the server state BASE and subsequently for a new user Mary in the server state COMPLETED.

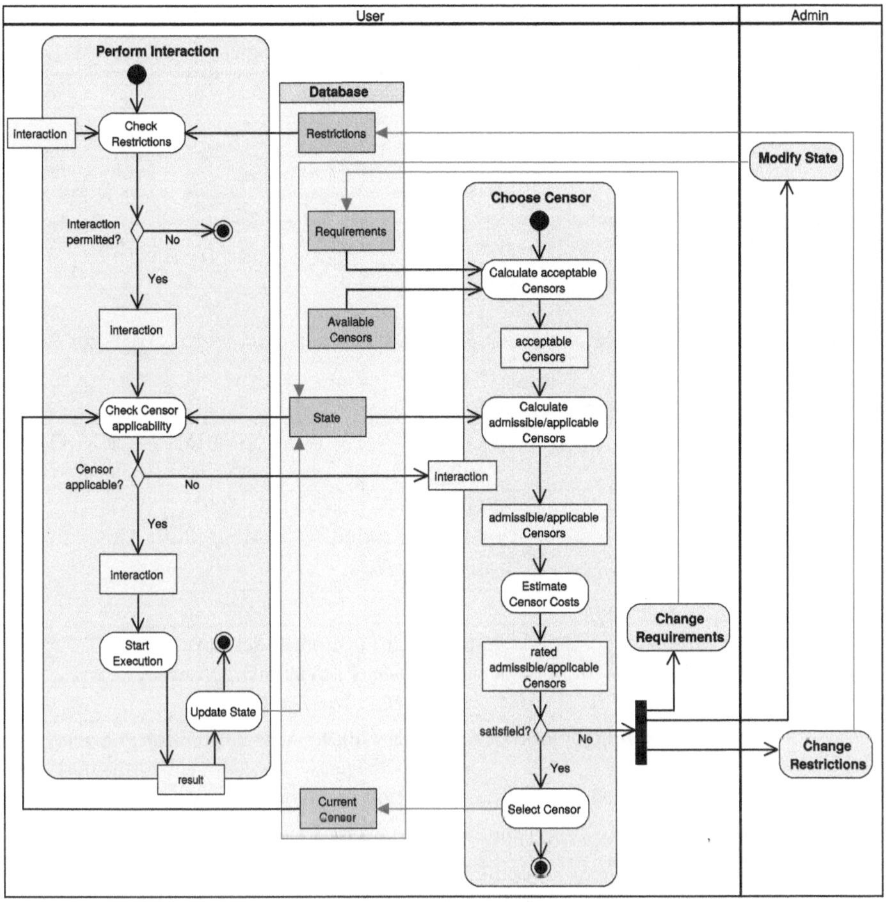

Fig. 4. Outline of the dynamic censor selection and employment functionality: circles denote activities, black (solid) arrows visualize control flow including an object depicted as a yellow rectangle, and green (gray) arrows indicate data flows into a component of the maintenance database and/or of a surrogate, depicted as a green rectangle. (Color figure online)

Table 1. A healthcare database instance.

ILL	Name	Diagnosis
	Lisa	Flu
	Mary	Aids
	Pete	Aids
	Theo	Aids
	Kate	Cancer

TREAT	Name	Prescription
	Lisa	MedB
	Mary	MedA
	Mary	MedB
	Pete	MedA
	Pete	MedB
	Theo	MedA
	Kate	MedC

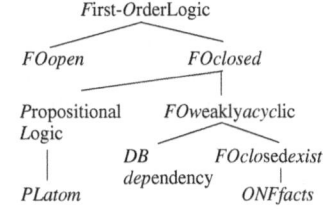

Fig. 5. Expressibility ordering of some sublanguages.

Table 2. Postulated and some further censors, together with their descriptors.

Censor	Ref	dbm.	dbs.	dbi.	distort.	backsubc.	logsubc.	logstatus	psecsubc.	disjclo.	aware.	operator	subclass
GenRefClo	[4]	rel.	⊤		com.	refusal	⊤	⊤	correct	FOclosed	⊤	known	QUE	FOclosed
GenRefOpe	[6]	rel.	⊤		com.	refusal	⊤	⊤	correct	FOclosed	⊤	known	QUE	FOopen
OptRefClo	[7]	rel.	ONF		com.	refusal	DBdep	FOclo.exist	correct	ONFfacts	⊤	known	QUE	FOclo.exist
GenLyiClo	[4]	rel.	⊤		com.	lying	⊤	⊤	⊤	FOclosed	yes	known	QUE	FOclosed
GenLyiOpe	[6]	rel.	⊤		com.	lying	⊤	⊤	⊤	FOclosed	yes	known	QUE	FOopen
ViewLyi	[10]	rel.	⊤		com.	lying	⊤	FOw.acyc.	⊤	FOw.acyc.	⊤	known	VIE/QUE	−/FO
UnkRefClo	[5]	rel.	⊤		com.	refusal	⊤	⊤	correct	FOclosed	⊤	unk.	QUE	FOclosed
LyiUpdate	[8]	prop.	⊤		com.	lying	⊤	⊤	⊤	PL	yes	known	VUP	PLatom
IncRef	[9]	prop.	⊤		inc.	refusal	⊤	⊤	⊤	PL	yes	known	QUE	PL
...	[3]	...	...	...	...	...	...	...	...	...	...	...	...

Table 3. The security officer's actions for global settings and user settings for Mary.

Server State	Setting/Decision	Input
BASE	*Constraints*	FORALL X,Y (treat(X,Y) IMPL (EXISTS Z ill(X,Z)))
	PriorAll	FORALL X ((treat(X,'MedA') AND treat(X,'MedB')) IMPL ill(X,'Aids'))
	Check/Commit	*successful/yes*
COMPLETED	*User Domains*	...
	PriorUser	none (with automatic derivation of [*logsubclass* : *dependency*] and [*logstatus* : *correct*])
	ConfidentialityPolicy	EXISTS X (ill(X,'Aids') OR ill(X,'Cancer')) and [*awareness* : *known*] (with automatic derivation of [*disjclosed* : *yes*])
	Restrictions	[*operator* : ⊤] and [*subclass* : ⊤]
	Requirements	[*distortion* : *refusal*]
	Check	*successful*
	Choose Censor/ Activate	**GenRefClo**/ yes

Finally, in Table 4 we present the inputs of the user Mary and the reactions of the security server while the dynamic-selection functionality is executed, complemented with the measured time needed by the prototype implementation running on a standard PC (intel i7-4770 processor/32GB memory/Ubuntu 14.04.4 LTS operating system) and using the Apache Derby DBMS with the in-memory option. The reactions of the security server are based on the dynamic development of the descriptors of Mary's surrogate state reported in Table 5, and the matchings with the static descriptors of the censors, shown in Table 2.

Table 4. The user inputs and system reactions during dynamic censor selection.

Step	Mary's Input	Server Reaction	Time [msec]
1a/b	QUE EXISTS X (ill(X,'Aids') OR ill(X,'Cancer'))	applicable: **GenRefClo**/mum	99
2a/b	QUE EXISTS X (treat(X,'MedA') AND treat(X,'MedB'))	applicable: **GenRefClo**/mum	97
3a	QUE treat(X,Y)	applicable: **GenRefOpe**	81 + 81
3b	change *Requirements*: [*distortion* : *lying*]	treat(Mary,MedA), treat(Lisa,MedB), treat(Pete,MedA), treat(Kate,MedC), treat(Theo,MedA) pertinent completeness sentence, see [6]	80 + 664
4a	VIE	applicable: **ViewLyi**	40
4b	choose censor: **ViewLyi**	materialized view generated	623
4c	QUE ill(X,Y)	ill(Theo, Cold), ill(Mary,Cold), ill(Pete,Diag1), ill(Lisa,Flu), ill(Kate,Diag2) implicit pertinent completeness sentence	40 + 81

7   Sketch of a Verification

Having the problems to be addressed in mind, in principle we have to formally verify the actual achievements of introducing descriptors and using them like security labels for monitoring a user's knowledge state and controlling the reactions on the user's requests over the time. Since a full elaboration of such a verification requires detailed case-by-case inspections of all the included censors and their possible interferences, we only sketch a general outline.

As a prerequisite, the previously used *slight variants* of a formal definition of confidentiality in terms of the indistinguishability of the actual (possibly harmful) situation from an alternative harmless situation under all sequences of *functional* interactions [3,15] have to be adapted. First, we have to suitably *unify* these definitions with an appropriate parametrization, and then we have to extend the parameterized unified form to capture also *control* interactions, which comprise the selection of censors and the corresponding notifications.

Then, for each of the included individual censors, we should first *adapt the existing proof* of the preservation of confidentiality to the unified and extended definition and then formally confirm that the unified control decisions based on descriptors *correctly implement* the previously stated application condition.

Next, inspecting each designed *notification* about a censor selection, we have to verify its compliance with the extended definition of confidentiality.

Finally, while previous proofs of confidentiality only refer to specific kinds of interactions, mostly only queries, we have to formally confirm the *compositionality* of these results under the unified representation of application requirements and their pertinent extensions by means of descriptors.

Table 5. Fixed and dynamic descriptor components relevant for user Mary.

Kind	Domain	Initial	Step 1	Step 2	Step 3	Step 4
global	*dbmodel*	*relational*	*relational*	*relational*	*relational*	*relational*
global	*dbschema*	⊤	⊤	⊤	⊤	⊤
global	*dbinstance*	*complete*	*complete*	*complete*	*complete*	*complete*
knowledge	*backsubclass*	*DBdep*	*DBdep*	*DBdep*	*DBdep*	*DBdep*
knowledge	*logsubclass*	*FOw.acyc.*	*FOw.acyc.*	*FOw.acyc.*	*FOw.acyc.*	*FOw.acyc.*
knowledge	*logstatus*	*correct*	*correct*	*correct*	*unreliable*	*unreliable*
policy	*psecsubclass*	*FOw.acyc.*	*FOw.acyc.*	*FOw.acyc.*	*FOw.acyc.*	*FOw.acyc.*
policy	*disjclosed*	*yes*	*yes*	*yes*	*yes*	*yes*
policy	*awareness*	*known*	*known*	*known*	*known*	*known*
restriction	*operator*	⊤	⊤	⊤	⊤	⊤
restriction	*subclass*	*FO*	*FO*	*FO*	*FO*	*FO*
requirement	*distortion*	*refusal*	*refusal*	*refusal*	*lying*	*lying*
interaction	*operator*	–	*QUE*	*QUE*	*QUE*	*VIE/QUE*
interaction	*subclass*	–	*FOclosed*	*FOclosed*	*FOopen*	*-/FOclosed*

8   Conclusions

Preserving confidentiality by inference control for sequences of interactions with a logic-oriented relational database requires sophisticated administration of global and user-specific settings and careful selections of applicable censors. The main challenges arise from the number of relevant parameters regarding the underlying database, the users and their interactions on the one hand and the variety of censors on the other hand.

We demonstrated how the stated requirement and its challenges can be partly automatically and partly interactively mastered by means of partially ordered descriptors of the relevant items. A censor selection can then algorithmically be decided based on the matching of the joint descriptor characterizing the wanted activity with the descriptor describing the inference control mechanism.

There are many further issues. For the *design* phase, a complete formal model of the compositional structure of the security server in terms of descriptors and states and a thorough verification would be worthwhile. For the initial *configuration* phase including subsequent reconfigurations, the installation of another censor should be fully automated, based on the formal model. For the *administration* phase, the already available conceptual part should be complemented by an operational part for setting additional parameters for data structures, algorithms, and heuristics. For the *interaction* phase, the so far purely conceptual steering should be complemented by automated runtime optimizations.

References

1. Abiteboul, S., Hull, R., Vianu, V.: Foundations of Databases. Addison-Wesley, Reading (1995)
2. Bell, D.E., LaPadula, L.J.: Secure computer systems: A mathematical model, volume II. J. Comput. Secur. **4**(2/3), 229–263 (1996). reprint of MITRE Corporation 1974
3. Biskup, J.: Inference-usability confinement by maintaining inference-proof views of an information system. Int. J. Comput. Sci. Eng. **7**(1), 17–37 (2012)
4. Biskup, J., Bonatti, P.A.: Lying versus refusal for known potential secrets. Data Knowl. Eng. **38**(2), 199–222 (2001)
5. Biskup, J., Bonatti, P.A.: Controlled query evaluation for enforcing confidentiality in complete information systems. Int. J. Inf. Sec. **3**(1), 14–27 (2004)
6. Biskup, J., Bonatti, P.A.: Controlled query evaluation with open queries for a decidable relational submodel. Ann. Math. Artif. Intell. **50**(1–2), 39–77 (2007)
7. Biskup, J., Embley, D.W., Lochner, J.-H.: Reducing inference control to access control for normalized database schemas. Inf. Process. Lett. **106**(1), 8–12 (2008)
8. Biskup, J., Gogolin, C., Seiler, J., Weibert, T.: Inference-proof view update transactions with forwarded refreshments. J. Comput. Secur. **19**, 487–529 (2011)
9. Biskup, J., Weibert, T.: Keeping secrets in incomplete databases. Int. J. Inf. Sec. **7**(3), 199–217 (2008)
10. Biskup, J., Wiese, L.: A sound and complete model-generation procedure for consistent and confidentiality-preserving databases. Theor. Comput. Sci. **412**, 4044–4072 (2011)
11. Ciriani, V., De Capitani di Vimercati, S., Foresti, S., Samarati, P.: k-Anonymity. In: Yu, T., Jajodia, S. (eds.) Secure Data Management in Decentralized Systems. Advances in Information Security, vol. 33, pp. 323–353. Springer, Heidelberg (2007). doi.10.1007/978-0-387-27696-0_10
12. Dolzhenko, E., Ligatti, J., Reddy, S.: Modeling runtime enforcement with mandatory results automata. Int. J. Inf. Sec. **14**(1), 47–60 (2015)
13. Farkas, C., Jajodia, S.: The inference problem: a survey. SIGKDD Explor. **4**(2), 6–11 (2002)
14. Fung, B.C.M., Wang, K., Fu, A.W.-C., Yu, P.S.: Introduction to Privacy-Preserving Data Publishing - Concepts and Techniques. Chapman & Hall/CRC, Boca Raton (2011)
15. Halpern, J.Y., O'Neill, K.R.: Secrecy in multiagent systems. ACM Trans. Inf. Syst. Secur. **12**(1), 5.1–5.47 (2008)
16. McCune, W.: Prover9 and Mace4. http://www.cs.unm.edu/~mccune/prover9/, 2005–2010

Privacy-Preserving Abuse Detection in Future Decentralised Online Social Networks

Álvaro García-Recuero[1,2]([✉]), Jeffrey Burdges[1], and Christian Grothoff[1]

[1] INRIA Rennes - Bretagne Atlantique, Rennes, France
{alvaro.garcia-recuero,jeffrey.burdges,christian.grothoff}@inria.fr
[2] Université de Rennes 1, Rennes, France
alvaro.garcia-recuero@univ-rennes1.fr

Abstract. Future online social networks need to not only protect sensitive data of their users, but also protect them from abusive behavior coming from malicious participants in the network. We investigate the use of supervised learning techniques to detect abusive behavior and describe privacy-preserving protocols to compute the feature set required by abuse classification algorithms in a secure and privacy-preserving way. While our method is not yet fully resilient against a strong adaptive adversary, our evaluation suggests that it will be useful to detect abusive behavior with a minimal impact on privacy.

1 Introduction

Users of online social networks (OSNs) currently face two systemic issues to their well-being: mass-surveillance and abusive behavior. Mass-surveillance in OSNs is a real threat for modern liberal societies [7]. OSN platform providers do not just need to self-impose limits on users' behavior[1], but now also avoid governments imposing draconian penalties to participants[2]. Abusive behavior where users in the OSN platform [9] or governments [14] send messages designed to harm potential victims, has been established as a significant risk factor for suicide [13] and a previous study is reporting it almost doubling the number of attempted suicides [8].

Future decentralised OSN designs such as [11] propose to protect users against censorship and mass-surveillance by decentralizing the OSN; namely establishing secure end-to-end encrypted communication between all participants, hiding meta data at the network level, and allowing pseudonymous interactions between participants. Thus it becomes plausible to address mass-surveillance threats. However, at the same time one would expect that threats from abusive behavior are likely to increase: Major centralised OSNs provide some safeguards, such as the Facebook-Imune-System (FIS) [15], to detect and block abusive behavior. Naturally, these centralised solutions typically exploit the comprehensive data available about the platform's users. Thus, these existing techniques will not work in a privacy-preserving decentralised OSNs,

---

[1] https://twitter.com/rules.
[2] http://www.bbc.com/news/technology-16810312.

© Springer International Publishing AG 2016
G. Livraga et al. (Eds.): DPM and QASA 2016, LNCS 9963, pp. 78–93, 2016.
DOI: 10.1007/978-3-319-47072-6_6

where some of the data is not supposed to be exposed due to privacy constraints, and other data may be easily falsified by an adversary.

In this paper, we describe key building blocks for building a privacy-preserving abuse detection system for future decentralised OSNs. As starting point we evaluate our abuse detection system with data from a centralised OSN, specifically the second largest one as of today, Twitter. Our assumption is that the interaction culture would remain similar between today's Twitter and a future decentralised OSN, and thus the results for analyzing abusive vs. non-abusive interaction patterns would carry over. Like the FIS, we use supervised learning to classify messages as acceptable or abusive. By incorporating a broad set of features based on publicly available data from Twitter, we establish a baseline for the accuracy of the method without privacy-preservation or adversarial adaptation to the method. We then study which features could be securely obtained without unduly exposing sensitive data about users. Here, we propose two new privacy-preserving protocols for secure set intersection, showing how efficient secure multiparty computation can assist in obtaining key features for abuse detection. We finally evaluate supervised learning using the resulting restricted feature set to demonstrate the utility of the method.

2   Defining Abuse

Before we can evaluate abuse detection methods, we need a definition of abusive behavior. From the rich literature on abuse, we found the Joint Threat Research Intelligence Group (JTRIG) of the British Government Communication Head Quarter (GCHQ) provided the most comprehensive and still reasonably simple definition in their characterization of their own work. JTRIG manipulates global opinion using techniques that they characterize with the four Ds: [14].

- Deny: They encourage self-harm to others users, promoting violence (direct or indirect), terrorism or similar activities. (This denies the victim health or even life, which are human rights.)
- Disrupt: They disrupt activities they disagree with using distracting provocations, denial of service, flooding with messages and generally promoting abuse of the intended victim.
- Degrade: They disclose personal and private data of others without their approval as to degrade their public image/reputation.
- Deceive: They deceive by spreading false information, including supplanting a known user identity (impersonation) for influencing other users behavior and activities, or assuming false identities. (The use of pseudonyms that are recognizable as such is not a deception.)

We will now argue that these four terms nicely cover common characterizations of abusive behavior.

Several studies have defined cyber-bullying as the act of harassing another person via any form of digital communications. This behavior is intended to *degrade* the self-esteem or image of the victim [10].

According to[3], an "Internet troll" or "cyber-troll" is a member of an online community who posts abusive comments at worst or divisive information at best to repeatedly create controversy. These actions are covered by the terms *disrupt* and possibly *deceive*.

Trolldor[4] allows users to search for the statistics of a particular user in Twitter, and report him as "troll". Key reasons Trolldor lists for users to report a Twitter profile as a "troll" to Trolldoor include:

– Provocation: users who just look to provoke for fun (*disrupt*)
– Creep: users who fill other users timeline on a daily basis with messages worshiping their idols, friends, relatives and colleagues. (*disrupt*)
– Retweeter/Favoriter: users who never create their own content and just retweet and favorite other peoples messages.
– Insult/Threat: users who insult or threaten other users. (threats *deny*)
– False identity: profiles that seek to usurp anothers identity (*deceive*)

Twitter's guidelines on abusive behavior explicitly prohibit: violent threats (*deny*), harassment (*degrade*), hateful conduct (*deny*), multiple account abuse (*deceive*), private information disclosure (*degrade*), impersonation (*deceive*), promotion of self-harm (*deny*), and spam (*disrupt*).

The examples demonstrate that the four *Ds* cover common definitions of abusive behavior.

3   Data Model

We consider two directed graphs whose set of vertices $\mathcal{V}$ represent the about one million user profiles collected from the OSN, Twitter. Let $\mathcal{G}_f=(\mathcal{V}, \mathcal{E}_f)$ be a directed graph of subscription relationships, where an edge $(a, b) \in \mathcal{E}_f$ represents that user a is subscribed to posts from user b.

Let $\mathcal{G}_m=(\mathcal{V}, \mathcal{E}_m)$ be a directed multi-graph of messaging relationships, where an edge $(a, b) \in \mathcal{E}_m$ implies that a directed a message specifically to b (on Twitter, this is done by either mentioning @b or by responding to a message from b). Note that $\mathcal{E}_m$ does not contain all messages that a broadcasts to all its subscribers, so it models the messages that are shown in the notifications of the user mentioned (@b), and which are thus a vector for potential abusive behavior.

To establish ground truth about abuse, we asked six reviewers to use JTRIG's four *Ds*-definition to manually annotate about 1000 Twitter messages as abusive, acceptable or undecided. The resulting data set (Table 3) provides the ground truth for supervised learning and evaluation of the methods presented in this paper.

Reviewers frequently disagreed about a message. For the *# agreement* value, we computed the agreement among the *other* reviewers and then checked whether this reviewer was in agreement with the rest of the reviewers about a tweet.

---

[3] What does Troll mean? http://www.techopedia.com/definition/429/troll.
[4] http://trolldor.com.

Table 1. Human baseline statistics. The c-values are explained in this Sect. 3.

reviewer	# reviews	% abusive	% accept	# agreement	c-abusive	c-accept	c-overall
1	754	3.98	83.55	703	0.71	0.97	0.93
2	744	4.30	82.79	704	0.66	0.97	0.94
3	559	5.01	83.90	526	0.93	0.95	0.94
4	894	4.03	71.92	807	0.61	0.94	0.90
5	939	5.54	69.54	854	0.88	0.90	0.91
6	1003	5.68	69.79	875	0.95	0.89	0.87
average	815	4.76	76.92	**745**	**0.79**	**0.94**	**0.92**
std. dev	162	0.76	7.18	130	0.15	0.03	0.03

On average, reviewer's ratings matched with the agreement among the other reviewers 745 times, corresponding to 92 % of the reviewed messages (*c-overall*). The value of *c-abusive* provides the agreement on abusive messages and *c-accept* the agreement on acceptable ones. As expected, agreement on abusive messages is significantly lower: the reviewers agreed on about 79 % of the abusive messages, and on over 94 % of the acceptable messages (Table 1).

4   Learning Without Privacy

At a high-level, the system has each user locally compute whether a message is likely to be abusive, and then allowing the user's software to take appropriate action, such as giving messages that are likely to be abusive a lower relevance in the user's timeline ranking. For this computation, the decision process should only use data that is available in the vicinity of the respective user. This approach ensures that the computation is compatible with decentralised OSNs that lack a central service provider.

Table 2 summarizes the feature set we used to evaluate abusive behavior. We experiment with various supervised models [1] from *scikit-learn*[5]. We present data from those classifiers that performed best. Specifically, we compare decision trees (DT), random forest (RF), extra trees (ET) and the gradient boosting (GB) classifier [3]. We also configure all our classifiers with a "depth" of eight, and using "balanced" for the "class weight" option. While we tried other supervised earning algorithms such as logistic regression, k-means clustering and NB-trees, the aforementioned tree-based methods performed best, and thus we limit our presentation to those.

A lower bound for the performance of the classifiers is provided by a base rate classifier (BR), where each messages is classified according to the most predominant class (acceptable in our case). This classifier classifies all abusive messages incorrectly, and all acceptable messages correctly. An upper bound for our performance expectations is the human baseline classifier (HB), described

---

[5] http://scikit-learn.org/stable/supervised_learning.html.

Table 2. Features, ordered following use in Sect. 5

	Feature	Description
5.1	# lists	how many lists the sender has created
	# subscriptions	number of subscriptions of the sender
	$\frac{\text{\# subscriptions}}{\text{age}}$	ratio of subscriptions made in relation to age of sender account
	$\frac{\text{\# subscriptions}}{\text{\# subscribers}}$	ratio of subscriptions to subscribers of sender
5.2	# mentions	number of mentions in the message
	# hashtags	number of hashtags in the message
	$\frac{\text{\# mentions}}{\text{\# messages}}$	ratio of mentions made in relation to messages written the sender
	# retweets	number of retweets the sender has posted
	# favorited messages	number of messages favorited by sender
5.3	message invasive	false if sender subscribed to receiver and receiver subscribed to sender
5.4	$\frac{\text{\# messages}}{\text{age}}$	ratio number of messages in relation to age of sender account
5.5	age of account	days since sender account creation
5.6	# subscribers	number of subscribers to public feed of the sender
	$\frac{\text{\# subscribers}}{\text{age}}$	ratio of subscribers in relation to age of sender account
5.7	subscription ∩ subscription	size of the intersection among subscriptions of sender and receiver
5.8	subscriber ∩ subscriber	size of the intersection among subscribers of sender and receiver
5.9	subscriber^r ∩ subscription^s	size of the intersection among subscribers of receiver and subscriptions of sender
	subscription^r ∪ subscriber^s	size of the intersection among subscriptions of receiver and subscribers of sender

Table 3. Evaluation of classifiers trained using 5-fold cross validation

Classifier	Metric	Arithmetic mean	Geometric mean	Only acceptable	Only abusive
HB	Precision	0.87 ± 0.09	0.86 ± 0.07	0.94 ± 0.03	0.79 ± 0.15
	Recall	0.76 ± 0.06	0.72 ± 0.03	0.98 ± 0.01	0.53 ± 0.10
	F-score	0.80 ± 0.07	0.78 ± 0.05	0.96 ± 0.02	0.63 ± 0.12
BR	Precision	0.48 ± 0.00	0.00 ± 0.00	0.95 ± 0.01	0.00 ± 0.00
	Recall	0.50 ± 0.00	0.00 ± 0.00	1.00 ± 0.00	0.00 ± 0.00
	F-score	0.49 ± 0.00	0.00 ± 0.00	0.98 ± 0.00	0.00 ± 0.00
DT	Precision	0.66 ± 0.10	0.59 ± 0.04	0.98 ± 0.01	0.35 ± 0.19
	Recall	0.77 ± 0.09	0.76 ± 0.10	0.94 ± 0.06	0.61 ± 0.18
	F-score	0.70 ± 0.10	0.64 ± 0.07	0.96 ± 0.03	0.43 ± 0.18
RF	Precision	0.73 ± 0.08	0.69 ± 0.04	0.98 ± 0.01	0.49 ± 0.17
	Recall	0.74 ± 0.10	0.70 ± 0.11	0.97 ± 0.05	0.51 ± 0.24
	F-score	0.73 ± 0.05	0.68 ± 0.04	0.97 ± 0.02	0.48 ± 0.10
ET	Precision	0.62 ± 0.07	0.51 ± 0.04	**0.99** ± 0.01	0.26 ± 0.14
	Recall	**0.82** ± 0.14	0.81 ± 0.12	0.89 ± 0.06	**0.74** ± 0.26
	F-score	0.66 ± 0.10	0.59 ± 0.08	0.93 ± 0.04	0.38 ± 0.16
GB	Precision	**0.87** ± 0.25	0.87 ± 0.07	0.98 ± 0.01	**0.77** ± 0.49
	Recall	0.74 ± 0.05	0.70 ± 0.05	**0.99** ± 0.04	0.49 ± 0.06
	F-score	**0.78** ± 0.12	0.75 ± 0.07	**0.98** ± 0.02	**0.58** ± 0.22

in Sect. 3. While the classification algorithms have additional data available to them, it is unrealistic for them to perform better than the individual reviewers who provided the ground truth. Table 3 summarizes the results of the evaluation. The key result is that even without extensive tuning, extra trees (ET) and gradient boosting (GB) perform surprisingly well, with accuracies comparable to those of individual reviewers.

5   Privacy-Preserving Learning

We now consider how to adapt the abuse detection algorithm to a decentralised privacy-preserving OSN, where we face an adaptive adversary who will change his behavior to evade detection. In this setting, we need to consider how to obtain the numeric value in a way that respects the privacy constraints, and how to make it difficult for an attacker to *forge or falsify* the value of a given feature.

5.1   Account Properties

Various features reflect properties of the sender's account that are entirely under the control of the sender. This includes the number of lists the user has created and the set of subscriptions made by the sender. Given an adaptive adversary who knows how the abuse detection algorithm uses these features, we have to assume that the adversary can freely adapt these properties and thus deliberately manipulates all such features.

5.2   Message Properties

This feature simply counts the number of times a message contains some of the special functions available in existing OSNs, such mentioning users (@user) or highlighting a topic (#hashtags) in Twitter.

These two are examples of message properties that are trivial to evaluate locally. The first one (mentions) seem to have negative implications for privacy when the computation is performed by the receiver, while the latter does not.

In case of mentions, adaptive adversaries may again shape their messages as to avoid a true positive in abuse classification, but possibly at the expense of being less effective at hurting the victim (e.g., not being able to mention her, thus not disrupting).

5.3   Message Is Invasive

The feature "message invasive" is a predicate that is false if sender and receiver of the message are mutual subscribers, that is both the sender subscribes to the receiver, and the receiver subscribes to the sender. If either party is not subscribed to the other,

Table 4. Relationship between abusive behavior and invasiveness.

	Acceptable	Abusive
invasive	440	31
non-invasive	196	1

the message is considered "invasive". Table 4 shows that messages that are invasive are more likely to be abusive.

The predicate is trivial to evaluate locally, as both parties know their subscriptions and their subscribers. While an attacker can easily subscribe to the victim, it would be hard to convince a victim to subscribe to the attacker's feed.

5.4   Messages Over Age

The feature "messages over age" represents the number of public messages sent in average by a user to all of its subscribers each day. The CCDF shows no clear trend as to whether abusive users in our data set send fewer or more messages per day (Fig. 1). To establish this value securely, a user could subscribe to the public feed and observe the message stream. As these are public messages, there is no privacy concern. Subscribing would—with some delay—provide an accurate count of the number of messages made per day.

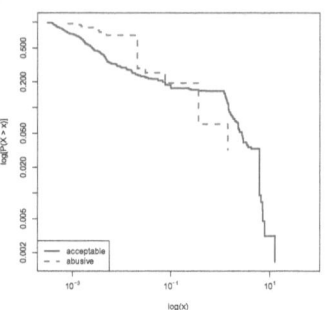

Fig. 1. CCDF of messages/day.

By supporting anonymous subscriptions and gossip-based message distribution, an OSN could make it difficult for an adversary to give the victim an inaccurate view of the public message stream of the adversary.

Naturally, the adversary may be able to adapt by sending fewer or more messages, but this may have an adverse and indirect impact into other features, particularly the adversary subscriber base. A similar analysis holds for features like "retweets" and "favorited messages".

5.5   Age of Account

The "age of account" feature considers how many days ago the account was created. The classifiers generally assume that older accounts are less likely to exhibit abusive behavior (which is supported by the CCDF in Fig. 2). Thus, an adversary has an interest in making his accounts look old. Using the age of an account is not privacy sensitive, as it hardly can be considered to be sensitive personal information about the user.

In a fully decentralised network, a time-stamping service [6] can be implemented to prevent malicious participants from backdating the

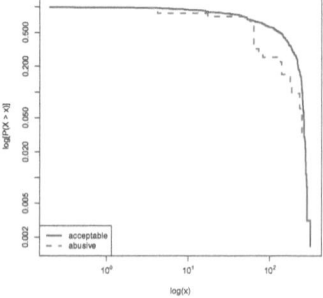

Fig. 2. CCDF of age of account.

time at which their account was created. Naturally, a time-stamping service does not prevent an adversary from creating dormant accounts to be used at a later time for attacks. However, time-stamping raises the bar in terms of required planning, and is thus unlikely to be defeated by non-professional trolls.

5.6   Number of Subscribers

The feature "subscribers count" represents the number of subscribers of the user sending the message. Figure 3 shows that there is no clear trend in our data set between abusive and non-abusive senders. It is conceivable that this is because the feature is trivial to manipulate: creating new accounts is generally relatively cheap, and there are even existing blackmarkets for Twitter [16].

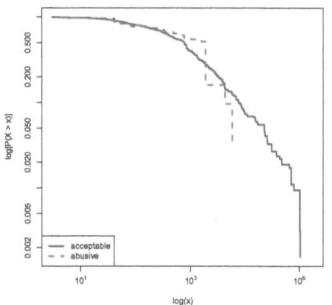

Fig. 3. CCDF of # of subscribers.

Assuming that abusive accounts do need to artificially inflate their subscriber base, one could use proof-of-work based group size estimation methods [5] to increase the cost of faking a large subscriber base. However, the network size estimation method presented in [5] would reveal the public keys of some of the subscribers. Still, this is easily mitigated by having each subscriber use a fresh pseudonym for each subscription, limiting the use of this special pseudonym to the group size estimation protocol. This has the drawback that the proof-of-work computation would have to be performed again for each subscription.

In any case, we do not expect such methods to work particularly well: an adversary can typically be expected to be willing to spend significant energy to create fake accounts. As a result, preventing fake accounts from being created by increasing the complexity is likely to deter normal users from using the system long before this would become an effective deterrent for a determined adversary.

5.7   Subscription ∩ Subscription

The "subscription ∩ subscription" feature is measuring the size of the intersection among the set of subscriptions of the sender and the receiver in relation; it is normalized by dividing it by the sum of the number of subscriptions of the receiver and the sum of subscriptions of the sender. Subscriptions are likely private information, and thus neither sender nor receiver can be expected to simply provide this information in a privacy-preserving OSN set up. In our data set, the resulting number of this feature is substantially less for messages classified as abusive (Fig. 4), thus an adversary would attempt

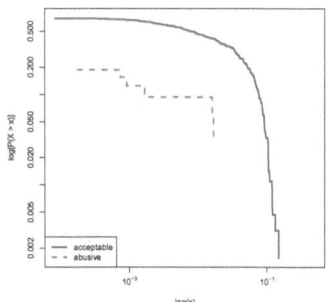

Fig. 4. CCDF of subscription intersection.

to increase the value. This requires the adversary to guess which subscriptions the victim may have, and then to create (or pretend to have made) the same subscriptions. We expect this to be costly, but not computationally hard: by watching the victim's public activity, it is likely possible to deduce quite a bit of information about the victim's subscriptions.

Our Protocol Part 1. We provide a new privacy-preserving protocol to compute the size of the set intersections, which is a variation of the PSI-CA protocol of [4]. Suppose each user has a private key c_i and the corresponding public key is $C_i := g^{c_i}$ where g is some generator. Let $\mathcal{A}$ be the set of public keys representing Alice's subscriptions and $\mathcal{B}$ be the set of keys representing Bob's subscriptions. Fix a cryptographic hash function h. For any list or set Z, define $Z' := \{h(x)|x \in Z\}$. We also assume a fixed system security parameter $\kappa \geq 1$ has been agreed upon.

Suppose Alice wishes to know $n := |\mathcal{A} \cap \mathcal{B}|$. First, she generates an ephemeral private scalar $x_A \in \mathbb{Z}/p\mathbb{Z}$ and sends Bob

$$\mathcal{X}_{\text{Alice}} := \mathsf{sort}\left[C^{x_A} \mid C \in \mathcal{A} \right] \tag{1}$$

Second, Bob picks ephemeral private scalars $t_{\text{Bob},j} \in \mathbb{Z}/p\mathbb{Z}$ for $j \in 1,\ldots,\kappa$ and computes

$$\mathcal{X}_{\text{Bob},j} := \mathsf{sort}\left[C^{t_{\text{Bob},j}} \mid C \in \mathcal{B} \right] \tag{2}$$

$$\mathcal{Y}_{\text{Bob},j} := \mathsf{sort}\left[\overline{C}^{t_{\text{Bob},j}} \mid \overline{C} \in \mathcal{X}_{\text{Alice}} \right] \tag{3}$$

He then sends commitments $\mathcal{X}'_{\text{Bob},i}$ and $\mathcal{Y}'_{\text{Bob},i}$ for $i \in 1,\ldots,\kappa$ to Alice. Third, Alice picks a non-empty random $J \subseteq \{1,\ldots,\kappa\}$ and sends J to Bob. Fourth, Bob sends Alice his scalar $t_{\text{Bob},j}$ for $j \notin J$, as well as $\mathcal{X}_{\text{Bob},j}$ for $j \in J$. Fifth, Alice checks the $t_{\text{Bob},j}$ matches the commitment $\mathcal{Y}'_{\text{Bob},j}$ for $j \notin J$. She also verifies the commitment to $\mathcal{X}_{\text{Bob},j}$ for $j \in J$. She then computes for $j \in J$

$$\mathcal{Y}_{\text{Alice},j} := \left\{ \hat{C}^{x_A} \mid \hat{C} \in \mathcal{X}_{\text{Bob},j} \right\} \tag{4}$$

Finally, Alice computes the result from $|\mathcal{Y}'_{\text{Alice},j} \cap \mathcal{Y}'_{\text{Bob},j}| = n$ for $j \in J$, checking that all $|J| \geq 1$ values agree.

We note that the same privacy-preserving protocol also applies for computing the overlap between the sender's subscriptions and the receiver's subscribers. However, in this case it is even easier for the adversary to manipulate the outcome, as the adversary can simply create fake accounts to subscribe to the victim, and it is trivial for the adversary to subscribe to these fake accounts. As a result, the adversary can increase the overlap for the "subscriber"-subscription^s" feature limited only by the number of fake accounts. As with the "number of subscribers" (Sect. 5.6), this attack can again be slightly mitigated by making account creation expensive.

5.8   Subscriber ∩ Subscriber

The "subscriber ∩ subscriber" feature is measuring the size of the intersection among the set of subscribers of the sender and the receiver; it is again normalized by the sum of the number of subscribers of sender and receiver. Unlike their subscription set, a user cannot freely determine the set of their subscribers: A user needs to actually convince other users that they should subscribe to their public channel. We assume the channel owner knows its subscribers, and that the subscribers are willing to cryptographically sign a message saying that they are subscribed to the user's channel.

Given this, we create a stronger version of the protocol from Sect. 5.7, which uses signatures that allow Bob to prove to Alice that his input consists really of his subscribers. The tricky part here is that the identities of the subscribers are still sensitive private information, so we need to use a particular signature scheme for our privacy-preserving computation of the overlap in subscriber sets. The fact that subscribers provide the signatures and not a certification authority is a key difference to the private set intersection with certificate authority (PSI-CA) of [4].

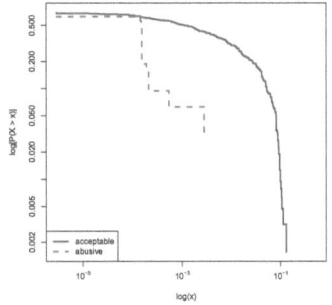

Fig. 5. CCDF of subscriber intersection.

The Boneh-Lynn-Shacham (BLS) Signature Scheme. We first outline the BLS signature scheme [2], which begins with a Gap co-Diffie-Hellman group pair (G_1, G_2) of order p with an efficiently-computable bilinear map $e: G_1 \times G_2 \to G_T$, a generator g_2 of G_2, and a cryptographic hash function $H : \{0,1\}^* \to G_1$.

In the BLS scheme, a private key consists of a scalar $c \in \mathbb{Z}/p\mathbb{Z}$, while the corresponding public key is $C := g_2^c$, and a signature on a message m by C is $\sigma := H(m)^c$.

A signature σ is verified by checking that $e(H(m), C) = e(\sigma, g_2)$. If $\sigma = H(m)^c$ then this holds by bilinearity of c.

Our Protocol Part 2. We again define $Z' := \{h(x) | x \in Z\}$ whenever Z is some set under discussion, and assume a fixed system security parameter $\kappa \geq 1$ has been agreed upon. Each participant is identified by a public key pair $C = g_2^c$ for the BLS signature scheme. Each participant A has a subscriber list L_A consisting of tuples $(C, \sigma_{A,C})$ where $\sigma_{A,C} := H(A, \text{date})^c$ is a BLS signature affirming that $C = g_2^c$ was subscribed to A until some expiration date, the specifics of which depend on the application. We envision these signatures being provided in advance so that Bob's subscribers need not be online when running the protocol.

Suppose Alice wishes to know $n := |L_{\text{Alice}} \cap L_{\text{Bob}}|$. First, she generates an ephemeral private scalar $x_A \in \mathbb{Z}/p\mathbb{Z}$ and sends Bob

$$\mathcal{X}_{\text{Alice}} := \text{sort}\left[C^{x_A} \mid (C, \sigma_{A,C}) \in L_{\text{Alice}} \right] \tag{5}$$

Second, Bob picks ephemeral private scalars $t_{\text{Bob},j} \in \mathbb{Z}/p\mathbb{Z}$ for $j \in 1,\ldots,\kappa$ and computes

$$\mathcal{X}_{\text{Bob},j} := \texttt{sort}\left[\left(C^{t_{\text{Bob},j}}, \sigma_{B,C}^{t_{\text{Bob},j}}\right) \,\middle|\, (C, \sigma_{B,C}) \in L_{\text{Bob}}\right] \tag{6}$$

$$\mathcal{Y}_{\text{Bob},j} := \texttt{sort}\left[\overline{C}^{t_{\text{Bob},j}} \,\middle|\, \overline{C} \in \mathcal{X}_{\text{Alice}}\right] \tag{7}$$

He then sends commitments $\mathcal{X}'_{\text{Bob},i}$ and $\mathcal{Y}'_{\text{Bob},i}$ for $i \in 1,\ldots,\kappa$ to Alice. Third, Alice picks a non-empty random $J \subseteq \{1,\ldots,\kappa\}$ and sends J to Bob. Fourth, Bob sends Alice his scalar $t_{\text{Bob},j}$ for $j \notin J$, as well as $\mathcal{X}_{\text{Bob},j}$ for $j \in J$. Fifth, Alice checks the $t_{\text{Bob},j}$ matches the commitment $\mathcal{Y}'_{\text{Bob},j}$ for $j \notin J$. She also verifies the commitment to as well as the signatures in $\mathcal{X}_{\text{Bob},j}$ for $j \in J$. The signatures in $\mathcal{X}_{\text{Bob},j}$ validate because we employ the BLS pairing based signature scheme where:

$$e(C^{t_{\text{Bob},j}}, H(m)) = e(C, H(m))^{t_{\text{Bob},j}}$$
$$= e(P_1, \sigma_{B,C})^{t_{\text{Bob},j}} = e(P_1, \sigma_{B,C}^{t_{\text{Bob},j}})$$

Alice then computes for $j \in J$

$$\mathcal{Y}_{\text{Alice},j} := \left\{\hat{C}^{x_A} \,\middle|\, \hat{C} \in \mathcal{X}_{\text{Bob},j}\right\} \tag{8}$$

Finally, Alice obtains the result from $|\mathcal{Y}'_{\text{Alice},j} \cap \mathcal{Y}'_{\text{Bob},j}| = n$ for $j \in J$, checking that all $|J| \geq 1$ values agree.

An attack on this blinded signature scheme translates into an attack on the underlying BLS signature scheme. If Bob tries to manipulate to increase the overlap, the cut-and-choose part detects this with probability $1 : 2^\kappa$.

Assessment. In our data set, the size of the subscriber set intersection is again substantially lower for messages classified as abusive (Fig. 5), thus an adversary would attempt to increase the value. It is hard for an adversary to try to get the subscribers of the victim to subscribe to the adversary's feed, especially given that the subscribers are typically unknown to the adversary as subscriptions are private information.

It is again possible for the adversary to create fake accounts which subscribe to both the adversary and the victim. While these accounts may be relatively new, the "age of account" feature only considers the age of the sender's account, not the age of the accounts of subscribers. As with the "subscribers count" feature, proof-of-work techniques may increase the cost of this attack.

5.9 Subscriber^s $\cap$ Subscription^r

Finally, we consider the size of the intersection among the set of subscribers of the sender and the subscriptions of the receiver. Figure 6 shows that, an adversary would try to increase the intersection of their subscribers (subscriber^s) with the subscriptions of the receiving victim (subscription^r). This feature is particularly interesting, as the sending attacker cannot easily influence set of subscriptions of the receiver, and will similarly have a hard time obtaining subscriptions from the user's to whom the victim is subscribed to. Unlike "subscriber $\cap$ subscriber", creating fake accounts is ineffective unless the receiver subscribes to these fake accounts.

Naturally, computing the subscriber^s-subscription^r overlap is again dependent on privacy-sensitive information. However, the protocol from the previous section can be trivially adapted to the situation where Alice uses her set of subscriptions instead of her set of subscribers.

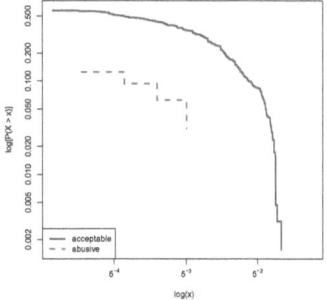

Fig. 6. CCDF of subscriber^s-subscription^r intersection.

6 Evaluation

We have shown how to obtain some of the key features from our original abuse detection heuristic even in a privacy-preserving decentralised OSN. While many

Table 5. Summary of how difficult it would be for an adversary to manipulate features in Sect. 5.

Feature	Falsification/Adaptation	Crypto helps?
# lists	trivial	n/a
# subscriptions	trivial	n/a
$\frac{\#\,subscriptions}{age}$	trivial	n/a
$\frac{\#\,subscriptions}{\#\,subscribers}$	trivial	n/a
# mentions	costly	n/a
# hashtags	costly	n/a
$\frac{\#\,mentions}{age}$	costly	yes
$\frac{\#\,mentions}{\#\,messages}$	costly	n/a
# retweets	costly	n/a
# favorited messages	costly	n/a
message invasive	**hard**	n/a
$\frac{\#\,messages}{age}$	costly	yes
age of account	**hard**	yes
# subscribers	possible	minimally
$\frac{\#\,subscribers}{age}$	possible	minimally
subscription $\cap$ subscription	costly	w. privacy
subscriber $\cap$ subscriber	possible	w. privacy
subscriber^s $\cap$ subscription^r	**very hard**	yes
subscription^s $\cup$ subscriber^r	possible	w. privacy

of the features can be inherently manipulated by a sophisticated adversary, others can be made robust even against strong and adaptive attacks.

We now evaluate the abuse detection system in the context of an adaptive adversary. In particular, we assume that the adversary can *trivially* adapt all of the account properties of the sender's account, *possibly* create fake accounts (Sybils) and fake subscriptions, and is willing to make *costly* behavioral adaptations, e.g. by adapting the text of messages to avoid message properties as mentions' Sect. 5.2 and the frequency at which messages of any type are sent (Table 5). However, the adversary is unable to manipulate the age of accounts (by breaking the timeline service) or to break the cryptographic primitives used in the protocols presented in this paper.

Given this adversary model, only three features remain: the age of the account, the subscriber^r ∩ subscription^s intersection size, and the invasive predicate. All other features need to be excluded from the classification algorithm's inputs, as we have to assume that the adversary will adapt to provide the worst-case input, thereby making abusive messages seem more benign.

We evaluated the accuracy of the supervised learning techniques presented in Sect. 4 on this modified feature set. Table 6 summarizes the results for the various classifiers. As before, the ET and GB classifiers generally perform better than DT and RF for our data set; however, the high variance means that this comparison may not generalize. The reduced feature set largely impacts the precision for abusive messages, cutting it by a bit more than a third in the best case scenario, and more than two-thirds in a worst case one (e.g., DT). Still, even with this strong adaptive adversary, the GB classifier performs at slightly more than half the precision and nearly the same recall of a human reviewer for abusive messages.

Figures 7 to 10 provide the ROC curve, precision-recall (P-R) curves and the confusion matrix (CM). In terms of relative importance (RI), the age of account

Table 6. Classifiers trained with 5-fold cross validation and hard to forge features

Classifier	Metric	Arithmetic Mean	Geometric Mean	Only Acceptable	Only Abusive
DT	Precision	0.64 ± 0.09	0.54 ± 0.04	0.98 ± 0.01	0.30 ± 0.17
	Recall	0.78 ± 0.12	0.76 ± 0.14	0.91 ± 0.08	0.64 ± 0.26
	F-score	0.67 ± 0.11	0.62 ± 0.09	0.95 ± 0.05	0.40 ± 0.18
RF	Precision	0.67 ± 0.12	0.59 ± 0.05	0.98 ± 0.01	0.36 ± 0.24
	Recall	0.76 ± 0.08	0.74 ± 0.09	0.94 ± 0.09	0.58 ± 0.19
	F-score	0.69 ± 0.12	0.64 ± 0.10	0.96 ± 0.05	**0.43** ± 0.20
ET	Precision	0.58 ± 0.05	0.40 ± 0.04	**0.99** ± 0.02	0.16 ± 0.08
	Recall	**0.80** ± 0.17	0.79 ± 0.16	0.79 ± 0.08	**0.80** ± 0.33
	F-score	0.58 ± 0.08	0.49 ± 0.08	0.88 ± 0.05	0.27 ± 0.13
GB	Precision	**0.71** ± 0.10	0.66 ± 0.04	0.97 ± 0.01	**0.45** ± 0.20
	Recall	0.70 ± 0.07	0.64 ± 0.07	**0.97** ± 0.03	0.42 ± 0.15
	F-score	**0.70** ± 0.08	0.64 ± 0.05	**0.97** ± 0.02	0.42 ± 0.14

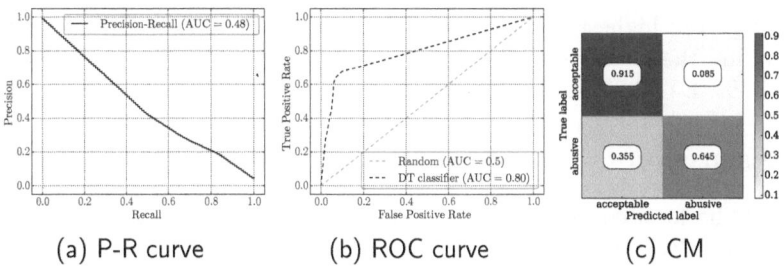

Fig. 7. Evaluation for decision trees (with strong adaptive adversary)

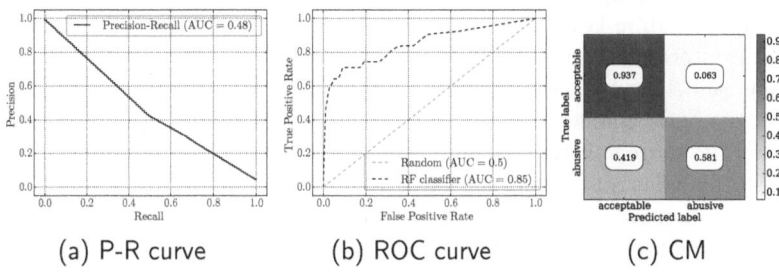

Fig. 8. Evaluation for random forest (with strong adaptive adversary)

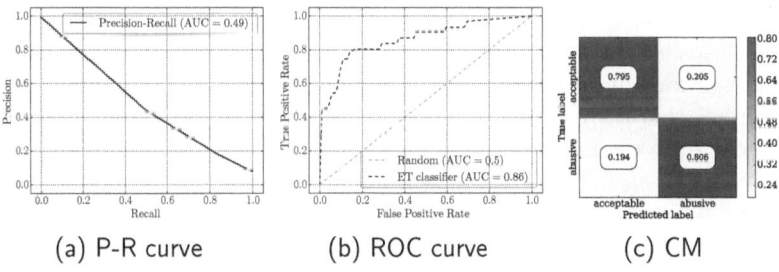

Fig. 9. Evaluation for extra trees (with strong adaptive adversary)

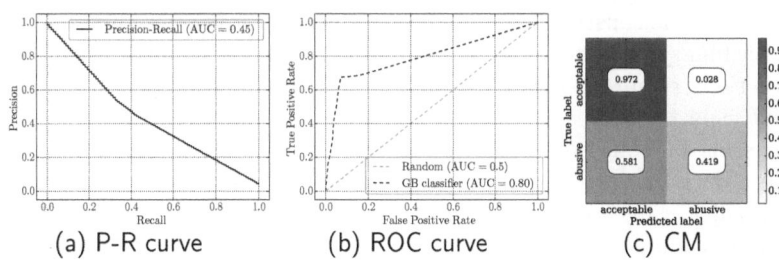

Fig. 10. Evaluation for gradient boosting (with strong adaptive adversary)

has always the highest importance (DT: 0.64 %, RF: 0.59 %, ET: 0.44 %, GB: 0.80 %) and the invasive predicate ranks pretty low in importance (DT: 0.00 %, RF: 0.07 %, ET: 0.27 %, GB: 0.01 %).

7 Discussion

Many of the features we originally considered could not be effectively secured against an adversary creating fake accounts and fake subscriptions. It might be possible to use some of these features if we additionally considered the age of the accounts: given a time-stamping service, the adversary may be able to create fake accounts, but it would be very hard to back-date them. Combining timestamped public keys with the privacy-preserving set intersection protocols is thus an interesting open problem for future work.

That said, even if we included some of these features that could be secured, the performance of the privacy-preserving classifiers did not significantly improve. The more substantial gains seem to depend on features involving basic account properties and sender behavior which fundamentally cannot be secured against an adaptive adversary as they are under full control of the adversary. Real-world deployments will thus have to figure out whether including those features would help (because real-world adversaries are not that adaptive) or hurt (because real-world adversaries would adapt to use these features to their advantage).

We envision that future decentralised privacy-preserving OSNs will use the sort of abuse classifiers discussed here as part of ranking messages in the user's *timeline*, not for binary filtering of messages for an inbox. By *timeline*, we mean any interface that displays short message summaries ordered so that users never feel the desire to read all listed messages. After browsing only a brief portion of their timeline, a user should firstly feel they have skimmed enough summaries to be up to date on any topics about which they consult the application, and secondly not have spent time on matters they might later regret, such as responding to abusive messages.

We have treated abuse as a binary classification problem in this article, but actually one would prefer the different features to report back a numerical risk score for timeline construction. As a result, the concerns around bias one encounters with binary classifiers [12] seem unnecessary here. Instead, actual timeline constructions requires integrating an array of features with both positive and negative aspects.

In terms of concrete deployments, we envision that future OSNs would include a decision tree baked into the code and not expect users to train their own classifier. This will simplify the deployed software, improve usability and avoid users running expensive training algorithms.

8 Conclusion

Our results show how to combine local knowledge with private set intersection and union cardinality protocols (with masking of BLS signature to protect identity of signers/subscribers) to privately derive feature values from users in OSNs. Given an adaptive adversary that would be able to manipulate most features we propose in our supervised learning approach, it is surprising that with just three features resistant to adversarial manipulation, the algorithms still provide useful classifications.

Acknowledgments. We thank the Renewable Freedom Foundation for supporting this research, the volunteers who annotated abuse and the anonymous reviewers. Special thanks to Cristina Onete for pointing us towards PSI protocol literature.

References

1. Bishop, C.M.: Pattern Recognition and Machine Learning, 1st edn. Springer, New York (2006)
2. Boneh, D., Lynn, B., Shacham, H.: Short signatures from the weil pairing. In: Boyd, C. (ed.) ASIACRYPT 2001. LNCS, vol. 2248, pp. 514–532. Springer, Heidelberg (2001)
3. Breiman, L.: Arcing the edge. Technical report, Technical Report 486, Statistics Department, University of California at Berkeley (1997)
4. De Cristofaro, E., Gasti, P., Tsudik, G.: Fast and private computation of cardinality of set intersection and union. In: Pieprzyk, J., Sadeghi, A.-R., Manulis, M. (eds.) CANS 2012. LNCS, vol. 7712, pp. 218–231. Springer, Heidelberg (2012)
5. Evans, N.S., Polot, B., Grothoff, C.: Efficient and secure decentralized network size estimation. In: IFIP International Conferences on Networking (2012)
6. Gipp, B., Meuschke, N., Gernandt, A.: Decentralized trusted timestamping using the crypto currency bitcoin. In: iConference. iSchools (2015)
7. Grothoff, C., Porup, J.M.: The NSA's SKYNET program may be killing thousands of innocent people. ARS Technica UK (2016). https://hal.inria.fr/hal-01278193
8. Hinduja, S., Patchin, J.W.: Bullying, cyberbullying and suicide. Arch. Suicide Res. **14**(3), 206–221 (2010)
9. Kramer, A., Guillory, J., Hancock, J.: Experimental evidence of massive-scale emotional contagion through social networks. In: Proceedings of the National Academy of Sciences of the United States of America (2013)
10. Langos, C.: Cyberbullying: The challenge to define. Cyberpsychology Behav. Soc. Networking **15**, 285–289 (2012)
11. v. Loesch, C., Toth, G.X., Baumann, M.: Scalability & paranoia in a decentralized social network. In: Federated Social Web. Berlin, Germany (2011)
12. López, V., Fernández, A., García, S., Palade, V., Herrera, F.: An insight into classification with imbalanced data: Empirical results and current trends on using data intrinsic characteristics. Inf. Sci. **250**, 113–141 (2013)
13. Luxton, D., June, J., Fairall, J.: Social media and suicide: A public health perspective. Am. J. Public Health **102**, 195–200 (2012)
14. Mandeep K. Dhami, P.: Behavioural Science Support for JTRIG's Effects and Online HUMINT Operations March 2011. http://www.statewatch.org/news/2015/jun/behavioural-science-support-for-jtrigs-effects.pdf
15. Stein, T., Chen, E., Mangla, K.: Facebook immune system. In: Proceedings of the 4th Workshop on Social Network Systems, p. 8. ACM (2011)
16. Thomas, K., McCoy, D., Grier, C., Kolcz, A., Paxson, V.: Trafficking fraudulent accounts: the role of the underground market in twitter spam and abuse. In: USENIX Security Symposium (2013)

Privacy-Preserving Targeted Mobile Advertising: Formal Models and Analysis

Yang Liu[✉] and Andrew Simpson

Department of Computer Science, University of Oxford,
Wolfson Building, Parks Road, Oxford OX1 3QD, UK
yang.liu@cs.ox.ac.uk

Abstract. Targeted Mobile Advertising (TMA) has emerged as a significant driver of the Internet economy. TMA gives rise to interesting challenges: there is a need to balance privacy and utility; there is a need to guarantee that applications' access to resources is appropriate; and there is a need to ensure that the targeting of ads is effective. As many authors have argued, formal models are ideal vehicles for reasoning about privacy, as well as for reasoning about the relationship between privacy and utility. To this end, we describe how the formal notation Z has been used to develop formal models to underpin a prototype privacy-preserving TMA system. We give consideration to how formal models can help in underpinning the prototype system, in analysing privacy in the context of targeted mobile advertising, and in allowing users to specify control of their personal information.

1 Introduction

Targeted Mobile Advertising (TMA) is an important part of the Internet economy. By analysing personal information, organisations can deliver ads for specific goods and services that may be of interest to users. In [3], Beales indicates that the average quarterly pricing data for targeted advertising of 12 advertising networks was twice that for standard advertising in 2009. Further, in [17], Yan *et al.* suggest that the click-through rate of ads can be improved by, on average, 670 % via the application of appropriate behavioural targeting strategies. However, TMA gives rise to privacy concerns: while users can take advantage of useful services, they are concerned about the misuse of their personal information and wish to not be 'tracked' [4]. The balance between concerns is, therefore, a delicate one.

There are two schools of thought with respect to trying to achieve this balance, with each school taking one 'side' or the other. On the one hand, researchers on the 'side' of corporations have tended to propose solutions that improve the collection of personal data and develop new analytical techniques to improve the accuracy of targeting (e.g. [2] and [18]). On the other hand, those on the users' 'side' tend to propose solutions that limit the ability of corporations to collect personal data (e.g. [5] and [8]). Our focus is a solution that tries to steer a middle path and that has the potential to be palatable to both users and corporations.

© Springer International Publishing AG 2016
G. Livraga et al. (Eds.): DPM and QASA 2016, LNCS 9963, pp. 94–110, 2016.
DOI: 10.1007/978-3-319-47072-6_7

To this end, we have prototyped a system called *Privacy-Preserving Targeted Mobile Advertising* (PPTMA) [12], with a view to users taking advantage of targeted ads without their privacy being compromised and organisations benefiting from higher response rates than would be possible via a solution that took a more anti-corporate stance.

Such a system gives rise to a number of interesting challenges. First, there is a need to balance privacy and utility — and to do so in a way in which all parties can have confidence. Second, and relatedly, there is a need to ensure that all access to underlying resources by applications is appropriate. Finally, there is a need for a framework to support principled and effective selection of ads.

As argued by Tschantz and Wing [16], formal models have many roles to play in reasoning about privacy in a variety of contexts. As an example, in [1], Abe and Simpson illustrate how formal models can be helpful in providing assurances of privacy in the context of data sharing. In terms of "privacy-specific needs", Tschantz and Wing argue the following:

"We want to allow users to control how much of their information is released to others, but we want to make it easy for them to specify this control, and even more challenging, to understand the implications of what they specify and to be able to change the specifications over time." [16]

This contribution is in the spirit of that argument.

Formal models can be beneficial in many ways. In this paper, we give consideration to how formal models can help in underpinning our prototype system, PPTMA, in analysing privacy in the context of, and in allowing users to specify control of their personal information. The underpinning models have been developed in terms of the schema language of Z [10]. The Z notation has been used due to its accessibility: it is widely taught and its structures have much in common with those of the relational model of data. In addition, Z has good tool support in the form of ProZ [13], which supports both animation and model-checking.

We present our models in stages. We start by formalising important aspects of current TMA systems, which enables us to identify the features of such systems that can impact users' privacy. A further specification then describes our solution and helps to underpin our design. The final model is then applied in a mainstream ad selection mechanism to show how the balance between utility and privacy can be reasoned about, and how users can understand (and, to an extent, specify) the extent to which their personal information is shared.

2 Motivation and Background

2.1 An Abstract TMA System

A TMA system automatically selects ads that are most relevant to the target user's profile and then presents those ads on their mobile device. The targeting process is based on the user's data, which includes personal information, the record of their online behaviour, the current context they are in, and so on.

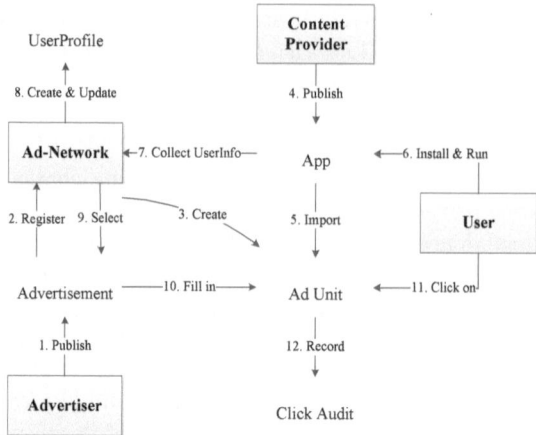

Fig. 1. A typical TMA workflow

For example, for a user who has installed a sports-related app on their mobile, and who frequently searches sports-related websites, the TMA system could present an ad of a sports store close to the user's current location.

There are four main kinds of actors in the system: advertisers, who publish ads for their products; content providers, who place those ads in their own apps; ad-networks, who collect ads from advertisers and serve them to content providers; and users, who interact with their mobile devices and click on ads.

Figure 1 shows key elements of an abstraction of current TMA systems, together with a typical workflow (consisting of five phases) between these actors:

1. An advertiser publishes a new ad and registers it to an ad-network; meanwhile, the ad-network creates some ad units for registered ads (steps 1–3).
2. A content provider develops a new app, and imports ad units into the app for the ads to be displayed (steps 4 and 5).
3. A user installs the app onto a mobile device and runs it, the app then collects the user's personal information and submits it to the ad-network (steps 6 and 7). The ad-network then creates a user profile to track the user's interests, and regularly updates it with new personal data (step 8).
4. With user profiles, the ad-network selects the most relevant ads for particular users and fills ads into ad units in the active app (step 9 and 10).
5. If the user is interested in the displayed ads and performs click operations, the operations are recorded as click-audits by the ad-network. The audits can then be used as references for charging money from the advertiser and for sharing the payment with the content provider (steps 11 and 12).

Users' personal information is mainly collected and analysed in Phase 3 (steps 6–8) and Phase 5 (steps 11 and 12), while the process of targeting is handled in Phase 4 (steps 9 and 10). Our prototype solution and related models focus primarily on the privacy issues involved in these phases.

2.2   Motivation

The inherent tension between corporations and users is delicate: some researchers concern themselves with improving the performance of TMA systems (e.g. [2] and [18]), while others are concerned with the rights of users (e.g. [5] and [8]). Broadly, previous contributions in this area have sought to address the following questions:

1. *How to enhance the mobile advertising effectiveness for corporations?*
2. *How to preserve privacy for mobile users?*

Contributions that address problem 1 tend to disregard potential hostility from users; contributions that address problem 2 can lead to reduced benefits for all parties as a result of, for example, utilising fake user data.

In attempting to address these issues, some contributions also consider the following questions:

1R. *How to enhance the mobile advertising effectiveness for corporations, and reduce users' hostility?*
2R. *How to preserve privacy for mobile users, and enable them to take advantage of useful advertising services?*

A number of contributions (such as [6,8,9] and [15]) serve ads with a hybrid personalisation mechanism   pre-downloading ads from the ad server with a generalised context and selecting the most relevant one with respect to a fine-grained user profile maintained on the client. The hybrid approach allows corporations to deliver personalised ads without compromising mobile users' privacy. In addition, users can receive ads that are particularly useful; however, it is not easy for users to specify control over released personal information nor to understand the implications of the operations they perform in the ad-selection process. This gives rise to a further question:

3. *How to make the control of personal information easily specified by mobile users, and enable users to understand the effects of their decisions?*

These questions represent the primary motivation for this contribution — to present formal models that characterise a privacy-preserving TMA solution that has the potential to address questions 1R, 2R and 3. The models give confidence in our prototype solution and help to underpin the decision-making process (both in terms of ad selection and in terms of access control). To this end, the formal models serve the following purposes.

1. They help to reason about the balance between potential benefits.
2. They help to provide assurance with respect to the preservation of privacy when using TMA, and to measure the balance between utility and privacy.
3. They help support the access control decision-making process, allowing users to understand (and, to an extent, specify) how much of their personal information is shared.
4. They underpin the ad-selection process, so that it takes into account a wide range of data — but only data that users have granted access to.

3   A Privacy-Preserving Solution

We now briefly introduce PPTMA [12]. At a high level, PPTMA is a service-based solution that works as a piece of middleware positioned between untrusted third-party apps and the underlying database on mobile systems. The service runs in the background of the system, and serves the following key functions.

1. **Personal data management.** Users' personal data can be managed manually with PPTMA. The system enables users to create different copies of their particular personal information and edit them separately.
2. **Access control.** A fine-grained access control mechanism allows users to decide what kinds of data or which copies of their personal information can be made available to third parties. Users can customise the data that is collected in Phase 3 (steps 6–8) of the TMA workflow of Fig. 1.
3. **Local ad selection and click-audit obfuscating.** PPTMA can serve as a local TMA system that performs ad selection on mobile devices: personal information is stored and analysed on mobile devices, rather than submitted to the servers of ad-networks. In addition, click-audit information that helps to trace users can be obfuscated in PPTMA before being submitted to ad-networks. The features addresses the privacy issues involved in Phases 4 (steps 9 and 10) and 5 (steps 11 and 12) of the workflow of Fig. 1.

Functions 1 and 2 enable users to take control over their personal information; function 3 offers a way of serving targeted ads without users' personal information being collected.

We have implemented an initial prototype of PPTMA on the Android platform [12]. Some of the core challenges are handled as follows.

1. **API hooking.** Calling APIs is the main method for apps to collect users' personal information or execute permissions on the Android system. Therefore, we hook sensitive APIs at run-time to implement the functions of access control and monitoring of malicious apps.
2. **Feature library comparing.** Apps use ad-SDKs of ad-networks to collect user data and present ads on mobiles. To make use of ad-SDKs, content providers have to register their apps with ad-networks and import their libraries. By comparing feature codes of these libraries, we can deduce the particular ad-networks related to an app, the kinds of ad styles it contains, the potential behaviour it involves, etc.
3. **Ad-SDKs integration.** Feature library comparing enables the discovery of ad-SDKs contained by apps. For cooperative ad-networks, PPTMA imports the limited versions of their ad-SDKs to perform the basic functions for local TMA — pre-downloading ads lists by providing only limited anonymous user information and submitting view or click reports without specific user identifiers.

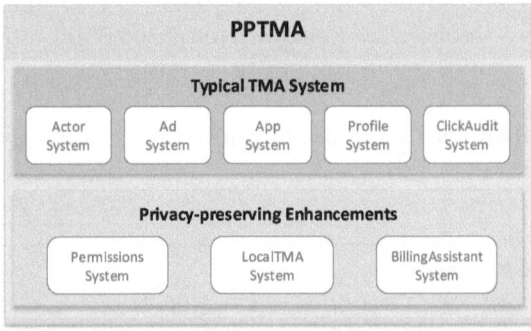

Fig. 2. The composition of the PPTMA system

4 Formal Models

We now present brief overviews of the formal models of the PPTMA system and discuss how the formal models can help reason about issues of privacy. Figure 2 shows the composition of the overall system at a high level of abstraction. We start by considering the initial model of typical TMA systems to identify privacy-related behaviours.

4.1 A Model of TMA

A typical TMA system is built up from many smaller components. In order to make our specification easier to grasp, we identify and describe the components separately in five subsystems, and then combine them. To this end, we present the possible states of the following subsystems respectively. For the sake of brevity, we have omitted type definitions and constraints on state schemas.

1. *ActorSystem* maintains information pertaining to the four kinds of actors: advertisers, ad-networks, content providers, and users.

> ┌─ *ActorSystem* ──────────────────────
> *advertiser* : *AdvertiserId* ↠ *Advertiser*
> *adNetwork* : *AdNetworkId* ↠ *AdNetwork*
> *contentProvider* : *ContentProviderId* ↠ *ContentProvider*
> *user* : *UserId* ↠ *User*
> └──────────────────────────────────

2. *AdSystem* is concerned with publishing and registering new ads. Newly published ads should be set to a particular format, assigned to target audiences, and associated with one or more keywords and categories.

$$UserBasicInfo \;\widehat{=}\; [\, gender : Gender;\; age : Age;$$
$$location : Location;\; language : Language\,]$$

$$Ad \cong [\, format : AdFormatId;\ targetAudience : \mathbb{P}\ UserBasicInfo;$$
$$keyword : \mathbb{P}\ Keyword;\ category : \mathbb{P}\ AdCategoryId\,]$$

$$AdUnit \cong [\, format : AdFormatId;\ adNetwork : AdNetworkId\,]$$

```
┌─ AdSystem ──────────────────────────────────────────
│ ad : AdId ⇸ Ad
│ adCategory : AdCategoryId ⇸ AdCategory
│ adUnit : AdUnitId ⇸ AdUnit
│ adFormat : AdFormatId ⇸ AdFormat
│ adInAdNetwork : AdNetworkId ⇸ ℙ AdId
└─────────────────────────────────────────────────────
```

3. *AppSystem* models the system for content providers to publish new apps and register their apps to particular ad-networks by importing related ad-plugins.

```
┌─ AppSystem ─────────────────────────────────────────
│ app : AppId ⇸ App
│ adUnitOfApp : AdUnitId ⇸ AppId
└─────────────────────────────────────────────────────
```

4. *ProfileSystem* models how ad-networks collect users' personal data, create profiles for them, deduce their interests, etc.

$$UserProfile \cong$$
$$[\, userBasicInfo : UserBasicInfo;$$
$$searchBrowseInfo : \mathbb{P}\ SearchBrowseInfo;$$
$$selfMadeDocument : \mathbb{P}\ SelfMadeDocument\,]$$

```
┌─ ProfileSystem ─────────────────────────────────────
│ userProfile : UserProfileId ⇸ UserProfile
│ userInterest : UserProfileId ⇸ ℙ AdCategoryId
│ profileOfUser : UserProfileId ⇸ UserId
│ profileInAdNetwork : UserProfileId ⇸ AdNetworkId
└─────────────────────────────────────────────────────
```

5. *ClickAuditSystem* records all users' click operations (including view operations for some ad-networks) on ads. Ad-networks make use of the records to settle accounts, and to update relevant users' behavioural profiles.

$$ClickAudit \cong [\, userId : UserId;\ adId : AdId;$$
$$adUnitId : AdUnitId;\ date : Date\,]$$

```
┌─ ClickAuditSystem ──────────────────────────────────
│ clickAudit : ClickAuditId ⇸ ClickAudit
│ clickAuditInAdNetwork : ClickAuditId ⇸ AdNetworkId
└─────────────────────────────────────────────────────
```

Combining these subsystems, we define a TMA system thus.

$$System \; \widehat{=} \; [\, ActorSystem;\; AdSystem;$$
$$AppSystem;\; ProfileSystem;\; ClickAuditSystem\,]$$

To make the notion of privacy accessible in the TMA system, we propose a relatively simple definition within our model: users' natural properties (e.g. age, gender, interests), which are stored in *ProfileSystem*, and users' behavioural data (e.g. browsing websites, clicking ads), which are stored in both *ProfileSystem* and *ClickAuditSystem*, are at the heart of the issues of privacy with which we concern ourselves. Thus, by tracking the data flow involved in the two subsystems, we can specify how much of a user's personal information is released to others.

A user profile is a series of records created by an ad-network for a particular user that stores the user's personal data and deduced information. The maintenance process associated with user profiles is reflected in steps 6–8 of the TMA workflow of Fig. 1. As the process takes place in the servers of the ad-networks, the users are unable to intervene in it. Therefore, the user's personal information is released to the ad-network without their control.

Ad selection is the core feature of the TMA system. Relevant ads can be selected by considering one or more factors: the user's hobbies and location; the most suitable format of ads for the active app and device; the ad budget; etc. The selection process is shown in steps 9 and 10 of the TMA workflow of Fig. 1.

The last steps of the TMA workflow involves recording users' clicks on ads. Since the click operations could reflect users' preferences (by assuming that users only click on ads that attract them), they can also be used as evidence for targeting and should be considered as a privacy-related feature. Again, users are unable to control the flow of their personal information within this process.

4.2   A Model of PPTMA

The model of the typical TMA system described in the previous subsection can help users understand how much of their personal information is disclosed. However, in this model, users' ability to control access to their personal information is limited — they can specify the released information and involved operations, but cannot intervene in the process.

We now refine the initial model by importing a permissions mechanism, a local TMA mechanism, and a billing assistant system. This helps us to describe the core features of PPTMA. The model of PPTMA allows users to control how much of their information is released, and helps to balance privacy and utility in the ad-selection process.

The permissions mechanism described (and implemented in our prototype) is consistent with the access control mechanism of Android 6.0 — enabling permissions held by apps to be modified after the apps are installed. This mechanism also enables apps to work properly with corresponding permissions granted by users. The enhancement gives users the ability to control which parts of their information can be released to which apps, as well as to the related ad-networks. The subsystem *PermissionsSystem* allows us to capture this feature.

```
┌─ PermissionsSystem ──────────────────────────────────────────
│ permission : PermissionId ⇸ Permission
│ installedApp : UserId ⇸ ℙ AppId
│ permissionRequiredOfApp : AppId ⇸ ℙ PermissionId
│ permissionRequiredOfAdNetwork : AdNetworkId ⇸ ℙ PermissionId
│ permissionHeldOfInstalledApp : (UserId × AppId) ⇸ ℙ PermissionId
└──────────────────────────────────────────────────────────────
```

With this subsystem, users can prevent ad-networks from collecting user data and delivering targeted ads by revoking all permissions required by related apps. This mechanism However, this compromises the ability of the advertisers and ad-networks — as their inaccurate ads might not be clicked, nor even displayed. To this end, we have implemented another extension to the model. The core mechanism creates coarse-grained copies of user profiles, pre-downloads ads to the mobile devices, then selects relevant ads from the pool of local ads according to local user profiles. The enhancement enables user profiles and targeted ads (the most significant privacy-related elements of the system) to be handled locally inside the mobile device. This mechanism is introduced by *LocalTMASystem*.

```
┌─ LocalTMASystem ─────────────────────────────────────────────
│ customUserProfile : UserProfileId ⇸ UserProfile
│ localAds : UserId ⇸ (AdNetworkId ⇸ seq AdId)
└──────────────────────────────────────────────────────────────
```

The function *customUserProfile* represents different user profiles edited manually by the users. The function *localAds* describes the pre-downloaded ads inside the device. It is important to note that the custom user profile, which is maintained by the user and not accessible to the ad-networks, differs from the actual user profile. Thus, the user's personal data stored in *LocalTMASystem* will not be released to ad-networks — unless the user chooses to share the coarse-grained or fine-grained version of it. The model, therefore, helps the user to make decisions pertaining to what extent they are willing to disclose their personal information.

The final extension to the TMA model is the billing assistant system. Click-audits are obfuscated in this subsystem before being submitting to the servers of ad-networks. This feature helps to record click operations without exposing the user's information.

```
┌─ BillingAssistantSystem ─────────────────────────────────────
│ obfuscatedClickAudit : ObfuscatedClickAuditId ⇸ ClickAudit
│ clickAuditMapping : ObfuscatedClickAuditId ⇸ ClickAuditId
└──────────────────────────────────────────────────────────────
```

The PPTMA model is based on the three new subsystems, together with the model of the original TMA system.

$$PPTMA \mathrel{\widehat{=}} [\,System;\ PermissionsSystem;$$
$$LocalTMASystem;\ BillingAssistantSystem\,]$$

It follows that ad-selection operations are composed of two stages. The first stage involves selecting and pre-downloading potential ads on remote servers with respect to coarse-grained copies of user profiles. In the second stage the most relevant ads are selected from the pre-downloaded ads by analysing the fine-grained user profiles on local client. These operations can be implemented (in both stages) via custom algorithms.

The click-audit is obfuscated in *BillingAssistantSystem* before being submitted to an ad-network. The original *UserId* value is replaced with a random single-use identifier to ensure that the ad-network cannot identify the specific user. The mappings of the original and the obfuscated click-audits are maintained locally to enable the tracing of click-fraud attacks. The obfuscated click-audit is sent to an ad-network from the *BillingAssistantSystem* rather than the mobile users. Therefore, the meta-information of the connection cannot be used to identify the original users.

5   Application of the PPTMA Model

Having described the PPTMA model, we now present audience targeting as an instance to show how a mainstream ad-selection mechanism can be applied in a privacy friendly way with our models. For the sake of brevity, we discuss only one instance of several different tests of the models. The instance illustrates how (the implementations of) these models can assist users in controlling how much of their personal information should be released to the ad-network, and help them to specify which particular operations disclose corresponding information.

5.1   The First Stage of the Ad-Selection Process: Pre-download Ads

By analysing a user's profile, ad-networks can assign the user to a particular audience segment, then recommend relevant ads for the user. The segment indicates the basic information and interests of associated users.

$$AudienceSegment \mathrel{\widehat{=}} [\,userBasicInfo : UserBasicInfo;$$
$$interestKeywords : \mathbb{P}\,Keyword\,]$$

We introduce one type explicitly — *Age* — to demonstrate the role that formal models can play in obfuscation.

$$Age:: =\ actual\langle\!\langle\mathbb{N}\rangle\!\rangle \mid range\langle\!\langle\mathbb{N} \times \mathbb{N}\rangle\!\rangle$$

Here, an age can either be a specific age, or drawn from a range.

We assume that there is a user whose basic information is described as follows.

$$UserBasicInfo1 = \langle\!\langle\, gender == Male, age == actual(25),$$
$$location == Oxford, language == English \,\rangle\!\rangle$$

We assume that profile ID of this user is $UserProfileId1$. The user is interested in $Basketball$ (which we assume has the associated identifier $IdForBasketball$); therefore, in $ProfileSystem$ the following predicate holds.

$$IdForBasketball \in userInterest(UserProfileId1)$$

The first stage of ad selection then consists of the following processes.

1. *Generate coarse-grained copy of the user's profile.*
   The schema $AudienceSegment$ suggests that the user's basic information $UserBasicInfo1$ and interest $IdForBasketball$ might be released in the following operations. The user chooses to only submit coarse-grained information to the ad-network, rather than his precise profile. Therefore he generates a custom user profile with following basic information:

   $$UserBasicInfo2 = \langle\!\langle\, gender == DeclineToState, age == range(20, 30),$$
   $$location == UK, language == English \,\rangle\!\rangle$$

   The custom profile is associated with $UserProfileId2$. Instead of disclosing his interest of Basketball, he only share his interests at a higher level as *Team Sports*. Therefore we have:

   $$IdForTeamSports \in userInterest(UserProfileId2)$$

2. *Assign the user to a relevant audience segment.*
   Based on the submitted profile — $UserProfileId2$ — the user will be assigned to the audience segment $AudienceSegment2$. By contrast, the original profile $UserProfileId1$ will lead the user to $AudienceSegment1$.

   $$AudienceSegment1 = \langle\!\langle\, userBasicInfo == UserBasicInfo1,$$
   $$interestKeywords == \{Basketball\} \,\rangle\!\rangle$$
   $$AudienceSegment2 = \langle\!\langle\, userBasicInfo == UserBasicInfo2,$$
   $$interestKeywords == \{TeamSports\} \,\rangle\!\rangle$$

   By analysing the two copies of audience segments, the user can understand which parts of his personal information is released (and to what extent).
3. *Select potential ads for the user.*
   A set of potential ads related to the segment can be selected via the following operation.

$\underline{\ SelectAdsByAudienceSegment}$ _____
$\Xi PPTMA$
$as? : AudienceSegment$
$anId? : AdNetworkId$
$ads! : \mathbb{P}\ AdId$
_____
$ads! = \{i : AdId\ |$
$\qquad i \in (adInAdNetwork\ anId?)\ \wedge$
$\qquad as?.userBasicInfo \in (ad\ i).targetAudience\ \wedge$
$\qquad as?.interestKeywords \cap (ad\ i).keyword \neq \emptyset\}$

Here, the ad-network applies *AudienceSegment2*, which is abstracted from the coarse-grained user profile, as the input *as?*. Therefore, ads associates with *TeamSports* (e.g. Football, Basketball, Baseball, Handball, etc.) will be selected. In addition, these ads are all applicable to a person who is aged 20 to 30, lives in the UK, and speaks English.

4. *Rank and deliver ads.*
   The selected ads are ranked on the servers without disclosing particular ranking strategies (e.g. ads can be sorted by remaining ad budgets, publish date, distance from the current location, etc.) that are applied by different ad-networks. The ordered list is then pre-downloaded to the user's device.

5.2 The Second Stage of the Ad-Selection Process: Local Ad Selection

Assuming that, via the first stage of ad selection, the user has obtained 100 ads related to different team sports located in different places in the UK, the local ad-selection stage can then help to pick the most relevant ads according to the user's precise profile. The processes are described as follows.

1. *Generate the precise audience segment from the fine-grained user profile.*
   As discussed in Sect. 5.1, *AudienceSegment1*, which is more precise than *AudienceSegment2*, can be abstracted from the original user profile associated with *UserProfileId1*. Since *UserProfileId1* and *AudienceSegment1* are both maintained locally in the user's mobile device, no personal information is released in this process.
2. *Select the most relevant ads.*
   With the precise audience segment, less relevant ads can be filtered out from the list of potential ads. For example, since we know the user's precise interest is Basketball, ads associated with Football, Baseball and Handball can all be removed from the list. In the same way, ads based in the UK, but outside of Oxford can also be filtered out. Note that the formats of selected ads should be consistent with the ad units of the active app.

```
┌─ SelectMostRelevantAds ──────────────────────────────────────
│ ΞPPTMA
│ uId? : UserId
│ as? : AudienceSegment
│ auId? : AdUnitId
│ adsSet! : ℙ AdId
│ adsList! : seq AdId
├───────────────────────────────────────────────────────────────
│ uId? ∈ dom localAds ∧ auId? ∈ dom adUnit
│ adsSet! = { i : AdId |
│              (i ∈ ran((localAds uId?) ((adUnit auId?).adNetwork))
│              ∧
│              as?.userBasicInfo ∈ (ad i).targetAudience
│              ∧
│              as?.interestKeywords ∩ (ad i).keyword ≠ ∅
│              ∧
│              (ad i).format = (adUnit auId?).format)}
│ adsList! =
│       ((localAds uId?) ((adUnit auId?).adNetwork)) ↾ adsSet!
└───────────────────────────────────────────────────────────────
```

Finally, we obtain a shortlist of ads with their relative ranks decided by the ad-network. The top ads on the list can then be displayed in apps as the most relevant ads. The two-stage ad-selection process helps to balance privacy and utility: ad-networks can only obtain the coarse-grained information that users would like to disclose, and users are able to obtain the most relevant ads based on their fine-grained profile.

5.3 Click-Audit Obfuscating and Click-Fraud Detecting

Finally, the user clicks on the displayed ad, and a click-audit record is created. As opposed to the second stage of the ad-selection process, the click operation and audit should be submitted to the ad-network, rather than stored in the mobile device. Thus, the user's interest might be deduced by analysing the clicked ad.

In order to prevent information leakage, the click-audit needs to be processed before being delivered to the ad-network. The click-audit obfuscating and click-fraud detecting mechanisms are described as follows.

1. *Obfuscate user identifier for an ad click report.*
   As discussed in Sect. 4.2, a random user identifier, *RandomId*1, is generated in the billing assistant system to replace the original user identifier, *UserId*1. *ClickAudit*2, the obfuscated copy of *ClickAudit*1, will then be submitted to the server of related ad-network. The mappings of the two copies are stored in the subsystem for later use.

$$ClickAudit1 = \langle\!| \; userId == UserId1, adId == AdId1,$$
$$adUnitId == AdUnitId1, date == Date1 \; |\!\rangle$$
$$ClickAudit2 = \langle\!| \; userId == RandomId1, adId == AdId1,$$
$$adUnitId == AdUnitId1, date == Date1 \; |\!\rangle$$
$$BillingAssistantSystem =$$
$$\langle\!| \; obfuscatedClickAudit ==$$
$$\{ObfuscatedClickAuditId1 \mapsto ClickAudit2\},$$
$$clickAuditMapping ==$$
$$\{ObfuscatedClickAuditId1 \mapsto ClickAuditId1\} \; |\!\rangle$$

2. *Detect click-fraud attacks.*
   The feature of click-audit obfuscating will not affect original click-fraud detecting mechanisms applied by ad-networks. As an example, bait ads [6,7] are hardly clicked by humans, but regularly clicked by automated bots. For example, the content of an ad is completely related to *Football*, but all attributes hidden behind the ad might be assigned to *Basketball*. A human user who is interested in Basketball might deem this ad a failed recommendation and ignore it. On the other hand, a bot performing click-fraud will be more likely to click on the ad without realising the inconsistent content. Thus, the ad-network can use click-audits of bait ads to trace suspected malicious users.

   Given an obfuscated click-audit of a bait ad, the real user can be identified with the permission from *BillingAssistantSystem*.

$\boxed{\begin{array}{l}
\underline{\;ClickFraudDetect\;} \\
\Xi PPTMA \\
ocId? : \mathbb{P} \; ObfuscatedClickAuditId \\
uId! : \mathbb{P} \; UserId \\
\hline
ocId? \subseteq \text{dom } obfuscatedClickAudit \\
uId! = \{u : UserId \;| \\
\qquad (\forall \, o? : ObfuscatedClickAuditId \bullet \\
\qquad\qquad u = (clickAudit \, (clickAuditMapping \, o?)).userId)\}
\end{array}}$

6   Analysis

We have used ProZ to analyse our model. ProZ allows its users to control the order in which operations are performed after the model is initialised. It also provides the ability to animate randomly.

We first performed operations involved in the TMA workflow, then animated new features associated with PPTMA. The result suggests new features merge well with the original TMA system and gives confidence in our prototype solution.

We paid particular attention to our main focus, which is how these models (and the related implementations) might help users to control how much of their

Table 1. Analysis on released personal information and related effects: example

Involved operations	User-held information example	Released information example	AdNetwork-held information example	Effects
Pre-download operations	*UserId*1 *Male* 25 *Oxford* *English* *Basketball*	1. Obfuscation: Age, Location, Interest 2. Disclosure: Language	*Null* *Null* 20 − 30 *UK* *English* *TeamSports*	1. Ad-networks obtain the coarse-grained data of *someone* who cannot be identified. 2. Related ads are selected for the *someone*.
Local ad selection operations	As above	No data is released	As above	1. The precise information is well preserved. 2.The most relevant ads can be selected.
Click-audit operations	As above, and: *UserId*1 *AdId*1 *AdUnitId*1 *Date*1	1. Obfuscation: UserID 2. Disclosure: ClickedAd, AdUnit, Date	As above, and: *RandomId*1 *AdId*1 *AdUnitId*1 *Date*1	Ad-networks cannot deduce the original user's interests by analysing click-audits.

personal information is released to the ad-network, to specify which particular operations release corresponding information, and to understand how their control might affect the ad-selection and user-tracking processes. Table 1 illustrates this. The analysis is based on the instance described in Sect. 5. Furthermore, all states and operations can be traced back by checking the state properties and the operation history list. Therefore, we can identify the source of each ad, ad unit, app and user profile involved in the process, which, in turn, provides the ability for us to detect malicious operations such as click-fraud attacks.

7   Conclusions

On the one hand, TMA provides significant financial benefits for advertisers. On the other hand, it gives rise to privacy concerns that users' personal information might be misused. Previous work in targeted advertising area (both on PCs and on mobile devices), such as Adnostic [15], Privad [6] and MobiAd [8], has typically tried to achieve the balance with a hybrid personalisation mechanism.

In this paper, we have shown how formal models might be used in helping to reason about the balance between benefits of mobile users and advertising corporations in the context of TMA. In particular, we have shown, in the spirit of Tschantz and Wing's contribution [16], the beneficial roles that formal models can play in reasoning about privacy. In our specific context, formal models allow users to specify the control of their personal information, and help them to understand how this control would affect the processes of ad selection and user tracking.

Next steps will involve the development of a privacy-preserving ad-selection framework and related protocols, building on the existing prototype of [12]. The ad-selection framework allows ad-networks to apply their own algorithms in the pre-download and local selection processes; additional privacy-preserving protocols will be developed to ensure that no profile can be exposed in the communication between devices and ad-networks. We will also explore means of refining our access control model by leveraging work on user-driven access control (see, for example, [14]). Furthermore, we will continue to use our models to underpin model-based testing [11] as we further refine our prototype implementation.

References

1. Abe, A., Simpson, A.C.: Formal models for privacy. In: Proceedings of the 9th International Workshop on Privacy and Anonymity in the Information Society (PAIS 2016). Bordeaux, France (2016)
2. Ahn, H., Kim, K.J., Han, I.: Mobile advertisement recommender system using collaborative filtering: MAR-CF. In: Proceedings of the 2006 Conference of the Korea Society of Management Information Systems, pp. 709–715. The Korea Society of Management Information Systems (2006)
3. Beales, H.: The value of behavioral targeting (2010). http://www. networkadvertising.org/pdfs/Beales_NAI_Study.pdf Accessed April 2015
4. Farahat, A.: Privacy preserving frequency capping in Internet banner advertising. In: Proceedings of the 18th International Conference on World Wide Web (WWW 2009), pp. 1147–1148. ACM, Madrid, Spain (2009)
5. Goldfarb, A., Tucker, C.E.: Privacy regulation and online advertising. Manag. Sci. **57**(1), 57–71 (2011)
6. Guha, S., Cheng, B., Francis, P.: Privad: Practical privacy in online advertising. In: Proceedings of the 8th USENIX Conference on Networked Systems Design and Implementation (NSDI 2011), pp. 169–182. Boston, MA, USA (2011)
7. Haddadi, H.: Fighting online click-fraud using bluff ads. ACM SIGCOMM Comput. Commun. Rev. **40**(2), 21–25 (2010)
8. Haddadi, H., Hui, P., Brown, I.: MobiAd: Private and scalable mobile advertising. In: Proceedings of the 5th ACM International Workshop on Mobility in the Evolving Internet Architecture (MobiArch 2010), pp. 33–38. ACM, Chicago, IL, USA (2010)
9. Hardt, M., Nath, S.: Privacy-aware personalization for mobile advertising. In: Proceedings of the 2012 ACM Conference on Computer and Communications Security (CCS 2012), pp. 662–673. ACM, Raleigh, NC, USA (2012)
10. ISO/IEC: ISO/IEC 13658: Information Technology – Z Formal Specification Notation – Syntax, Type System and Semantics. ISO/IEC (2002)
11. Jacky, J.: Model-based testing with spec#. In: Davies, J., Schulte, W., Barnett, M. (eds.) ICFEM 2004. LNCS, vol. 3308, pp. 5–6. Springer, Heidelberg (2004)

12. Liu, Y., Simpson, A.C.: Privacy-preserving targeted mobile advertising: Requirements, design, and a prototype implementation. Software: Practice and Experience (2016). http://dx.doi.org/10.1002/spe.2403

13. Plagge, D., Leuschel, M.: Validating Z specifications using the PROB animator and model checker. In: Davies, J., Gibbons, J. (eds.) IFM 2007. LNCS, vol. 4591, pp. 480–500. Springer, Heidelberg (2007)

14. Roesner, F., Kohno, T., Moshchuk, A., Parno, B., Wang, H.J., Cowan, C.: User-driven access control: Rethinking permission granting in modern operating systems. In: Proceedings of the 2012 IEEE Symposium on Security and privacy (SP 2012), pp. 224–238. IEEE, San Francisco, CA, USA (2012)

15. Toubiana, V., Narayanan, A., Boneh, D., Nissenbaum, H., Barocas, S.: Adnostic: Privacy preserving targeted advertising. In: Proceedings of the 17th Annual Network and Distributed System Security Symposium (NDSS 2010). San Diego, CA, USA (2010), April 6, 2016. https://www.isoc.org/isoc/conferences/ndss/10/pdf/05.pdf

16. Tschantz, M.C., Wing, J.M.: Formal methods for privacy. In: Cavalcanti, A., Dams, D.R. (eds.) FM 2009. LNCS, vol. 5850, pp. 1–15. Springer, Heidelberg (2009)

17. Yan, J., Liu, N., Wang, G., Zhang, W., Jiang, Y., Chen, Z.: How much can behavioral targeting help online advertising? In: Proceedings of the 18th International Conference on World Wide Web (WWW 2009), pp. 261–270. ACM, Madrid, Spain (2009)

18. Yuan, S.T., Tsao, Y.W.: A recommendation mechanism for contextualized mobile advertising. Expert Syst. Appl. **24**(4), 399–414 (2003)

Identification, Authentication, and Authorization

Searchable Encryption for Biometric Identification Revisited

Ghassane Amchyaa$^{(\boxtimes)}$, Julien Bringer, and Roch Lescuyer

Safran Identity and Security, Issy-Les-Moulineaux, France
`prenom.nom@safrangroup.com`

Abstract. Cryptographic primitives for searching and computing over encrypted data have proven useful in many applications. In this paper, we revisit the application of symmetric searchable encryption (SSE) to biometric identification. Our main contribution is two SSE schemes well-suited to be applied to biometric identification over encrypted data. While existing solution uses SSE with single-keyword search and highly sequential design, we use threshold conjunctive queries and parallelizable constructions. As a result, we are able to perform biometric identification over a large amount of encrypted biometric data in reasonable time. Our two SSE schemes achieve a different trade-off between security and efficiency. The first scheme is more efficient, but is proved secure only against non-adaptive adversaries while the second is proved secure against adaptive adversaries.

1 Introduction

Since the advent of cloud computing, more and more data are outsourced to remote cloud platforms, supplying efficient and rational data management, but also raising security and privacy issues.

Among the different tools supplied by the cryptographic community, a symmetric searchable encryption scheme (SSE) enables a client to store a private document collection on a remote server in such a way that (1) the server will not learn any useful information about the documents, and that (2) the server can search throughout the collection and return requested documents to the client. Symmetric searchable encryption techniques are more efficient than other primitives achieving a similar functionality, such as Private Information Retrieval (PIR) [15] or Oblivious Ram (ORAM) [14]. This efficiency often comes at the cost of a lower privacy, meaning that some information can leak. However, this leakage can be properly defined.

Biometric technologies [11] supply tools for authenticating and identifying persons based on their biometric characteristics. In the biometric identification paradigm, a fresh biometric trait, supplied by a client, is compared to a database of biometric references, owned by a server. The server returns the identity

---

G. Amchyaa—Part of this work was done while this author was an intern at Safran Identity and Security, and a student at Eurécom, Sophia-Antipolis, France.

G. Livraga et al. (Eds.): DPM and QASA 2016, LNCS 9963, pp. 113–129, 2016.
DOI: 10.1007/978-3-319-47072-6_8

(or a list of identities, possibly empty) of the user in the database whose biometric reference is close to the fresh biometric trait.

Biometric identification over encrypted data from SSE techniques has been proposed in [1]. The authors of this work use Locality Sensitive Hashing (LSH) [16] to construct a dictionary of keywords from biometric templates, then they use this dictionary as entry point for SSE techniques. Due to the SSE scheme they use [7], the communication performance and the storage complexity of their scheme are not optimal. The underlying SSE scheme only supports single-keyword queries and has a highly sequential design, leading to some overheads, in particular in terms of bandwidth.

In this paper, we improve on secure biometric identification and introduce new constructions, based on recent advances in the field of searchable encryption. We revisit the solution of [1] with more complex search pattern, namely queries supporting "at least t-out-of-n" conjunctive keyword search. That is, given a query consisting of n keywords, the server returns the documents for which at least t among the n keywords are associated with.

We also take advantage of the parallelism potential of the SSE design introduced in [5]. Motivated by the popularity of MapReduce and the parallel access it provides to blocks of data, we implemented our SSE-based biometric solution in MapReduce. We are then able to achieve identification over encrypted biometric data over a large amount of enrolled persons.

Related work. First SSE solutions [7] only handle static database and single keyword search, but recent constructions achieve more complex query pattern [6] and dynamic databases [5]. A related topic is fuzzy search on encrypted data [2], which have application to biometry. [12] enhances outsourced attribute-based encryption with keyword search capabilities.

Different cryptographic primitives have been used to achieve biometric identification over encrypted data. The work of [3] builds upon Private Information Retrieval [15], whereas [4] uses Oblivious RAMs [14]. Secure multi-party computation [10] and homomorphic encryption techniques [13] have also been used in the same context. While those solutions achieve more privacy properties than SSE, they are far less efficient.

Organization of the paper. In Sect. 2, we formally define the primitive we consider and also introduce the cryptographic tools we need in our constructions. In Sect. 3, we informally introduce our constructions. In Sect. 4, we give and analyse our scheme with non-adaptive security, and propose our scheme with adaptive security in Sect. 5. Finally, in Sect. 6, we discuss and revisit the application of searchable encryption to biometric identification.

2   Preliminaries

We first define symmetric searchable encryption, then introduce some useful tools needed in our constructions: locality sensitive hashing, pseudo-random functions and Bloom filters.

Notations. $x \leftarrow S$ denotes that element x is sampled from set S – according to uniform distribution, if not specified. $\nu(\cdot)$ denotes an unspecified negligible function, namely a function that decreases faster than any polynomial.

2.1 Symmetric Searchable Encryption

Index and keywords. An index is given by a tuple $(\mathcal{D}, \mathcal{W}, \mathcal{C})$, where $\mathcal{D}$ is set of documents, $\mathcal{W}$ a set of keywords, and $\mathcal{C}$ a subset of $\mathcal{W} \times \mathcal{D}$, denoting the correspondence between them. The term *document* here does not necessarily mean a text that contains the keywords. D might be a unique string identifying such a text, as a pointer. The set $\mathcal{C}$ induces two functions, DB that maps a keyword $w \in \mathcal{W}$ to a set of documents $DB(w) := \{D : (w, D) \in \mathcal{C}\}$, and KW that maps a document $D \in \mathcal{D}$ to a set of keywords $KW(D) := \{w : (w, D) \in \mathcal{C}\}$. Given a vector of keywords $\mathbf{w} = (w_1, \ldots, w_n) \in \mathcal{W}^n$, for $n \geq 1$, we note $DB(\mathbf{w}) := \cap_{i \in [1,n]} DB(w_i)$ (we assume that each document is associated with at least one keyword).

Algorithms description. A symmetric searchable encryption scheme (SSE) between a client and a server over a set $\mathcal{D}$ of documents is given by four algorithms Keygen, BuildIndex, Trapdoor, Search as follows.

- *Key generation.* Keygen is a probabilistic algorithm run to setup the scheme. It takes as input a security parameter λ and outputs a secret key K.
- *Encryption of the index.* BuildIndex is a (possibly probabilistic) algorithm run by the client to build an encrypted index EDB. It takes as input a secret key K and an index $\mathcal{I} = (\mathcal{D}, \mathcal{W}, \mathcal{C})$, and outputs EDB.
- *Generation of the queries.* Trapdoor is a deterministic algorithm run by the client to generate a trapdoor for a given query. It takes as input a secret key K and a query Q, and outputs a trapdoor T (called encrypted query).
- *Search in the encrypted index.* Search is a deterministic algorithm run by the server to look for documents in $\mathcal{D}$ that contains the query Q. It takes as input an encrypted index EDB and a trapdoor T, and outputs a response R.
  In some cases, a post-processing phase (noted Decrypt) might be performed by the client to extract a set of documents from the response R.

Queries in our schemes have the form $Q := (t, w_1, \ldots, w_n)$ where $1 \leq t \leq n$. It asks for the documents that contain at least t among the n keywords $w_1, \ldots, w_n$. Putting $t = n$ gives conjunctive queries: it asks for the documents that contain the all keywords $w_1, \ldots, w_n$. Putting $t = n = 1$ gives single keyword search.

Simulation-based security for SSE. We use standard simulation-based security definitions for SSE following the real-ideal paradigm [5,7]. The t-out-of-n case does not impact the standard security definition for SSE, since we include the threshold t into the query. A leakage function $\mathcal{L}$ describes what a secure protocol may leak. Security against a non-adaptive adversary means that the adversary is not allowed to see the encrypted index EDB or the trapdoors of any keywords before it had generated the index $\mathcal{I}$ and the queries $(Q_1, \ldots, Q_q)$ it wants to look

NonAdapReal$_{\mathsf{A}}^{\mathrm{SSE}}(\lambda, q)$	NonApIdeal$_{\mathsf{A}}^{\mathcal{S},\mathcal{L}}(\lambda, q)$

- $(\mathcal{I}, Q_1, \ldots, Q_q, st_{\mathsf{A}}) \leftarrow \mathsf{A}(1^\lambda)$
 - $K \leftarrow \mathrm{SSE.Keygen}(1^\lambda)$
 - $\mathrm{EDB} \leftarrow \mathrm{SSE.BuildIndex}(K, \mathcal{I})$
 - for $i = 1, \ldots, q$:
     • $T_i \leftarrow \mathrm{SSE.Trapdoor}(K, Q_i)$
     • $R_i \leftarrow \mathrm{SSE.Search}(\mathrm{EDB}, T_i)$
 - $b \leftarrow \mathsf{A}(st_{\mathsf{A}}, \mathrm{EDB}, T_1, R_1, \ldots, T_q, R_q)$
 - return b
	- $(\mathcal{I}, Q_1, \ldots, Q_q, st_{\mathsf{A}}) \leftarrow \mathsf{A}(1^\lambda)$
	 - $(\mathrm{EDB}, T_1, R_1, \ldots, T_q, R_q)$
	              $\leftarrow \mathcal{S}(\mathcal{L}(\mathcal{I}, Q_1, \ldots, Q_q))$
	 - $b \leftarrow \mathsf{A}(st_{\mathsf{A}}, \mathrm{EDB}, T_1, R_1, \ldots, T_q, R_q)$
	 - return b

Fig. 1. Non-adaptive security game for symmetric searchable encryption

AdapReal$_{\mathsf{A}}^{\mathrm{SSE}}(\lambda, q)$	AdapIdeal$_{\mathsf{A}}^{\mathcal{S},\mathcal{L}}(\lambda, q)$

- $(\mathcal{I}, st_{\mathsf{A}}) \leftarrow \mathsf{A}(1^\lambda)$
 - $K \leftarrow \mathrm{SSE.Keygen}(1^\lambda)$
 - $\mathrm{EDB} \leftarrow \mathrm{SSE.BuildIndex}(K, \mathcal{I})$
 - for $i = 1, \ldots, q$:
     • $(Q_i, st_{\mathsf{A}}) \leftarrow$
         $\mathsf{A}(st_{\mathsf{A}}, \mathrm{EDB}, \{(T_j, R_j)\}_{j \in [1, i-1]})$
     • $T_i \leftarrow \mathrm{SSE.Trapdoor}(K, Q_i)$
     • $R_i \leftarrow \mathrm{SSE.Search}(\mathrm{EDB}, T_i)$
 - $b \leftarrow \mathsf{A}(st_{\mathsf{A}}, \mathrm{EDB}, \{(T_i, R_i)\}_{i \in [1, q]})$
 - return b
	- $(\mathcal{I}, st_{\mathsf{A}}) \leftarrow \mathsf{A}(1^\lambda)$
	 - $\mathrm{EDB} \leftarrow \mathcal{S}(\mathcal{L}(\mathcal{I}))$
	 - for $i = 1, \ldots, q$:
	     • $(Q_i, st_{\mathsf{A}}) \leftarrow$
	         $\mathsf{A}(st_{\mathsf{A}}, \mathrm{EDB}, \{(T_j, R_j)\}_{j \in [1, i-1]})$
	     • $(T_i, R_i) \leftarrow \mathcal{S}(\mathcal{L}(Q_1, \ldots, Q_{i-1}))$
	 - $b \leftarrow \mathsf{A}(st_{\mathsf{A}}, \mathrm{EDB}, \{(T_i, R_i)\}_{i \in [1, q]})$
	 - return b

Fig. 2. Adaptive security game for symmetric searchable encryption

for. To the contrary, the adversary in the adaptive game is allowed to choose the queries adaptively, meaning that the choice of a query can based on the output of the previous queries.

A scheme SSE is said indistinguishable against non-adaptive adversaries according to a leakage $\mathcal{L}$ if for all polynomial-size A and polynomial q, there exists a simulator $\mathcal{S}$ such that

$$\left| \Pr[\mathsf{NonAdapReal}_{\mathsf{A}}^{\mathrm{SSE}}(\lambda, q(\lambda)) \Rightarrow 1] - \Pr[\mathsf{NonApIdeal}_{\mathsf{A}}^{\mathcal{S},\mathcal{L}}(\lambda, q(\lambda)) \Rightarrow 1] \right| < \nu(\lambda),$$

where the real and ideal games are defined in Fig. 1. SSE is indistinguishable against adaptive adversaries according to a leakage $\mathcal{L}$ if for all polynomial-size adversaries A and all polynomial q, there exists a simulator $\mathcal{S}$ such that

$$\left| \Pr[\mathsf{AdapReal}_{\mathsf{A}}^{\mathrm{SSE}}(\lambda, q(\lambda)) \Rightarrow 1] - \Pr[\mathsf{AdapIdeal}_{\mathsf{A}}^{\mathcal{S},\mathcal{L}}(\lambda, q(\lambda)) \Rightarrow 1] \right| < \nu(\lambda),$$

where the real and ideal games are defined in Fig. 2.

2.2 Useful Tools

Locality sensitive hashing. The basic idea of Locality Sensitive Hash functions (LSH) [16] is that similar items are hashed to similar values with high probability. Let (B, d) be a metric space, U a set of smaller dimensionality. Let $\mu \geq 1, r_1, r_2 \in \mathbb{R}, p_1, p_2 \in [0, 1]$ such that $p_1 > p_2$. A family $H = \{h_1, \ldots, h_\mu\}, h_i : B \to U$ is (r_1, r_2, p_1, p_2)-LSH, if for all $h \in H$, $x, x' \in B$:

$$\Pr\left[h(x) = h(x') \mid d(x, x') < r_1\right] > p_1$$
$$\Pr\left[h(x) = h(x') \mid d(x, x') > r_2\right] < p_2$$

Pseudo-random functions. Pseudo-random functions (PRF) achieve a computational relaxation of random functions. They are required to look random only in front of polynomial-time adversaries. Let $\lambda, n, m \geq 1$. A function $f : \{0, 1\}^\lambda \times \{0, 1\}^n \to \{0, 1\}^m$ is *pseudo-random* if for all polynomial-time A,

$$\left| \Pr\left[\mathsf{A}^{f(K, \cdot)} \Rightarrow 1 \mid K \leftarrow \{0, 1\}^\lambda\right] - \Pr\left[\mathsf{A}^{g(\cdot)} \Rightarrow 1 \mid g \leftarrow \mathsf{Func}[n, m]\right] \right| \leq \nu(\lambda),$$

where $\mathsf{Func}[n, m]$ denotes the set of functions mapping n-bit strings to m-bit strings, and where the probabilities are taken over the choice of K and g. A pseudo-random permutation (PRP) is a bijective PRF.

Bloom filters. A Bloom filter is a data structure providing an efficient test for the group membership. It consists of an m-bit array W standing for a set $S = \{s_1, \ldots, s_n\}$. Initially, all bits in the array W are set to 0. Let $H_1, \ldots, H_k$ be k independent hash functions mapping strings to integers between 1 and m. When inserting an element $s \in S$ into W, all bits $W[H_i(s)]$ are set to 1, for $i \in [1, k]$. To test whether an element s is a member of the set S or not, return yes if $\forall i \in [1, k] : W[i] = 1$, otherwise return no. Bloom filters do not introduce false negatives, but false positives may happen.

3 High-Level Descriptions of Our Schemes

In the following two sections, we propose two SSE schemes. In this section, we introduce global parameters, common to both schemes. We also give some high-level explanation of the schemes before giving the technical details.

Global parameters. Let $\lambda, \kappa, \mu, k, m \in \mathbb{N}$ be some non-negative integer parameters. Our schemes use:

- some pseudo-random functions
  - $PRF_\ell : \{0, 1\}^\lambda \times \{0, 1\}^\mu \to \{0, 1\}^\lambda$
  - $PRF_w : \{0, 1\}^\lambda \times \mathcal{W} \to \{0, 1\}^\lambda$ (for the 1-NA scheme)
  - $PRF_w : \{0, 1\}^\lambda \times \{1, 2\} \times \mathcal{W} \to \{0, 1\}^\lambda$ (for the 2-A scheme)
- a symmetric encryption scheme
  - $\mathsf{Encrypt} : \{0, 1\}^\lambda \times \{0, 1\}^\kappa \to \{0, 1\}^\mu$

- Decrypt : $\{0,1\}^\lambda \times \{0,1\}^\mu \to \{0,1\}^\kappa$
- k hash functions $H_i : \{0,1\}^\lambda \times \{0,1\}^\mu \to [1,m]$ for $i \in [1,k]$.

High-level view. For the easiness of the exposition, let us begin by explaining the adaptive 2-A scheme. It is inspired by the approach introduced in [5], in which entries of the encrypted index are of the form (label, data). Each entry depends on a particular keyword-document association. As a result, the size of the encrypted database is given by the number of keyword-document mappings.

Labels are derived from the keywords with the pseudo-random function PRF_ℓ. For each keyword w, there exists $|DB(w)|$ corresponding entries in the encrypted index, one per associated document. For each (label, data) entry, we construct the 'data' field as a pair (filter, ciphertext) of a Bloom filter and a ciphertext. The ciphertext is a symmetric encryption F of the document D, using Encrypt, under a key derived from the keyword. The Bloom filter represents the set of the keywords $KW(D)$ associated to the document. It is filled as follows. For each keyword $w \in KW(D)$, a random value τ is derived with the pseudo-random function PRF_w from w. Then the k hash functions $\{H_i\}_{i\in[1,k]}$ are applied to the token τ and the encrypted document F.

This achieves the high-level view of the encrypted index. Now, given n keywords, the client computes an encrypted query with the pseudo-random function PRF_w. Given this encrypted query, the server retrieves the entries (label, (filter, ciphertext)) for which label maps one of the elements in the query, then performs checks in the Bloom filter and return, or not, the (decrypted) document according to some threshold.

Careful choices of the key derivations and the domains for the pseudo-random functions enable to prove security with respect to adaptive adversaries.

The 1-NA scheme is a variant of the 2-A scheme there is only a single entry per document in the encrypted database. That is, an entry of the encrypted database is of the form (filter, ciphertext). Labels are dropped. We lose the adaptive security, but the scheme is more efficient, and we still manage to prove its security with respect to non-adaptive adversaries if the decryption is performed by the client.

Assumptions on the number of keywords. Our schemes are not proven secure in the general sense of the definition given Sect. 2.1. However, we prove their security if each document is linked with a constant-sized set of keywords (which is the case in our application to biometric identification).

- Assumption A1. $\exists n \in \mathbb{N}, |KW(D)| = n$ for all $D \in \mathcal{D}$.

We enhance the definition of the index to include such an n: $\mathcal{I} := (\mathcal{D}, \mathcal{W}, \mathcal{C}, n)$.

4   A Non-adaptive Scheme

In this section, we introduce a scheme called 1-NA and prove its security against non-adaptive attacks. 1-NA is not secure against adaptive adversaries, but more efficient than the 2-A scheme. It provides then a trade-off between security and efficiency.

4.1   Algorithms Description

Key generation. Pick and return two random keys $K_w, K_E \leftarrow \{0,1\}^\lambda$.

Encryption of the index. Given an index $\mathcal{I} = (\mathcal{D}, \mathcal{W}, \mathcal{C})$:

1. initialize the encrypted index $\mathsf{EDB} := \{\}$
2. for each document $D \in \mathcal{D}$:
   (a) encrypt the document $F := \mathtt{Encrypt}(K_E, D)$
   (b) initialize the Bloom filter $W := [0, \dots, 0] \in \{0\}^m$
   (c) for each keyword $\mathsf{w} \in KW(D)$:
       i. compute a token $\tau := PRF_w(K_w, \mathsf{w})$
       ii. fill in the filter: for each $H \in \{H_1, \dots, H_k\}$: $W[H(\tau, F)] := 1$
   (d) update the encrypted index $\mathsf{EDB} := \mathsf{EDB} \cup \{(W, F)\}$
3. return the encrypted index EDB

Query generation algorithm. Given a key (K_w, K_E), a threshold t, and keywords $(w_1, \dots, w_n)$, return $T := (t, PRF_w(K_w, w_1), \dots, PRF_w(K_w, w_n))$.

Search over encrypted index. Given an encrypted query $T = (t, \tau_1, \dots, \tau_n)$:

1. initialize the response $R := \{\}$
2. for each (filter, encryption) pair $(W, F) \in \mathsf{EDB}$:
   (a) initialize a counter $c := 0$; then for $j := 1, \dots, n$:
       i. if $[(W[H(\tau_j, F)] = 1)$ for all $H \in \{H_1, \dots, H_k\}]$: $c++$
   (b) if $(c \geq t)$: update the response $R := R \cup \{F\}$
3. return the response R

Given R and K, the client gets the set of documents $\{\mathtt{Decrypt}(K_E, F) : F \in R\}$.

4.2   Leakage Analysis of the 1-NA Scheme

Let us now analyse the leakage of the 1-NA scheme. That is, following the simulation-based definition of Sect. 2.1, we must define an appropriate leakage function under which we will prove our construction secure. On input an index $\mathcal{I} = (\mathcal{D}, \mathcal{W}, \mathcal{C}, \mathsf{n})$ and a sequence $Q_1, \dots, Q_q$, the leakage function $\mathcal{L}_{NA}$ returns $(N := |\mathcal{D}|, \mathsf{n}, SP(Q_1, \dots, Q_q), AP(Q_1, \dots, Q_q))$, where the search pattern SP and the access pattern AP are defined as follows.

Search pattern. The 1-NA scheme leaks whether the same keyword is repeated in the queries. Given a sequence $Q_1, \dots, Q_q$ where $Q_i := (t_i, w_{i:1}, \dots, w_{i:n_i})$ for $i = 1, \dots, q$, the search pattern SP is given by:

$$SP(Q_1, \dots, Q_q) := \{(t_i, n_i, V_i, S_{i:1}, \dots, S_{i:n_i}) : i \in [1, q]\}$$

where $V_i := \{j : \exists j' \neq j, w_{i:j} = w_{i:j'}\}$ and $S_{i:j} := \{(i, j) \in [1, i-1] \times \mathbb{N} : w_{i:j} = w_{i:j}\}$. Depending on the use-case, it might be useless to ask twice the same word in a query, but, formally, this case remains allowed by the definition.

Access Pattern. The scheme 1-NA leaks whether a document is returned through several responses. We must properly simulate the responses according to the index, but also according to the false positives of the Bloom filters. To this aim, the leakage function computes the responses $R_1, \ldots, R_q$ as follows:

1. for $i = 1, \ldots, q$:
   - (a) parse Q_i as $(t_i, w_{i:1}, \ldots, w_{i:n_i})$
   - (b) $\mathsf{R} := \{(D, J) \in \mathcal{D} \times \mathcal{P}([1, n_i]) : J = \{j \in [1, n_i] : D \in DB(w_{i:j})\} \wedge |J| \geq t_i\}$ // *if* $t_i = n_i$, *then* J *is useless and* $\mathsf{R} = DB(w_{i:1}) \cap \cdots \cap DB(w_{i:n_i})$
   - (c) set $R_i := \mathsf{R}$; for each document $D \in \mathcal{D}$ not in R:
     - i. initialize $T := [0 \ldots 0] \in \{0\}^{n_i}$
     - ii. for $j = 1, \ldots, n_i$: set $T[j] := 1$ with probability $\left(1 - \left(1 - \frac{1}{m}\right)^{k \cdot n}\right)^k$
     - iii. set $J := \{j \in [1, n_i] : T[j] = 1\}$
     - iv. if $(|J| \geq t_i)$: add (D, J) to R_i

Then, the access pattern $AP(Q_1, \ldots, Q_q)$ is given by

$$AP := \{A_D : D \in \mathcal{D}\},$$
$$A_D := \{(i, J) \in [1, q] \times \mathcal{P}(\mathbb{N}) : (D, J) \in R_i\}.$$

4.3   A Simulator for the 1-NA Scheme

We now construct a simulator $\mathcal{S}_{NA}$ allowing to prove security with respect to the leakage $\mathcal{L}_{NA}$ above against non-adaptive attacks. Given $\mathcal{L}_{NA}$ $(\mathcal{I}, Q_1, \ldots, Q_q) = (N, \mathsf{n}, (SP_1, \ldots, SP_q), AP)$, where $SP_i := (t_i, n_i, V_i, S_{i:1}, \ldots, S_{i:n_i})$ for all $i = 1, \ldots, q$, the simulator $\mathcal{S}_{NA}$ first simulates the queries according to the search pattern. $\mathcal{S}_{NA}$ maintains a map $\mathbf{T}$, where the keys of $\mathbf{T}$ are the entries in EDB.

1. for $i = 1, \ldots, q$: for $j = 1, \ldots, n_i$:
   - (a) if $(\exists(\mathsf{i}, \mathsf{j}) \in S_{i:j})$: $Q_i[j] := Q_i[\mathsf{j}]$,
   - (b) else if $(j \in V_i$ and $\exists \mathsf{j} \in V_i, \mathsf{j} < j)$: $Q_i[j] := Q_i[\mathsf{j}]$,
   - (c) else: $Q_i[j] \leftarrow \{0, 1\}^\lambda$

Then, the encrypted index and responses are simulated w.r.t. the access pattern.

2. initialize $\mathsf{EDB} := \{\}$; then for each $A_D \in AP$:
   - (a) set $F \leftarrow \{0, 1\}^\mu$; initialize $W := [0, \ldots, 0] \in \{0\}^m$
   - (b) $\forall (i, J) \in A_D$: $\forall j \in J$: $\forall H \in \{H_1, \ldots, H_k\}$: set $W[H(Q_i[j], F)] := 1$
   - (c) set $\mathbf{T}[(W, F)] := |\{Q_i[j] : (i, J) \in A_D, j \in J\}|$ // *Note: it is a set (not a multi-set), so the simulation is consistent with respect to the repetitions in the search pattern*
   - (d) $\mathsf{EDB} := \mathsf{EDB} \cup \{(W, F)\}$
3. for $i = 1, \ldots, q$:
   - (a) parse Q_i as $(t_i, \tau_1, \ldots, \tau_n)$; initialize $R_i := \{\}$; for each $(W, F) \in \mathsf{EDB}$:

  i. $c := 0$; for each $\tau \in \{\tau_1, \ldots, \tau_n\}$:
   A. if $[\,(W[H(\tau, F)] = 1)$ for all $H \in \{H_1, \ldots, H_k\}\,]$: $c++$
  ii. if $(c \geq t_i)$: $R_i := R_i \cup \{F\}$

At this point we are sure that the number of documents per responses is consistent with the access pattern. However, the Bloom filters in the database may not contain the correct number of elements. We must fill in the Bloom filters while ensuring that we do not add new documents in the responses.

4. complete the filters (an algorithm for this is given Fig. 4 in Appendix)
5. return $(\mathsf{EDB}, (Q_1, R_1), \ldots, (Q_q, R_q))$.

  Once the simulator is described, the remaining of the proof of security is classical. It consists of a sequence of 3 games. In the first hop we replace PRF_w by a random function. In the second hop we replace the encryption function $\mathtt{Encrypt}$ by a random function.

5 An Adaptive Scheme

We now introduce a scheme called 2-A and prove its security against adaptive attacks, in the random oracle model.

5.1 Algorithms Description

Key generation algorithm. Pick and return a random key $K \leftarrow \{0,1\}^\lambda$.

Encryption of the index. Given an index $\mathcal{I} = (\mathcal{D}, \mathcal{W}, \mathcal{C})$:

1. initialize an encrypted index $\mathsf{EDB} := \{\}$
2. for each keyword $w \in \mathcal{W}$:
 (a) set the keys $K_\ell := PRF_w(K, 1, w)$ and $K_E := PRF_w(K, 2, w)$
 (b) for each document $D \in DB(w)$:
  i. encrypt the document $F := \mathtt{Encrypt}(K_E, D)$
  ii. initialize the Bloom filter $W := [0, \ldots, 0] \in \{0\}^m$
  iii. for each keyword $\mathsf{w} \in KW(D)$ associated to the document:
   A. compute a token $\tau := PRF_w(K, 1, \mathsf{w})$
   B. fill in the filter: for each $H \in \{H_1, \ldots, H_k\}$: $W[H(\tau, F)] := 1$
  iv. set $\ell := PRF_\ell(K_\ell, F)$ and $\mathsf{EDB} := \mathsf{EDB} \cup \{(\ell, (W, F))\}$
3. return the encrypted index EDB

Query generation algorithm. Given K and $(t, w_1, \ldots, w_n)$, it returns $(t, (\tau_1, \chi_1), \ldots, (\tau_n, \chi_n))$ where $(\tau_j, \chi_j) := (PRF_w(K, 1, w_j), PRF_w(K, 2, w_j))$ for $j \in [1, n]$.

Search over encrypted index. Given a query $Q = (t, (\tau_1, \chi_1), \ldots, (\tau_n, \chi_n))$:

1. initialize $R := \{\}$

2. for each $(\ell, (W, F)) \in$ EDB:
   (a) if [$\exists(\tau, \chi) \in Q$ s.t. $\ell = PRF_\ell(\tau, F)$]: // Or: if [$\ell = PRF_\ell(\tau_1, F)$]:
      i. initialize $c := 0$; then for $i := 1, \ldots, n$:
         A. if [$(W[H(\tau_i, F)] = 1)$ for all $H \in \{H_1, \ldots, H_k\}$]: $c++$
      ii. if $(c \geq t)$: $R := R \cup \{\texttt{Decrypt}(\chi, F)\}$
3. return the response R

There is no post-processing step here, so the SSE.Decrypt function can be seen as the identity function. On step (2a), an optimisation is possible. In some cases, only a test on one (or a subset) of the tokens is sufficient. The incidence on the simulation is indicated in the proof.

5.2   Leakage Analysis of the 2-A Scheme

Let $\mathcal{L}_A$ be the following leakage function for adaptive experiments.

- On input the index $\mathcal{I} := (\mathcal{D}, \mathcal{W}, \mathcal{C}, \mathsf{n})$, $\mathcal{L}_A$ initializes a counter $p := 1$, an empty list $\mathcal{Q} := \{\}$, and returns (N, n), where $N := \sum_{w \in \mathcal{W}} |DB(w)|$.
- For a search query $Q := (t, w_1, \ldots, w_n)$, $\mathcal{L}$ appends $(p, t, n, w_1, \ldots, w_n)$ to $\mathcal{Q}$, increments p and returns $(SP(Q, \mathcal{Q}), AP(Q, \mathcal{Q}))$ where SP and AP are defined as follows.

Search Pattern. The 2-A scheme leaks whether the same keyword is repeated in the search queries. The search pattern of a query $Q = (t, w_1, \ldots, w_n)$ with respect to the set $\mathcal{Q}$ is given by $SP(Q, \mathcal{Q}) := (t, n, V, S_1, \ldots, S_n)$ where $S_j := \{(\mathsf{i}, \mathsf{j}) : \exists(t_i, w_{i:1}, \ldots, w_{i:n_i}) \in \mathcal{Q}, w_{i:j} = w_j\}$ for all $j = 1, \ldots, n$, and $V := \{j \mid \exists j' \neq j, w_j = w_{j'}\}$. Again, depending on the use-case, it might be useless to ask twice the same word in a query, but, formally, this case remains allowed by the definition.

Access Pattern. The 2-A scheme leaks the documents associated to each token and the documents returned. The access pattern $AP(Q, \mathcal{Q})$ of a search query $Q = (t, w_1, \ldots, w_n)$ with respect to the set $\mathcal{Q}$ is given by $(DB(w_1), \ldots, DB(w_n), FP)$ where FP are the false positives due to the Bloom filter. The response of the query is then $(DB(w_1) \cap \cdots \cap DB(w_n)) \cup FP$. The simulation of the false positives is done by the leakage function as follows.

1. $FP := \{\}$; for $D \in (DB(w_1) \cup \cdots \cup DB(w_n)) \setminus (DB(w_1) \cap \cdots \cap DB(w_n))$:
   // Or, with optimisation: for each $D \in DB(w_1) \setminus (DB(w_1) \cap \cdots \cap DB(w_n))$:

   (a) $T := [0 \ldots 0]$; $\forall j \in [1, n]$: set $T[j] := 1$ with prob. $\left(1 - \left(1 - \frac{1}{m}\right)^{k \cdot n}\right)^k$.
   (b) if $(|\{j \in [1, n] : T[j] = 1\}| \geq t)$: add D to FP

A document D is a false positive here in the sense that one can say the document is not associated with *all* keywords in the query. However the scheme ensures that D is associated with at least one keyword (otherwise, the line in the database would not have been parsed).

5.3   A Simulator for the 2-A Scheme

To prove the security against adaptive queries, we will need to see the ℓ-PRF, the encryption scheme and the hash functions for the Bloom filter as random oracles. We do not need to see the w-PRF as a random oracle, only that it achieves indistinguishability from random. Let $H_\lambda : \{0,1\}^\lambda \times \{0,1\}^\mu \to \{0,1\}^\lambda$, $H_\mu : \{0,1\}^\lambda \times \{0,1\}^\kappa \to \{0,1\}^{\mu-\lambda}$, $H_m : [1,k] \times \{0,1\}^\lambda \times \{0,1\}^\mu \to [1,m]$ be three random oracles. The following instantiations are plugged in the 2-A scheme.

- for the pseudo-random function:
  $PRF_\ell (K, x) := H_\lambda (K, x)$
- $\text{Encrypt}(K, x) := [\text{ pick } r \in \{0,1\}^\lambda ; \text{ return } (r, H_\mu(K, r) \oplus x)]$
- for the Bloom filter: $H_i(\tau, F) := H_m(i, \tau, F)$ for $i = 1, \ldots, k$

Now the simulation of the encryption of the index is done as follows. Given a leakage $\mathcal{L}_A(\mathcal{I}) = (N, \mathsf{n})$, the simulator $\mathcal{S}_A$ carries out:

1. initializes $\mathsf{EDB} := \{\}$; for $e = 1, \ldots, N$:
   (a) set $\ell_e \leftarrow \{0,1\}^\lambda$; $F_e \leftarrow \{0,1\}^\mu$; $W_e := [1, \ldots, 1] \in \{1\}^m$
   (b) for $j = 1, \ldots, m$: set $W_e[j] := 0$ with probability $\left(1 - \frac{1}{m}\right)^{k \cdot \mathsf{n}}$
   (c) $\mathsf{EDB} := \mathsf{EDB} \cup \{(\ell_e, (W_e, F_e))\}$
2. return the encrypted index EDB

Due to the definition of Bloom filters, and due to the specific assumption that exactly n keywords are associated with each document, EDB is perfectly simulated. In the following, the simulated EDB is enumerated by indices $e = 1, \ldots, N$.

Then the adaptive simulation of the queries $\mathcal{S}_A (\mathcal{L}_A (Q_1, \ldots, Q_p))$ for $p = 1, \ldots, q$ is done as follows.

$\mathcal{L}_A(Q_1, \ldots, Q_p)$ is parsed as $(L_1, \ldots, L_p)$. To maintain consistency, the simulator maintains auxiliary tables $\mathbf{Q}, \mathbf{T}, \mathbf{D}$. $\mathbf{Q}$ records the tokens appearing in the query. $\mathbf{T}$ records the entries in EDB assigned to the token. $\mathbf{D}$ records the document assigned to the entry.

1. parse L_p as $((t, n, V, S_1, \ldots, S_n), (A_1, \ldots, A_n, FP))$
2. [Simulation of the tokens] for $j = 1, \ldots, n$:
   (a) if $(\exists (i, j) \in S_j)$: $T_p[j] := T_i[j]$,
   (b) else if $(j \in V$ and $\exists j \in V, j < j)$: $T_p[j] := T_p[j]$,
   (c) else: set $T_p[j] \leftarrow \{0,1\}^\lambda \times \{0,1\}^\lambda$; $\mathbf{Q}[p] := \mathbf{Q}[p] \cup \{T_p[j]\}$
3. [Assigning entries to tokens and documents to entries]
   for each $A \in \{A_1, \ldots, A_n, FP\}$: if $T_p[j] \in \mathbf{Q}[p]$:
   (a) set $\mathsf{D} := A$; for $i = 1, \ldots, |\mathsf{D}|$:
       i. pick e in $\mathsf{EDB} \setminus \{e \mid \mathbf{D}[e] \neq \bot\}$; set $\mathbf{T}[T_p[j]] := \mathbf{T}[T_p[j]] \cup \{e\}$
       ii. pick a random $D \in \mathsf{D}$;   set $\mathsf{D} := \mathsf{D} \setminus \{D\}$;   set $\mathbf{D}[e] := D$

The simulator must now program the random oracles to match with all introduced tokens. We must do this for all information the adversary can deduce when seeing a query.

4. *[Programming the random oracles]* for each $(\tau, \chi) \in \mathbf{Q}[p]$:
   (a) for each $e \in \mathbf{T}[\tau]$:
       i. retrieve the eth entry $(\ell, (W, F))$ in EDB
       ii. set $\mathsf{H}_\lambda(\tau, F) := \ell$ *– abort if already defined*
       iii. set $\mathsf{H}_\mu(\chi, F_1) := F_2 \oplus (\mathbf{D}[e])$ *– abort if already defined*
       iv. set $W := \{u \in [1, m] \mid W[u] = 1\}$ and $W' := \{\}$; then for $i = 1, \ldots, |W|$:
           A. pick $u \leftarrow W \setminus W'$; set $\mathsf{H}_m(i, \tau, F) := u$ *– abort if already defined*
           B. $W' := W' \cup \{u\}$
       v. if $(k > |W|)$, then for $i = |W| + 1, \ldots, k$:
           A. pick $u \in W$; set $\mathsf{H}_m(i, \tau, F) := u$ *– abort if already defined*
5. *[Computing the response]* $R_p := (A_1 \cap \cdots \cap A_n) \cup FP$
6. return (T_p, R_p).

The probability for a random oracle to be defined before seeing a particular (τ, χ) is negligible in λ, so the simulator aborts with negligible probability.

Once the simulator is described, the remaining of the proof of security is classical. It consists of a sequence of $k + 4$ games. In the first hop we replace the encryption by a random function. In the second hop, we replace the w-PRF by a random function. In the third hop, we replace the ℓ-PRF by a random function. In the last hops, we replace the Bloom filter hash functions by random functions.

6 Application to Biometric Identification

Let us now turn our attention to biometric identification, and assume a client supplying a fresh acquisition of a biometric trait and a server owning several biometric references stored in a database. The notion of closeness between templates is determined by the computation of similarity scores between them, then by comparison to a threshold parameter.

We first informally discuss the application of SSE to biometric identification in Sect. 6.1, then we formally describe a solution in Sect. 6.2, before reporting some experiments in Sect. 6.3.

6.1 Biometric Identification from SSE

Initial application of SSE to biometric identification. The basic idea of [1] to achieve biometric identification over encrypted data from searchable encryption is to associate a set of keywords to each biometric data thanks to a LSH family, then to use a symmetric searchable encryption scheme to perform keyword search over the encrypted biometric database. The LSH family is chosen so that similar biometric data will share several keywords with non negligible probability, enabling to compute a similarity score in the encrypted domain. The work of [1] describes a concrete solution by using the adaptively SSE scheme of [7] for single keyword search. In the resulting construction, the client needs to evaluate $\mathsf{max} \cdot \mu$ PRP to generate the query, where $\mathsf{max} := \max_{w \in \mathcal{W}} \{|DB(w)|\}$.

Looking for optimisations. As a first optimisation, more recent schemes for single keyword search, published after [1], could be used. For instance, using the scheme $\Pi_{\text{bas}}^{\text{ro}}$ from [5], the client computes only $2 \cdot \mu$ PRF to get the trapdoors. However, this first optimisation still uses a naive approach to perform a conjunctive search.

A further approach would then to use a SSE scheme supporting conjunctive queries such as the OXT scheme [6]. However, the latter construction does not give the best biometric performance, because of the fuzziness of the biometric data. To see this, note that a matching template never shares all the extracted keywords with a database reference, they share only some keywords in common. Retrieving $DB(w)$, for some w in a conjunctive query, gives a false negative error if the yet close template is not associated with w. The server only returns the documents in which all the keywords specified by the search query appear.

This motivated the use of "t-out-of-n-word" queries, instead of "all-keyword-or-nothing" as supplied by conjunctive queries. We first worked on a "t-out-of-n-word" version of the OXT scheme [6]. This scheme uses operation in a group of prime order. We realized that we could drop out the group of prime order and use fast primitives, as Bloom filters, at the cost of a certain fuzziness. When applied to biometric identification, this fuzziness is not a matter of concern. All parameters of the solution might be balanced (cf. Sect. 6.3 below).

6.2   The Biometric Identification Protocol

More formally, let λ be a security parameter, (B, d) be a normed vector space (possibly depending on λ) where d be the distance associated to the norm and t, λ_{min}, λ_{max} some thresholds. Let SSE be a SSE scheme, some $p_1, p_2 \in [0, 1]$, t such that $0 < t \leq \frac{1}{2}$, and a $(\mu, \lambda_{\text{min}}, \lambda_{\text{max}}, p_1, p_2)$-LSH family over B such that $\mu \geq \lambda$.

Let us assume that a biometric reference database DB is given by a set of pairs (b, ID) such that $b \in B$ and ID is some (fixed-length) identifier. These identifiers might be pointers enabling to retrieve the references, or encrypted user data, *etc.* In the latter case, a client step might be added below in the post-processing to decrypt them.

Given a database DB, an index $\mathcal{I}^{\text{BI}} = (\mathcal{D}^{\text{BI}}, \mathcal{W}^{\text{BI}}, \mathcal{C}^{\text{BI}})$ is defined as follows:

$$\mathcal{D}^{\text{BI}} := \{ID \mid \forall (b, ID) \in \text{DB}\},$$
$$\mathcal{W}^{\text{BI}} := \{(h_j(b), j) \mid \forall j \in [1, \mu], \forall (b, ID) \in \text{DB}\},$$
$$DB^{\text{BI}} := w \in \mathcal{W}^{\text{BI}} \mapsto \{ID \mid \exists b, \exists j, (b, ID) \in \text{DB} \ \wedge \ w = (h_j(b), j)\},$$
$$\mathcal{C}^{\text{BI}} := \{(w, DB^{\text{BI}}(w)) \mid \forall w \in \mathcal{W}^{\text{BI}}\}.$$

Let now BI be the following biometric identification scheme over encrypted data.

- During the setup phase, the client calls the key generation SSE.KeyGen(1^λ).
- During the enrolment, it defines the index $\mathcal{I}^{\text{BI}}$ as above, then it stores the encrypted index EDB := SSE.BuildIndex($K, \mathcal{I}^{\text{BI}}$) on the server.
- During the identification, given a query $Q = (t, (h_1(b), 1), \ldots, (h_\mu(b), \mu))$, the client sets an encrypted query $T = (t, \tau_1, \ldots, \tau_\mu) = $ SSE.Trapdoor(K, Q). The server then performs $R :=$ SSE.Search(EDB, T). The client defines the multi-set $F :=$ SSE.Decrypt(K, R) and returns the identities $\{ID \mid \#ID \geq t \cdot \mu\}$.

F must be a multi-set: with the 2-A scheme, false positive are expected to appear, but correct documents are expected to appear with greater multiplicity.

Optimisation in the case of the 2-A scheme. When the whole encrypted database is read in parallel (as in our MapReduce experiments; cf. Sect. 6.3 below), and the 2-A scheme is used (cf. Sect. 5.1, note about (2a)), the following optimisation gives better performance: instead of launching a query $(t, w_1, \ldots, w_\mu)$ and performing μ tests for each entry, a random subset J of $\{w_1, \ldots, w_\mu\}$ of size p, for some parameter p, is drawn and p queries (t, w) are launched in parallel, for all $w \in J$ (or a query (t, J) is performed).

Note on the security in presence of LSH functions. Although the security properties of our SSE schemes are properly defined and analysed, the biometric identification protocol still lack a proper analysis due to the use of LSH functions. The use of LSH functions for fuzziness in encrypted data is an important, open problem (see [2]). We leave this tricky analysis outside the scope of this paper. Our main goal was to improve on the use of SSE for biometric identification.

6.3   Experiments

Parameters. Table 1 sums up the different parameters of our schemes. LSH and Bloom filters parameters determine a proportion of false positives in the answer. However, other parameters allow to compensate the number of false positive. Typical values we used in our experiments are $b = 2048$, $\mu = 128$, $\beta = 4$, $\lambda = 128$. The number of false positive in a Bloom filter is given by the formula $\approx (1 - e^{\frac{-k \cdot \mu}{m}})^k$. A theoretical optimum is reached when $\mu \cdot k \approx 0.7 \cdot m$. However, our experiments show that (i) the effect of the parameters heavily depends on the number of enrolled users, and (ii) overall, a value of m bigger than the theoretical estimation gives better accuracy.

Table 1. Summary of the parameters

b	Length of the binarized biometric data	λ	Security parameter (keys length)
μ	Number of LSH functions	β	LSH hashes size
k	Number of Bloom filters hash functions	m	Bloom filter size
t	Threshold for the 't-out-of-μ' queries	t	Threshold for the accuracy
$\lambda_1, \lambda_2, p_1, p_2$	Parameters of the LSH family	p	Number of queries in parallel

MapReduce programming model. We implemented our algorithms on the MapReduce framework. MapReduce (MR) is a programming model and a framework for processing and generating large data sets in a parallel, distributed fashion. MR was first published by two Google researchers [8] in 2004 before it becomes an Open Source project later. The MR framework supplies two functions `map` and `reduce`. The `map` function takes as input a set of key/value pairs and produces a set of intermediate key/value pairs and the `reduce` function takes the intermediate values associated with the same key to produce the final result of the MapReduce job. Additional algorithms are `parse`, for parsing blocks, `partition`, for conveying outputs of the mappers to inputs of the reducers, and `merge`, for merging the outputs of the reducers.

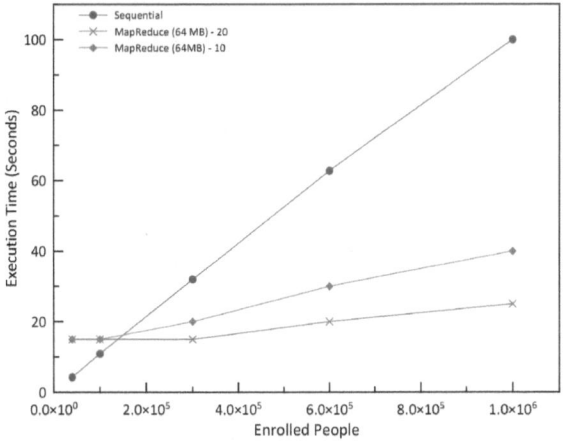

Fig. 3. Experiments. Sequential vs. parallel.

MapReduce implementations. Programming the algorithms of Sects. 4 and 5 in the MR model is particularly straightforward: the "for" steps (for each entry in the database) are implemented in parallel by the map tasks when parsing the blocks. The experiments we conducted had run in a Hadoop [9] single-node virtual cluster with a 2 GB RAM and 2.27 GHz CPU machine. We compared a sequential execution of a biometric identification algorithm to a parallel implementation. Figure 3 also reports the execution time of the two types executions. The red curve corresponds to a cloud cluster of 20 machine (10 machines for the blue curve). For large indexes, a parallel implementation is considered to be more interesting. Increasing the number of available machines lowers more the computation time. Hence the big advantage of a public elastic cloud platform that gives the client the ability to allocate more machines when it is needed.

Acknowledgement. This work has been partially funded by the French ANR-12-CORD-0014 project SECULAR and the European H2020 TREDISEC project under the Grant Agreement 644412.

Appendix

- for each $(W, F) \in \mathsf{EDB}$ {
  - set $v := \mathbf{T}[(W, F)]$; if $(v < \mathsf{n})$: update (W, F) as follows {
    - while $(v < \mathsf{n})$ { repeat k times {
      - set $\mathsf{B} := [1, m]$; cont := true; do {
        - pick a random $u \leftarrow \mathsf{B}$
        - if $(W[u] = 1)$: set cont := false; else {
          - set $W[u] := 1$; pb := false ; $\forall i = 1, \ldots, q$ {
            - if $(F \in R_i)$: continue
            - parse T_i as $(t_i, \tau_1, \ldots, \tau_n)$; set $c := 0$;
            - $\forall \tau \in \{\tau_1, \ldots, \tau_n\}$:
            - if $[(W[H(\tau, F)] = 1)\ \forall H \in \{H_1, \ldots, H_k\}]$: $c{+}{+}$
            - if $(c \geq t_i)$: pb := true } (end for)
          - if (pb) {
            - set $\mathsf{B} := \mathsf{B} \setminus \{u\}$; $W[u] := 0$
          } else: cont := false } (end else)
      } while (cont) } (end repeat)
    - $v{+}{+}$ } (end while) } (end if) } (end for)

Fig. 4. Completion of Bloom filters in the non-adaptive simulator

References

1. Adjedj, M., Bringer, J., Chabanne, H., Kindarji, B.: Biometric identification over encrypted data made feasible. In: Prakash, A., Sen Gupta, I. (eds.) ICISS 2009. LNCS, vol. 5905, pp. 86–100. Springer, Heidelberg (2009)
2. Boldyreva, A., Chenette, N.: Efficient fuzzy search on encrypted data. In: Cid, C., Rechberger, C. (eds.) FSE 2014. LNCS, vol. 8540, pp. 613–633. Springer, Heidelberg (2015)
3. Bringer, J., Chabanne, H., Kindarji, B.: Identification with encrypted biometric data. Secur. Commun. Netw. **4**(5), 548–562 (2011)
4. Bringer, J., Chabanne, H., Patey, A.: Practical identification with encrypted biometric data using Oblivious RAM. In: ICB 2013, pp. 1–8. IEEE (2013)
5. Cash, D., Jaeger, J., Jarecki, S., Jutla, C.S., Krawczyk, H., Rosu, M., Steiner, M.: Dynamic searchable encryption in very-large databases: data structures and implementation. In: NDSS 2014. The Internet Society (2014)
6. Cash, D., Jarecki, S., Jutla, C., Krawczyk, H., Roşu, M.-C., Steiner, M.: Highly-scalable searchable symmetric encryption with support for boolean queries. In: Canetti, R., Garay, J.A. (eds.) CRYPTO 2013, Part I. LNCS, vol. 8042, pp. 353–373. Springer, Heidelberg (2013)
7. Curtmola, R., Garay, J.A., Kamara, S., Ostrovsky, R.: Searchable symmetric encryption: improved definitions and efficient constructions. In: CCS 2006, pp. 79–88. ACM (2006)

8. Dean, J., Ghemawat, S.: MapReduce: simplified data processing on large clusters. Commun. ACM **51**(1), 107–113 (2008)
9. Apache Hadoop Project. http://hadoop.apache.org/
10. Huang, Y., Malka, L., Evans, D., Katz, J.: Efficient privacy-preserving biometric identification. In: NDSS 2011. The Internet Society (2011)
11. Jain, A.K., Ross, A., Prabhakar, S.: An introduction to biometric recognition. IEEE Trans. Circ. Syst. Video Technol. **14**(1), 4–20 (2004)
12. Li, J., Lin, X., Zhang, Y., Han, J.: KSF-OABE: outsourced attribute-based encryption with keyword search function for cloud storage. IEEE Trans. Serv. Comput. **PP**(99), 1 (2016)
13. Melchor, C.A., Fau, S., Fontaine, C., Gogniat, G., Sirdey, R.: Recent advances in homomorphic encryption: a possible future for signal processing in the encrypted domain. IEEE Sig. Process. Mag. **30**(2), 108–117 (2013)
14. Ostrovsky, R.: Efficient computation on oblivious rams. In: ACM Symposium on Theory of Computing - STOC 1990, pp. 514–523. ACM (1990)
15. Ostrovsky, R., Skeith, W.E.: A survey of single-database private information retrieval: techniques and applications. In: Okamoto, T., Wang, X. (eds.) PKC 2007. LNCS, vol. 4450, pp. 393–411. Springer, Heidelberg (2007). doi:10.1007/978-3-540-71677-8_26
16. Wang, J., Shen, H.T., Song, J., Ji, J.: Hashing for similarity search: a survey. In: CoRR, abs/1408.2927 (2014)

On the User Acceptance of Privacy-Preserving Attribute-Based Credentials – A Qualitative Study

Ahmad Sabouri[(✉)]

Deutsche Telekom Chair of Mobile Business and Multilateral Security,
Goethe University Frankfurt, Theodor-W.-Adorno-Platz 4, 60323 Frankfurt, Germany
ahmad.sabouri@m-chair.de

Abstract. Privacy and data protection are critical aspects of today's use of Internet services. Privacy-preserving Attribute-based Credentials (Privacy-ABCs), also known as anonymous credentials, are elegant techniques to allow security and privacy go hand-in-hand. In this paper, we report on the results of our structured interviews with users who tried a prototype of Privacy-ABC identity card. We questioned their observations of benefits and barriers to use such technologies as well as their desired application. Moreover, we investigated their trust believes and anchors and inquired their preferred implementation scheme. Our results shed lights on the direction that must be followed to foster adoption of Privacy-ABCs.

Keywords: Privacy-preserving Attribute-based Credentials · Anonymous credentials · Trust in privacy-abcs · Perceived benefits · Perceived barriers

1 Introduction

With the widespread use of online services, the users need to manage various credentials for authentication towards those services. Today's online services are typically protected by username and password. Nevertheless, there are services requiring higher level of security, such as for accessing governmental and corporate networks. Those may benefit from digital certificate for strong authentication of the users. Identity Federation and Single-Sign-On techniques have come to relieve the users from the burden of managing multiple credentials.

Enhancing strong authentication schemes to respect privacy has been in the focus of the research community. More specifically, efforts have been dedicated to design schemes for providing data minimization, unlinkability and untraceability during an authentication session. In this regard, *Privacy-preserving Attribute-based Credentials (Privacy-ABCs)*, also known as anonymous credentials, have been in the focus of various recent research projects such as Prime [5], PrimeLife [6], FutureID [2], and ABC4Trust [1]. From the different flavours of Privacy-ABCs, the IBM Idemix [3] and Microsoft U-Prove [4] are among the most prominent ones.

© Springer International Publishing AG 2016
G. Livraga et al. (Eds.): DPM and QASA 2016, LNCS 9963, pp. 130–145, 2016.
DOI: 10.1007/978-3-319-47072-6_9

While the theoretical advantages of privacy enhancing technologies like Privacy-ABCs are clear, in practice less adoption is observed [8]. Moreover, there have been only a few number of user studies with Privacy-ABCs with regard to their adoption. Therefore, in this experiment we took a different approach than the previous research works in this domain and conducted "structured interviews" to investigate the users' perceptions after allowing them to use a prototype implementation in a relatively privacy-sensitive scenario.

The rest of this paper is organized as follows. Section 2 elaborates on the contribution of this work. In Sect. 3, we review how Privacy-ABCs work. A brief overview of the related work is provided in Sect. 4. We explain the experiment design and the applied methodology in Sect. 5 and present the results in Sect. 6. Limitations and conclusion of this work are provided in Sects. 7 and 8, respectively.

2 Contribution

This paper aims to shed light on the direction which one has to follow to foster adoption of Privacy-ABCs. Here we report on an empirical study that consists of a practice part and an interview. Our findings are based on the results of interviews with 40 users. We first implemented a platform so that the users can practice privacy-enhanced authentication with Privacy-ABCs. We called our mock-up Privacy-ABC identity card as "ID+" and let the users try it in our experiment portal, "Politiks.eu". We guided the participants through a task list demonstrating them various features of Privacy-ABCs, namely pseudonymity, selective disclosure and unlinkability. Afterwards, we interviewed them with structured questions to investigate their perceptions. More specifically, the following questions were in the focus of the interview:

1. What do you see as the benefits of using ID+?
2. What do you see as the barriers to use ID+?
3. For what services do you prefer to use ID+ to login? Why?
4. What makes you believe that ID+ or any similar technology keeps its promises for privacy protection?
5. Who would you rely to certify that the technology does what it says?
6. If you have two options, one to use smartcard as the ID Wallet, or use a Cloud-based Wallet (which stores your certificates data somewhere on the Internet), which one do you prefer? Why?

3 How Privacy-ABCs Work

In this section, we provide a brief overview of Privacy-ABCs and their mechanisms. A *Credential* is defined to be "a certified container of attributes issued by a credential Issuer to a User" [7]. An *Issuer* vouches for the correctness of the attribute values for a *User* when issuing a credential for her. In an example

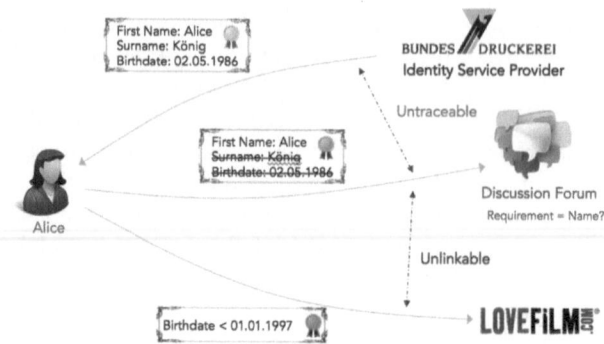

Fig. 1. A sample Privacy-ABC issuance and usage scenario

scenario (show in Fig. 1), Alice as a *User*, contacts the Bundesdruckerei (the German authority responsible for issuing electronic IDs) and after a proper proof of her identity (e.g. showing her old paper-based ID), she receives a digital identity credential containing her first name, surname and birth-date. In the next step, she can seek to access an online Discussion Forum. The service provider (the Discussion Forum) provides Alice with the *Presentation Policy* that requires her to deliver an authentic proof of her first name. Using Privacy-ABCs features, Alice has the possibility to derive a minimal authentication token from her identity credential that contains only the first name. As a result, her privacy is preserved by not disclosing unnecessary information (i.e. surname and birth-date). Note that the commonly used digital certificates do not offer such capability as any change in those certificates invalidates the issuers' signature. Another example where Alice could use her Privacy-ABC might be with an online movie rental website, which requires age verification. Alice is able to provide such a proof without actually disclosing her exact birth-date. The proof is done based on complex cryptographic concepts that can show her birth-date attribute in her credential is before a certain date.

It is worth noting that the authentication tokens based on Privacy-ABCs are cryptographically proven to be unlinkable and untraceable. Thus, the service providers cannot tell whether two tokens were generated by the same user or not. Also the issuers cannot trace tokens back to the issuance phase and the person behind it, unless the disclosed attributes contains some identifying information.

4   Related Works

There has been only a few number of studies in the literature concerning the human aspects of Privacy-ABCs. Wästlund et al. [17] were the first ones who reported about the challenges to design user-friendly interfaces that convey the privacy benefits of Privacy-ABCs to users. They observed that users were still unfamiliar with the new and rather complex concept of Privacy-ABCs, since no obvious real-world analogies existed that could help them create the correct mental models. Benenson et al. [8,9] investigated one of the ABC4Trust trials [12] using the Technology Acceptance Model (TAM) [10]. The trial allowed them to involve students from the University of Patras who used a real implementation of Privacy-ABCs during one semester and submitted their course evaluation forms online using the privacy-preserving evaluation portal. Benenson et al. discovered significant negative correlation of Perceived Risk with the Intention to Use, the Perceived Usefulness for the first and secondary goals, the Perceived Ease of Use and the Trust. In the same study, they found the Perceived Risk to be dependent to Perceived Anonymity.

An experts survey was conducted in [13] to predict the factors influencing adoption of Privacy-ABCs. The results show that Business Model Dependency to Data Collection, Complexity for User, Top Management Support, Observability, Trialability, Cost of Integration, Regulations for Data Collection, and Complexity for Developers are the most important or influential factors impacting the decision of the service providers to employ Privacy-ABCs. That work can be seen as the counter part of the contribution of this paper, as we here focus on the users' perspective rather than the service providers.

The closest study to our work was conducted for German new Identity Card [11]. The scholars studied why the German nPA is receiving little adoption as a privacy-preserving authentication technology, even though the technical capabilities are excellent. The results of their work reveal six main barriers, namely no added value/no motivation, complexity, control, comfort, insufficient information and cost. Their interviewees stated that they would prefer it for governmental and banking e-services, for insurances, eCommerce websites as well as for identity confirmation purposes. These results are very well aligned with the relevant findings in this paper. Compared to [11], we covered a broader scope of topics including building trust and discovering implementation preferences because Privacy-ABCs are still in the trial and pre-adoption phase while they studied an already rolled-out service.

5   Experiment Design

We conducted the experiment through the network of the students at the Goethe University Frankfurt in October and November 2015. In the following sections, we explain the details of our process.

5.1   Experiment Platform Setup

A precondition for our experiment was to set up a platform where scenarios for authenticating with Privacy-ABCs could be tried out. The ABC4Trust EU project has provided a reference implementation (RI) of Privacy-ABCs. However, some part of the RI, such as the smartcard software, are specific to the ABC4Trust trials. Moreover, the user interfaces of the RI encompasses all the features of Privacy-ABCs, which makes it a complex GUI and it could have prevented our participants from focusing on the experiment goals. Consequently, we decided to develop a mock-up prototype which presents the workflow of authenticating with Privacy-ABCs with a more friendly interface and better integration to the web browser.

Privacy-ABCs are user-centric and users need a so-called "User Agent" to support them managing their credentials and performing proofs of their attributes. The ABC4Trust RI implements the User Agent as a web-based application running on the users' computer and it will be invoked within the browser when it is needed. As our experiment use-cases were focused on authentication in the web, we decided to implement the User Agent as a Firefox plugin and integrate it into the browser. We added a button, called "ID" into the toolbar (Fig. 2) of the Firefox browser, which upon clicking, it would show the users' identity credential in case the smartcard was connected to the computer. In the experiment, the authentication was emulated, therefore the smart card was employed to provide the feeling of a real process but the users' attributes were actually stored in the browser configurations. A small Java application was developed to run in the background in order to check the status of the smartcard, which allowed the browser plug-in to query the status via a Restful web-service call.

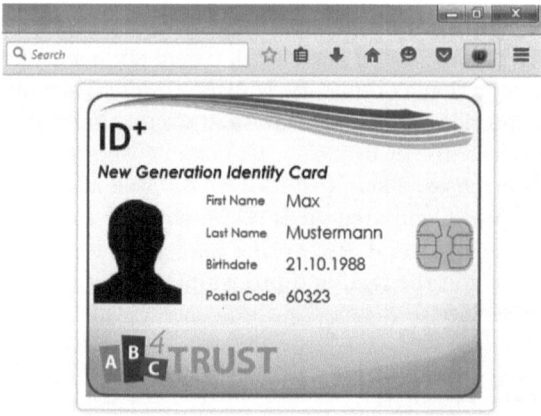

Fig. 2. Screenshot of the GUI for communicating with ID+ within firefox

The plugin was designed to attach specific Javascript codes to the html content of the web-page when opening the experiment portal URL. The Javascript codes provided the possibility of communicating with the plugin in order to invoke the GUI for authentication with Privacy-ABCs. When a button on the web-page triggers login with Privacy-ABCs, the message is communicated to the plugin. The GUI would pop up as a small window next to the "ID" button if the smart card is present. The window guides the user through the steps of authentication and upon completion the user is redirected to the requested page.

1. Open Firefox
2. Plug your smart card into the reader
3. Check your data on the card
4. What information about your is stored on the ID+ smart card?
5. Close the ID+ window
6. Question: *How can you check your data again if you want?*
7. Open "http://politiks.eu"
8. *The portal is introduced!*
9. Login to the "Frankfurt Mayor" discussion
10. Follow the authentication steps
11. What is happening now?
12. Question: *What is the website going to learn about you?*
13. Have a look at the posts
14. Write a post and send it
15. Check your post
16. Log out
17. Login to the "Drug" discussion
18. Follow the authentication steps
19. Question: *What is the website going to learn about you?*
20. Have a look at the posts
21. Write a post and send it.
22. Check your post
23. Log out
24. Login to the "Mayor" discussion again
25. Follow the authentication steps
26. Have a look at your previous posts
27. Write a new post and send it
28. Check your post
29. Log out.

Fig. 3. User tasks list

Fig. 4. Authentication with Privacy-ABCs using ID+

5.2   Conducting the Experiment

The experiment was conducted within the student community of the Goethe university Frankfurt. The only constraint was to limit the age to be between 18 and 34. All participants received a brief introduction of ID+ and its privacy-enhancing features. Afterwards, the participants were given a smartcard and were asked to open Firefox and browse to the experiment portal, "http://politiks. eu". In order to urge the need for privacy, we decided to deliver political discussion as the main content of the portal. Two forums were initiated in the portal; one about mayoral election in the city of Frankfurt, and one about legalizing drugs. Each forum required the user to authenticate with her ID+ in order to get access to the discussion. The process of authenticating with ID+ is shown in Fig. 4. Upon clicking on "Login with ID+" the respective GUI would pop up to guide the participant through the authentication process. The Frankfurt mayoral election forum asked the users to deliver a proof for "Your Postal code is between 59999 and 61000" and the forum on legalizing drugs, would request the users a proof of "Your birth date is before the 01.01.1997". The former policy semantically means that the participant is living in the Frankfurt am Main area as the postal code is following 60xxx format, and therefore the forum ensures that she is a stakeholder. The latter also proves that the participant is older than 18 (by the time of the experiment) and consequently allowed to discuss about drugs.

The participants were guided through a task list (presented in Fig. 3) to interact with the portal. In the end, each participant was interviewed with the questions we explained in Sect. 2.

5.3   Data Analysis Methodology

This paper uses a sample of 40 interviewees, 24 male and 16 female. 21 participants were between 18 and 25, and 19 were between 25 and 34 years old. The education of the participants is the following: 7 High School graduates (18 %), 16 Bachelor graduates (40 %), 16 Master graduates (40 %) and 1 Doctorate (2 %). As for their experience with online services, the sample spent on average 32 hours ($\sigma = 20$) on the Internet per week. Almost all of them used the Internet for surfing on the websites and exchanging emails, 80 % used online banking, 86 % performed online shopping, 95 % utilized social networks and 58 % used online storage services. The profile of their privacy-aware behaviour on the Internet is demonstrated in Fig. 5. The audio recordings were transcribed and statements subsequently assigned to the general questions introduced previously. To present the results, we report statements from the questions and the respective participants are referred to as P1 to P40.

The data analysis is based on coding according to Strauss and Corbin [15]. The coding consists of three stages, which are explained below.

Open Coding: According to Strauss and Corbin [15] the process starts with the open coding. Thereby, the researcher goes line-by-line through the interview or the protocol and analyses the texts. The idea is about constant comparison of the texts to figure out concepts, achieved by an integration of codes [14–16]. A code is the name for an empirical incident in the data that is observed or described. Repetitions of codes lead to a first impression on what seems to be relevant because it occurs more often. In addition, it allows to identify different contexts in which the identical code is used. Further, the goal is to identify categories based on the concepts as well as their properties and relationships to each other.

Axial Coding: In the second coding step, the categories are analysed in more detail. Of main interest are the relationships between the identified categories. This leads to a better understanding and clarification of each category. Therefore, the coding takes place around the axes of the categories. The result of this step is the identification of the main categories.

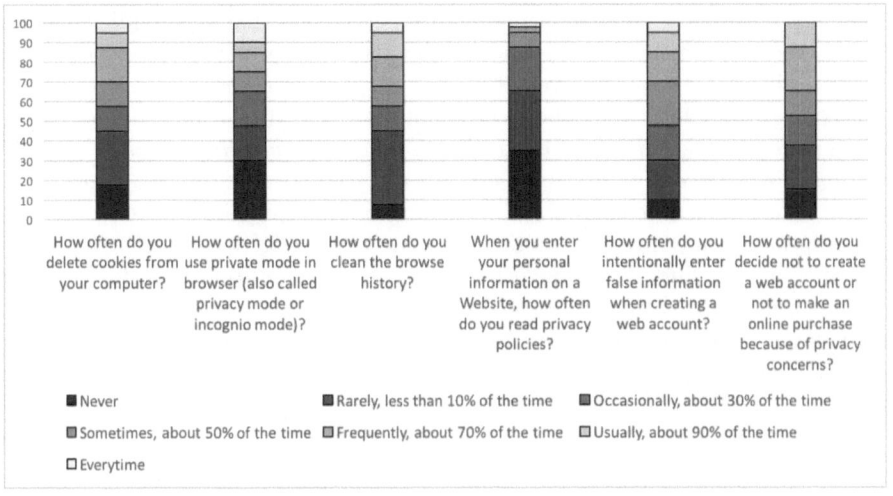

Fig. 5. Privacy-aware behaviour profile of the participants

Selective Coding: The selective coding finishes the coding process in a systematic way. Strauss and Corbin describe a shift of the coding focus to the main categories that are central for the theoretical model, occur very often in the data and explain most of the variation. The other categories and concepts are subordinated to the main categories. This step is not considered in our work as building a theoretical model was not in the scope of our research.

6   Results

In this section, we present the results of processing the interviews using the aforementioned coding methodology. The results are presented according to the respective research questions.

6.1   Perceived Benefits:

We started the interviews by asking the participants about their general feeling of ID+ and continued by specifically questioning their perception of benefits of using such technology. The results indicate that almost all the participants highlighted the privacy protection features of ID+ to be the main benefits. Around 23 % mentioned explicitly that **Selective Disclosure** is one of the main benefits. For instance, P3 pointed *"... you have your data on this card, and this card can pick which data is relevant for the login. It is good, that you don't have to give too much information"*. Similarly P18 mentioned *"I can use online services which require personal information about me without disclosing them in detail. I think it is the biggest benefit. I didn't use some technology like this before, so for me it*

is already very good. ". Another aspect of Privacy-ABCs that was implicitly prac-
tised in the experiment was the **anonymity/pseudonymity**. The participants
received different identifiers every time they logged into the discussion forums.
This concept was noticed by the participants as referred by P28: *"... each time I
logged in, I got a different name like Steven or Harry or Dilian, I can remember.
So I mean if it's really trustworthy and it's not possible to figure out who I really
am, in case I'm writing a comment, it's a pretty good thing"*. However some participants found the provided anonymity as a double-edge sword; P27 expressed
her concern by saying *"The benefit is that no one can connect the statements you
give to your name. That can be positive, but can also be negative.[...] I think if
you login not with your real name many people easily go to insult people, because
they don't have to fear anything, if they can't be linked to the person."*. Another
interesting impression of the benefits was about **Transparency**. Providing a
clear statement about the information that the user is going to disclose was
appreciated by some participants. In this regards, P40 said *"the main benefit I
think is that it is clear to the user what information the website is getting from
you"*.

Beside the privacy protection aspects, the participants also pointed to the
convenience and usability features. The fact that personal data stored on the
ID+ relieve the user from the burden of registration in different services, was
perceived as one of the main benefits. P11 favoured the **Registration-Free**
authentication by stating *"We have private information on the card, if we login
in website or something like that, we don't have to type it down."*. P19 also had
a similar perception: *"first of all, it will save a lot of time. Because if you login
some website, you need to fill a lot of forms about yourself. You are required to
put a lot of information on this website. When you use this ID[+] card, you just
need to set it up once. The cards will get more information, when you login some
website, the website will just catch out what they need if you use ID[+] card"*.
Even though the experiment only presented one credential (identity credential)
and used it upon only one service (the discussion forum), the possibility of
having various credentials on the same card and using it towards various service
providers was resembled in the minds of some participants. Therefore, **Multi-
Purpose Usage** was also another dimension of usability and convenience which
was noted as the main benefits of ID+. This opinion was raised clearly by P1:
*"I'd say, you only have one central device where all you relevant information is
stored and you can use that device to login to a variety of different portals and
websites"*.

The third type of perceived benefits was due to the use of smartcard. The
participants felt a kind of **Security** with regard to their personal data as they
were stored on a secure token, which is in hands of the owner. For instance P8
responded *"I think it is safer, because you have an additional device you cannot
copy. A password can be stolen from you but the card is a physical hardware"*.

6.2   Perceived Barriers to Use:

An often stated barrier is the **Lack of Information**. P7 raised his concern by saying *"I would need more information to trust ID+. I as a user would not trust ID+ completely because the information supported to me is not enough"*. The lack of information includes missing information about the technology itself, how it works and how it achieves all its privacy protection goals. For instance, P21 clearly stated *"I think there need to be more information about how does it hide my information"*. An interesting request in this regard was to highlight differences to the traditionally used mechanisms as P9 said *"[...] compared to the old fashion way"*. Another dimension which was questioned frequently concerns the operator of ID+. The participants were missing information about who will provide the technology, and who is controlling the information. P8 referred to this issue when mentioning *"I think the most important information would be who controls the information."*. P23 responded more comprehensively pointing to all the dimensions: *"the main problem is really not knowing [...] the issuer of the technology and not understanding the technology or not having information about the technology"*.

Lack of Trust was nominated as one of the main barriers to use ID+ by several respondents. As a completely new technology, the participants had difficulties to trust that ID+ is actually delivering what it is promising. P3 mentioned *"I don't know if I trust this device, because it displayed that it just transmit these information, but I'm not sure if it really just sends this information and not others"*. The concern was not only about privacy protection, but also about security, as inferred from statements like *"... maybe it can easily be hacked"* by P32. One of the interviewees related the lack of trust to the problem of demonstrating privacy protection and requested certification to gain trust of the users: *"They can't see the privacy protection. The users need more introduction and more proof to certify this card is safe"*.

The issue of **Adoption Inertia** was very well spotted by the respondents. The fact that service providers must in the first place allow authentication with such privacy-enhancing technologies for their services, was highlighted in the interviews. For example, P1 said *"a lot of websites and online shop companies have to adopt it. They need to agree that you can use it on the online shops and websites and there are not a lot of people who use it"*.

Another frequently mentioned barrier was about **Additional Hardware** to carry. The interviewees had the concern that they would need to have the card and the card reader all the time with them and they can use ID+ only wherever they have the possibility to set the hardware up. In another word, they will not be able to access their desired service if they do not have the card and the reader functional. P6 said *"The biggest barrier is, that you have to buy such a card reader and that you have to carry it with you. When you are on holiday and don't have the card with you, you cannot login"*. Equivalently, P10 expressed her worries as *"The first I would say, is the hardware you have to use. You always have to use the USB connection and the card"*. In summary, they found the use of smartcard contradicting with the principle of convenience and availability.

Some even had deeper thought and questioned the possibility of integrating into mobile devices as the trend is moving in this direction: *"[the] obstacle would be the switch to mobile, because most of the transactions in the future will go via the mobile and mobile payment in Germany will be the next big thing. So I cannot imagine how to use ID+ with the mobile payment"*, said P10.

Many of the participants raised the issue about the consequences and the situation when the smart card is broken, lost or stolen; as P7 said *"Normally you will think that the card is really important and what happens when you lose this card?"*. Therefore, **Compromised Smartcard** was specified among the main barriers. The interviewees were struggling with the fact that what will happen if they lose control of the card? How can they get access to the services for which they need ID+? How difficult is the process of getting a replacement card and set it up again?

One other highlighted barrier was about the **Costs**. P32 expressed her concerns as *"I assume you have to buy it and maybe it's expensive"*. The cost factor was mentioned not only with regard to the hardware itself but also for the services that would offer authentication with ID+. For instance, this matter was referred to explicitly by P16: *"... maybe some services will cost something to me."*.

6.3   Desired Application:

We inquired the participants about their desired use cases and application where they prefer to use ID+ to authenticate. The answers were very much correlated. The first answer was to use ID+ for **Online Payment**. Even though many of them used the term "online banking" in their explanation they did mean online payment rather than online-banking in terms of managing their bank account through online services by the bank. The participants were very much interested to benefit from ID+ in order to hide their bank account details from the online retailers and services. This is technically possible such as demonstrated in the ABC4Trust demo of privacy-preserving Hotel Booking[1]. In other words, the participants disliked storing the payment information on the service providers. For instance, P21 stated *"For online banking I think or if I do online transactions. I don't want my data to be stored."*. P31 similarly said *"I just would like to hide my bank accounts and the really important money stuff things, as I say"*.

The other side of the coin for online payment was the **Online Shopping** applications. Beside the payment related issues, the participants favoured the capabilities of avoiding targeted advertisements when staying anonymous and unlinkable across the websites. For instance, P2 sought separation of concerns when saying *"when I do online shopping they should get as less information as possible. Other things, like, which kind of music style I prefer and combine that with other topics or websites should not be possible. It should not be mixed. Music is music and politics is politics"*.

---

[1] https://abc4trust.eu/demo/hotelbooking.

The aforementioned benefit of registration-free authentication with ID+ was also reflected on online shops as they typically require creating an account. This was mentioned by P1 as follow: *"Especially I would use it, when doing online shopping, because for basically every new online shop you have to create a new ID and password and always have to remember those. With the ID+ card you can use the ID+ service to login to various shops"*.

Moreover, inspired by the experiment, using ID+ to participate in forums, blogs and polls were also frequently mentioned, which we can call all those scenarios as **eParticipation**. In all those scenarios, anonymity together with trustful verification of eligibility was desired. For instance, P20 said she would prefer to use ID+ for service *"like government politics, [where] they want to have an election,[or] they want to listen to the people's advice"*.

6.4   Trust to the Technology and Trust Anchors:

In the interviews, the participants were asked if they trust the ID+ to deliver its privacy protection promises. The majority responded that they do not trust it at the moment but showed directions on how to gain their trust. The minority who stated that they trust ID+, mentioned interesting reasons. Among them, some participants had similar reasons to believe the functionality of ID+. For instance, P2 said *"If you come up with such a system and the main issue you tell your customer is that everything will be private and safe and anyone finds out, that it is not true, the whole idea of an ID+ card would be nonsense"*. So they believed it because they consider privacy protection to be the unique selling point of ID+.

A conservative approach to put trust on ID+ was mentioned by P12, when saying *"Trust comes from time to time. If this card will show itself after some months, years. If it works well, not any problems, so l will believe and I will probably use this card"*. Therefore, **Flawless Operation over Time** seems to be a driver. Aligned with the analysis of perceived barriers, some required further **Transparency** to gain their trust. In this regard, P18 said *"I mean you have to check who is behind this technology and where my data is actually stored. It is actually on the card.[... and] the reputation of the agent behind this technology"*. One of the most frequent suggestions was to bind promises via **Contracts**. For instance, P13 said *"Maybe when they have like a contract, they are writing that my personal data are safe, and then I believe this"*. P26 also pointed *"[if] it's in their AGB[2] I would trust them"*. Another important action to enable their trust to the technology was to consider **Certification** for the claimed features. This was for instance raised by P19 mentioning *"If the company wants to introduce this technology into [the] market, I think the users need more introduction and proof from some certified organisations like government, big companies or research group"*.

To find out about the trust anchors who could potentially support gaining the trust of the users, we asked the participants about their preferred certification

---

[2] Allgemeine Geschäftsbedingungen (Terms of Service).

organization. The majority nominated **Governments** to be the most appropriate entity to verify such technologies and vouch for their correct functionalities; *"It should be certified by an official institution for example the state of Germany or the European Union"*, said P10. Some participants even had stronger opinion such as P14 who said *"Definitely government. The third party should be government and the government will take responsibility if we are well protected"*. Nevertheless, one should mentioned that this observation is highly dependent to the culture. In general, German citizens consider a high level of trust to the government in data protection aspects. At the same time, **Products Inspection Institutions** with good reputation of examining things in an independent way were proposed frequently; P1 stated *"It obviously has to be tested and certified by a third party - like institutions like the Stiftung Warentest[3] or something like that. A lot of or at least a few independent references"*. P18 pointed out in a similar way that *"There are some certification company in Germany like TÜV[4] who like to certify something"*. P37 also mentioned *"[...] for example chip.de, chip.com, when the websites say that ID+ is safe, I trust it"*. Another candidate for verification of these technologies was **Academia** as was mentioned by P6, *"[...] something like the Frauenhofer Institut in Germany"* , and P20, *"[...] and also like my university; If they want us to have it, I will believe it"*.

An interesting observation was that some participants mentioned **Diversity of Trust Anchors** to be necessary for them to believe in a technology. For example, P38 said *"[...] maybe if a few of them, more than one say so. So the government and one independent institution, so a combination and not when only one says: Yes it's safe, it's OK you can use it. I wouldn't be sure. But when there are a few of them, a group, that are not linked today, I would believe it"*.

6.5   Smartcard vs Cloud-Based Wallet:

Privacy-ABCs are typically bound to some secret keys during the issuance time and those keys will be needed when using the credentials to prove some attributes or facts about them. This essentially means that a secure mechanism is needed to store the secret keys. In such settings, smartcards are commonly used to store the secret keys and often perform the key-related computations. Consequently, it is not trivial to remove the role of such secure token without partially compromising the security.

Carrying a smartcard and a reader device were indicated by many of the participants to be a barrier to adopt ID+. In our interviews, we inquired their preferences to use smartcard or a cloud-based wallet, where they do not need to carry any additional device. Even though many of the participants mentioned that they did not find it convenient to have an additional device, more than 70 % said they prefer to use smartcard rather than a cloud-based wallet. There has been a general feeling of **Distrust Towards Cloud**. For instance, P2 said *"Definitely the ID wallet, because the cloud is something for me, which I know*

---

[3] A German consumer protection organization.

[4] Technischer Überwachungsverein (Technical Inspection Association).

what it is, but which is not transparent enough. I don't trust it like something I have in my pocket or in my wallet". In the same way P6 expressed her distrust as *"I would prefer the physical ID+ card, because I don't have trust in any cloud services"*.

Moreover, the participants very often felt more **Control** over their personal data when they have them on a device on which they can get hold. For instance, P23 mentioned *"I would choose the smartcard, because then I got the information on my smartcard and not stored on somebody's else server. Which means I decide what is done with my data at any time"*. Among the answers, the interviewees frequently indicated that they consider the smartcard to be **Safer** than the cloud option: *"I think [I will choose] smartcard wallet, because this machine[device] is much more secure than a cloud. So cloud could be hacked in a way"*, said P22.

The minority who opted for cloud-based wallet raised the flag for the **Usability** aspects. For example, P8 said *"If both would be at the same level in terms of safety and security I would prefer the cloud based wallet because with a cloud based wallet I don't need this additional device which reads the cards. I think cloud based systems are in general much easier to use"*. **Availability** of cloud services was also another reason not to go for smartcard option, such as for P40 who said *"Yeah definitely a cloud [...] because it's independent of whether I have it on me or not"*.

6.6   Summary

The participants of our experiment perceived *selective disclosure, anonymity / pseudonymity, additional transparency, registration-free* authentication, *multi-purpose usage* of the same credential, and *security* to be the main benefits of using such technologies. At the same time, they identified *lack of information* about the technical and organizational aspects of the technology, *lack of trust, adoption inertial* of the service providers, need for *additional hardware*, uncertainty about consequences of a *compromised smartcard* and possible enforced *costs* to be the main barriers for them to use ID+.

They expressed their preferences with regard to the usage of such technologies to be primarily for *online payment* and *online shopping* as well as *eParticipation* scenarios. In order to gain their trust, they consider *flawless operation over time, transparency*, binding *contracts* and *certification* for correct operation of the technology to be necessary. When it comes to certification, they can rely on *governments*, independent *product inspection institutes* with good reputation, and *academia*. Some of the participants prefer to have a combination of those certifying the technology.

With regard to the preferred implementation of the user wallet, the majority of the participants chose the smartcard implementation rather than a cloud-based approach because of their *distrust towards cloud* as well as their feeling of more *control* when physically holding the smartcard. Moreover, they also considered a smartcard to be generally *safer* than cloud for storing personal information. Nevertheless, the minority who favoured the cloud-based wallet, argued on the *usability* and *availability* of such implementation.

7   Limitations

We followed methodological approaches to perform our experiment. The experiment was conducted through the student network of the Goethe University Frankfurt. Moreover, the age of the participants were limited to 18–34 years old in order to avoid the lack of technical skills of using computer-based systems. Consequently, the results may not be generalizable to users who are significantly different from our sample group.

8   Conclusion

In this work, we conducted an experiment with 40 users. After a brief introduction, we let them use a mock-up implementation of Privacy-ABCs, called ID+, and guided them through a scenario by a task list. In the given chain of actions, they experienced selective disclosure, pseudonymity and unlinkability features. After the trial, we interviewed them using structured questions. Our findings show that the users were capable of perceiving the privacy protection benefits of using such technologies. They also caught the convenience dimensions as they can use the same credentials to authenticate towards various services. Therefore, it demonstrates our sample group had an appropriate mental model and were ready to capture the benefits of such complicated technologies. In this regard, communities with similar characteristics might be the appropriate entry points for diffusing such novel technologies.

However, efforts must be put to gain the trust of the potential adopters. This may require comprehensive introductory materials, explaining how privacy protection is achieved by those technologies. Moreover, certification and reviews by the trust anchors of the potential adopters and legal binding contracts delivering assurance and accountability seem to be crucial. Users will need service providers in the first place to adopt Privacy-ABCs so that the users can potentially use them. It is recommended to target online payment, online shopping, and eParticipation applications scenarios as the necessity of such privacy-enhancing features is more perceived for those services by the users. Additionally, as the costs were mentioned frequently to be a barrier, the technology shall be delivered with minimum cost or even free of charge in the roll-out phase. Nevertheless, transparency with regard to the business model of the operator is extremely important because the users get to know that their personal data is not being sold in a different way.

The paradox of security and usability is still challenging the users. While they consider additional hardware to introduce inconvenience and therefore be a barrier for adoption in their opinion, they feel better security when they have their personal data on a token in their pocket! In this regard, innovative solutions for maximising both aspects of security and usability will be needed.

References

1. Attribute-based Crednetials for Trust (ABC4Trust) EU Project. https://abc4trust. eu/
2. FutureID EU Project. http://www.futureid.eu/
3. Identity Mixer. http://idemix.wordpress.com/
4. Microsoft U-Prove. http://www.microsoft.com/uprove
5. PRIME - Privacy and Identity Management for Europe. https://www.prime-project.eu/
6. PrimeLife EU Project. http://primelife.ercim.eu/
7. Sabouri, A., (ed.): Architecture for Attribute-based Credential Technologies - Final Version. Deliverable D2.2, The ABC4Trust EU Project (2014). https://abc4trust. eu/download/Deliverable_D2.2.pdf, Accessed 2014–11-08
8. Benenson, Z., Girard, A., Krontiris, I.: User acceptance factors for anonymous credentials: An empirical investigation. In: Proceedings of the Workshop on the Economics of Information Security (WEIS) (2015)
9. Benenson, Z., Girard, A., Krontiris, I., Liagkou, V., Rannenberg, K., Stamatiou, Y.: User acceptance of privacy-ABCs: an exploratory study. In: Tryfonas, T., Askoxylakis, I. (eds.) HAS 2014. LNCS, vol. 8533, pp. 375–386. Springer, Heidelberg (2014). doi:10.1007/978-3-319-07620-1_33
10. Davis, F.D.: Perceived usefulness, perceived ease of use, and user acceptance of information technology. MIS Q. **13**, 319–340 (1989)
11. Harbach, M., Fahl, S., Rieger, M., Smith, M.: On the acceptance of privacy-preserving authentication technology: the curious case of national identity cards. In: De Cristofaro, E., Wright, M. (eds.) PETS 2013. LNCS, vol. 7981, pp. 245–264. Springer, Heidelberg (2013)
12. Liagkou, V., Metakides, G., Pyrgelis, A., Raptopoulos, C., Spirakis, P.G., Stamatiou, Y.C.: Privacy preserving course evaluations in greek higher education institutes: An e-participation case study with the empowerment of attribute based credentials. In: Privacy Technologies and Policy - First Annual Privacy Forum, ApPF 2012, Limassol, Cyprus, October 10–11, 2012, Revised Selected Papers, pp. 140–156 (2012)
13. Sabouri, A.: Understanding the determinants of privacy-ABC technologies adoption by service providers. In: Janssen, M., et al. (eds.) I3E 2015. LNCS, vol. 9373, pp. 119–132. Springer, Heidelberg (2015). doi:10.1007/978-3-319-25013-7_10
14. Seidel, S., Recker, J.C., Vom Brocke, J.: Sensemaking and sustainable practicing: functional affordances of information systems in green transformations. Manage. Inf. Syst. Q. **37**(4), 1275–1299 (2013)
15. Strauss, A., Corbin, J.: Basics of Qualitative Research: Techniques and Procedures for Developing Grounded Theory. Sage Publications Inc., Thousand Oaks (1998)
16. Strübing, J.: Grounded Theory: Zur sozialtheoretischen und epistemologischen Fundierung eines pragmatistischen Forschungsstils. Springer, Heidelberg (2014)
17. Wästlund, E., Angulo, J., Fischer-Hübner, S.: Evoking comprehensive mental models of anonymous credentials. In: Camenisch, J., Kesdogan, D. (eds.) iNetSec 2011. LNCS, vol. 7039, pp. 1–14. Springer, Heidelberg (2012). doi:10.1007/978-3-642-27585-2_1

Investigating the Animation of Application Permission Dialogs: A Case Study of Facebook

Yousra Javed and Mohamed Shehab[✉]

UNC Charlotte, Charlotte, USA
{yjaved,mshehab}@uncc.edu

Abstract. Third party applications play an important role in enhancing a social network user's online experience. These applications request various permissions from the users at install-time. However, these permissions are often ignored, and the users end up granting access to sensitive information. This motivates the need for techniques that can attract user attention towards the requested permissions and make users read and understand the permissions before authorizing them.

We investigate the animation of application permission dialogs. Using a real-life analogy of luggage screening at airport security checkpoints, we attempt to draw user attention towards application's requested permissions. We map the various elements involved at an airport security checkpoint to our context through the use of avatars, and present the permissions one by one. The user makes decision on a permission based on its provided details. The permission details include its description, type, and the user's personal information example to communicate the potential information disclosure in the event of its authorization. We developed a prototype of our proposed animated dialog design for Facebook applications, and compared it with Facebook's existing dialog designs. Our preliminary evaluation on 16 participants with the help of their eye-tracking data shows that the use of animation and personal information examples on a permission authorization dialog is effective.

Keywords: Habituation · Application permission dialogs · Animation

1 Introduction

Social network applications have gained a tremendous popularity over the last few years. On Facebook, these applications range from gaming to photo editing, shopping and other complex functionalities. The third party developers require user permissions to acquire read or write access to user data in accordance with the application's functionality. These permissions are presented to the user (through the scope parameter) on the login dialog as part of the authorization flow. The user authenticates and approves these permissions. Once the permissions are granted and the authorization flow is completed, the third party developer receives an access token to make API calls on behalf of the user, and retrieve user data.

© Springer International Publishing AG 2016
G. Livraga et al. (Eds.): DPM and QASA 2016, LNCS 9963, pp. 146–162, 2016.
DOI: 10.1007/978-3-319-47072-6_10

Authorizing permissions without reading and consenting to them, raises the risk of unintentional information disclosure to third parties. A Wall Street Journal study found numerous apps on Facebook extracting identifiable user information from the platform and sharing this bounty with advertising companies [12]. Due to the huge number of users of social network applications, they are also a tempting target for spammers and hackers. For example, *Facebook color changer* is a malicious application that steals the user's Facebook access tokens [9]. Similarly, lookalike applications of popular Facebook applications such as *Candy Crush Saga* have been used to target the users.

Most computer security warnings and authorization dialogs lack effectiveness in attention switch and maintenance; the very first stage of Communication-Human Information Processing (C-HIP) model proposed by Wogalter et al. [5]. The end-users are more focused on accomplishing the task at hand, than switching their attention towards the warning dialog and assessing the associated risks. Since access control is not the primary goal of users, many users simply click through the notices, ignoring the one important piece of information that alerts them about giving away their personal information to the third parties. Researchers have proposed various attractors to acquire user attention towards warning messages [3]. However, it still remains an unsolved problem. This suggests the need for other mechanisms of acquiring end-user attention and communicating security and privacy risks on warnings and authorization dialogs.

Moving elements are a powerful tool to attract users' attention [10]. Visuals are processed many times faster than text, and they quickly affect user's emotions, which in turn greatly affect their decision-making [1]. The use of computer animations is increasingly becoming popular for creating security awareness among the users and helping them understand information security. To the best of our knowledge, the use of animation to attract user attention towards permissions, and create awareness about them has not been explored in the context of application permission dialogs.

The incorporation of end-user's personal information examples on the application authorization dialogs has recently been claimed to be effective in communicating the security risks associated with authorizing an Android application's requested permissions. For example, displaying a stored photo along with the *read SD card* permission to communicate the user's personal data which the developer can access. Harbach et al. [8] state that users take longer to install applications when presented with personal information examples along with the permissions. Similarly, Serge et al. explored the display of user information verbatim on the Facebook connect dialog [6].

The use of personal information examples has not been studied extensively in the context of social network application permission dialogs. Moreover, to the best of our knowledge, there is no existing eye-tracking based research that investigates whether users read the authorization dialogs while installing third party applications.

In this paper, we contribute the following:

- We propose an animated permission dialog design for Facebook applications. We leverage the real-life analogy of luggage screening at airport security checkpoints, and incorporate the end-user's personal information examples to acquire user attention, and communicate the potential information disclosure associated with each permission. We chose Facebook, because of its widespread use, growing number of applications, and API to access the information of its large user base.
- We conduct a pilot study to evaluate our proposed dialog prototype through its comparison with the checkbox based dialog proposed by Wang et al. [13] and the dialog currently deployed by Facebook. We evaluate the effectiveness of our dialog and show that:
- The animated dialog design performs well on the first stage of C-HIP model— i.e., attention switch and maintenance. There are significantly more and longer eye-gaze fixations on the permission descriptions and personal information examples in the proposed dialog as compared to other dialogs.
- The personal information examples prove to be a good indicator in making the participants more aware and concerned about their personal information.
- Fewer number of permissions are authorized using the animated dialog as compared to the other dialogs.
- The animated dialog is easy to use and learnable.

2   Facebook Application Permission Dialogs

By default, a Facebook application has access to the underlying user's public profile information. This includes their id, name, username, gender, location, age_range, and any other information that the user has shared publicly. If a Facebook application requires access to other information, it needs to request permission from the user. These permissions are presented to the user on two separate dialogs during application authorization:

1. Required Permissions Dialog: This dialog displays the permissions necessary for the application to function properly. These permissions cannot be revoked in the dialog during installation, i.e., they are not optional for the users. They request read access to extended profile properties. The information asked for, can either be the underlying user's information or their friends'. Figure 1a shows the *Fortune Cookies* application's required permission dialog. In addition to the user's information, the *Fortune Cookies* application requests access to friends' information consisting of birthday, work histories, status updates, check-ins, events, current cities, photos and likes. For a detailed description of each permission, please refer to the "Permissions" section in [2].

2. Optional Permissions Dialog: This dialog displays permissions to more sensitive information, and the ability to publish and delete data. This dialog appears after the required permissions dialog. Figure 1b shows the optional permissions dialog for the *Fortune Cookies* application.

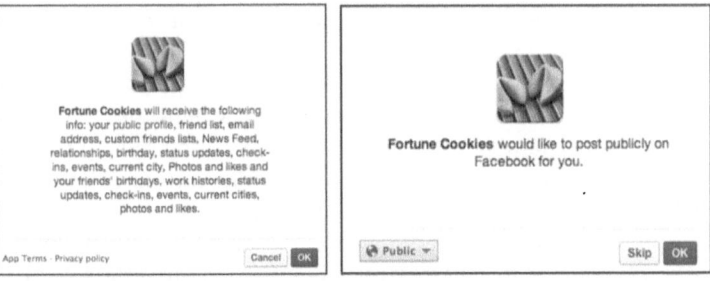

(a) Step 1. Required Permissions Dialog   (b) Step 2. Optional Permissions Dialog

Fig. 1. Facebook application authorization flow

3   Related Work

The literature most relevant to our work falls in two categories: user attention acquisition, and risk communication and informed consent.

3.1   User Attention Acquisition

Bravo-Lillo et al. [3] proposed five attractors to draw users' attention to a text field within a dialog. Among these, four were inhibitive attractors which prevent the user from proceeding until some time has passed (such as waiting for the text to gradually appear or become highlighted) or, the user performs a required action (such as moving the mouse over a field or typing the text). The authors studied their proposed attractors' resiliency to habituation. The two inhibitive attractors that forced the user to interact with the text field by moving the mouse over it or typing the text, proved to be effective even after increasing the level of habituation. We animate the permission text through a combination of avatar, font highlight and background color. We use a red font on the personal information examples to highlight their importance similar to their non-inhibitive attractor.

3.2   Risk Communication and Informed Consent

Several researchers have made efforts to improve the risk communication on the authorization dialogs. Egelman et al. [6] proposed design changes to the Facebook connect dialog by presenting the actual information requested by the public profile permission. However, their study showed that users are unlikely to notice small changes. Furman et al. [7] conducted an eye-tracking experiment on the Facebook connect dialog formats proposed by Egelman i.e., with and without information verbatim. Their results showed that although the participants who were shown information verbatim took longer to read the dialog, it did not affect their decision to authenticate using Facebook connect. We explore the similar idea in the context of Facebook application authorization dialogs. However, we use a playful approach and present each permission one by one instead of using a bulleted list.

Harbach et al. [8] proposed a modified Android application permission dialog for improving security risk communication to the end-user. They presented a personal information example along with each permission to help the user understand the permission and the risk associated with its authorization. Their study showed that participants who were presented with information examples for each permission spent more time on the dialog and seemed to become more aware of the security and privacy risks. However, they used sample data for their study and did not explore the use of actual user information. We incorporate information examples in our proposed dialog by extracting real user information using the Facebook API. Moreover, we present each permission and its information example one by one instead of all together on the dialog.

Several design enhancements have been proposed to the existing permission authorization dialogs for Facebook applications, to assist the end-users in making informed decisions. Wang et al. [14,15] proposed Fair Information Practice Principles (FIPPs) based interface designs for third party applications' authentication dialogs to overcome limitations of existing authorization dialogs and give users more control over their information. In [13], the authors have further studied the effectiveness of variations of their monochrome design. Although their design proved to be effective in fine-grained access control as compared to the default design, an eye-tracking based evidence of whether participants read the whole dialog before making decisions would be interesting. Moreover, this design lacks personal information examples.

4   Animated Dialog Design

We use a playful design approach on the application permission dialog, and leverage a real-life analogy—i.e., the screening of luggage items at the airport security checkpoints, to draw user attention towards permissions. The end-user plays the role of a security guard who monitors the scanned luggage on a computer screen. The permissions are presented to the user one by one in a manner analogous to how the luggage is screened. To maintain user attention long enough to read and evaluate the permissions, we explore the use of personal information examples with each permission to communicate the associated information disclosure.

4.1   Design Elements

We map various elements involved at an airport security checkpoint to our context through the use of avatars.

- Luggage— We refer to the user information requested by the application permissions as the luggage items to be scanned. Each permission—read, or write access to a user's information, is represented by a box-shaped avatar. A permission box has an icon to symbolize the requested resource. We use the

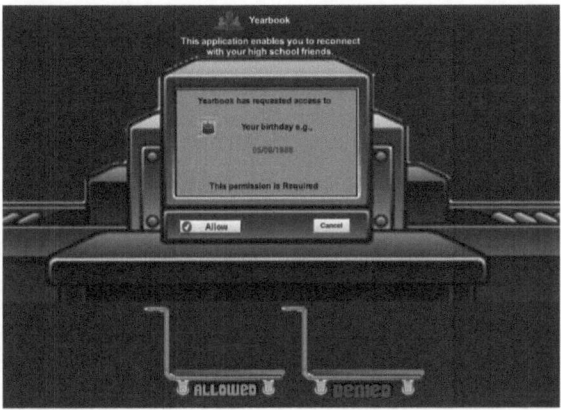

Fig. 2. Animated dialog design (Color figure online)

Facebook's existing icons for the information items requested by a permission. For example, for "access photos" and "access checkins" permissions, we use the photo and location icons present above the post sharing text box on the user's timeline.

– Scan Summary Screen— The permissions are scanned one by one. Once a permission is scanned, we display the permission's scan summary on a screen. The summary consists of the following pieces of information:

- Permission description: The type of user information being accessed
- Personal information example: An example of the actual user data being requested by the permission. The user data is extracted through Facebook API and presented beneath the permission description to highlight the actual user information disclosed as a result of granting the permission. For example, for the user photos and friend-lists permissions, we display one of user's album titles, and one of user's created friend-list's name respectively. The personal information is shown in red font to further emphasize its importance.
- Permission type: Whether the permission is required or optional to authorize

After the permission scanning is complete, the user is alerted by making the background color yellow, and the permission details are displayed on the screen. The user makes an authorization decision based on the provided summary by clicking the respective allow and deny buttons under the scan summary screen.

– Decision Options— The allow and deny buttons appear beneath the scan summary screen to grant or deny authorization for the permission. If the permission is a required permission, the deny button disappears. Therefore, only the optional permissions can be denied. To keep the design consistent with Facebook's existing design, and the other proposed designs, a cancel button

is displayed next to the allow and deny buttons to give the user an option to leave the application at any time.
- Permission Decision Carts— There are two decision carts—allowed, and denied. The allowed cart stores the permissions that have been authorized, similar to the luggage at security checkpoint that has been cleared. The denied cart stores the permissions that have been denied.

4.2 Dialog Prototype

We implemented an HTML prototype of our model and conducted a pilot study on 16 participants recruited from our university. Figure 2 shows a screenshot of our proposed application permission dialog prototype.

5   Pilot Study

We conducted a pilot study[1] for a preliminary evaluation of our proposed dialog design. We compared our animated dialog design with (1) the design currently deployed by Facebook and (2) the design proposed by Wang et al. [13]. Our study focuses on answering the following research questions:

- **Attention switch and maintenance-** Is the animated dialog design significantly different than the other designs in making the participants notice the permissions and pay attention towards them long enough to read them?
- **Comprehension-** Is the animated dialog's permission layout effective in helping the users easily read and differentiate permissions, and making them aware and concerned about the associated information disclosure?
- **Behavior-** Does the animated dialog have an impact on the users' installation decisions/allow-all permissions behavior?
- **Usability-** Is the animated dialog rated at least equal to the other dialog designs w.r.t ease of use and learnability?

5.1 Design

Conditions

- Control—This is the dialog currently deployed by Facebook (Figs. 3a and b).
- Treatment A (Checkbox)—This is the checkbox based dialog proposed by Wang et al. [13] (described in Sect. 3). To enable direct comparison of this dialog and the animated dialog w.r.t the effectiveness of personal information examples, we developed a modified version of this dialog by incorporating information examples. We also removed the additional columns that represent how the information is being accessed, for two reasons (i) this information is not yet incorporated in our proposed design (ii) it was hard to classify this information for every permission. Figure 3c shows our modified version of this dialog design. From now on, we will refer to this dialog as the checkbox based dialog design.

---

[1] Approved IRB Protocol #13-03-30.

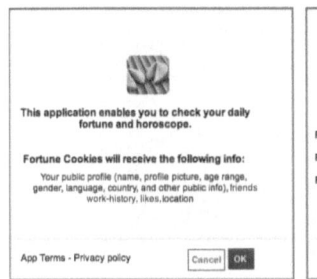  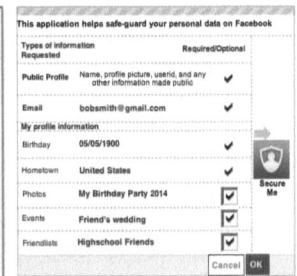

(a) Control—Required Permissions Dialog

(b) Control—Optional Permissions Dialog

(c) Checkbox Based Dialog

Fig. 3. Control and checkbox based dialog design

– Treatment B (Animated)—This is our proposed animated dialog design (Fig. 2).

We developed 6 Facebook applications from categories including fortune telling, games, comics, and others, to incorporate each of the three conditions in our experiment. Our applications were the lookalikes of 6 popular Facebook applications using their logo and description. Each application requested the same number of permissions—4 required and 3 optional.

Eye-Tracking Data. To collect evidence of whether the participants read/paid more attention to the animated dialog as compared to the other dialog designs, we logged eye-tracking data and analyzed the following information.

– **Eye-gaze fixation count**— An eye-gaze fixation refers to the maintenance of visual gaze at a single location. We used fixation counts to determine if the participants looked at the permission descriptions and information examples in the animated dialog more often than in the other dialogs.
– **Eye-gaze fixation duration**— We used fixation duration to study whether the participants looked at the permission descriptions and information examples in the animated dialog for a duration longer than the other dialogs.
– **Saccades/Eye-movement pattern**— A saccade is a rapid eye movement (a jump) which is usually conjugate (i.e. both eyes move together in the same direction) and under voluntary control. We studied whether the participant eye-movements follow the expected pattern i.e., from permission description to information example, and then the decision area. Figure 4b shows an example of eye-gaze fixations and saccades of a participant over our animated dialog. The yellow circles represent the fixations and the lines represent the saccades.

We used **The Eye Tribe**[2] eye-tracker to record eye-gaze data in our experiment. The participants completed a 9 point eye-calibration procedure at the

---

[2] https://theeyetribe.com.

 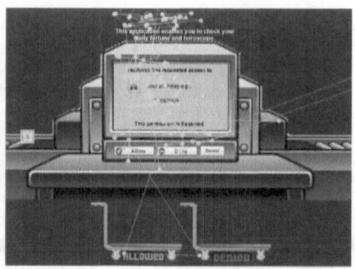

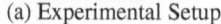

(a) Experimental Setup   (b) Eye-Gaze Fixations and Saccades
                                    of a Participant

Fig. 4. Experimental setup, and eye-gaze fixations/saccades on the animated dialog (Color figure online)

beginning of the study session.Our study was designed as a slideshow experiment using the open source *The Open Gaze and Mouse Analyzer (OGAMA)* [18]. Each application installation task and survey was designed as a separate web slide. OGAMA supports The Tribe Eye-Tracker and records the eye-gaze data from the underlying slideshow based experiment. To log eye-gaze data over specific areas on each dialog design, we created areas of interests (AOIs) on the preview image of the application installation web slides. These AOIs include permission descriptions, personal information examples, decision buttons, decision summary carts, application logo and description. Figure 4a shows our experimental setup. The eye-tracker was placed below the computer screen.

Surveys

– **Usability**— To evaluate the dialog designs w.r.t ease of use and learnability, we designed a questionnaire based on the System Usability Scale (SUS) [4].
– **Comprehension**— To study the effectiveness of permissions layout in each dialog design, we designed a Likert scale based survey focusing on the following:
    1. Ease of differentiating the required permissions from the optional permissions
    2. Ease of reading the permissions
    3. Extent to which personal information was informed
    4. Influence of personal information examples on authorization decision
    5. Increase of concern about personal information

Study Session. Our study used a within-subject design. After signing the consent form, participants completed the demographic survey. The participants then logged into their Facebook account, and were given the following instructions:

"You will be using and evaluating 6 Facebook applications. You will complete a short survey after every two applications. At the end of the study, you will

complete an exit survey". At the beginning of the session, the participants under-
went the eye-tracker calibration procedure. The participants were not informed
about the purpose of eye-tracking in our study. The participants were given a
brief tutorial on how to install an application using the three dialog designs.
The order of the dialog designs and the applications shown to a participant was
counterbalanced to prevent learning and practice effect.

5.2 Participants

We recruited our participants from the university through email announcements.
An email describing the purpose of the study was sent to all students. In order
to be eligible, the participants were required to have a Facebook account and be
users of Facebook applications. The eligible participants were invited to the lab
to complete the tasks, and received a $5 gift-card for participation.

A total of 16 participants successfully completed the study, 10 males and 6
females. Our participants were active Facebook users who were members for more
than 4 years. 70 % were between the ages of 25 to 30. 90 % had four or more
years of college education. 50 % of the participants frequently used Facebook
applications.

6 Results

6.1 Attention Switch and Maintenance

As mentioned in Sect. 5.1, we used eye-gaze fixation count and duration as metrics for measuring participant attention. We conducted a comparison of the
repeated measures using Friedman's test, showing a significant difference in the
fixation counts on permission description of the three dialogs at the $p<.05$ level
$[X^2(2) = 9.69, p = 0.004]$. Post-hoc analysis with Wilcoxon signed-rank test
was conducted with a Bonferroni correction, resulting in a significant difference
between the fixation counts on animated(mean = 5.1, SD = 2.7) and control
(mean = 3.1, SD = 1.7) dialog with an effect size of 0.4, and between animated
(mean = 5.1, SD = 2.7) and checkbox (mean = 3.8, SD = 2) based dialog with
an effect size of 0.31 (See Fig. 5a). Thus, the participants had significantly more
eye-gaze fixations on permissions (descriptions and permission type) when using
the animated dialog. Note that for the control dialog, we used fixations from
both required and optional permission dialogs.

Similarly, we conducted a Friedman's test for the effect of dialog design on
eye-gaze fixation duration over permission description. The experiment showed
significant differences in the fixation durations of the three dialogs at the $p<.05$
level $[X^2(2) = 7.24, p = 0.04]$ (See Fig. 5b). Post-hoc analysis with Wilcoxon
signed-rank test was conducted with a Bonferroni correction, resulting in a significant difference between the fixation durations on animated(mean = 167 ms,
SD = 288 ms) and control (mean = 128 ms, SD = 111 ms) dialog with an effect
size of 0.3. Thus, the participants had significantly longer eye-gaze durations on
permissions (descriptions and permission type) when using the animated dialog.

The higher number and longer eye-gaze fixations on permission descriptions in the animated dialog show that the animated dialog was able to switch and maintain the participants' attention towards the permissions. However, the higher fixations counts on animated dialog can be attributed to the sequential display of permissions, and the fact that participants have to look at a single piece of information at a time.

The participants had more eye-gaze fixations and of longer duration over personal information examples while using the animated dialog as compared to the checkbox based dialog. Wilcoxon signed-rank test showed significant differences between the eye-gaze fixation count on information examples of animated (mean = 14.81, SD = 14.73) and checkbox (mean = 3.69, SD = 5.21) dialog with p = 0.005 and an effect size of 0.63. Similarly, the Wilcoxon signed-rank test for eye-gaze fixation duration on information examples showed significant difference between the animated (mean = 287.39, SD = 193.49) and checkbox (mean = 181.66, SD = 134.71) dialog with p = 0.002 and an effect size of 0.49. Figure 6 shows the eye-gaze fixation counts and durations on animated and checkbox based dialogs. Thus, the participants paid more attention to the personal information examples on the animated dialog as compared to the checkbox based dialog. This can be attributed to the red font used to display the information in the animated dialog. The longer eye-gaze fixations on personal information examples in the animated dialog show that the animated dialog is able to maintain attention towards the permissions significantly more as compared to the checkbox based dialog.

We also analyzed the participants' eye-movement (saccade) patterns in order to get a better understanding of the attention paid towards the permissions before making a decision. Our hypothesis was that the participants will have more eye-movements from the permission description area to the decision (allow/deny/cancel button) area in the animated dialog than the other dialogs. We excluded the eye-movements towards and from the personal information examples areas. We performed a comparison of the repeated measures using Friedman's test on the effect of dialog design on saccade counts from the permission description area to decision area. However, the experiment showed no significant differences in the saccade counts of the three dialogs at the p<.05 level [$X^2(2) = 3.19, p = 0.18$] (see Fig. 7a). Therefore, the participants seemed to have equal number of eye movements from the permission description to the decision area in each dialog. A possible reason for why this pattern was not observed more frequently in the checkbox based and animated dialog is due to the presence of the personal information examples between the permission description and the decision area. Moreover, the animated dialog had many other elements which distracted the participant attention. For example, many participants also looked at the decision summary carts (containing their previous allowed and denied permissions), before making a decision on the current permission. Some participants also looked at the application logo and description to remind themselves about the application context. To verify this, we conducted another analysis on the checkbox and animated dialog to study the eye movements from the permission description to information examples.

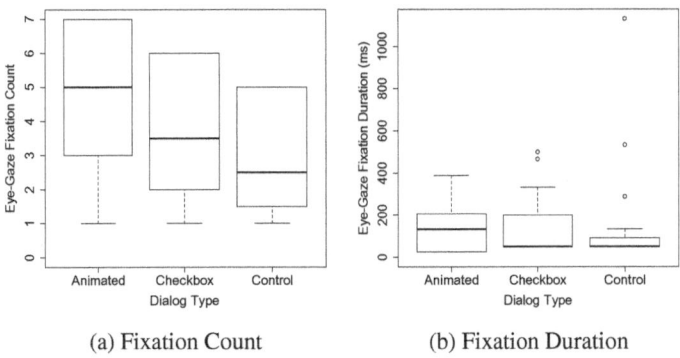

(a) Fixation Count   (b) Fixation Duration

Fig. 5. Eye-gaze fixations on permission descriptions

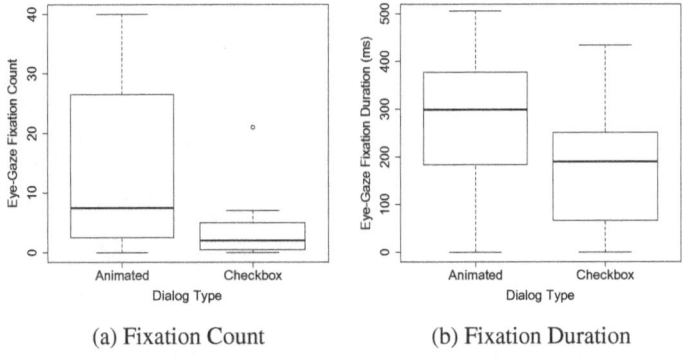

(a) Fixation Count   (b) Fixation Duration

Fig. 6. Eye-gaze fixations on information examples

Wilcoxon signed-rank test between the saccade counts from permission description to information example showed significant differences between the saccade count on animated(mean = 3.69, SD = 4.39) and checkbox(mean = 1.06, SD = 1.18) dialogs with p = 0.01 and an effect size of 0.57. Figure 7 shows the saccade counts of the participants using the checkbox based dialog and the animated dialog.

Heat map is a visualization technique derived from the eye-gaze fixation maps [11]. Heat map separates different levels of observation intensity better than the fixation maps. Color mapping is usually selected so that the longer the observation, the warmer the color used to represent it. Figure 8 shows the heat map of the eye-gaze fixations on various elements (permission description, information examples, and decision areas) of the three dialog designs. The heat map for the control dialog surprisingly covered the application logo, application description, permission descriptions, and the decision areas. However, the red region showing longer fixations did not cover any of these areas completely. The optional permissions dialog in the control design were not included in the calculation because a few participants chose not to install the application by clicking cancel on the first dialog, and therefore did not see the optional dialog.

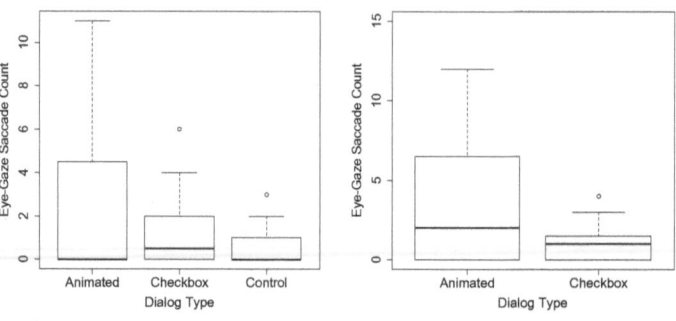

(a) Permission Description to Decision

(b) Permission Description to Information Example

Fig. 7. Participants eye-gaze saccades

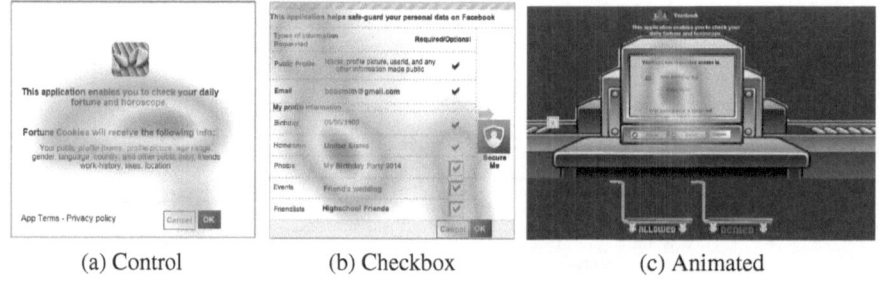

(a) Control   (b) Checkbox   (c) Animated

Fig. 8. Heatmaps of eye-gaze fixations on the three dialog designs (Color figure online)

The heat map for checkbox based dialog had good coverage, with the participants paying more attention to the personal information examples, and the decision areas for the optional permissions. The permission descriptions were not looked at that much probably because the information examples seemed enough for making decisions. The heat map for animated dialog was quite unexpected and did not have the extent of dialog coverage as we had expected. The red region shows that participants the paid most attention to the personal information examples and the permission descriptions in the animated dialog. This could have attracted the most attention because it showed the most important information to the participants. Moreover, this area was animated—the information appeared and disappeared, and the fonts and background color changed.

6.2   Permission Comprehension

Next, we evaluated the effectiveness of permission layout in our proposed dialog w.r.t helping the users easily read and differentiate permissions, and making them aware and concerned about the associated information disclosure.

We analyzed the (Likert scale based) participant ratings of the permission layout and personal information examples for each dialog using their responses to the permission comprehension survey presented to them at the end of the study.

Table 1 shows the average participant ratings for the permission layout and information examples presented on each dialog. In order for the participant to make a decision, it is important that they understand the permissions from which they can opt out. The ratings show that the participants found it easier to differentiate the required permissions from the optional permissions on the animated dialog, primarily due to the explicit mention of permission type under each permission. The participants found it easier to read the permission descriptions on the control dialog design, possibly due to lesser amount of time required to read them.

The participant ratings for the personal information examples show that the inclusion of examples had an impact on their decision to allow or deny a permission. This rating is higher for the animated dialog than that of the checkbox based dialog. Moreover, the participants indicated that if the personal information examples were included in the control dialog, it would have made an impact on their authorization decisions.

As compared to the checkbox based, and control dialog, the animated dialog had a higher average rating for how well it informed the participants of their personal information. Both the checkbox based dialog and the animated dialog made the participants feel more concerned about their personal information as compared to the control dialog.

Table 1. Average participant ratings for the effectiveness of permission layout and information examples in each dialog

Dialog Type	Ease of differentiating required & optional permissions	Ease of reading the permissions	Personal information examples (would have) influenced the authorization decision	Informed about the personal	Increased the concern about personal information
Control	3	5	5	3.66	3
Checkbox	3.33	3	4	4.33	4.33
Animated	4.33	4.33	4.66	4.66	4.33

6.3   Permission Authorization Behavior

To analyze the animated dialog's influence on users' installation decisions, and the deviation from **allow-all permissions** behavior, we measured the extent to which the participant's openness to authorize permissions differed for the applications installed using the three dialogs.

The participant permission openness for an application was calculated as the number of permissions allowed out of the total number of permissions requested by the application. Therefore, the openness ranged from 0 to 1. We conducted a comparison of the repeated measures using Friedman's test, showing a significant

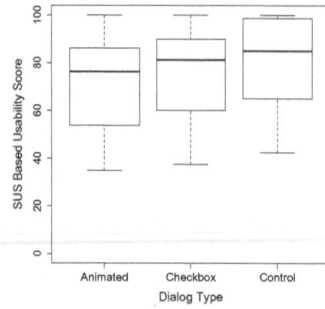

Fig. 9. Usability scores of the three dialogs

Table 2. Average visit duration on each dialog

Dialog Type	Mean (ms)	Standard deviation (ms)
Control	30.76	17.57
Checkbox	26.98	24.82
Animated	96.12	77.13

effect of dialog design on the permission openness at the p<.05 level for the three conditions $[X^2(2) = 8.481$, p= 0.0012]. Since the p value of 0.0012 is less than 0.05, we conclude that there is sufficient evidence to support the claim that the dialog used to install the application had a significant affect on the number of permissions authorized by the participants irrespective of the type of application showed. Post-hoc analysis with Wilcoxon signed-rank test was conducted with a Bonferroni correction, indicating that the mean permission openness for the animated dialog (M = 0.35, SD = 0.47) was significantly different from that of the checkbox based dialog (M = 0.66, SD = 0.41) with an effect size of 0.10, and from the control dialog (M = 0.79, SD = 0.49) with an effect size of 0.41.

6.4   Ease of Use and Learnability

Based on the participant responses to the usability surveys, we calculated an aggregated System Usability Scale (SUS) score of the ease of use and learnability for each dialog using the method described in [4]. Our hypothesis was that the participants will rate the usability of animated dialog equal to that of the checkbox and control dialog designs. To test this hypothesis, a comparison of the repeated measures was performed using Friedman's test. The test showed no significant differences in the SUS scores of the three dialogs at the p<.05 level, $(X^2(2) = 1.66$, p =0.45) (see Fig. 9)

A few participants complained that the animated dialog is slower than the other designs for application installation (see Table 2 for average visit duration per dialog). The likability of the animations was also subjective, with some participants indicating that it suits their style and some stating that they prefer the simpler text based design. A few participants liked the control dialog design because of its simplicity. However, they preferred to see a single dialog instead of two. Some participants stated that the checkbox based dialog had too much information, and found it to be confusing. A few participants suggested to use colors to differentiate permissions.

7   Discussion

Our results show that the animated dialog is able to switch and maintain participant attention towards permissions. Unlike Bravo-Lillo et al. [3] we find that our non-inhibitive attractor—red font based highlight on the information examples along with the background color beneath the text attracted the participants' attention. However, we did not incorporate habituation in our study. The focus of our study was to investigate the viability of animation on permission dialogs as potential attention attractors, and how the users perceive it. Our future work involves conducting a habituation based study on a larger sample (to represent the broader Internet population).

Similar to the eye-tracking results on Facebook connect dialog by Furman et al. [7], we find that participants had significantly more eye-fixations on the permission descriptions and information examples in the animated dialog as compared to the control dialog. However, they found no difference in participants' decision to authorize the dialogs in the three conditions. Our results on the other hand, show a significant difference in the participants' permission authorization decisions in the control and treatment conditions. Our results also correlate with those of Harbach et al. [8] and show that the personal information examples are effective in making the users concerned about their information.

Our results support the conclusions claimed by Wang et al. [13]. The checkbox based dialog also had an impact on participants' information disclosure as compared to the control dialog design. The personal information examples and decision areas were found to be the primary attractors in the checkbox based design. Therefore, we believe that the inclusion of personal information examples in the actual design proposed by Wang et al. [13] will further improve its effectiveness.

8   Conclusion

We explored the use of animation on application authorization dialogs as a possible attention attractor towards permissions.

Our preliminary study on the proposed animated dialog showed promising results. The participants had significantly more and longer eye-gaze fixations on permission descriptions in the animated dialog. The participants also looked longer at the personal information examples on the animated dialog as compared to the checkbox based dialog. The personal information examples in particular, made the participants more concerned about their information, and motivated them to read and evaluate the permissions. This was further observed in the participants' permission authorization decisions which were significantly more conservative compared to that of the other dialog designs. The participant ratings for the ease of use and learnability of the animated dialog were not significantly different than those of the other dialog designs.

References

1. Power of visual communication (2014). http://blog.wyzowl.com/power-visual-communication-infographic
2. Permissions with facebook login (2016). https://developers.facebook.com/docs/facebook-login/permissions/v2.2
3. Bravo-Lillo, C., Komanduri, S., Cranor, L.F., Reeder, R.W., Sleeper, M., Downs, J., Schechter, S.: Your attention please: Designing security-decision uis to make genuine risks harder to ignore. In: SOUPS. New York, USA, July 2013
4. Brooke, J.: Sus-a quick and dirty usability scale. Usability evaluation in industry (1996)
5. Conzola, V.C., Wogalter, M.S.: A communication-human information processing (c-hip) approach to warning effectiveness in the workplace. J. Risk Res. **4**(4), 309–322 (2001)
6. Egelman, S.: My profile is my password, verify me!: the privacy/convenience trade-off of facebook connect. In: SIGCHI, pp. 2369–2378. ACM (2013)
7. Furman, Susanne, Theofanos, Mary: Preserving privacy – more than reading a message. In: Stephanidis, Constantine, Antona, Margherita (eds.) UAHCI 2014. LNCS, vol. 8516, pp. 14–25. Springer, Heidelberg (2014). doi:10.1007/978-3-319-07509-9_2
8. Harbach, M., Hettig, M., Weber, S., Smith, M.: Using personal examples to improve risk communication for security and privacy decisions. In: CHI. ACM, Toronto, Canada (2014)
9. Mobile, C.: Facebook security issue: Facebook color scam (2014). http://www.cmcm.com/blog/2014-08-07/348.html
10. Pratt, J., Radulescu, P.V., Guo, R.M., Abrams, R.A.: It's alive! animate motion captures visual attention. Psychol. Sci. **21**, 1724–1730 (2010)
11. Špakov, O., Miniotas, D.: Visualization of eye gaze data using heat maps (2007)
12. Steel, E., Fowler, G.A.: Facebook in privacy breach (2010). http://www.wsj.com/articles/SB10001424052702304772804575558484075236968
13. Wang, N., Grosuklags, J., Xu, H.: An online experiment of privacy authorization dialogues for social applications. In: ACM CSCW, pp. 261–272 (2013)
14. Wang, N., Xu, H., Grosuklags, J.: Third-party apps on facebook: Privacy and the illusion of control. In: ACM CHIMIT. New York, NY (2011)
15. Xu, H., Wang, N., Grosuklags, J.: Privacy by redesign: Alleviating privacy concerns for third-party apps (2012)

Security and Secure Applications

Securing Multiparty Protocols
Against the Exposure of Data to Honest Parties

Peeter Laud[1]([✉]) and Alisa Pankova[1,2,3]

[1] Cybernetica AS, Tartu, Estonia
{peeter.laud,alisa.pankova}@cyber.ee
[2] Software Technologies and Applications Competence Centre (STACC),
Tartu, Estonia
[3] University of Tartu, Tartu, Estonia

Abstract. We consider a new adversarial goal in multiparty protocols, where the adversary may corrupt some parties. The goal is to manipulate the view of some honest party in a way, that this honest party learns the private data of some other honest party. The adversary itself might not learn this data at all. This goal, and such attacks are significant because they create a liability to the first honest party to clean its systems from second honest party's data; a task that may be highly non-trivial. Cleaning the systems is essential to prevent possible security leaks in future.

Protecting against this goal essentially means achieving security against several non-cooperating adversaries, where only one adversary is active, representing the real attacker, and each other adversary is passive, corrupting only a single party. We formalize the adversarial goal by proposing an alternative notion of universal composability. We show how existing, conventionally secure multiparty protocols can be transformed to make them secure against the novel adversarial goal.

1 Introduction

Data is a toxic asset [1]. If it has been collected, then it has to be protected from leaking. Hence one should not collect data that one has no or a little use of. To make sure that one is not collecting such data, one should try to never learn that data in the first place. In existing models of multiparty protocols, the security goals of a party are not violated if it learns too much: according to the model, an honest party may simply ignore the messages not meant to it or the data it has learned because of the misbehaviour of some other party. In practice, such forgetting of data may be a complex and expensive process, involving thorough scrubbing or destruction of storage media.

An honest party's attempt to not learn the data that it is not supposed to learn, brings about an adversarial goal that has not been considered so far. The adversary may deliberately try to cause some honest party to learn some other honest party's private data. The adversary's inability to learn such data itself does not imply the impossibility of such attacks.

In formalizing such attacks and security against them, we want to cover only leaks that are due to the protocol itself. A protocol always runs in the context of

© Springer International Publishing AG 2016
G. Livraga et al. (Eds.): DPM and QASA 2016, LNCS 9903, pp. 165–180, 2016.
DOI: 10.1007/978-3-319-47072-6_11

some larger system and we must be careful to exclude the side channels unrelated to the protocol from the security definition.

The security of protocols is often proved in the universal composability (UC) framework [2] which ensures that the protocol is secure not only when considered alone, but also when run in several sessions or in parallel with some other protocols. This framework assumes that there is a single monolithic adversary that controls all the corrupted parties. This model is not well-suited for defining the property we have in mind because an honest party trying to not learn other honest parties' data should really be modeled as passively corrupted, but independent from the "real" adversary.

If we care about the views of honest parties, we could treat each honest party as an independent adversary. There exist some alternative definitions of UC that support multiple adversaries, such as CP (Collusion Preserving) computation [3] or LUC (Local UC) [4]. These models are used to prove the protocol property of *preserving collusions*, meaning that the parties cannot use the protocol to exchange more information that they could do without the protocol. Treating each honest party as a separate adversary, collusion-preserving property would be sufficient to protect against leaking information to honest parties. However, technical details prevent us from using CP or LUC as the basis for defining when the adversary cannot make one honest party's secrets leak to another honest party. Namely, CP and LUC consider the joint view of all the adversaries as the environment output. If each party is controlled by an adversary, then the environment eventually gets the joint view of all the parties on the protocol. Hence a number of techniques are unusable as the building blocks of protocols deemed secure. Threshold secret sharing is one of the techniques ruled out, since the environment gets all the shares and may reconstruct the shared secret. We need a model where we can state that an honest party will never collude with the other parties its view may be treated as being completely separated from the other adversaries' views. For this, we need a model weaker than CP or LUC.

Our contribution. We define a "weak CP" (WCP), which splits the adversary into mutually exclusive coalitions. The motivation behind splitting the adversary to coalitions is to treat each honest party and the attacker as separate entities that are not trying to collaborate. Instead of bounding the total number of corrupted parties, we only bound the sizes of coalitions. Our model does not focus on preventing the attacker from sending arbitrary data directly to the honest parties, but rather on detecting the flaws in protocols where an honest party is obliged to leak its secret to another honest party at some point. More formally, we split the adversary $\mathcal{A}$ into $\{\mathcal{A}_1^H, \ldots, \mathcal{A}_n^H\}$ and $\mathcal{A}^L$, each $\mathcal{A}_i^H$ representing a separate adversarial coalition. Only $\mathcal{A}_i^H$ may get messages from the parties corrupted by it, but the attacks on the protocol are performed by $\mathcal{A}^L$. We are interested in attacks that can be performed by $\mathcal{A}^L$ without taking into account the messages that $\mathcal{A}_i^H$ received from the protocol. We see if $\mathcal{A}^L$ succeeds in leaking information received by $\mathcal{A}_i^H$ to *another* adversary $\mathcal{A}_j^H$. This allows to capture the attacks where both $\mathcal{A}_i^H$ and $\mathcal{A}_j^H$ represent the views of some honest parties.

After reviewing some preliminaries in Sect. 2 and related work in Sect. 3, we give a formal definition of WCP and prove its composability in Sect. 4. In Sect. 5 we give examples of new attacks that WCP detects. In Sect. 6 we show that although UC emulation implies WCP emulation in presence of a passive adversary, it is not the case for fail-stop, covert, and active adversaries. We also present some transformations that make a protocol that is secure in UC model also secure in WCP model.

2   Preliminaries

We give a brief review of the basic UC model [2]. UC considers systems of Interactive Turing Machines (ITM) connected to each other by input and output communication tapes. Throughout this work, on the figures, ITMs are represented by boxes, and the communication tapes by arrows.

A protocol π consists of ITMs M_i (i is a unique identifier in the given protocol session) that mutually realize some functionality $\mathcal{F}$. They may be connected to each other, and may also use some "trusted" resource ITM R to mediate their communication or even compute something for them. A special ITM $\mathcal{A}$ represents the *adversary* that may corrupt some M_i and get access to their internal states. There is a special ITM $\mathcal{Z}$, the *environment*, that chooses the inputs for each M_i and receives their outputs. This $\mathcal{Z}$ may contain the parties P_i sitting behind the machines M_i, or any other protocols running in parallel or sequentially with π, probably even some other sessions of π. $\mathcal{Z}$ also communicates with $\mathcal{A}$ and sees which information it has extracted from the protocol.

In security proofs, one defines a functionality $\mathcal{F}$ represented by a "trusted" ITM and describes what it computes exactly and which data is insensitive enough to be output to the adversary deliberately. On the other hand, there is a protocol π that has exactly the same communication ports with $\mathcal{Z}$ as $\mathcal{F}$ has, but that consists of untrusted machines M_i and optionally some other smaller resource R. Since π is usually more realistic than $\mathcal{F}$, the goal is to show that π is secure enough to be used instead of $\mathcal{F}$, and this can be done by proving that any attack (represented by $\mathcal{A}$) against π can be converted to an attack (represented by some $\mathcal{A}s$) against $\mathcal{F}$. Formally, one proves that no environment $\mathcal{Z}$ is able to distinguish whether π (with $\mathcal{A}$) or $\mathcal{F}$ (with $\mathcal{A}s$) is running, regardless of the adversary $\mathcal{A}$.

In our model, we treat different kinds of adversaries:

- **Passive (honest-but-curious):** the corrupted party follows the protocol as an honest party would do, but it shares all its internal state with $\mathcal{A}$.
- **Fail-Stop** [5]: the corrupted party follows the rules, but at some moment it may try to stop the protocol, so that the computation fails. In this paper, we use the definition where the party may stop the protocol only if it will not be caught (by being caught we mean that all the honest parties of the protocol consistently agree that this party is guilty).
- **Covert** [6]: the corrupted party may misbehave, but only as far as it will not be caught.
- **Active (malicious):** the corrupted party does whatever it wants.

3   Related Work

The problem of leaking a secret to an honest party is not new. The multiparty computation protocol of [7] is provided with a description of an attack that allows the malicious party to leak a secret value of one honest party to a different honest party. Very shortly, one considers three parties where at most one can be maliciously corrupted. In the protocol, the first party generates a key and sends it to the second party, which uses it to encrypt a secret and send it to the third party. If the first party maliciously generates a weak key then the third party will learn the second party's secret. This attack remains unnoticed by the traditional UC framework [2], and it could be detected using some other model that assumes the existence of two distinct adversaries: the malicious one and the semihonest one.

The abstract cryptography framework [8] does take into account multiple adversaries. The more concrete frameworks [9–11] study the collusion-freeness property of protocols whose main goal is to prevent smaller adversarial coalitions from forming larger coalitions using subliminal channels. A *collusion-free* protocol prevents the parties from any communication. A *collusion-preserving* protocol ensures that the parties cannot exchange more information that they could without executing the protocol.

Extending the traditional UC framework [2] to multiple adversaries has been considered in [3,4]. In CP (Collusion Preserving computation) [3], there is a separate adversary $\mathcal{A}_i$ for each party P_i. The adversaries communicate with the protocol π using a communication resource R which in turn contributes to defining the adversarial behaviour. The idea is that, in the real protocol, the adversaries should be able to exchange only as much information as they could in the ideal protocol. In LUC (Local UC) [4], each party P_i may be corrupted by $n-1$ adversaries $\mathcal{A}_{(i,j)}$ that can deliver messages to the party P_i where the sender identity of the delivered messages must be P_j. This model can be used to express more interesting properties than CP allows.

In CP and LUC, the environment gets the joint view of all the adversaries. Assigning an adversary to each honest party results in leaking all the data of honest parties to the environment, and so an honest party gets turned into a passively corrupted party. A secure protocol would have to be secure in the setting where all the parties are corrupted.

One way to prevent the communication between the honest and the corrupted parties is to assume that the environment is split into distinct parts with constrained information movement. For example, [12] formalizes *information confinement* property of a protocol. It splits the environment $\mathcal{Z}$ into *high* and *low* subenvironments $\mathcal{Z}_\mathcal{H}$ and $\mathcal{Z}_\mathcal{L}$ where data is allowed to move from $\mathcal{Z}_\mathcal{L}$ to $\mathcal{Z}_\mathcal{H}$, but not the other way around. The confinement property is formally achieved if $\mathcal{Z}_\mathcal{L}$ cannot guess a bit generated by $\mathcal{Z}_\mathcal{H}$ with non-negligible advantage. This property needs to be checked in addition to ordinary UC security. We use a simpler and cleaner solution in this paper, putting constraints onto the adversary instead of the environment. This allows to embed the confinement property into the definition of emulation.

4   Weak Collusion Preservation

In this section we present a model that allows to formalize the problems we presented in Sect. 1. We need to define more formally what it means that the protocol does not allow sensitive information to be leaked to honest parties.

4.1   Definitions

In this subsection we first repeat some definitions of UC and CP, and then adjust them to WCP. In this paper, the simulation does not mean the transformation of the adversary as $S(\mathcal{A})$, but the parallel composition $(S\|\mathcal{A})$, meaning that the simulator S translates the messages moving between the real adversary $\mathcal{A}$ and the ideal functionality $\mathcal{F}$, but S does not get access to the other communication ports of $\mathcal{A}$. The reason is that although there is no difference for UC and CP definitions, in our model getting control over all the ports of $\mathcal{A}$ may give too much power to the simulator. We discuss it in more details when we define WCP.

Let $EXEC_{\pi,\mathcal{A},\mathcal{Z}}$ be the probability ensemble of outputs of the environment $\mathcal{Z}$ running the protocol π with the adversary $\mathcal{A}$. Recall the definition of standard UC emulation.

Definition 1 (UC emulation [2]). *Let π and ϕ be PPT (probabilistic polynomial time) protocols. We say that π UC-emulates ϕ if there exists a PPT machine S, such that for any PPT adversary $\mathcal{A}$, and for any PPT environment $\mathcal{Z}$, the probability ensembles $EXEC_{\pi,\mathcal{A},\mathcal{Z}}$ and $EXEC_{\phi,(S\|\mathcal{A}),\mathcal{Z}}$ are indistinguishable (denoted $EXEC_{\pi,\mathcal{A},\mathcal{Z}} \approx EXEC_{\phi,(S\|\mathcal{A}),\mathcal{Z}}$).*

If the protocol ϕ is defined in a way that executing some ideal functionality $\mathcal{F}$ is the only thing that the parties do, we may also say that the protocol π UC-realizes $\mathcal{F}$. Since Definition 1 does not specify the adversary type, we will further explicitly specify whether a protocol emulates the functionality passively, covertly, or actively.

We base our work on the collusion preserving (CP) computation of [3]. Although CP is based on *generalized universal composability* (GUC) [13], which assumes that the protocols may use some shared global setup, we first give a simplified definition based on common UC. Differently from Definition 1, instead of one monolithic adversary there are n adversaries $\mathcal{A}_1,\ldots,\mathcal{A}_n$, one for each party. It is assumed that they do not interact with the protocol directly, but use some kind of communication resource. All the adversaries are connected with the environment $\mathcal{Z}$, and hence potentially may use it for communication.

We give the definition of CP emulation in its simplified form (without shared resources and the global setup).

Definition 2 (CP emulation [3]). *Let π and ϕ be PPT n-party protocols. We say that π CP-emulates ϕ if there exist mutually isolated PPT machines $S_1,\ldots,S_n$, such that for any PPT adversaries $\mathcal{A}_1,\ldots,\mathcal{A}_n$ for any PPT environment $\mathcal{Z}$, for $\mathcal{A} = \{\mathcal{A}_1,\ldots,\mathcal{A}_n\}$, $\mathcal{A}_S = \{(S_1\|\mathcal{A}_1),\ldots,(S_n\|\mathcal{A}_n)\}$, the probability ensembles $EXEC_{\pi,\mathcal{A},\mathcal{Z}}$ and $EXEC_{\phi,\mathcal{A}_S,\mathcal{Z}}$ are indistinguishable.*

In CP model, all the adversaries may still communicate through the environment, and so the values seen by any corrupted party may eventually get there. We want to modify the construction in such a way that it would take into account that the distinct adversarial coalitions will never use $\mathcal{Z}$ to communicate. Instead of assigning an adversary to each *party*, we assign an adversary to each *coalition*. We put some additional constraints on the adversary that ensure that the outputs of *only one* of these coalitions reach the environment.

Definition 3 (*t*-**coalition split adversary**). *Let n be the number of parties, and let $[n] = \{1, \ldots, n\}$. A t-coalition split adversary $\mathcal{A}$ is a set of PPT machines $\{\mathcal{A}_1^H, \ldots, \mathcal{A}_n^H, \mathcal{A}^L\}$ defined as follows.*

1. *The adversary $\mathcal{A}$ is defined as a set PPT ITMs $\{\mathcal{A}_1^H, \ldots, \mathcal{A}_n^H\}$ ("high") and $\mathcal{A}^L$ ("low") where $\mathcal{A}_i^H$ [resp. $\mathcal{A}^L$] does not receive inputs from $\mathcal{Z}$ [resp. π] nor give outputs to π [resp. $\mathcal{Z}$]. Any communication inside $\mathcal{A}$ goes from ITM $\mathcal{A}^L$ to ITMs $\mathcal{A}_i^H$.*
2. *The active adversary $\mathcal{A}_1^H$ may corrupt up to t parties. Each party P_i that is not corrupted by $\mathcal{A}_1^H$ is corrupted by some passive adversary $\mathcal{A}_j^H$.*
3. *There is some $j \in [n]$, such that for all $i \in [n] \backslash \{j\}$, the internal state of $\mathcal{A}_i^H$ does not depend on the inputs coming from π. We call $\mathcal{A}_j^H$ the true adversary and the other $\mathcal{A}_i^H$-s the false adversaries.*

The t-coalition split adversary is depicted on Fig. 1.

The property (1) lets the information moving from $\mathcal{Z}$ to π to be controlled by a single adversary $\mathcal{A}^L$, and it splits the information moving from π to $\mathcal{Z}$ amongst different receiving adversaries. The property (2) constructs an actively corrupted coalition of size at most t, and lets each honest party be controlled by a separate passive adversary. The property (3) guarantees that the views of different coalitions will not be merged.

Let $C(k)$ be the set of party indices corrupted by $\mathcal{A}_k^H$. The execution model of a t-coalition split adversary is the following.

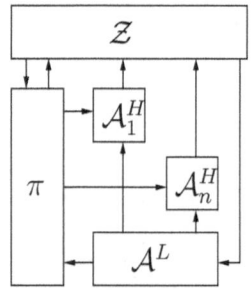

Fig. 1. t-coalition split adversary

- The corruption of a machine M_i into the coalition handled by $\mathcal{A}_j^H$ is determined by $\mathcal{A}^L$, which sends a message (corrupt, i, j) to the protocol. After the machine M_i receives that message, it forwards its internal state and all further received messages to the adversary $\mathcal{A}_j^H$.
- Any message m sent by M_i for $i \in C(1)$, can be substituted by $\mathcal{A}^L$ with an arbitrary message m^*. Alternatively, $\mathcal{A}^L$ may substitute m with $\bot$, which denotes cancelling delivery of m, or with $\top$, which denotes that m remains unchanged. The message $\top$ is need to enable $\mathcal{A}^L$ to proceed with honest protocol execution even if does not receive m.

We could define WCP emulation analogously to Definition 2, just replacing *any* adversary with a *t-coalition split* adversary. However, we now need to be careful with the simulator definition. If we allow S to be an arbitrary PPT machine, then it may happen that $(S\|\mathcal{A})$ is no longer a t-coalition split adversary. Hence we need to constrain the class of simulators.

Definition 4 (split simulator). *A split simulator $S = \{S_1^H, \ldots, S_n^H, S^L\}$ consists of PPT machines S_i^H and S^L where*

- *the communication is allowed from S^L to S_i^H for all $i \in [n]$, but not the other way around;*
- *the input ports of S_i^H are connected to π, and its output ports to $\mathcal{A}_i^H$;*
- *the input ports of S^L are connected to $\mathcal{A}^L$, and its output ports to π.*

We need to ensure that $(S\|\mathcal{A}) = \{(S_1^H\|\mathcal{A}_1^H), \ldots (S_n^H\|\mathcal{A}_n^H), (S^L\|\mathcal{A}^L)\}$ is also a t-coalition split adversary, since otherwise it may happen that we give more power to the adversary that attacks an ideal functionality than to the adversary that attacks a real functionality, and that would result in weaker security proofs.

Lemma 1. *Let $\mathcal{A} = \{\mathcal{A}_1^H, \ldots, \mathcal{A}_n^H, \mathcal{A}^L\}$ be a t-coalition-split adversary, and let $S = \{S_1^H, \ldots, S_n^H, S^L\}$ be a split simulator. Then the parallel simulation $\mathcal{A}\mathsf{s} = \{(S_1^H\|\mathcal{A}_1^H), \ldots, (S_n^H\|\mathcal{A}_n^H), (S^L\|\mathcal{A}^L)\}$ is also a t-coalition split adversary.*

The proof of Lemma 1 can be found in the full version of this paper [14].

Definition 5 (t-WCP emulation). *Let π and ϕ be n-party protocols. We say that π WCP-emulates ϕ if there is a PPT split simulator $S = \{S_1^H, \ldots, S_n^H, S^L\}$, such that for any PPT t-coalition split adversary $\mathcal{A} = \{\mathcal{A}_1, \ldots, \mathcal{A}_n\}$, and for any PPT environment $\mathcal{Z}$, for a t-coalition split adversary $\mathcal{A}\mathsf{s} - \{(S_1^H\|\mathcal{A}_1^H), \ldots, (S_n^H\|\mathcal{A}_n^H), (S^L\|\mathcal{A}^L)\}$, the probability ensembles $EXEC_{\pi, \mathcal{A}, \mathcal{Z}}$ and $EXEC_{\phi, \mathcal{A}\mathsf{s}, \mathcal{Z}}$ are indistinguishable.*

The definition is correct by Lemma 1. The t-WCP emulation is depicted on Fig. 2. We emphasize that we intentionally require blackbox simulatability, i.e. the same simulator S must be suitable for an arbitrary adversary $\mathcal{A}$. Intuitively, in this case the simulator does not know which $\mathcal{A}_i^H$ is the true adversary, and

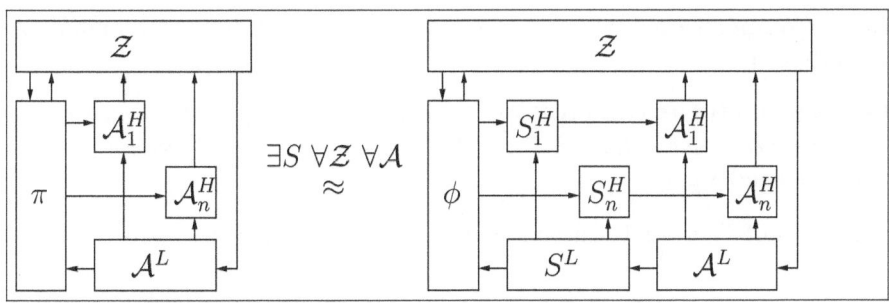

Fig. 2. t-WCP emulation

hence each S_i^H needs to simulate a proper view to all $\mathcal{A}_i^H$, not only to the true one. This is one reason why we use the parallel composition $(S_i^H \| \mathcal{A}_i^H)$ for the simulation, and not the transformation $S_i^H(\mathcal{A}_i^H)$ where the code of $\mathcal{A}_i^H$ could potentially tell S_i^H directly whether $\mathcal{A}_i^H$ is true or false adversary.

4.2   Composition Theorem

Dummy Lemma. The composition proofs of UC are simpler if instead of an arbitrary adversary $\mathcal{A}$ we consider the dummy adversary $\mathcal{D}$ that only forwards the messages between the protocol and the environment. This kind of adversary is in some sense the strongest one since it delegates all the attacks to the environment $\mathcal{Z}$, and it just gives to $\mathcal{Z}$ the entire view of the corrupted parties. In WCP model, the false adversaries are not allowed to forward the messages. If we replace a false adversary with $\mathcal{D}$, it will be too strong since the environment $\mathcal{Z}$ becomes able to forward its inputs through $\mathcal{D}$. We conclude that the dummy lemma of UC (that works also for CP and LUC) is not straightforwardly applicable to WCP. Nevertheless, it holds if $\mathcal{D}$ satisfies the t-coalition adversary definition.

Definition 6 (k-dummy t-coalition split adversary). *Let n be the number of parties, and let $k \in [n]$. The k-dummy t-coalition split adversary $\mathcal{D}k = \{\mathcal{D}k_1^H, \ldots, \mathcal{D}k_n^H, \mathcal{D}k^L\}$ is a t-coalition split adversary, where:*

- *$\mathcal{D}k^L = \mathcal{D}$ is just a message forwarding ITM;*
- *$\mathcal{D}k_k^H = \mathcal{D}$ is also a message forwarding ITM, but $\mathcal{D}k_i^H$ for $i \neq k$ does not forward the inputs that come from π (this is a actually a part of Definition 3).*

For n parties, there are n different k-dummy adversaries $\mathcal{D}1, \ldots, \mathcal{D}n$.

Lemma 2 (t-dummy lemma). *Let π and ϕ be n-party protocols. Then π t-WCP-emulates ϕ according to Definition 5 if and only if it t-WCP-emulates ϕ with respect to all k-dummy t-coalition split adversaries for all $k \in [n]$.*

The proof of Lemma 2 can be found in the full version of this paper [14].

WCP Composition Theorem. We prove that WCP definition is composable, similarly to UC.

Theorem 1 (WCP composition theorem). *Let ρ, ϕ, π be protocols such that ρ uses ϕ as subroutine, and π t-WCP-emulates ϕ. Then protocol $\rho[\phi \to \pi]$ t-WCP-emulates ρ.*

The proof of Theorem 1 can be found in the full version of this paper [14].

4.3 Relations to the Existing Notions

We show that t-WCP-emulation implies UC-emulation, and hence our security definition is stronger. However, failure in achieving t-WCP-specific properties does not provide an immediate UC security fallback in general (as in the case of CP), but on the assumption that only t parties remain corrupted.

Since the ports between π and $\mathcal{A}$ are different for UC and WCP, we need to define a transformation between UC and WCP functionalities, as it was done for CP and LUC. The transformation is analogous, and it either splits the monolithic adversary to distinct coalitions, or merges the coalitions into one monolithic adversary. The formal definitions of these transformations are given in the full version of this paper [14].

Theorem 2. *Let π be a protocol that t-WCP emulates a protocol ϕ. Then π also UC emulates ϕ in presence of at most t corrupted parties. However, there exists protocols π and ϕ, such that π UC-emulates ϕ in presence of at most t corrupted parties, but does not t-WCP emulate it.*

The proof of Theorem 2 can be found in the full version of this paper [14].

We would also like to compare WCP and CP. In general, CP security is stronger since a t-coalition split adversary is an instance of CP adversary where the entire $\mathcal{A}^L$ can be pushed into $\mathcal{Z}$, and the collaboration of coalitions can be also arranged through $\mathcal{Z}$. The simulators S_i of CP could be used as S_i^H in WCP. The only problem is that the simulator S_i of CP translates the messages between $\mathcal{A}_i$ and ϕ in both directions, while WCP allows S_i^H to only forward messages from ϕ to $\mathcal{A}_i^H$. Using a single S^L for simulating the other direction may fail without knowing certain inputs that S_i^H has got from ϕ.

Hence we could straightforwardly use only such functionalities ϕ that do not give to the adversary any outputs before they have already received from it all the inputs.

Definition 7 (one-time input protocol). *A protocol ϕ is called one-time input if all the inputs that it gets from the adversary $\mathcal{A}$ are obtained before any output is given by ϕ to $\mathcal{A}$.*

We show that, assuming that the number of corrupt parties is the same, and ϕ is one-time input protocol, then CP emulation implies WCP emulation. However, depending on the choice of t, it may happen that t-WCP is strictly weaker than CP.

Theorem 3. *Let t be the total number of corrupted parties. Let π be a protocol that CP emulates a one-time input protocol ϕ. Then π also t'-WCP emulates ϕ for any $t' \leq t$. However, there exists a $t' < t$ and protocol π and ϕ, such that π t'-WCP emulates ϕ, but does not CP emulate it.*

The proof of Theorem 3 can be found in the full version of this paper [14].

5   Attacks Detected in WCP Model

In this section we show why WCP is a suitable model for pointing out the problems we mentioned in Sect. 1. We present some properties related to leaking information to an honest party that can be captured by t-WCP, but not by UC, CP, LUC. Since CP lets the adversaries to communicate through an arbitrary resource R, the security in CP model may be dependent on the particular choice of R, which allows it to be stronger as well as weaker than the other models. In order to make the definitions similar, we assume that R delivers to $\mathcal{A}_i$ the internal state of M_i, and the adversary $\mathcal{A}_i$ may also replace any message m sent by M_i by a message m* of $\mathcal{A}_i$'s own choice.

The relations of our protocols and functionalities with the adversaries are described as $\mathcal{A}(i)$, where i is some party identifier, and $\mathcal{A}(i)$ corresponds to *all i-related adversaries*, which is just $\mathcal{A}$ for UC, $\mathcal{A}_i$ for CP, $\mathcal{A}_{c(i)}$ for WCP, and $\mathcal{A}_{i,1}, \ldots, \mathcal{A}_{i,n}$ for LUC. More details about transformations between different adversaries can be found in the full version of this paper [14].

We now present an ideal functionality $\mathcal{F}_0$ and two of its possible realizations π_1 and π_2. We see that, while for UC, CP, LUC these realizations either both realize or do not realize $\mathcal{F}_0$, they are different in t-WCP model.

Let $Enc(key, message)$ be some symmetric computationally secure encryption scheme that is secure with respect to a uniformly distributed key.

Ideal. The ideal functionality $\mathcal{F}_0$ takes a secret s from a certain party P_i. If P_i is actively corrupted, then $\mathcal{F}_0$ outputs s to each $\mathcal{A}(j)$ for $j \in [n]$. The adversary is allowed to abort the protocol. If it does not, $\mathcal{F}_0$ outputs 0 to each party.

Protocol 1. Consider the protocol π_1 where a (symmetric) key is generated as $k = \sum_{\ell \in \mathcal{I}} k_\ell$ where $\mathcal{I}$ is a set of arbitrarily chosen t parties that are supposed to generate k_ℓ from uniform distribution. All k_ℓ are sent to the party M_i that encrypts a secret s with this key and sends $Enc(k, s)$ to some party M_j. If any party refuses to send its message, the protocol aborts.

Protocol 2. Consider an analogous protocol π_2 which works in exactly the same way, but where M_i itself generates one more share k_{t+1} of k, and sends it to all other parties.

We now compare these protocols in various models.

UC: Assuming that the total number of corrupted parties is at most t, both π_1 and π_2 UC-realize $\mathcal{F}_0$. If M_i is corrupted, then S gets s from $\mathcal{F}_0$ and can simulate everything. Otherwise, the adversary either gets only the key k (if P_j is not corrupted), or it gets $Enc(k, s)$ and up to all shares of k except one (if P_j is corrupted). If the number of corrupted parties is at least $t + 1$, then both protocols are insecure since all the key shares and the $Enc(k, s)$ may leak to $\mathcal{Z}$.

CP, LUC: If M_i is corrupted, then the key generating parties may use their shares of k as side channels for collaborating with $\mathcal{A}(i)$, and hence neither π_1 nor π_2 does not realize $\mathcal{F}_0$. Let M_i be honest. Assuming that the total number of corrupted parties is at most t, the functionalities π_1 and π_2 both realize $\mathcal{F}_0$.

If at least one key generating party is honest, the simulator $S(j)$ only needs to simulate $Enc(k, s)$ as if the key was uniform. If all the key generating parties are corrupt, then k might not be uniform, but in this case P_j is uncorrupted, and S_j does not have to simulate anything. If the total number of corrupted parties is at least $t + 1$, then both the k and $Enc(k, s)$ may leak to $\mathcal{Z}$, and hence π_1 and π_2 are both insecure, similarly to UC.

WCP: The protocol π_2 does t-WCP-realize $\mathcal{F}_0$, but π_1 does not. If M_i is corrupted, then all S_j^H get s from $\mathcal{F}_0$, and S^L gets from $\mathcal{A}^L$ all the shares of k that S^L delivers to all S_j^H, so these side-channels are not taken into account by WCP. Let M_i be honest. In π_1, if all the t key generating parties are corrupted, then S_j^H has to simulate $Enc(k, s)$ based on the bad key k that no longer comes from uniform distribution and might be known by $\mathcal{Z}$. Although S^L might have sent the bad key k to S_j^H, it still does not know s, and hence cannot simulate $Enc(k, s)$. In π_2, the key k comes from a uniform distribution in any case, since at least one share is generated by the uncorrupted M_i itself. The question is whether k may leak to $\mathcal{Z}$ if all the key generating parties are controlled by an adversarial coalition of size t, as they also get the final share k_{t+1} at some moment. We care about the simulation by S_j^H only if $\mathcal{A}_j^H$ is the true adversary. In this case, the entire key generating coalition has been controlled by a false adversary that never leaks the final share k_{t+1} to $\mathcal{Z}$.

An analysis of a particular multiparty computation protocol of [7] related to bad key generation, and another example of an attack captured by WCP model, are given in the full version of this paper [14].

6   Achieving t-WCP Security

We start from a protocol that is secure against $t < n/2$ passively corrupted parties. In this section, we show how such a protocol can be made secure against $t < n/2$ actively corrupted parties, allowing up to all the other parties to be passively corrupted (i.e. "semihonest majority" assumption).

6.1   Adversaries Weaker Than Active

First, we show that UC and t-WCP emulations are equivalent definitions if the UC model allows at least t parties to be corrupt, and the adversary is passive. This shows that it does not make sense to define a special transformation for making a protocol passively secure in t-WCP model.

Theorem 4. *Let π be a protocol that passively UC-emulates a protocol ϕ in presence of t corrupted parties. Then π also passively t-WCP emulates ϕ.*

The proof of Theorem 4 is based on the fact that a passive adversary will not interact with the protocol, and so all the false adversaries do not interact with the protocol at all. The only true adversary is handled as in the UC model. A more formal proof be found in the full version of this paper [14].

A fail-stop adversary [5] follows the protocol as the honest parties do, but it also may force the corrupt parties to abort the protocol. Differently from the passive adversary case, the measures taken in the case when some party attempts to stop the protocol may result in leaking a secret to some honest party.

As a simple example, let us take the transmission functionality $\mathcal{F}_{tr}$ that has been used in [15,16] to prevent the protocol from aborting by pointing out the exact party that has aborted the protocol. This helps against a fail-stop adversary that does not want to be accused in cheating. Suppose that a party P_i should be sending a message m_{ij} to another party P_j. If P_i refuses to send the message to P_j, then there is no way for neither party to prove whether P_i is indeed silent, or P_j has already received m_{ij} but just accuses P_i. The realization of $\mathcal{F}_{tr}$ works on the assumption that the majority of parties follows the protocol. If there is a fail-stop conflict between P_i and P_j, then the message should just be broadcast by P_i to all the parties, so that they get the evidence that P_j indeed received it. Now if P_i decides to abort the protocol, then it will be blamed by everyone. The definition of $\mathcal{F}_{tr}$ is given in Fig. 3.

Let $[n] = \{1, \ldots, n\}$, where n is the number of parties. Let $\mathcal{A}s = \{\mathcal{A}s_1^H, \ldots, \mathcal{A}s_n^H, \mathcal{A}s^L\}$ be the ideal t-coalition split adversary. Let $c(i)$ be the index of the coalition to which the party P_i belongs.

$\mathcal{F}_{tr}$ works with unique message identifiers mid, encoding a sender $s(mid) \in [n]$ and a receiver $r(mid) \in [n]$. Some (n, t) threshold sharing scheme is defined.

Secure transmit: Receiving (transmit, mid, m) from $P_{s(mid)}$ and (transmit, mid) from all (semi)honest parties, store $(mid, m, r(mid))$, mark it as undelivered, and output $(mid, |m|)$ to all $\mathcal{A}s_i^H$. If the input of $P_{s(mid)}$ is invalid (or there is no input), and $P_{r(mid)}$ is (semi)honest, then output (corrupt, $s(mid)$) to all parties.

Secure broadcast: Receiving (broadcast, mid, m) from $P_{s(mid)}$ and (broadcast, mid) from all (semi)honest parties, store (mid, m, bc), mark it as undelivered, output $(mid, |m|)$ to all $\mathcal{A}s_i^H$. If the input of $P_{s(mid)}$ is invalid, output (corrupt, $s(mid)$) to all parties.

Synchronous delivery: At the end of each round, for each undelivered (mid, m, r) send (mid, m) to P_r; mark (mid, m, r) as delivered. For each undelivered (mid, m, bc), send (mid, m) to each party and all $\mathcal{A}s_i^H$; mark (mid, m, bc) as delivered.

Fig. 3. Ideal functionality $\mathcal{F}_{tr}$

Compared to [15,16], we need to modify the realization of $\mathcal{F}_{tr}$ in such a way that it would be secure in t-WCP model. Namely, P_i may no longer broadcast the message to all the parties, since some honest party P_k may receive a message that P_i and P_j would exchange privately.

We propose a slight modification to the realization of $\mathcal{F}_{tr}$ given in [15]. Now for each message bitstring m_{ij} transmitted from P_i to P_j, there is a random bit mask q_{ij}^m that is known by both P_i and P_j, but not anyone else (this can be done by sharing a common randomness between each pair of parties). In the case of conflict, P_i signs and broadcasts $m'_{ij} = m_{ij} \oplus q_{ij}^m$ to all the parties, and P_j computes $m'_{ij} \oplus q_{ij}^m$.

Let $[n] = \{1, \ldots, n\}$, where n is the number of parties. Let $\mathcal{As} = \{\mathcal{As}_1^H, \ldots, \mathcal{As}_n^H, \mathcal{As}^L\}$ be the ideal t-coalition split adversary. Let $c(i)$ be the index of the coalition to which the party P_i belongs. By Def. 3, let 1 be the index of the actively corrupted coalition (in this way, $C(1)$ is the set of indices of actively corrupted parties). $\mathcal{F}_{vmpc}$ works with session identifiers sid, where $\boldsymbol{r}_i[sid]$ is the randomness of P_i, $\bar{\boldsymbol{x}}_i[sid]$ are all the inputs of P_i committed so far, and $\bar{\boldsymbol{m}}_i[sid]$ are all the messages received by P_i so far, and $\boldsymbol{m}_{ij}[sid, \ell]$ are the committed outputs of P_i to P_j (there can be several such outputs for the same sid, representing different rounds).

Random tape generation On input $(\mathsf{gen\_rnd}, sid, i)$ from all (semi)honest parties, $\mathcal{F}_{vmpc}$ randomly generates $\boldsymbol{r}_i$. It outputs $\boldsymbol{r}_i$ to P_i and also sends $(\mathsf{randomness}, i, \boldsymbol{r}_i)$ to $\mathcal{As}_{c(i)}^H$. $\mathcal{F}_{vmpc}$ treats $\boldsymbol{r}_i$ as the committed randomness for P_i's computation. Alternatively, a message $\perp$ may come from $\mathcal{As}^L$, and in this case the randomness generation fails.

Input commitment On input $(\mathsf{commit\_input}, sid, i, \boldsymbol{x}_i)$ from the party P_i and $(\mathsf{commit\_input}, sid, i)$ from all (semi)honest parties, $\mathcal{F}_{vmpc}$ appends $\boldsymbol{x}_i$ to $\bar{\boldsymbol{x}}_i[sid]$. For $i \in C(1)$, it sends $(\mathsf{input}, i, \boldsymbol{x}_i)$ to $\mathcal{As}_{c(i)}^H$. Alternatively, a message $(\mathsf{corrupt}, j)$ may come from $\mathcal{As}^L$ with $j \in C(1)$. $\mathcal{F}_{vmpc}$ defines $\mathcal{B}_0 = \{j \mid (\mathsf{corrupt}, j) \text{ has been sent by } \mathcal{As}^L\}$.

Message commitment On input $(\mathsf{commit\_msg}, sid, i, j, \ell, \boldsymbol{m})$ from the party P_i and $(\mathsf{commit\_msg}, (sid, \ell), i, j)$ from all (semi)honest parties, $\mathcal{F}_{vmpc}$ stores $\boldsymbol{m}_{ij}[sid, \ell] = \boldsymbol{m}$. Alternatively, a message $(\mathsf{corrupt}, j)$ may come from $\mathcal{As}^L$ with $j \in C(1)$. $\mathcal{F}_{vmpc}$ defines $\mathcal{B}_0 = \{j \mid (\mathsf{corrupt}, j) \text{ has been sent by } \mathcal{As}^L\}$.

Verification On input $(\mathsf{verify}, sid, C, i, j, \ell)$ from all (semi)honest parties, where C is the description of circuit that corresponds to the computation of a message for P_j by P_i, $\mathcal{F}_{vmpc}$ checks if $\boldsymbol{m}_{ij}[sid, \ell]$ and all the values $\bar{\boldsymbol{x}}_i[sid]$, $\boldsymbol{r}_i[sid]$, $\bar{\boldsymbol{m}}_i[sid]$ necessary for computing $C(\bar{\boldsymbol{x}}_i[sid], \boldsymbol{r}_i[sid], \bar{\boldsymbol{m}}_i[sid])$ are committed. If they are, $\mathcal{F}_{vmpc}$ computes $\boldsymbol{m}'_{ij} = C(\bar{\boldsymbol{x}}_i[sid], \boldsymbol{r}_i[sid], \bar{\boldsymbol{m}}_i[sid])$. If $\boldsymbol{m}'_{ij} = \boldsymbol{m}_{ij}[sid, \ell]$, then $\mathcal{F}_{vmpc}$ outputs $(\mathsf{approved}, sid, C, i, j, \ell, \boldsymbol{m}_{ij}[sid, \ell])$ to P_j and $(\mathsf{approved}, sid, C, i, j)$ to all other parties. It appends $\boldsymbol{m}_{ij}$ to $\bar{\boldsymbol{m}}_j[sid]$ and outputs $\boldsymbol{m}_{ij}$ to $\mathcal{As}_{c(j)}^H$. If $j \in C(1)$, then $\mathcal{F}_{vmpc}$ appends $\boldsymbol{m}'_{ij}$ to $\bar{\boldsymbol{m}}_j[sid]$ even if $\boldsymbol{m}'_{ij} \neq \boldsymbol{m}_{ij}$. In any case, it outputs C to each adversary $\mathcal{A}_k^H$. $\mathcal{F}_{vmpc}$ defines $\mathcal{M} = \mathcal{B}_0 \cup \{i \in [n] \mid \exists j : \boldsymbol{m}'_{ij} \neq \boldsymbol{m}_{ij}[sid, \ell]\}$. For all $i \notin C(1)$, $\mathcal{As}^L$ sends $(\mathsf{blame}, i, \mathcal{B}_i)$ to $\mathcal{F}_{vmpc}$, with $\mathcal{M} \subseteq \mathcal{B}_i \subseteq C$. $\mathcal{F}_{vmpc}$ outputs $(\mathsf{blame}, sid, \ell, \mathcal{B}_i)$ to P_i.

Fig. 4. The ideal functionality for verifiable computations

Lemma 3. *Assuming that the majority of parties are at least semihonest, there exists an realization of $\mathcal{F}_{tr}$ that is secure in t-WCP model.*

Lemma 3 is proven by construction of a certain realization of $\mathcal{F}_{tr}$ in the full version of this paper [14].

If all the communication in the protocol is performed using $\mathcal{F}_{tr}$, then UC security implies WCP security for any fail-stop adversary. This result can be easily extended to any covert adversary [6] that will not cheat if it will be caught with a non-negligible probability. If the initial protocol is able to detect any covert adversary in the UC model, we may assume that a covert adversary will act as passive anyway, and $\mathcal{A}^L$ will not attempt to modify the flow of π since otherwise it will be detected. Hence we may be sure that, if a covert adversary will not attempt to cheat, then UC-emulation implies t-WCP emulation. Nevertheless, it is more difficult to reason about fallback security, i.e. what happens if the

Let $\boldsymbol{x}_i$ be the vector of inputs of the party P_i in the protocol π. Let $\boldsymbol{r}_i$ be the randomness used by P_i.

1. *Random tape generation.* When activating WCP-Comp(π) for the first time with session identifier sid, all (semi)honest parties send (gen_rnd, sid, i) to $\mathcal{F}_{vmpc}$ for all $i \in [n]$.

2. *Activation due to new input.* When activated with input $(sid, \boldsymbol{x}_i)$, party P_i proceeds as follows.

   (a) *Input commitment:* At any moment when a party P_i should commit an input, all the (semi)honest parties send (commit_input, sid, i) to $\mathcal{F}_{vmpc}$. P_i sends (commit_input, $sid, i, \boldsymbol{x}_i$) to $\mathcal{F}_{vmpc}$ and adds $\boldsymbol{x}_i$ to the list of inputs $\bar{\boldsymbol{x}}_i$ (this list is initially empty and contains P_i's inputs from the previous activations of π). P_i then proceeds to the next step.

   (b) *Protocol computation:* Let $\bar{\boldsymbol{m}}_i$ be the series of messages that were transmitted to P_i in all the activations of π until now ($\bar{\boldsymbol{m}}_i$ is initially empty). P_i runs the code of π on its input list $\bar{\boldsymbol{x}}_i$, messages $\bar{\boldsymbol{m}}_i$, and random tape $\boldsymbol{r}_i$. If π instructs P_i to transmit a message, P_i proceeds to the next step.

   (c) *Outgoing message transmission:* Let $\boldsymbol{m}_{ij}^\ell$ be the outgoing message that P_i sends in π to P_j on ℓ-th round. As soon as the ℓ-th round starts, all the (semi)honest parties send (commit_msg, sid, i, j, ℓ) to $\mathcal{F}_{vmpc}$ for all $i, j \in [n]$. P_i sends (commit_msg, $sid, i, j, \ell, \boldsymbol{m}_{ij}^\ell$) to $\mathcal{F}_{vmpc}$.

3. *Activation due to incoming message* Let C_{ij}^ℓ be the description of the arithmetic circuit representing the computation of P_i on the ℓ-th round that finally outputs $\boldsymbol{m}_{ij}^\ell$ to P_j. As soon as each party has finished with its computation of the ℓ-th round, it sends (verify, $sid, C_{ij}^\ell, i, j, \ell$) to $\mathcal{F}_{vmpc}$. Upon receiving a message (approved, $sid, C_{ij}^\ell, i, j, \ell, \boldsymbol{m}_{ij}^\ell$) from $\mathcal{F}_{vmpc}$, P_j appends $\boldsymbol{m}_{ij}^\ell$ to $\bar{\boldsymbol{m}}_j$ and proceed with the Step 2b above. All the other (semi)honest parties wait for the message (approved, $sid, C_{ij}^\ell, i, j, \ell$) from $\mathcal{F}_{vmpc}$ to proceed with the Step 2b.

   In addition, $\mathcal{F}_{vmpc}$ outputs a message (blame, $sid, \ell, \mathcal{B}_i$) to each (semi)honest $\mathcal{B}_i$. The way in which (semi)honest parties handle the set $\mathcal{B}_i$ depends on the particular protocol π.

4. *Output:* Whenever π generates an output value, WCP-Comp(π) generates the same output value.

Fig. 5. The compiled protocol WCP-Comp(π)

adversary does not follow the protocol regardless of being punished. There may be still more attacks in the t-WCP model than in the UC model, and this will be discussed in more details in Sect. 6.2.

We conclude our discussion about the weaker than active adversary with the following theorem.

Theorem 5. *Let π be a protocol where the parties use the functionality $\mathcal{F}_{tr}$ for communication. Let π UC-emulate a protocol ϕ in presence of t covertly corrupted parties. If the majority of parties is at least semihonest, then π also t-WCP emulates ϕ, assuming that the strongest adversaries are at most covert.*

The proof of Theorem 5 can be found in the full version of this paper [14].

6.2   Active Adversary

For constructing a multiparty protocol secure against active adversaries, we follow the general pattern used in other related works [17,18]. Initially, there is a multiparty protocol secure only against a passive adversary. In order to make it secure against an active adversary, on each round, each party needs to provide a zero-knowledge proof that it has followed the protocol rules.

On Fig. 4, we present a functionality $\mathcal{F}_{vmpc}$ that we use to compute one protocol round. In the full version of this paper [14], we give a protocol that t-WCP realizes $\mathcal{F}_{vmpc}$. The implementation relies on Byzantine agreement, and so it works only under (semi)honest majority assumption.

We use $\mathcal{F}_{vmpc}$ to construct a protocol transformation WCP-Comp (Fig. 5) that uses $\mathcal{F}_{vmpc}$ to compute each round. The transformation is analogous to Comp of [18,19]). Having WCP-Comp, we may prove the following theorem.

Theorem 6. *Let π be a protocol that passively UC-emulates a protocol ϕ in presence of t corrupted parties. Assuming that the majority of parties is at least semihonest, the protocol* WCP-Comp(π) *t-WCP emulates ϕ in presence of a coalition of t active adversaries.*

The proof of Theorem 6 can be found in the full version of this paper [14].

7   Conclusions

We have defined WCP model, which a stronger version of UC that additionally allows to capture the cases where the information leaks to some honest party. It makes the protocol reliable not on some participants' unconditional honestness, but rather on their non-collusion which seems a more realistic assumption. The definition is weak enough to make WCP security relatively easily achievable. We have proposed a scheme transforming passively secure protocols with one adversary up to actively secure protocols with semihonest majority and multiple adversaries. Our transformation relies on semihonest majority assumption.

References

1. Schneier, B.: Data is a toxic asset, March 2016. https://www.schneier.com/blog/archives/2016/03/data_is_a_toxic.html
2. Canetti, R.: Universally composable security: a new paradigm for cryptographic protocols. In: FOCS, pp. 136–145. IEEE Computer Society (2001)
3. Alwen, J., Katz, J., Maurer, U., Zikas, V.: Collusion-preserving computation. In: Safavi-Naini, R., Canetti, R. (eds.) CRYPTO 2012. LNCS, vol. 7417, pp. 124–143. Springer, Heidelberg (2012)
4. Canetti, R., Vald, M.: Universally composable security with local adversaries. In: Visconti, I., De Prisco, R. (eds.) SCN 2012. LNCS, vol. 7485, pp. 281–301. Springer, Heidelberg (2012)

5. Galil, Z., Haber, S., Yung, M.: Cryptographic computation: secure fault tolerant protocols and the public-key model. In: Pomerance, C. (ed.) CRYPTO 1987. LNCS, vol. 293, pp. 135–155. Springer, Heidelberg (1988)
6. Aumann, Y., Lindell, Y.: Security against covert adversaries: efficient protocols for realistic adversaries. J. Cryptol. **23**(2), 281–343 (2010)
7. Mohassel, P., Rosulek, M., Zhang, Y.: Fast, secure three-party computation: the garbled circuit approach. In: Proceedings of the 22nd ACM SIGSAC Conference on Computer and Communications Security (CCS 2015), pp. 591–602, New York, NY, USA. ACM (2015)
8. Maurer, U., Renner, R.: Abstract cryptography. In: Chazelle, B., (ed.) Innovations in Computer Science - ICS, 7–9 January 2011, Tsinghua University, Beijing, China, pp. 1–21. Tsinghua University Press (2010)
9. Alwen, J., Shelat, A., Visconti, I.: Collusion-free protocols in the mediated model. In: Wagner, D. (ed.) CRYPTO 2008. LNCS, vol. 5157, pp. 497–514. Springer, Heidelberg (2008)
10. Alwen, J., Katz, J., Lindell, Y., Persiano, G., shelat, a, Visconti, I.: Collusion-free multiparty computation in the mediated model. In: Halevi, S. (ed.) CRYPTO 2009. LNCS, vol. 5677, pp. 524–540. Springer, Heidelberg (2009)
11. Lepinski, M., Micali, S., Shelat, A.: Collusion-free protocols. In: Gabow, H.N., Fagin, R., (eds.) Proceedings of the 37th Annual ACM Symposium on Theory of Computing, Baltimore, MD, USA, 22–24 May 2005, pp. 543–552. ACM (2005)
12. Halevi, S., Karger, P.A., Naor, D.: Enforcing confinement in distributed storage and a cryptographic model for access control. IACR Cryptology ePrint Archive 2005, p. 169 (2005)
13. Canetti, R., Dodis, Y., Pass, R., Walfish, S.: Universally composable security with global setup. In: Vadhan, S.P. (ed.) TCC 2007. LNCS, vol. 4392, pp. 61–85. Springer, Heidelberg (2007)
14. Laud, P., Pankova, A.: Securing multiparty protocols against the exposure of data to honest parties. Cryptology ePrint Archive, Report 2016/650 (2016). http://eprint.iacr.org/2016/650
15. Damgård, I., Geisler, M., Nielsen, J.B.: From passive to covert security at low cost. In: Micciancio, D. (ed.) TCC 2010. LNCS, vol. 5978, pp. 128–145. Springer, Heidelberg (2010)
16. Laud, P., Pankova, A.: Preprocessing-based verification of multiparty protocols with honest majority. Cryptology ePrint Archive, Report 2015/674 (2015). http://eprint.iacr.org/
17. Goldreich, O., Micali, S., Wigderson, A.: How to play any mental game or a completeness theorem for protocols with honest majority. In: STOC, pp. 218–229. ACM (1987)
18. Canetti, R., Lindell, Y., Ostrovsky, R., Sahai, A.: Universally composable two-party and multi-party secure computation. In: Reif, J.H., (ed.) Proceedings on 34th Annual ACM Symposium on Theory of Computing, 19–21 May 2002, Montréal, Québec, Canada, pp. 494–503. ACM (2002)
19. Canetti, R., Lindell, Y., Ostrovsky, R., Sahai, A.: Universally composable two-party and multi-party secure computation. IACR Cryptology ePrint Archive 2002, p. 140 (2002)

Secure Frequent Pattern Mining
by Fully Homomorphic Encryption
with Ciphertext Packing

Hiroki Imabayashi[✉], Yu Ishimaki, Akira Umayabara, Hiroki Sato,
and Hayato Yamana

Waseda University, 3-4-1 Okubo, Shinjuku-ku, Tokyo, Japan
{imabayashi,yuishi,uma,hsato,yamana}@yama.info.waseda.ac.jp

Abstract. We propose an efficient and secure frequent pattern mining
protocol with fully homomorphic encryption (FHE). Nowadays, secure
outsourcing of mining tasks to the cloud with FHE is gaining attentions.
However, FHE execution leads to significant time and space complexities. P3CC, the first proposed secure protocol with FHE for frequent pattern mining, has these particular problems. It generates ciphertexts for
each component in item-transaction data matrix, and executes numerous operations over the encrypted components. To address this issue, we
propose efficient frequent pattern mining with ciphertext packing. By
adopting the packing method, our scheme will require fewer ciphertexts
and associated operations than P3CC, thus reducing both encryption
and calculation times. We have also optimized its implementation by
reusing previously produced results so as not to repeat calculations. Our
experimental evaluation shows that the proposed scheme runs 430 times
faster than P3CC, and uses 94.7 % less memory with 10,000 transactions
data.

Keywords: Ciphertext packing · Fully homomorphic encryption ·
Frequent pattern mining · Privacy preservation · Cloud computing

1 Introduction

In the present era of big data, demand is increasing for outsourcing both data
storage and calculations to the cloud. Although such outsourcing is convenient
for users, there are security and privacy issues. Private information could be
obtained maliciously by data "snooping" or covert monitoring. Thus, secure and
privacy-preserving outsourced calculation has become indispensable, regardless
of whether or not users trust the cloud.

In this paper, we focus on privacy-preserving data mining for outsourced
calculations [7]. Previous research on such data mining is classified into three
approaches: (i) protecting input privacy, (ii) protecting output privacy, and (iii)
cryptosystems. Protecting input privacy preserves the input data on the user

© Springer International Publishing AG 2016
G. Livraga et al. (Eds.): DPM and QASA 2016, LNCS 9963, pp. 181–195, 2016.
DOI: 10.1007/978-3-319-47072-6_12

side by abstraction, noise-addition or randomization [6,16,19,21], while protecting output privacy preserves mining results on the cloud side by either noise-addition or perturbation [3,4]. The third approach, i.e., cryptosystems, preserves privacy by executing mining algorithms on encrypted data [11,12]. Each approach has its advantages and disadvantages. While the computational costs of the input and output privacy approaches are smaller than those of cryptosystems, full input and output privacy cannot be guaranteed. Furthermore, mining result may become ambiguous when input or output privacy is used. Finally, cryptosystems require excessive computational time, albeit that they assure both secure computation and mining accuracy. Based on the above considerations, we chose to adopt a cryptosystem to assure the full privacy.

A fully homomorphic cryptosystem is one that handles unlimited numbers of multiplications and additions of ciphertexts. Gentry [8] proposed Fully Homomorphic Encryption (FHE), which has been widely adopted by many data-mining researches for statistical calculations [15], machine learning algorithms [9,13], and the frequent pattern mining [11,14].

However, these FHE applications suffer from the limitations of the computational resources such as memory and storage. They also take excessively long to execute because of large size ciphertexts and the significant number of associated operations. The data mining process itself also involves a high computational cost when handling large data sets. As a secure mining protocol, Liu et al. [14] proposed the P3CC frequent pattern mining scheme over FHE, which was implemented over DGHV integer-based FHE by van Dijk et al. [20]. It encrypts plaintexts component-wise in the item-transaction matrix data, and then applies addition or multiplication operation to each ciphertext individually. Therefore, the total number of ciphertexts increases linearly with the matrix size, which results in the excessive memory/storage usage, communication costs, and the operational costs for encrypted data.

To solve the above problems, it is essential to execute mining tasks with both a reduced size of ciphertext and fewer encrypted-data operations. In order to realize this, we adopt the polynomial Chinese Reminder Theorem (CRT) packing method proposed by Smart and Vercauteren [17,18] with the Ring Learning With Errors (RLWE)-based BGV scheme [5]. With the packing method, we are able to pack multiple plaintexts into a ciphertext, followed by a parallelization of its element-wise vector multiplication. In comparison with P3CC, this results in smaller ciphertexts overall and fewer operations.

Our contribution is threefold. (i) To the best of our knowledge, this is the first implementation of the frequent pattern mining constructed with the FHE packing method. (ii) Our algorithm is optimized to pack the components column-wise in the item-transaction matrix data to reduce the number of ciphertexts and associated operations. Here, we define N as the number of transactions (i.e., the number of rows in the item-transaction matrix), and ℓ as the slot size (i.e., a ciphertext packs ℓ components of an item-column). In our algorithm, the number of ciphertexts required to pack all the components of an item column decreases from N to $\lceil N/\ell \rceil$, and hence the number of operations over all ciphertexts also decreases from N to $\lceil N/\ell \rceil$. (iii) Both parallelization and caching technique are adopted to speed up the execution: parallelization for file reading/writing, encryptions and calculations for each support value for encrypted data, and caching the previous results of the element-wise vector multiplication. FHE requires numerous multiplications among ciphertexts during such a multiplicative process, thus caching technique will work effectively.

The rest of this paper is organized as follows. We review related work in Sect. 2, and then introduce the background to the RLWE-based FHE scheme and the P3CC protocol in Sect. 3. We propose our scheme for efficient frequent pattern mining in Sect. 4, followed by its experimental evaluation in Sect. 5. Lastly, we conclude this paper in Sect. 6.

2 Related Work

In this section, we discuss related research on data mining with cryptosystems. We then describe P3CC, which is the work most related to ours on frequent pattern mining.

Works on data mining with cryptosystems [11,12] is classified into two categories: multi-party computation (MPC), and homomorphic encryption (HE). In MPC, Kapoor et al. [12] proposed an algorithm for pattern mining that targets distributed database while preserving privacy by MPC. In HE, Mohammed et al. [11] proposed a secure comparison technique with FHE in the case of two-party association rule mining. They then showed that MPC is not suitable for association rule mining due to its storage, communication, and computational limitations.

The Privacy Preserving Protocol for Counting Candidates (P3CC) by Liu et al. [14] is the work that is most related to ours. Liu et al. employed an integer-based FHE [20] by van Dijk et al. It uses component-wise encryption on all the individual binary-represented components in the item-transaction matrix data. Liu et al. proposed α-pattern uncertainty for security in frequent pattern mining. This method maps items to meaningless symbols, and then adds dummy itemsets to prevent identification. The limitations of P3CC are its time complexity and the availability of computational resources, i.e., memory and storage. In addition, P3CC time complexity depends linearly on the number of transactions because of its component-wise encryption scheme. As for the execution time of P3CC, it takes from 1,000 to 10,000 s even with 5,000 transactions, with the minimum support ranging from 10 % to 60 % [14].

3 Preliminaries

In this section, we explain four algorithms that are used in latter sections: (i) the Apriori algorithm, which is one of the best-known frequent pattern mining algorithms, (ii) the P3CC algorithm, (iii) polynomial CRT packing, and (iv) the TotalSum algorithm for summing up all the elements of CRT-represented ciphertexts.

Trans. ID	Item Set
T1	{I1, I3, I4}
T2	{I3, I5, I6}
T3	{I2, I4, I5, I6}
T4	{I1, I2, I5}
T5	{I3, I6}
T6	{I1, I4, I6}

(a) original database

Items / Trans	I1	I2	I3	I4	I5	I6
T1	1	0	1	1	0	0
T2	0	0	1	0	1	1
T3	0	1	0	1	1	1
T4	1	1	0	0	1	0
T5	0	0	1	0	0	1
T6	1	0	0	1	0	1

(b) item-transaction matrix database

Fig. 1. Item-transaction database

3.1 Apriori Algorithm

Agrawal and Srikant [2] proposed the now well-known algorithm called Apriori for mining frequent patterns. The transaction database, which consists of a set of items such as in Fig. 1(a), can be mapped to the bit-represented item-transaction matrix shown in Fig. 1(b). We show both the formal model of frequent patterns (Definition 1) [1] and the Apriori procedure (Algorithm 1) [14].

Definition 1 (Frequent Patterns). *Let $I = \{i_1, i_2, ..., i_m\}$ be a set of m non-identical items, and let T be a set of transactions. Each transaction $t \in T$ has a set of items from I, i.e., t is a subset of I, with $t[k] = 1$ if t contains i_k, and $t[k] = 0$ otherwise. Let a pattern p be a subset of I. We say that a transaction t satisfies p, if and only if $t[k] = 1$ for all items i_k in p. The support of p is equal to the number of transactions in T that satisfy p. We say that a pattern is frequent if and only if its support is equal to or greater than a given minimum threshold called minSup.*

Firstly, the Apriori algorithm sets the frequent patterns of unit length, as L_1 by counting each item's support (lines 1–4). It then obtains all the frequent patterns in the iteration (lines 6–13).

Secondly, Apriori generates the length-2 candidate itemset C_2 from the frequent itemset L_1 (line 7), e.g., it generates $C_2 = \{\{a, b\}, \{b, c\}, \{a, c\}\}$ from $L_1 = \{\{a\}, \{b\}, \{c\}\}$. Thirdly, Apriori counts each length-2 pattern's support (lines 8–10) to obtain a new frequent pattern itemset L_2 by comparing with minSup (line 11), e.g., it obtains $L_2 = \{\{a, b\}, \{b, c\}\}$ if only the support of items $\{a, c\}$ is lower than minSup. Lastly, Apriori joins L_2 to the set A (line 12), followed by the execution of lines 6–13 repeatedly until no more candidates are generated.

Function *countSupport* calculates each support of candidate $c \in C_{i+1}$ by executing the element-wise AND operations over the item columns of c, followed by summing up all bits. For example, suppose we count the support of $c = \{\mathbf{a}, \mathbf{b}\}$, where $\mathbf{a} = (1, 0, 1, 1, 0)^T$ and $\mathbf{b} = (1, 1, 0, 1, 1)^T$ are vectors, each of whose elements represents whether the ith transaction has $\mathbf{a}$ or $\mathbf{b}$. We first generate $(1, 0, 0, 1, 0)$ by executing element-wise AND operations, and then obtain a support of 2 by counting all unitary bits.

Algorithm 1. Apriori($I, TDB, minSup$) [14]

Input: Itemset I; Transaction database TDB; Minimum threshold $minSup$;
Output: Frequent pattern itemset A;

1: **for each** *candidate* $c \in I$ **do**
2:     $c.support :=$ countSupport(c, TDB);
3: **end for**
4: $L_1 := \{c \in I \mid c.support \geq minSup\}$;
5: $A \leftarrow L_1$
6: **for** $(i = 1; \|L_i\| > 1; i \leftarrow i + 1)$ **do**
7:     $C_{i+1} :=$ generateCandidatePatterns(L_i);
8:     **for each** *candidate* $c \in C_{i+1}$ **do**
9:         $c.support :=$ countSupport(c, TDB);
10:     **end for**
11:     $L_{i+1} := \{c \in C_{i+1} \mid c.support \geq minSup\}$;
12:     $A \leftarrow L_{i+1}$;
13: **end for**
14: **return** A;

3.2 P3CC and α-Pattern Uncertainty

P3CC as proposed by Liu et al. [14] adopts the "α-pattern uncertainty" algorithm, which decreases the probability of information leakage to attackers during P3CC server-client communication. Since FHE does not support comparison over encrypted data, P3CC has to return intermediate results of frequent pattern mining to the client. This is to both decrypt and compare them when numeric comparisons are required between each itemset's support and $minSup$.

Along with Algorithm 1, P3CC works as follows. (i) As a preparation step, the client generates both public and secret keys to encrypt the database. Then, the client sends both the public key and the encrypted database to the server. (ii) The server calculates each item's support over the encrypted data (lines 1–3) followed by sending the encrypted results back to the client. Then, the client obtains frequent items by comparing with $minSup$ after decrypting the results (line 4). (iii) The client generates a new candidate itemset, and then sends it to the server (line 7). (iv) The sever calculates each pattern's support (lines 8–10) over the encrypted data, and then sends the encrypted results back to the client. (v) The client decrypts the results to obtain the counted supports, and then compares each itemset's support with $minSup$ over plaintexts (line 11). For each length-$(i + 1)$ itemset, iterate processes (iii), (iv), and (v).

During the multiple occurrences of server-client communication described above, there exists a security issue whereby the server can infer the important itemsets by snooping on the candidate patterns obtained from the client. To prevent this, α-pattern uncertainty limits the server's certainty about frequent patterns. In other words, α-pattern uncertainty lowers the probability of an attacker inferring frequent patterns by employing dummy patterns. In this paper, we assume the α-pattern uncertainty achieves a *Semi-honest* model, where the server tries to distinguish true patterns from dummy patterns while following the protocol. The α-pattern uncertainty ensures that the server cannot infer true patterns more than the probability α. We do not discuss the security analysis in detail since it is not our objective. See the work by Liu et al. for further details [14].

3.3   Polynomial CRT Packing over FHE

Smart and Vercauteren [17,18] proposed the CRT packing method over FHE. This allows multiple plaintexts to be packed into one ciphertext, which results in fewer ciphertexts. The following two steps generate a ciphertext in the polynomial CRT representation: (i) multiple plaintexts are encoded into a single polynomial, i.e., CRT packing, and (ii) encrypting the polynomial generates a ciphertext.

A CRT-represented ciphertext generated from ℓ plaintexts can be considered as a vector consisting of ℓ slots, each of which contains one plaintext. Multiplication over the CRT-represented ciphertexts is performed slot-by-slot in parallel, i.e., element-wise vector multiplication. See the work by Smart and Vercauteren [17,18] for the mathematical construction of polynomial CRT packing with FHE.

3.4   Total Summation over CRT-represented Ciphertext

With the polynomial CRT packing method [17,18], the FHE scheme needs to handle a ciphertext encrypted from multiple plaintexts, i.e., CRT-represented ciphertext. The following TotalSums proposed by Halevi and Shoup [10] is used for summing up all slots of a CRT-represented ciphertext. It takes a ciphertext encrypted from $(v_1, v_2, \ldots, v_n)$ as its input, and outputs a ciphertext that encrypts $(u, u, \ldots, u)$, where $u = \Sigma_{k=1}^{n} v_k$. The procedure is shown in Algorithm 2. See the work by Halevi and Shoup for detailed explanation of the algorithm and the implementation [10].

4   Efficient Frequent Pattern Mining Algorithm over FHE

In this section, we propose an efficient frequent pattern mining algorithm that uses Apriori over FHE. It has minimal time and space complexities, and uses the polynomial CRT packing method and our caching technique. To begin with, we prepare an item-transaction binary-represented matrix data as shown in Fig. 2. Each column and row contains transactions and items, respectively. We use N_{trans} as the number of transactions, N_{item} as the number of items, and ℓ as the slot size of a ciphertext.

Since P3CC [14] encrypts plaintexts individually for each components in the item-transaction matrix data (as circled with heavy lines in Fig. 2a), it uses significant storage space and accrues excessive operational costs for encrypted data. This is because component-wise encryption increases the total size of ciphertexts

---

Algorithm 2. TotalSums(v) [10]

Input: Encrypted array v;
Output: Encrypted array u;

1: $u := v$, $e := 1$, $n := \|v\|$;
2: $k := \text{numBits}(n)$; # number of bits in n, e.g., numBits(5)=3
3: **for** $(j := k - 2; j \geq 0; j \leftarrow j - 1)$ **do**
4:   $u \leftarrow u + (u \gg e)$; # $\gg$: rotate operation
5:   $e \leftarrow 2 \cdot e$;
6:   $b := \text{bit}_j(n)$; # j-th bit of n, with bit 0 of LSB
7:   **if** $(b = 1)$ **then**
8:     $u \leftarrow v + (u \gg e)$;
9:     $e \leftarrow e + 1$;
10:   **end if**
11: **end for**
12: **return** u

---

linearly with the matrix size. In particular, P3CC generates $N_{item} \times N_{trans}$ ciphertexts in total, which requires $\Sigma_{i=1}^{m} p_i N_{trans}^{i-1}$ times multiplications to count the supports of all patterns, where p_i is the number of length-i candidate itemsets, N_{trans}^{i-1} is the $(i-1)^{th}$ power of N_{trans}, and m is the maximum length of the candidate itemset.

To reduce the time and space complexities, it is essential to execute mining tasks with smaller ciphertexts and fewer associated operations. In order to achieve this, we tune Apriori over FHE in two ways. Firstly, we adopt polynomial CRT packing [17,18], which not only reduces the total ciphertext size, but also enables element-wise vector multiplication over ciphertexts in parallel, i.e., batching. Secondly, the execution of our scheme is accelerated by caching the previous results of the element-wise vector multiplication.

4.1   Polynomial CRT Packing and Batching

To reduce the time and space complexities of Apriori algorithm over FHE, polynomial CRT packing is adopted. We first port the framework of FHE from the P3CC integer-based DGHV scheme [20] to the RLWE-based BGV scheme [5], so that our scheme is able to handle the polynomial CRT packing. As in Sect. 3.3, an FHE scheme with packing generates a ciphertext in the polynomial CRT representation, which packs multiple plaintexts in the ciphertext slots.

To implement the packing method with Apriori, we choose to pack binary components column-by-column, where each column has N_{trans} components for all N_{items} columns and each ciphertext packs ℓ components of their components. That is, our scheme requires $\lceil N_{trans}/\ell \rceil$ ciphertexts to pack all N_{trans} components in one item-column as shown in Fig. 2(b). Here, when N_{trans} is indivisible by ℓ, its remaining r components are packed into another ciphertext along with $\ell - r$ dummy zero components, as shown in Fig. 3.

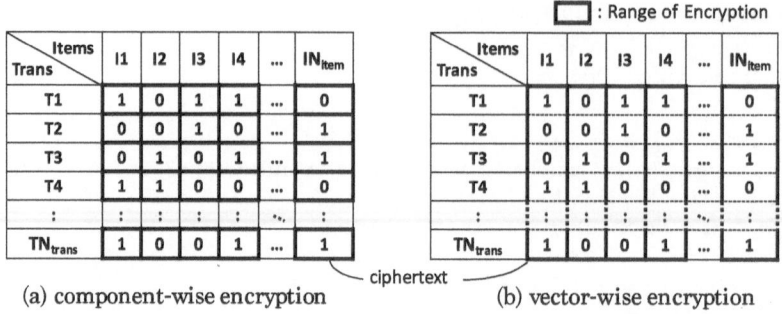

□ : Range of Encryption

(a) component-wise encryption   **(b)** vector-wise encryption

Fig. 2. Encryption strategy of item-transaction database

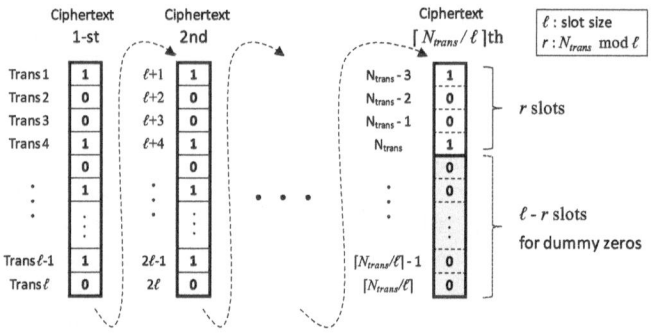

Fig. 3. Ciphertext-packing of item-column-components

With its polynomial CRT packing method, our scheme has two advantages. Firstly, the number of ciphertexts to represent all components in the database decreases from $N_{trans} \cdot N_{items}$ to $\lceil N_{trans}/\ell \rceil \cdot N_{items}$. Likewise, the costs of both memory/storage and communication between the client and the server decrease from $N_{trans} \cdot N_{items}$ to $\lceil N_{trans}/\ell \rceil \cdot N_{items}$, given that the space usage and communication cost arises from the ciphertext size. Secondly, the number of multiplications required to count the supports of all patterns decreases from $\Sigma_{i=1}^{m} p_i N_{trans}^{i-1}$ to $\Sigma_{i=1}^{m} p_i \lceil N_{trans}/\ell \rceil^{i-1}$, where p_i, N_{trans}^{i-1}, and m are defined above.

4.2 Optimization by Caching

We propose a caching technique to omit redundant operations when counting the support of each candidate in the Apriori algorithm with FHE. As described in Sect. 4.1, counting the support of each candidate requires $\Sigma_{i=1}^{m} p_i \lceil N_{trans}/\ell \rceil^{i-1}$ element-wise vector multiplications. In particular, with a length-$(i+1)$ candidate itemset $c = \{c_1, c_2, \ldots, c_{i+1}\}$, the operation $\otimes_{j=1}^{i+1} c_j$ is required for calculating its support, where $\otimes$ is the element-wise vector multiplication. For example, when we calculate the support of a length-4 candidate itemset $\{a, b, c, d\}$, element-wise vector multiplications of $a \otimes b \otimes c \otimes d$ are required. However, the supports

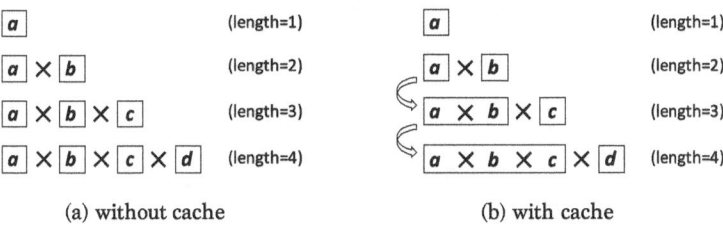

(a) without cache   (b) with cache

Fig. 4. Support calculation with caching technique.

of the length-3 candidate itemsets (i.e., $a \otimes b \otimes c$, $a \otimes b \otimes d$, $a \otimes c \otimes d$, and $b \otimes c \otimes d$) have been calculated before for the length-4 one $\{a,b,c,d\}$, because of the Apriori algorithm described in Sect. 3.1. To take the full advantage of this phenomena, we adopt a caching technique to reuse the previously calculated element-wise vector multiplication results.

During the execution of the $(i+1)^{th}$ iteration, we will reuse the cached result from the ith iteration. In the example above, our algorithm caches the results $a \otimes b \otimes c$, $a \otimes b \otimes d$, $a \otimes c \otimes d$, and $b \otimes c \otimes d$ with indexation by items when counting the supports for length-3 patterns, and reuse them in the next iteration for length-4, as shown in Fig. 4(b).

With the proposed caching technique, our algorithm requires only one time element-wise vector multiplication per support calculation in the ith iteration. As described in Sect. 4.1, the total number of element-wise vector multiplications decreases from $\Sigma_{i=1}^{m} p_i \lceil N_{trans}/\ell \rceil^{i-1}$ without caching to $\Sigma_{i=1}^{m} p_i \lceil N_{trans}/\ell \rceil$ with it, where p_i and m are defined at the beginning of Sect. 4. The server's total computational order is equal to the computational order of the support counting, which decreases from $\mathcal{O}(\lceil N_{trans}/\ell \rceil^{i-1})$ to $\mathcal{O}(\lceil N_{trans}/\ell \rceil)$.

Our new algorithm for counting supports with caching technique is shown in Algorithm 3. The caching technique works when the pattern length is greater than two. In addition, we adopt the TotalSums function described in Sect. 3.4 to sum up all elements, i.e., slots of the CRT-represented ciphertext.

5 Experimental Evaluation

In this section, we evaluate the effectiveness of both (i) adopting the packing scheme implemented with Apriori, and (ii) optimization by our caching technique. Furthermore, we confirm that our optimized scheme works acceptably with α-pattern uncertainty and relatively large data sizes.

The dataset we used for the experimental evaluations was one that was generated artificially by the IBM Quest Synthetic Data Generator[1]. This generator produces various patterns of datasets by changing the parameters $\{T, I, N, D, L\}$, where T is the average length of items per transaction, I is the average length of the maximal pattern, N is the number of different items in a

---

[1] http://fimi.ua.ac.be/data/.

Algorithm 3. CountSupport by FHE with Cache $(ETDB, C, CD)$

Input: Encrypted transaction database $ETDB$; Candidate itemsets C;
   Associative array for caching data CD;
Output: Support array of candidate itemsets S; Updated CD;

 1: $S := \emptyset$;
 2: **for each** candidate itemset $\boldsymbol{c} \in C$ **do**
 3:   $i := \|\boldsymbol{c}\|$;
 4:   $itemID := \boldsymbol{c}[i-1]$; # $i-1$: last element
 5:   $\boldsymbol{c'} := \boldsymbol{c}[0, 1, \ldots, i-2]$; # length-$(i-1)$ itemset
 6:   $\boldsymbol{col} := \text{getItemColumnfromETDBbyID}(itemID)$;
 7:   $hashKey := \text{setHashKeyfromItemset}(\boldsymbol{c'})$;
 8:   $\boldsymbol{cache} := \text{getCachedDatabyKey}(CD, hashKey)$;
 9:   $\boldsymbol{res} := \text{elementwiseVectorMultiply}(\boldsymbol{cache}, \boldsymbol{col})$; # $\boldsymbol{cache} \cdot \boldsymbol{col}$
 10:   $support := \text{TotalSums}(\boldsymbol{res})$; # sum up all elements of $\boldsymbol{res}$
 11:   $newHashKey := \text{makeNewHashKey}(\boldsymbol{c})$;
 12:   $\text{cacheNewData}(\text{ makePair}(newHashKey, \boldsymbol{res}))$;
 13:   $S.\text{append}(support)$;
 14: **end for**
 15: **return** S, CD;

---

transaction, D is the number of transactions, and L is the number of possible frequent patterns that can be generated.

In addition, our scheme is implemented both with the public FHE library HElib[2] that supports the BGV RLWE cryptosystem [5], and with the NTL mathematical library[3] over the GMP multiple-precision arithmetic library[4]. The GMP is used for the long integer arithmetic and the NTL is for handling polynomials over the integers. HElib builds an FHE scheme with parameters $\{p, r, k, l, c, w\}$, where p^r denotes the plaintext space, k is the security parameter, l is the number of levels in the modulus chain, c is the number of columns in the key-switching matrices, and w is the Hamming weight of the secret key.

The platform used in the evaluation consists of two machines: a client with an Intel Xeon CPU E5-2643 v3 running at 3.4 GHz and with 512 GB of memory, and a server with an Intel Xeon CPU E7-8880 v3 running at 2.3 GHz and with 1 TB of memory, both of which are equipped with CentOS6.6.

For comparison with the component-wise encryption scheme of P3CC, we implemented our method over the RLWE-based FHE, and then use it in the following evaluations. As for the HElib parameters, we set $\{p, r, k, l, c, w\}$ to $\{2, 14, 80, 10, 3, 64\}$ in the following evaluations. The plaintext space 2^{14} is higher than the largest value of D we use, the level $l = 10$ is to enable at least four multiplications per ciphertexts, and k, w, and c are default values for the security and the key-switching matrix.

---

[2] http://shaih.github.io/HElib/index.html.
[3] http://www.shoup.net/ntl/.
[4] https://gmplib.org/.

5.1   Experiment with Ciphertext Packing

To evaluate the effectiveness of our scheme with the ciphertext packing (i.e., a vector-wise encryption scheme), we compared it with our implementation of P3CC (i.e., a component-wise encryption scheme), from the viewpoints of both execution time and maximum memory usage. We choose the small dataset, T10I6N50D100L1k, for the comparative experiment, since the component-wise encryption scheme over the RLWE-based FHE takes a relatively long time to run.

Figure 5 shows the execution times of both the component-wise and the vector-wise encryption schemes with variation of the minimum support. We first ran the experiment on a single thread (Fig. 5a), and then adopted parallelization by multi-thread file reading/writing, encryption, and calculation of each pattern's support (Fig. 5b). The client executed file writing and encryption on 12 threads, and the server executed file reading and calculations on 24 threads.

As shown in Fig. 5(a), compared to the component-wise encryption scheme, our vector-wise one is 13.4 times faster with 10 % minsup, and 7.26 times faster on average over the range 10 % $\leq$ minsup $\leq$ 40 %. With parallelization, our scheme is 14.9 times faster with 10 % minsup, and 7.97 times faster on average, as shown in Fig. 5(b). The maximum memory usage decreases by 90.7 %.

5.2   Optimization by Caching

To evaluate our optimized scheme with both ciphertext packing and the caching technique, we compare it with the non-optimized scheme, i.e., only with ciphertext packing, which was evaluated in Sect. 5.1. We used the same dataset to compare them for the same criteria.

Figure 6 shows the execution times of both the optimized and non-optimized schemes with variation of the minimum support. We ran these on a single thread (Fig. 6a), and then on multiple threads (Fig. 6b). The number of threads and the target of multi-threading were the same as those of the evaluations in Sect. 5.1.

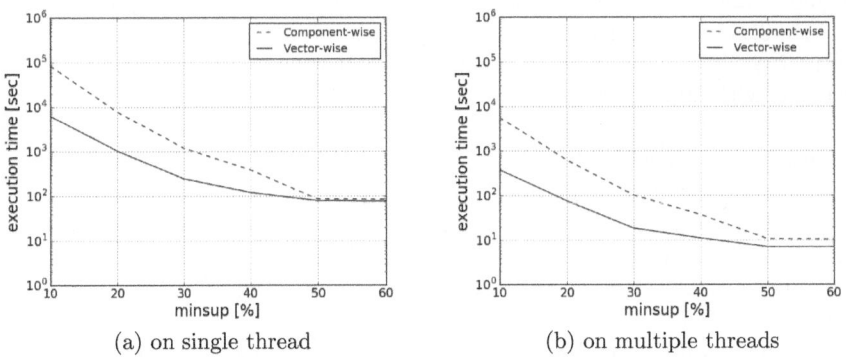

(a) on single thread   (b) on multiple threads

Fig. 5. Comparison of packing and non-packing schemes

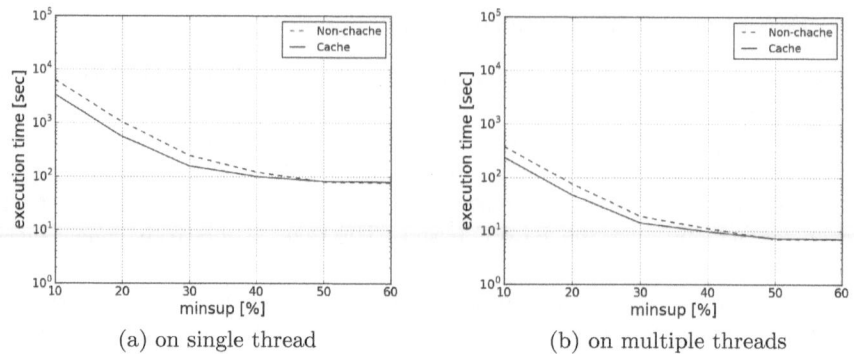

(a) on single thread   (b) on multiple threads

Fig. 6. Comparison of caching and non-caching schemes

As shown in Fig. 6(a), compared to the non-cached scheme, our scheme is 1.86 times faster with 10 % minsup, and 1.62 times faster on average over the range 10 % $\leq$ minsup $\leq$ 40 %. With parallelization, our scheme is 1.58 times faster with 10 % minsup, and 1.42 times faster on average, as shown in Fig. 6(b). The maximum memory usage decreases by 14.5 %. In total, our optimized scheme is 23.6 times faster, and the memory usage decreases by 92.1 % with 10 % minsup in comparison with the multi-threaded component-wise encryption scheme in Sect. 5.1.

5.3   Security and Data Size

We test the scalability of our optimized scheme (i.e., with packing and caching) for (i) the size of the data, and (ii) α-pattern uncertainty security as described in Sect. 3.2. The latter determines the server's uncertainty over true patterns in the candidate itemset by adding dummy patterns.

We evaluate the first case by measuring the execution times and memory usages of both our optimized scheme and the component-wise encryption scheme, while varying the transaction data size. We first set the dataset to T10I6N50D1kL1k, and then vary the parameter D from 1k to 10k as shown in Fig. 7(a). The experiment is multi-threaded with the same conditions as in Sect. 5.1, with 20 % minsup.

As shown in Fig. 7(a), the difference in the execution times between the schemes increases with the transaction size. This result is attributed to the number of ciphertexts generated in each scheme by the ciphertext packing, as described in Sect. 4.1. Compared to the component-wise encryption scheme, our scheme is 430 times faster with $D = 10k$, and 180 times faster on average over the range 1k $\leq D \leq$ 10k. In addition, the maximum memory usage of our scheme decreases by 94.7 %.

We then evaluate the second case by measuring both the execution time and the memory usage of our optimized scheme, with α-pattern uncertainty as described in Sect. 3.2. The parameter α is the probability of inferring the true

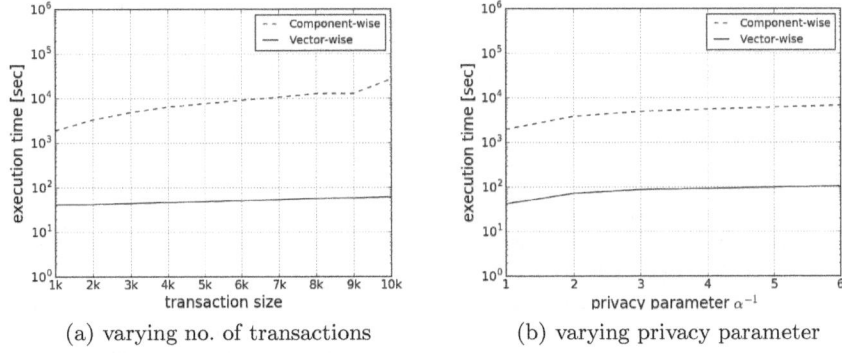

(a) varying no. of transactions   (b) varying privacy parameter

Fig. 7. Optimized scheme with security and relatively large data sizes

patterns in the candidate set with dummy patterns. In other words, if as α increases, the security becomes weaker. Therefore, we can consider α^{-1} to be a privacy parameter. We first set the dataset to T10I6N50D1kL1k and α^{-1} to 1 (i.e., no dummy patterns), then vary the parameter α^{-1} from 1 to 6 as shown in Fig. 7(b). Compared to the component-wise encryption scheme, our scheme is 56.8 times faster on average over the range $1 \leq \alpha^{-1} \leq 6$. In addition, the maximum memory usage decreases by 82.8 %. There is a trade-off between the execution time and the security due to the additional calculations for the dummy patterns.

6 Conclusions and Future Work

We proposed an efficient and secure frequent pattern mining by adopting both the polynomial CRT packing method and a caching technique. Our experimental results shows that the proposed scheme has lower time and space complexities in comparison with those of the previous P3CC scheme. When the transaction size is 10,000, our optimized scheme is 430 times faster and the memory usage decreases by 94.7 %.

Future work will include attempting to reduce the communication costs by comparing larger and smaller ciphertexts. To achieve this, bootstrapping procedures will have to be implemented, since such comparisons require numerous homomorphic operations. Moreover, we will consider a new security idea that should work for the aforementioned comparative scenario.

Acknowledgements. This work was supported by the CREST program of the Japan Science and Technology Agency. We would like to thank Mr. Takumi Takahashi, who implemented our scheme experimentally.

References

1. Agrawal, R., Imieliński, T., Swami, A.: Mining association rules between sets of items in large databases. In: ACM SIGMOD record, vol. 22, pp. 207–216. ACM (1993)
2. Agrawal, R., Srikant, R., et al.: Fast algorithms for mining association rules. In: Proceedings of the 20th international conference on very large data bases, VLDB, vol. 1215, pp. 487–499 (1994)
3. Atzori, M., Bonchi, F., Giannotti, F., Pedreschi, D.: Anonymity preserving pattern discovery. VLDB J. **17**(4), 703–727 (2008). Springer
4. Bhaskar, R., Laxman, S., Smith, A., Thakurta, A.: Discovering frequent patterns in sensitive data. In: Proceedings of the 16th ACM SIGKDD International Conference on Knowledge Discovery and Data Mining, pp. 503–512. ACM (2010)
5. Brakerski, Z., Gentry, C., Vaikuntanathan, V.: (leveled) fully homomorphic encryption without bootstrapping. In: Proceedings of the 3rd Innovations in Theoretical Computer Science Conference, pp. 309–325. ACM (2012)
6. Evfimievski, A., Gehrke, J., Srikant, R.: Limiting privacy breaches in privacy preserving data mining. In: Proceedings of the 22th ACM SIGMOD-SIGACT-SIGART Symposium on Principles of Database Systems, pp. 211–222. ACM (2003)
7. Gellman, R.: Privacy in the clouds: risks to privacy and confidentiality from cloud computing. In: Proceedings of the World Privacy Forum, 23 February 2012
8. Gentry, C.: Fully homomorphic encryption using ideal lattices. In: Proceedings of the 41th Annual ACM Symposium on Theory of Computing, pp. 169–178. ACM (2009)
9. Graepel, T., Lauter, K., Naehrig, M.: ML Confidential: machine learning on encrypted data. In: Kwon, T., Lee, M.-K., Kwon, D. (eds.) ICISC 2012. LNCS, vol. 7839, pp. 1–21. Springer, Heidelberg (2013)
10. Halevi, S., Shoup, V.: Algorithms in HElib. In: Garay, J.A., Gennaro, R. (eds.) CRYPTO 2014. LNCS, vol. 8616, pp. 554–571. Springer, Heidelberg (2014). doi:10.1007/978-3-662-44371-2_31
11. Kaosar, M.G., Paulet, R., Yi, X.: Fully homomorphic encryption based two-party association rule mining, vol. 76, pp. 1–15. Elsevier (2012)
12. Kapoor, V., Poncelet, P., Trousset, F., Teisseire, M.: Privacy preserving sequential pattern mining in distributed databases. In: Proceedings of the 15th ACM international conference on Information and knowledge management, pp. 758–767. ACM (2006)
13. Khedr, A., Gulak, G., Vaikuntanathan, V.: Shield: Scalable homomorphic implementation of encrypted data-classifiers. In: IEEE Transactions on Computers. IEEE (2015)
14. Liu, J., Li, J., Xu, S., Fung, B.C.M.: Secure outsourced frequent pattern mining by fully homomorphic encryption. In: Madria, S., Hara, T. (eds.) DaWaK 2015. LNCS, vol. 9263, pp. 70–81. Springer, Heidelberg (2015). doi:10.1007/978-3-319-22729-0_6
15. Naehrig, M., Lauter, K., Vaikuntanathan, V.: Can homomorphic encryption be practical? In: Proceedings of the 3rd ACM Workshop on Cloud Computing Security Workshop, pp. 113–124. ACM (2011)
16. Qiu, L., Li, Y., Wu, X.: Protecting business intelligence and customer privacy while outsourcing data mining tasks. Knowl. Inf. Syst. **17**(1), 99–120 (2009). Springer
17. Smart, N.P., Vercauteren, F.: Fully homomorphic encryption with relatively small key and ciphertext sizes. In: Nguyen, P.Q., Pointcheval, D. (eds.) PKC 2010. LNCS, vol. 6056, pp. 420–443. Springer, Heidelberg (2010). doi:10.1007/978-3-642-13013-7_25

18. Smart, N.P., Vercauteren, F.: Fully homomorphic simd operations. Des. Codes Crypt. **71**, 57–81 (2014). Springer
19. Tai, C.H., Yu, P.S., Chen, M.S.: k-support anonymity based on pseudo taxonomy for outsourcing of frequent itemset mining. In: Proceedings of the 16th ACM SIGKDD International Conference on Knowledge Discovery and Data Mining, pp. 473–482. ACM (2010)
20. Dijk, M., Gentry, C., Halevi, S., Vaikuntanathan, V.: Fully homomorphic encryption over the integers. In: Gilbert, H. (ed.) EUROCRYPT 2010. LNCS, vol. 6110, pp. 24–43. Springer, Heidelberg (2010). doi:10.1007/978-3-642-13190-5_2
21. Wang, Y., Wu, X.: Approximate inverse frequent itemset mining: Privacy, complexity, and approximation. In: 5th IEEE International Conference on Data Mining (ICDM), pp. 482–489. IEEE (2005)

Isabelle Modelchecking for Insider Threats

Florian Kammüller$^{(\boxtimes)}$

Middlesex University, London, UK
f.kammueller@mdx.ac.uk

Abstract. The Isabelle Insider framework formalises the technique of social explanation for modeling and analysing Insider threats in infrastructures including physical and logical aspects. However, the abstract Isabelle models need some refinement to provide sufficient detail to explore attacks constructively and understand how the attacker proceeds. The introduction of mutable states into the model leads us to use the concepts of Modelchecking within Isabelle. Isabelle can simply accommodate classical CTL type Modelchecking. We integrate CTL Modelchecking into the Isabelle Insider framework. A running example of an IoT attack on privacy motivates the method throughout and illustrates how the enhanced framework fully supports realistic modeling and analysis of IoT Insiders.

1 Introduction and Overview

Insider threats pose a serious problem for security and privacy that is inherently hard to control since the attack comes from a user within the security perimeter. Techniques to tackle these challenges need to be application oriented and yet thorough. We propose in this paper to further explore the rigorous modeling and analysis of Insider attacks including infrastructures based on logics: we extend the Isabelle Insider framework with Modelchecking thus combining the practical advantages of policy invalidation with mathematical proof and expressive models. We validate our extension on a case study of a privacy attack on the IoT performed by an Insider.

The original invalidation idea [18] uses the advantages of Modelchecking to find attacks by Insiders on infrastructures. Starting from an invalidated policy, the attempt to modelcheck fails producing an attack vector. The Isabelle Insider framework [20] implements the process of social explanation inspired by Max Weber's work on sociology to model and analyse Insider threats. This framework is a general tool to integrate logical rigour and automated reasoning at the infrastructure level validated on major Insider patterns identified by the CERT Insider guide. Preliminary applications of the Isabelle Insider framework, for example, to Insider threats in the IoT [16] or to Insider threats in aviation [15], show that the framework is capable of expressing realistic case studies. However, to support a systematic identification of detailed attacks from known general attack cases or patterns, more details from the context of the application, e.g. the physical infrastructure, need to be integrated into the model.

© Springer International Publishing AG 2016
G. Livraga et al. (Eds.): DPM and QASA 2016, LNCS 9963, pp. 196–210, 2016.
DOI: 10.1007/978-3-319-47072-6_13

The integration of attack trees into the Isabelle Insider framework [14,24] is an important first step to exemplify attack vectors. Attack trees refine an attack case into more detailed sub-attacks which are then successors in the attack tree but they do not provide clues how to find these refinements. For a given attack vector, however, we need a more systematic way to explore the infrastructure graph with its associated actors, policies and credentials, to constructively identify the Insider attack.

In this paper, we revisit the invalidation approach by providing a substantial extension of the Isabelle Insider framework to accommodate Modelchecking of infrastructures. Our contribution is an extension of the Insider framework by a notion of graph-based state and state-transition. In addition, we embed Kripke-structures and the temporal logic CTL into Isabelle to analyse Insider attacks by Modelchecking. Thereby, we finally provide the missing link of the Isabelle Insider framework to the invalidation approach. The extended framework is motivated by and illustrated on an IoT Insider attack.

2   Background

In formal analysis of technical scenarios, the motivation of actors and the resulting behaviour of humans is often not considered because the complexity is beyond usual formalisms. The Isabelle Insider framework [20] provides expressiveness to model infrastructures, policies, and humans while keeping up the level of proof automation. In this section, we give a short summary of this framework for modeling and analysing Insider attacks. A detailed technical introduction is given in [20] and the sources are online [1]. We also present the IoT case study in the current section.

2.1   Social Explanation in Isabelle

The Isabelle Insider framework [20] is based on a logical process of sociological explanation [12] inspired by Weber's *Grundmodell*, depicted in Fig. 1, to explain Insider threats by moving between societal level (macro) and individual actor level (micro).

The standard example to illustrate the process of macro-micro-macro transitions in the spirit of Max Weber is to explain the relationship between 'protestant ethic' and 'the spirit of capitalism'. Protestantism has lead to changes in familial socialization, a 'familial revolution' (macro to micro-level). The change of educational style employed by protestant parents (micro-level) has equipped their children with 'strong internalized achievement drives'. This has created the spirit of capitalism back on the collective, the macro-level, and has lead to the spread of a new type of actor, the entrepreneur.

In the application of the steps (a–c) of the logic of explanation, the insider's move over the 'tipping' point is seen as (a), the actual Insider attack as step (b) and the damages caused by the attack as step (c) in Fig. 1.

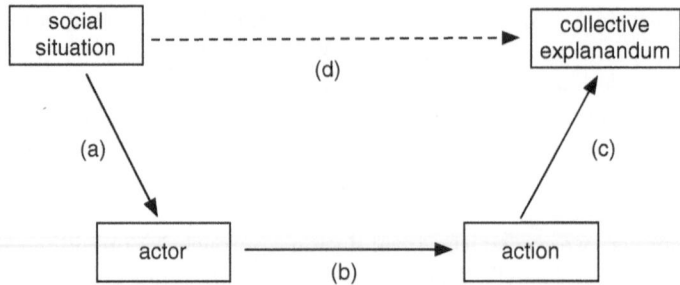

Fig. 1. The 'Grundmodell' of sociological explanation [10]: a macro-micro-macro-transition explains sociological phenomena by breaking down the global facts from the macro level (a) onto a more refined local view of individual actors at the micro-level (b). Finally those micro-steps are generalized and lifted back onto the macro-level (c) to explain the global phenomenon.

The interpretation into a logic of explanation is formalized in Isabelle's Higher Order Logic. This Isabelle formalisation constitutes a tool for proving security properties using the assistance of the semi-automated theorem prover [20]. Isabelle/HOL is an interactive proof assistant based on Higher Order Logic (HOL). Applications can be specified as so-called object-logics in HOL providing reasoning capabilities for examples but also for the analysis of the meta-theory. Examples reach from pure mathematics [17] to software engineering [13]. An object-logic contains new types, constants and definitions. These items reside in a theory file, *e.g.*, the file `Insider.thy` contains the object-logic for social explanation of Insider threats (see [1,20]). This Isabelle Insider framework is a *conservative extension* of HOL. This means that our object logic does not introduce new axioms and hence guarantees consistency.

The micro-level and macro-level of the sociological explanation give rise to a two-layered model in Isabelle, reflecting first the psychological disposition and motivation of actors and second the graph of the infrastructure where nodes are locations with actors associated to them. Security policies can be defined over the agents, their properties, and the infrastructure graph; properties can be proved mechanically with Isabelle. We demonstrate the application of the Isabelle Insider framework in Sect. 3.1 on an IoT Insider case study presented next.

2.2   Challenge IoT Insider

The Internet-of-Things (IoT) denotes the combination of physical objects with a virtual representation in the Internet. It consists not only of humans but a variety of "Things" as well. From a security and privacy perspective, at this point the IoT could be perceived as a hopeless case since all prevention aspects of security (confidentiality, integrity, and availability) are inherently weak, and unwanted tracking and monitoring throws the doors wide open to privacy attacks. Insiders using the IoT represent a significant challenge for enterprises. The paper [23] assesses this problem in detail, and outlines several vectors through which insiders may attack their employers. The structure of [23] draws on the VERIS 4A approach to define cyber attacks [27]. This includes understanding the *assets* at risk in the attack, the *actors* (or insiders) that launch the attack, the *attributes* (or impact) of the attack on the asset, and the specific *actions* involved in the attack. Below, we present two of the attack vectors (AVs) from [23] in the broad context of the VERIS approach; the first one perpetrated by a malicious insider (MI) and the second by an unintentional insider (UI) threat. They give a gist of Insider attack cases and the informality of their description. The former one MI-A4 is used as a basis for modeling and analysis throughout this paper in the form of the "Employee Blackmail" case as presented below.

MI-AV4: Using the storage system on a smart device, the insider is able to copy sensitive data (*e.g.*, IP or files) from the organisation's computers to the device and remove it from the enterprise. Bluetooth or NFC may be preferred for this attack as organisations now tend to monitor USB connections. This attack is possible with any IoT device with a storage capability.

UI-AV7: As a result of improperly configured or inadequately protected insider smart devices (*e.g.*, a smart-watch and a paired smartphone), the communications channel between them is compromised by a malicious third-party. This party then gathers enterprise data via the notifications, schedules, messages synchronised across devices. Further detail on such attacks on wearables can be found in [25]. We note that this attack could be conducted by another insider as well. This attack is possible with any device with a notification and storage capability.

2.3 Example – Employee Blackmail

The insider in this case is an employee in the IT department of a manufacturing company. He has received a formal warning from the CEO because there had been reports that the employee had abused colleagues. This warning has been contrived by the CEO himself who had an extramarital liaison with one of the employees with whom the insider had been flirting with. Following that, the IT employee heard rumours that he might be dismissed, which constituted the precipitating event that made him an insider: he planned his revenge.

From a report by an online security blog, the Bitdefender Research Team [4], the insider knew that it was possible to eavesdrop on and intercept communications between a smart-watch and a smartphone. The vulnerability was described in some detail on the blog. So, when the CEO purchased a smart-watch paired with his smartphone, the insider then exploited the vulnerability using additional methods found on hacking forums. He could move freely in the offices and could thus get into close range to collect data communicated between the CEO's smartphone and smart-watch. Although the communicated data has been encrypted before being transmitted via the Bluetooth protocol, the encryption used a 6-digit PIN code as a key in addition to data obfuscation (adding redundant "padding" to the clear text). Using publicly available decryption algorithms, the insider was thus able to get the key information.

Once the encryption was broken, the Insider could use this credential to collect data on incoming phone calls, SMS and emails, and personal and work related calendar. Finally, the insider blackmailed the CEO with the stolen information that also implied the CEO's liaison with a colleague: he threatened to show it to his wife and children unless he would receive a large severance package and good references. The 4As for this case are as follows:

- *Assets*: Sensitive company and personal information;
- *Actors*: Malicious insider;
- *Attributes*: Unauthorised data access then used for blackmail and fraud; and
- *Actions*: Attack Vector UI-AV7 (where an insider is the perpetrator).

This case highlights a key weakness in IoT devices, i.e., the limited security features with these devices and a clever attack building on personal knowledge helped by current reports and malicious Web forums.

3   IoT Case Study in Isabelle Insider Framework

3.1   Infrastructure Graph and Policies

We now present the formalisation of the 'Employee blackmail' in the Isabelle Insider framework. Isabelle sources of this case study are available [1]. For the application to the office scenario, we only model two identities, **Boss** and **Employee** representing an employee and his boss. The actors that are legal participants of the scenario are summarized in the following set of office actors as a locale definition **office_actors**. The full Isabelle/HOL syntax for a locale definition uses **fixes** and **defines** sections but in all subsequent definitions we omit these and also drop the types for conciseness of the exposition. The double quotes ''s'' create a string in Isabelle/HOL;

```
fixes office_actors :: identity set
defines office_actors_def: office_actors ≡ {''Boss''}
```

In a similarly simplified abstraction, we consider the offices architecture as a simple graph having three locations: employee's office, boss office, and smartphone defined as locale definitions and summarized in the set **office_locations**.

```
sphone ≡ Location 2
boss0 ≡ Location 1
employee0 ≡ Location 0
office_locations ≡ { employee0 , boss0, sphone }
```

As the topology of the infrastructure, we define the following graph where the actors Boss and Employee reside in their respective offices. A graph is quite naturally given as a set of nodes of locations and the actors residing at certain locations are specified by a function associating lists of nodes with the locations.

```
ex_graph ≡  Lgraph {(boss0, employee0), (employee0, sphone)}
            (λ x. if x = boss0 then [''Boss'']
                else (if x = employee0 then [''Employee''] else []))
```

In an infrastructure, the actors can have credentials like PINs or they can have roles. We define the assignment of the credentials as predicate over actors. These predicates are true for actors that have these credentials. For the office scenario, the credentials express that the office actor **Boss** possess the PIN for the encryption to the smartphone.

```
ex_creds ≡ (λ x. if x = Actor ''Boss'' then has (x,''PIN'') else True)
```

Similarly, the locations can have features attached to them, like locks. The possible states of the smart phone are *encrypted* or *cracked*. The Isabelle Insider framework provides an additional predicate **isin** that checks the value of a location against string values, here the location **sphone** against the string values ''encrypted'' or ''cracked''. The following **ex_locks** defines the smart phone to be encrypted.

```
ex_locs ≡ (λ x. if x = sphone then (isin x ''encrypted'') else True))
```

Changing the position of the sphone to **cracked**, i.e., using the PIN of the phone to decypher messages, corresponds to being able to perform a **put** action in the boss's office. The global policy is thus 'no one except the boss can put anything in the boss's office':

```
global_policy I a ≡  a ∉ office_actors ⟶
                     ¬(enables I boss0 (Actor a) put)
```

To guarantee this global policy, local policies need to be defined accordingly. These local policies are attached to locations in the organization's graph using a function that maps each location to the set of the policies valid in this location. The policies are again pairs: the first element of these pairs are predicates over actors specifying necessary conditions on actors; the second elements are sets of actions that are authorized in this location for actors authenticated by the predicates. In the following definition of local policies for each node in the office scenario, we additionally include parameters **G**, **ts** and **ls** to refer to the graph, the actors' credentials, and the locations' features. The predicate @$_G$ checks whether an actor is at a given location in the graph G.

```
local_policies G ts ls ≡
 (λ x.  if x = employee0 then {(λ y. True,{get, put, move}) }
        else (if x = boss0 then {((λ y. has (y, ''PIN'')), { put}),
                                 (λ y. True, {move})}
            else (if x = sphone then
                    {((λ y. (∃ n. (n @_G boss0) ∧ Actor n = x) ∧
                    ls sphone = isin sphone ''cracked'',  {get, put}))}
                 else {})))
```

This policy expresses that any actor can move to the employee's and the boss's office but places the following restrictions on the boss's one.

put: to perform a **put** action, i.e., put the PIN and thus crack the phone, an actor must have the PIN;

move: to perform a **get** or **put** action at location sphone, i.e., intercept its messages, an actor must be at the position **boss0**, be at position **boss0**, i.e., in the boss's office, and **sphone** must be in state **cracked**.

Although this policy abstracts from the smart watch, and a few other technical details, it contains the essential features of the 'Employee blackmail' scenario. The smart watch and the communication between the watch and the phone is seen in this abstraction as part of the smart phone. The main reason for this coarse abstraction is the conciseness of the exposition in this paper and the fact that PIN and encryption are shared parameters of the combined smart phone-watch system.

The graph, credentials, and features are plugged together with the policy into the infrastructure **Office_scenario**.

```
Office_scenario ≡ Infrastructure ex_graph
                  (local_policies ex_graph ex_creds ex_locs)
                  ex_creds ex_locs
```

3.2   Analysis of Security and Privacy Properties

Note, that all the above definitions have been implemented as local definitions using the locale keywords **fixes** and **defines** [21]. Thus they are accessible whenever the locales **scenarioOffice** is invoked but are not axioms that could endanger consistency. We now also make use of the possibility of locales to define local assumptions. This is very suitable in this context since we want to emphasize that the following formulas are not general facts or axiomatic rules but are assumptions we make in order to explore the validity of the infrastructure's global policy. The first assumption provides that the precipitating event has occurred which leads to the second assumption that provides that Employee can act as an insider:

```
assumes Employee_precipitating_event: tipping_point(astate ''Employee'')
assumes Insider_Employee: Insider ''Employee'' {''Boss''}
```

The above definitions and assumptions provide the model for the Employee blackmail Insider attack. We can now state theorems about the security of the model and interactively prove them in our Isabelle/HOL framework. We first prove a sanity check on the model by validating the infrastructure for the "normal" case. For the boss as an office actor, everything is fine: the global policy does hold. The following is an Isabelle/HOL theorem **ex_inv** that can be proved automatically followed by the proof script of its interactive proof. The proof is achieved by locally unfolding the definitions of the scenario, *e.g.*, **Office_scenario_def** and applying the simplifier:

```
lemma ex_inv: global_policy Office_scenario ''Boss''
  by (simp add: Office_scenario_def global_policy_def office_actors_def)
```

However, since the `Employee` is at tipping point, he will ignore the global policy. This insider threat can now be formalised as an invalidation of the global company policy for ''`Employee`'' in the following "attack" theorem named `ex_inv1`:

```
theorem ex_inv1:  ¬ global_policy Office_scenario ''Employee''
```

The proof of this theorem consists of a few simple steps largely supported by automated tactics. Thus `Employee` can get access to the data and blackmail the boss. The attack is proved above as an Isabelle/HOL theorem. Applying logical analysis, we thus exhibit that under the given assumptions the organisation's model is vulnerable to an insider.

This analysis follows closely the analysis of Insider attack patterns, like the Entitled independent [20], and applications to Airplane safety and security. The formalization and proofs are very similar. This overall procedure uses the strong assumption that the employee can impersonate the boss thus being able to provide all credentials and act like the boss. The attack stays abstract without explaining in detail how the employee finds the means to get hold of the PIN that then enables him to crack the smart phone. For a more refined approach we would like to be able to demonstrate how it is possible that the employee finds the PIN and breaks the encoding of the smart phone communication with the smart watch.

4   Extensions of Sociological Explanation to State Change

The original approach of invalidation of a global policy based on local policies of infrastructure scenarios [18] uses the idea of Modelchecking: the attempt to prove a security property fails but provides a trace of steps in the infrastructure leading to a state in which the property is violated but more importantly providing a refined attack trace providing detailed steps leading to the attack.

4.1   Refined Attack Scenario

The scenario representing the office in danger, has a graph in which the actor Employee is in the boss's office rather than his own.

```
ex_graph' ≡  Lgraph {(boss0, employee0), (employee0, sphone)}
              (λ x. if x = boss0 then [''Boss'', ''Employee'']
                  else (if x = employee0 then [] else []))
```

The credentials of the actors encode now that the employee has the PIN.

```
ex_creds' ≡ (λ x. if x = Actor ''Boss'' then has (x,''PIN'')
                  else (if x = Actor ''Employee'' then has (x,''PIN'')
                  else True))
```

The location features' settings now encode that the smart phone is cracked.

```
ex_locs' ≡ (λ x. if x = sphone then (isin x ''cracked'') else True))
```

The local policies stay the same as before but we use the updated graph and location settings when re-defining the scenario.

```
Office_in_danger ≡ Infrastructure ex_graph'
                   (local_policies ex_graph' ex_creds' ex_locs')
                   ex_creds' ex_locs'
```

Analysing this new scenario, we can prove that – as before – the insider attack by employee is possible, i.e., the global policy does not hold.

```
¬ global_policy Office_in_danger ''Employee''
```

Note, however, that in this changed infrastructure, the proof is possible without invoking the Insider assumption for Employee. In fact, in this changed infrastructure the employee has already managed – using his privileges as an insider – to get hold of the necessary credentials and use them to manipulate the smart devices and their communication.

The extension that we propose here is to define a notion of state transition between those different states office_scenario and office_in_danger represented by the respective infrastructure graphs. In introducing the extension to state transition, we will get the benefits of the invalidation approach to Insider attacks that lies in discovering attacks by changing the models – here the infrastructures.

4.2   Infrastructure Graph State Transition

At this point, we have seen that the Isabelle Insider framework allows to model and analyse the IoT scenario by using the standard methodology. However, we have also seen that a detailed analysis of the existing and the changed policies necessitates to change to scenario Office_in_danger. This is a scenario that we have extracted from an actual insider attack. How can we ensure that there are no other scenarios that would invalidate the new policy?

The approach taken in the Isabelle Insider framework explores the possible behaviours of actors by a logical exploration of the enables predicate. This exploration starts from one specific infrastructure. As we have seen in this case study, we can model different scenarios by adapting the infrastructure. In the remainder of this section, we want to sketch an extension of the Isabelle Insider framework that generalizes this approach.

We introduce a relation on infrastructures as an inductive predicate called state_transition and introduce the syntactic infix notation $I \rightarrow_i I'$ to denote that infrastructures I and I' are in this relation.

```
inductive state_transition ::
          [infrastructure, infrastructure] ⇒ bool ("_  →ᵢ _")
```

The definition of this inductive relation is given by a set of rules. To give an impression of this definition, we show here just the rule for the move action.

```
move: ⟦ G = graphI I; a @_G l; l ∈ nodes G; l' ∈ nodes G;
         a ∈ actors_graph(graphI I); enables I l (Actor a) move;
         I' = Infrastructure (move_graph_a a l l'
                               (graphI I))(delta I)(tspace I)(lspace I)
     ⟧ ⟹ I →_i I'
```

The rule for get allows an actor a' to 'nick' something from another actor a
that is in the same location l; in I' actor a' "has" z.

```
get : ⟦ G = graphI I; a @_G l; has (Actor a, z);
        a' @_G l; enables I l (Actor a) get;
        I' = Infrastructure (graphI I)(delta I)
             (λ x. if x = Actor a' then (has (Actor a', z))
                   else (tspace I x))(lspace I)
    ⟧ ⟹ I →_i I'
```

The rule for put allows an actor who is in a location and for whom the put action
is enabled to change the state of that location encoded in the isin predicate for
some specific location feature of an application.

```
put : ⟦ G = graphI I; a @_G l; enables I l (Actor a) put;
        I' = Infrastructure (graphI I)(delta I)(tspace I)
             (λ x. if x = l then (isin l z) else (lspace I x))
    ⟧ ⟹ I →_i I'
```

We show next how Modelchecking in Isabelle can be constructed over this state
transition of the state graph of an infrastructure.

4.3 Modelchecking for Insider Attacks in Isabelle

A very nice and practical feature of Modelchecking is that if the proof of a property fails, a counterexample can be provided automatically. This counterexample
consists of a series of steps from the transition relation from an initial state to a
state in which the CTL property is violated. In security applications, for example security protocol verification, these sequences of steps correspond to attack
sequences. This advantage also goes for Insider attacks and has been exploited
in the invalidation approach [18].

   Modelchecking is in practice very successful mainly due to its full automation. It is often advertised as a 'push-button' technique in contrast to automated
verification techniques, for example with Isabelle, where the user has to interact
with the tool to verify properties (although, for example, the applications in the
Isabelle Insider framework are mostly performed by quite standard sequences of
automatic proof procedures). A major problem of Modelchecking is the exponential growth of the number of states – and the notorious 'state explosion'
problem that arises as a consequence as soon as infinite data domains are considered (which is very common in almost all applications). The practical success
of Modelchecking is despite these limitation due to an extension called Symbolic Modelchecking (SMC) which consists in two main technical advances. First

SMC represent the next step relation not by explicit states but only by 'symbolic' states that use variables, e.g. x, y. The next step transition relation R then needs to be expressed by specification in terms of these variables using x', y' to denote the successor state of variable x, y. The second technical advance of SMC is the effective representation of boolean formulas over state variables x, y, x', y' in the so called (Ordered) Binary Decision Diagram representation ((O)BDD). (O)BDD are directed acyclic graphs that allow a concise representation for any boolean formula.

Due to the expressiveness of HOL, Isabelle allows us to formalise within HOL the notion of Kripke structures, temporal logic, and formalise the semantics of Modelchecking by directly encoding the fixpoint definitions for each of the CTL operators.

Our encoding of Modelchecking is available online [1]. This encoding is not meant as a competitor for Modelchecking in general but tries to use its good concepts for the analysis of Insider threats. Therefore, the representation of (O)BDD is not important for us here. (O)BDD serves SMC for the efficiency of representation of formulas and we are not concerned about this since Isabelle's Higher Order Logic provides for formula representation. Also, we do not attempt to provide Symbolic Model Checking because to a large extent our representation is largely symbolic since we can use the powerful symbolic language of Higher Order Logic. In addition, we are in fact very specifically interested in some concrete states of certain variables like has (x, ''PIN'') for the specification of critical states of infrastructures. Using Isabelle with an embedding of Modelchecking, will on the other hand provide us with the means to explore Kripke structures. The Kripke structures are defined by taking different states of an infrastructure as its states and the state transition relation $\rightarrow_i$ as transition relation R. Via explicit evaluation of temporal logic formulas, the possible paths in the Kripke structure may reveal attacks. Also, it is important to note that the definitions are constructive thus allowing to use Isabelle's code generation technique. Hence, we could actually derive an executable Modelchecker. Another interesting observation is that we can formalise the classic semantic definitions of CTL-operators one-to-one in the context of Higher Order Logic although these operators are defined for propositional logic only. To verify the correctness of our approach, we use some simple implications of essential theorems of Tarski's theory of fixpoints [26] which we can prove in Isabelle (formalisation is available online [1]).

Based on the state transition $\rightarrow_i$ over the infrastructures, we define the CTL-operators EX and AX expressing that property f holds in some or all next states, respectively.

```
AX f ≡ { s. {f0. s →ᵢ f0 } ⊆ f }
EX f ≡ { s. ∃ f0 ∈ f. s →ᵢ f0 }
```

The CTL formula AG f means that on all paths branching from a state s the formula f is always true (G stands for 'globally'). It can be defined using the Tarski fixpoint theory (see the formalisation available online [1]) by applying the greatest fixpoint operator.

AG $f \equiv$ gfp(λ Z. $f \cap$ AX Z)

In a similar way, the other CTL operators are defined. Finally, the labeling function for states can be defined for the Isabelle Insider framework as a predicate over infrastructures I based on the behaviour definition **enables**.

L I $\equiv \exists$ a l c. enables I a l c

Modelchecking a formula f in a Kripke structure M for Insiders can now be defined formally in Isabelle by stating that the initial states of the Kripke structure **init** M need to be contained in the set L s of all states **states** M that imply f.

M $\vdash$ f $\equiv$ init M $\subseteq$ { s $\in$ (states M) . s $\in$ f $\wedge$ (L s) }

The set of states of the Kripke structure can be defined as the set of states reachable by the infrastructure state transition from the initial state Office_scenario.

Office_states $\equiv$ { I. Office_scenario $\rightarrow_i$^* I }

The relation $\rightarrow_i$^* is the reflexive transitive closure – an operator supplied by the Isabelle theory library – applied to the relation $\rightarrow_i$.

The **Kripke** constructor combines the constituents initial state, state set, state transition relation $\rightarrow_i$ and labeling function L.

Office_Kripke $\equiv$ Kripke Office_states {Office_scenario} $\rightarrow_i$ L

When we now try to verify the global security policy, the attempt to prove fails.

Office_Kripke $\vdash$ AG global_policy

In order to explore more precisely where it fails, we prove the complementary property.

Office_Kripke $\vdash$ EF $\neg$ global_policy

This final proof reveals the chain of actions that leads to the attack state Office_in_danger: from the initial state Office_scenario a state transition (by rule **move**) moves the boss to the employee's office. Then, employee can get the PIN – corresponding to a transition with rule **get**. Finally, the employee can move to the boss's office and is in the possession of the PIN leading to the infrastructure Office_in_danger. Besides showing the trace of actions, this chain of actions also highlights the different state graphs traversed by the state transition relation $\rightarrow_i$ on the way from the initial Office_scenario Office_in_danger. The integration of the contextual information into the graphical model permits the systematic exploration of the actions' effects on the infrastructure leading to the attack state. Summarizing, the Modelchecking approach to invalidation can be integrated into the Isabelle Insider framework.

5   Related Work and Conclusions

In this paper, we have provided an extension of the Logical Explanation for Insider Threats with the Isabelle Insider framework to Modelchecking. As requirements elicitation we used the case study of an IoT Insider attack. We used the Isabelle Insider framework for the formal modeling showing where abstract models need more refinement in order to provide sufficient detail to document the attack and make it more realistic. The introduction of mutable states into the model has lead us to use the concepts of Modelchecking. We have then shown how Isabelle can be extended to accommodate classical CTL type Modelchecking and how this extension can be smoothly integrated into the Isabelle Insider framework. The case study of the IoT attacker illustrates how the enhanced framework now fully supports realistic modeling and analysis of IoT Insiders.

The Insider threat patterns provided by CERT [6] use the System Dynamics models, which can express dependencies between variables. The System Dynamics approach has also been successfully applied in other approaches to Insider threats, for example, in the modeling of unintentional insider threats [11]. Axelrad et al. [2] have used Bayesian networks for modelling Insider threats in particular the human disposition. In comparison, the model we rely on for modeling the human disposition is the Isabelle Insider framework, a simplified classification following the taxonomy given in [22]. On the other side, compared to all these approaches, the Isabelle Insider framework provides an additional model of infrastructures and policies allowing reasoning at the individual and organisational level.

On the formal side within the Insider threat community in general, the work by Bishop et al. [3] is relevant to the Isabelle Insider framework since it also uses a formal model to analyse Insider threats. Bishop and colleagues use the LITTLE-JIL process description language, a general framework for Software Engineering. It allows the definition of activities, artifacts, and agent specifications. For the analysis, they use fault tree analysis and finite state verification. While resembling the Isabelle Insider framework concepts, in comparison, the Isabelle framework provides more support to express organisations' infrastructures. The ready made analysis procedures of LITTLE-JIL provide an easier to use analysis approach while Isabelle is superior in flexibility, expressivity and thus generality when it comes to properties.

Logical modeling and analysis of Insider threats has started off by investigating Insider threats with invalidation of security policies in connection with Modelchecking [18,19]. This early approach also uses infrastructure models of organisations, actors and policies but necessarily has to be simpler than the Isabelle Insider framework since model checking does only support finite models. The use of sociological explanation has been pioneered in [5] already with first formal experiments in Isabelle. Finally, the Isabelle Insider framework has been established [20] and has been validated on two of the main three Insider patterns the Entitled Independent and Ambitious Leader. Recently an application to IoT Insiders [16] has consolidated the applicability of the Isabelle Insider framework but also illustrated an extension of the framework to attack trees.

Attack trees have been added to the Isabelle Insider framework [24] to provide the possibility to refine attacks once they have been identified. This refinement is formalised together with the notion of attack trees as first introduced in [14]. Another extension towards probabilistic modeling using Bayes networks (BN) and Markov decision processes (MDP) has been explored in [7] but not within the Isabelle Insider framework. Although the work follows the concept of sociological explanation, the tool Matlab is used for the analysis of the micro-level BN and the Prism Modelchecker provides an analysis of the infrastructure's representation as MDP.

Beyond the current state of the Isabelle Insider framework, the application presented in this paper has shown that a more thorough Insider analysis might be achieved by generalising the approach of considering different infrastructures by defining an inductive relation on them. We have intentionally named this relation 'state transition' to refer to the idea of model checking that has initially inspired the logical approach. We have provided an embedding of the concepts of model checking in Isabelle. On top of the induction relation, a notion of validity of formulas in a Kripke structure in combination with temporal logic has been provided in Isabelle. Embedding Modelchecking into Isabelle has been done before, e.g. [9], but not in the context of Insider threat analysis. An interesting observation, however, is that the classical CTL model checking methodology usually restricted to propositional logic can be applied to Higher Order Logic formulas.

References

1. Kammüller, F.: Isabelle insider framework including modelchecking and examples (2016). https://www.dropbox.com/sh/rx8d09pf3lcv8bd/AAALKtaP8HMX642fi04Og4NLa?dl=0
2. Axelrad, E.T., Sticha, P.J., Brdiczka, O., Shen, J.: A Bayesian network model for predicting insider threats. In: IEEE Security and Privacy Workshops, SPW-WRIT (2013)
3. Bishop, M., Conboy, H.M., Phan, H., Simidchieva, B.I., Avrunin, G.S., Clarke, L.A., Osterweil, L.J., Peisert, S.: Insider threat identification by process analysis. In: IEEE Security and Privacy Workshops, SPW-WRIT (2014)
4. Bitdefender. Bitdefender research exposes security risks of android wearable devices (2014). http://www.darkreading.com/partner-perspectives/bitdefender/bitdefender-research-exposes-security-risks-of-android-wearable-devices-/a/d-id/1318005
5. Boender, J., Ivanova, M.G., Kammüller, F., Primiero, G.: Modeling human behaviour with higher order logic: insider threats. In: STAST 2014, Co-located with CSF 2014 in the Vienna Summer of Logic. IEEE (2014)
6. Cappelli, D.M., Moore, A.P., Trzeciak, R.F., The, C.: Guide to Insider Threats: How to Prevent, Detect, and Respond to Information Technology Crimes (Theft, Sabotage, Fraud). Addison-Wesley, Boston (2012)
7. Chen, T., Kammüller, F., Nemli, I., Probst, C.W.: A probabilistic analysis framework for malicious insider threats. In: Tryfonas, T., Askoxylakis, I. (eds.) HAS 2015. LNCS, vol. 9190, pp. 178–189. Springer, Heidelberg (2015)
8. Clarke, E.M., Grumberg, O., Peled, D.A.: Model Checking. MIT Press, Cambridge (1999)

9. Esparza, J., Lammich, P., Neumann, R., Nipkow, T., Schimpf, A., Smaus, J.-G.: A fully verified executable LTL model checker. In: Sharygina, N., Veith, H. (eds.) CAV 2013. LNCS, vol. 8044, pp. 463–478. Springer, Heidelberg (2013)

10. Esser, H.: Soziologie - Allgemeine Grundlagen. Campus, Frankfurt (1993)

11. Greitzer, F.L., Strozer, J.R., Cohen, S., Moore, A.P., Mundie, D., Cowley, J.: Analysis of unintentional insider threats deriving from social engineering exploits. In: IEEE Security and Privacy Workshops, SPW-WRIT (2014)

12. Hempel, C.G., Oppenheim, P.: Studies in the logic of explanation. Philos. Sci. **15**, 135–175 (1948)

13. Henrio, L., Kammüller, F., Rivera, M.: An asynchronous distributed component model and its semantics. In: de Boer, F.S., Bonsangue, M.M., Madelaine, E. (eds.) FMCO 2008. LNCS, vol. 5751, pp. 159–179. Springer, Heidelberg (2009)

14. Ivanova, M.G., Probst, C.W., Hansen, R.R., Kammüller, F.: Transforming graphical system models to graphical attack models. In: Mauw, S., Kordy, B., Jajodia, S. (eds.) GraMSec 2015. LNCS, vol. 9390, pp. 82–96. Springer, Heidelberg (2016)

15. Kammüller, F., Kerber, M.: Investigating airplane safety and security against insider threats using logical modeling. In: IEEE Security and Privacy Workshops, SPW-WRIT. IEEE (2016)

16. Kammüller, F., Nurse, J.R.C., Probst, C.W.: Attack tree analysis for insider threats on the IoT using isabelle. In: Tryfonas, T. (ed.) HAS 2016. LNCS, vol. 9750, pp. 234–246. Springer, Heidelberg (2016)

17. Kammüller, F., Paulson, L.C.: A formal proof of Sylow's theorem. J. Autom. Reasoning **23**(3), 235–264 (1999)

18. Kammüller, F., Probst, C.W.: Invalidating policies using structural information. In: IEEE Security and Privacy Workshops, SPW-WRIT (2013)

19. Kammüller, F., Probst, C.W.: Combining generated data models with formal invalidation for insider threat analysis. In: IEEE Security and Privacy Workshops, SPW-WRIT (2014)

20. Kammüller, F., Probst, C.W.: Modeling and verification of insider threats using logical analysis. IEEE Syst. J. **PP**(99), 1–12 (2016). Digital Espionage, and Counter Intelligence. Special issue on Insider Threats to Information Security

21. Kammüller, F., Wenzel, M., Paulson, L.C.: Locales - a sectioning concept for isabelle. In: Bertot, Y., Dowek, G., Hirschowitz, A., Paulin, C., Théry, L. (eds.) TPHOLs 1999. LNCS, vol. 1690, pp. 149–165. Springer, Heidelberg (1999)

22. Nurse, J.R.C., Buckley, O., Legg, P.A., Goldsmith, M., Creese, S., Wright, G.R.T., Whitty, M.: Understanding insider threat: a framework for characterising attacks. In: IEEE Security and Privacy Workshops, SPW-WRIT (2014)

23. Nurse, J.R.C., Erola, A., Agrafiotis, I., Goldsmith, M., Creese, S.: Smart insiders: exploring the threat from insiders using the internet-of-things. In: International Workshop on Secure Internet of Things (SIoT), in conjunction with ESORICS 2015, LNCS. Springer (2015, in print)

24. Probst, C.W., Kammüller, F., Hansen, R.R.: Formal modelling and analysis of socio-technical systems. In: Probst, C.W., Hankin, C., Hansen, R.R. (eds.) Semantics, Logics, and Calculi. LNCS, vol. 9560, pp. 54–73. Springer, Heidelberg (2016)

25. Symantec. How safe is your quantified self? Tech. Rep. (2014)

26. Tarski, A.: A lattice-theoretic fixpoint theorem and its applications. Pac. J. Math. **5**, 285–309 (1955)

27. VERIS. Veris: the vocabulary for event recording and incident sharing (2015). http://veriscommunity.net

DPM Short Papers

Managing and Presenting User Attributes over a Decentralized Secure Name System

Martin Schanzenbach$^{(\boxtimes)}$ and Christian Banse

Fraunhofer AISEC, Garching b. München, Germany
{schanzen,banse}@aisec.fraunhofer.de

Abstract. Today, user attributes are managed at centralized identity providers. However, two centralized identity providers dominate digital identity and access management on the web. This is increasingly becoming a privacy problem in times of mass surveillance and data mining for targeted advertisement. Existing systems for attribute sharing or credential presentation either rely on a trusted third party service or require the presentation to be online and synchronous. In this paper we propose a concept that allows the user to manage and share his attributes asynchronously with a requesting party using a secure, decentralized name system.

1   Introduction

Identity and Access Management today revolves around the presentation of attributes or credentials to services for authentication and authorization purposes. Third party identity providers (IdP), such as Google or Facebook are often used in case a service requires an asynchronous way to access user attributes. Often, users are required to share personal data, like email addresses, to use certain services (i.e., a mailing list). Such services only need the user's data when a particular action is executed (i.e., a mail is posted to the mailing list) and it must at that time be able to asynchronously access this data. Usually, this is achieved by persisting the data in a database upon registration or retrieving it from an IdP. In the first case, the data can become stale, unless the user manages the persisted data at the service. In the second case, the user and service must trust the third party IdP to provide fresh, authentic attribute data, to be available whenever needed and not to misuse attributes for user profiling.

In practice, served attributes have no freshness guarantees, the attributes are not verifiably unchanged from what the user provided and availability is either not guaranteed (in case of free offerings) or expensive. Further, IdPs have full access and control over personal, potentially sensitive data limited only by compliance laws and regulations [4], that are often subject to change or even ignored and challenged [3]. Users have no guarantee that IdPs do not indeed analyse and market personal data from attributes and requests. As digital identities are managed by a service oligopoly of two identity providers that claim over 85 % of

© Springer International Publishing AG 2016
G. Livraga et al. (Eds.): DPM and QASA 2016, LNCS 9963, pp. 213–220, 2016.
DOI: 10.1007/978-3-319-47072-6_14

the market[1], Big Data and targeted advertisement businesses make this a valid concern.

In this paper, we present a design and implementation of a system that addresses this issue and does not rely on a centralized IdP to serve attributes. Our solution is a *decentralized* system based on a name system. It can be used to selectively share user attributes asynchronously with other parties. The users manage their attributes and asserted credentials locally on their devices and can grant access to other parties for a limited amount of time over a chosen subset of user attributes.

2   Related Work

Existing technologies and protocols related to identity and access management such as OAuth2 [7] and OpenID-Connect (OIDC) [10] are designed as centralized services which are, in practice, operated by large corporations. Systems such as Idemix address the privacy deficiencies of OAuth2 and OIDC. Idemix is an "anonymous credential system" allowing "anonymous yet authenticated and accountable transactions between users and service providers" [2]. We emphasize here that Idemix's use case is different to ours. It supports the presentation of credentials asserted by a trusted third party to a service provider in an anonymous or pseudonymous manner without disclosing the information directly. However, asynchronous presentation of the actual data is not addressed. Instead, we propose a system that allows a user to asynchronously disclose and share personal data with a relying party.

In many ways, our system addresses User-Managed-Access (UMA) [5] use cases. UMA is a system to protect a user-controlled resource server using an OAuth2-based authorization protocol. UMA also allows asynchronous access to personal data, as it requires the user to manage the data on a dedicated central resource server. However, users are only in full control over their data and authorizations when hosting their own resource and authorization server. In contrast, we propose a completely decentralized system that allows the user to manage his data locally, and selectively share it without the need of a dedicated resource server.

Finally, NameID[2] is a decentralized identity management system built on the blockchain-based name system namecoin[3]. It allows a namecoin user to create identities in the same fashion as domain names and enables the user to authenticate using a simple public key authentication scheme. However, it has one significant drawback: The data stored in the blockchain is public information. As such, storing sensitive personal information is not viable. While our approach also uses a secure name system to store data, we do not require a global, public ledger.

---

[1] http://www.gigya.com/blog/the-landscape-of-customer-identity-q2-2015/, accessed 2016/02/20.

[2] https://nameid.org, accessed 2016/02/20.

[3] https://namecoin.info/, accessed 2016/02/23.

3   Design of a Decentralized Attribute Sharing System

Our approach extends on the concept of decentralized name systems. Specifically, we base our design on the GNU Name System (GNS) [11,12]. In GNS, a user can manage any number of namespaces and thus identities by creating key pairs – the owner of the private key is the authority of the respective namespace. In the following, we describe how our system can be used to share identity attributes in a decentralized way. It allows asynchronous sharing and provides stronger properties on authorization, availability, and freshness than current centralized IdPs, while removing the need to trust a third party.

In our design, user attributes are managed locally by the user and only published to the name system on demand in the form of *identity tokens*. This heavily relies on query privacy and non-traversable namespaces in GNS [11]. We leverage the fact that a record name in GNS can be treated as a shared secret between two parties that want to exchange information [11]. We call this shared secret name *grant* and it is used to achieve confidentiality of identity tokens. We refer to the entity that is requesting user attributes as the *client* and the entity that holds the data as the *user*. The user can authorize a client by generating a *ticket* and handing it to the client.

Our system aims to satisfy three security properties:

1. The grant is a shared secret between the user and an authorized client
2. An issued identity token cannot be retrieved by an unauthorized party
3. If the client is able to bind the user's public key to a trusted identity, our proposed authorization protocol also allows to authenticate the user.

3.1   User Attributes and Identity Tokens

Identity attributes are key-value pairs representing user attributes, for example an email address as "email=john@doe.com". For consistency and simplicity we use GNS as a local attribute data storage. We define the record type **ID_ATTR** for records that contain identity attributes. By default ID_ATTR records are stored as private records in GNS and are therefore not remotely resolvable. Their main purpose is to store and manage attributes that a user can eventually selectively share upon request in *identity tokens*.

Identity tokens are required because if clients access ID_ATTR records directly, revocation of access would become complex as the same attributes are also shared with other clients. An identity token is issued by the user when authorizing a client and contains the attributes requested by a client. We define a record type **ID_TOKEN** for storing identity tokens. The name of an identity token record is the *grant* which is the string representation of a random number. Clients can retrieve identity tokens by querying the respective grant in a particular GNS identity namespace. Grants must be kept confidential by the user and the client.

3.2   Tickets

A ticket is a container for a grant and allows the user to securely transfer a grant to a client identified by the public key P_{client}. The user is identified by a public key P_{user} of the GNS namespace that contains the identity token he intends to share. As there is no central entity that requires the client to authenticate, the grant contained in the ticket must be cryptographically secured in such a way that it can only be decrypted by the owner of the respective private key x_{client}. This is achieved by using static-ephemeral ECDHE [1] to establish a shared symmetric encryption key K_{ticket} derived from P_{client} and a generated ephemeral private key $K_{ECDHE,priv}$. The ticket is a triple (p, k, s) consisting of the encrypted payload p, an ephemeral ECDHE public key $k = K_{ECDHE,pub}$ and the cryptographic ECDSA signature $s = S_{ticket}$ over p and k using x_{user}. The payload p is a triple (l, n, P_{user}) containing the grant l, a nonce n to prevent replay attacks and the user public key P_{user}. It is encrypted using the symmetric key K_{ticket}.

3.3   Client Authorization Protocol

In the following we are using an example to illustrate the client authorization protocol. We assume that only the email address of a user is requested and that an ID_ATTR record $R_{P_{user},email}$ exists in the namespace of P_{user} under the name *email* with the record data "john@doe.com". First, the client creates a request to access the email address of the user. Such a request contains three parameters: The requested attribute names - In this case "email" -, a nonce that will be included in the ticket and the public key P_{client} of the client. When the user receives the request, he must first make a decision if P_{client} is a trusted client. This process is discussed in detail in Sect. 3.5. If the user decides that the client P_{client} is trustworthy, the user creates an identity token including the email attribute. This token also includes a representation of his public key P_{user} as well as expiration and signature information. The user signs the token with the private key x_{user} and encrypts token and signature using a symmetric key K_{token} derived using ECDHE from the client public key P_{client} and a new ECDHE private key $K'_{ECDHE,priv}$. As a result, only the authorized client will be able to decrypt the token. The user stores the ECDHE public key $K'_{ECDHE,pub}$ along with the encrypted data in the GNS record $R_{P_{user},l}$ and publishes it under the grant l. The user responds to the client authorization request with a ticket (p, k, s) containing the grant.

When the client receives the ticket, it must verify the signature s and decrypt the ticket payload p by calculating the symmetric key K_{ticket} using the public ECDHE key $k = K_{ECDHE,pub}$ and his private key x_{client}. After checking the nonce n, the client resolves the token record $R_{P_{user},l}$ from GNS using the grant l. To decrypt the token the client must calculate the symmetric key K_{token} using the client private key x_{client} and the public ECDHE key $K'_{ECDHE,pub}$ contained in the GNS record.

The client can now retrieve the identity attributes from the token. When the token expires the client can use the ticket grant again to retrieve a fresh token from GNS. If the token has been revoked or is not updated by the user it becomes invalid and must not be used any longer.

3.4   Token and Grant Management

The grants contained in tickets expire when the corresponding GNS record in the name system expires. The record expiration times are managed at the GNS-level using the respective operations and settings for records. Tokens have dedicated relative expiration times not directly related to the grant expiration time. If a token expires an updated token can be retrieved using the same grant until the grant is expired. New tokens that contain updated expiration times must be generated regularly by the user where token lifetime may be fixed or chosen by the user at issuance.

3.5   Trust Establishment

In our design we do not rely on a central authority, but on a decentralized public-key infrastructure where trust is not an absolute binary measure but rather a relational, subjective metric. This approach does not exclude the existence of highly trusted third parties, but it gives the user the option to choose what those parties are. For a user to make a reasonable decision whether or not to trust a client with a set of user attributes there must be a trust relationship between any of the user identities and the client. Technical details of trust establishment in GNS is sufficiently explained in [11] and the related work by Rivest et al. [9].

In GNS, a public key can be translated into a human-readable name by performing a reverse lookup. The result of a reverse lookup reveals the trust relationship between the user and the client. If the user has a direct trust relationship with the client, a reverse lookup will return a single name that the user himself assigned, for example: "bob". If the user only has an indirect trust relationship with the client, the name will contain multiple labels separated with a ".": For example: "bob.alice.carol".

If the user has no direct or indirect trust relationship with the client, only a readable representation of the client public key instead of a name is available. The user can recognize that the client is unknown and he can decide if a token should be issued and what data it contains.

The user's decision is expected to depend on the context and the requested set of attributes. For example it is perfectly reasonable that a mailing list provider is requesting access to an email address, even if the user does not have a direct trust relationship. On the other hand interaction with the user's financial institution might incline the user to require a previously established direct trust relationship.

4 Protocol and Implementation

We have implemented the system as a components in the GNUnet peer-to-peer framework[4]. The authorization protocol is realized on top of HTTP utilizing REST services for token issuance and retrieval.

Fig. 1. Identity and attribute management of the implementation prototype.

The system consists of a user-side issue endpoint and a client-side token endpoint that both interact with GNS for token issuance and lookup, respectively. A user-side service is keeping track of all issued tokens across all user namespaces and updates expired tokens. The system's functionality for token issuance and management is exposed through a JavaScript user interface (see Fig. 1). It is also used in the authorization protocol (see Fig. 2) to prompt the user for authorization consent. The interface and an example client have been implemented separately and are available online[5,6].

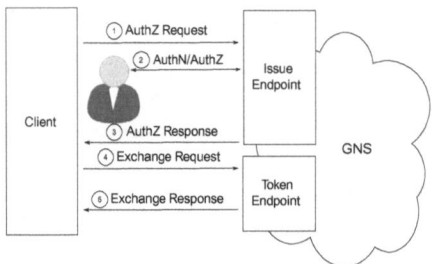

1. A client requests authorization to access identity attributes and redirects the user agent to the user interface
2. The user authorizes the client to access user attributes by instructing the issue endpoint to issue a ticket and an identity token.
3. The client receives an authorization response containing a ticket.
4. The client issues an exchange request and passes the ticket from the authorization response to his own token endpoint.
5. The client endpoint retrieves the token from GNS and passes it to the client.

Fig. 2. Client authorization protocol.

The initial authorization request is an HTTP redirect response sent by the client to the user agent when the user accesses a client resource that requires user

---

[4] https://gnunet.org/svn.
[5] https://github.com/schanzen/gnunet-webui.
[6] https://github.com/schanzen/gnuidentity-example-rp.

information, such as a web application. The redirect response contains the client public key P_{client}, the nonce n, the requested attributes as well as a redirect URI. As the client cannot know the domain name and URI of the end user endpoint, it uses a protocol handler in the redirect response. The protocol handler redirects the user agent to the user interface. To authorize the client, the user chooses an identity, selects the attributes to share and consents to the request. If the user chooses not to accept the authorization request the protocol will conclude with an HTTP redirect back to the redirect URI including an error response. If the user consents to the authorization request an issue request is sent to the end user issue endpoint. The request includes a token expiration time, the nonce provided by the client as well as the client public key. The endpoint creates the token and adds the respective records in GNS. The endpoint responds to the issue request with an HTTP redirect response and the user agent is redirected to the redirect URI along with a new ticket as URL parameter.

The client exchanges the ticket provided in the URL parameter for a token by issuing a token exchange request to its own token endpoint. The endpoint resolves the token from GNS using the grant. After decryption and validation it returns the token in the exchange response. Issued tickets are JSON objects containing the ticket payload p, the ECDHE public key k as well as the signature s. The identity token is implemented as a JSON-Web-Token (JWT) [6].

5   Conclusion

In this paper we have demonstrated how the secure name system GNS can be used for decentralized user attribute sharing. We designed a system that removes the need for central service providers or trusted authorities by securely sharing identity tokens via the name system and relying on its inherent PKI for trust establishment. We formally verified our proposed security properties (see Sect. 3) using the Casper [8] script in the Appendix.

Our system fills the gap that existing privacy-preserving credential systems such as Idemix do not address. The system's availability does not depend on a third party service and it provides a requesting party with attributes signed by the user that cannot be forged by an attacker. Finally, the system allows for attributes to expire transparently and allow the requesting party to request and retrieve updated attributes on demand.

Performance measurements were out of scope for this work but are a concern and should be evaluated further. In a next step, we are planning to investigate how users can be familiarized with the management of multiple identities and how attributes can be asserted by third parties to address distributed authorization scenarios.

Acknowledgment. This work has been partially funded in the project PARADISE by the German Federal Ministry of Education and Research under the reference 16KIS0422.

A   Appendix - Casper Sources

```
1      -- Only relevant sections included for brevity.
2      #Processes
3      INITIATOR(I , nc, CSK, CPK, G) knows
4                           PK, GNSENC
5      USER(U, grant, CPK, G, data) knows
6                           PK, SK(U), GNSENC       20    #Specification
7      GNS(G) knows PK, GNSENC                       21    Secret(U, grant, [I])
8                                                    22    Secret(U, data, [I, G])
9      #Protocol description                         23    Agreement(U, I, [G, data])
10     0. ->I: U                                     24
11     1.I->U:  nc, I                                25    #Intruder Information
12     2.U->G:  {{data}{CPK}}{GNSENC(grant, PK(U))}  26    Intruder = Mallory
13         % record                                  27    IntruderKnowledge =
14     3.U->I:  {nc, grant, PK(U)}{CPK},             28       {Gns, User, Mallory, nonce,
15              {{nc, grant, PK(U)}{CPK}}{SK(U)}     29       PK, SK(Mallory), cpk, GNSENC}
16     4.I->G:  {grant}{GNSENC(grant, PK(U))}
17         % query
18     5.G->I:  record %
19              {{data}{CPK}}{GNSENC(grant, PK(U))}
```

References

1. Brown, D.: Standards for efficient cryptography, sec 1: elliptic curve cryptography. Released Stan. Version 1, 2 (2009)
2. Camenisch, J., Van Herreweghen, E.: Design and implementation of the idemix anonymous credential system. In: Proceedings of the 9th ACM Conference on Computer and Communications Security, pp. 21–30. ACM (2002)
3. French data protection authority. Decision no. 2016–007 of January 26, 2016 issuing formal notice to FACEBOOK INC. and FACEBOOK IRELAND, January 2016
4. Gola, P., Schomerus, R., Klug, C.: BDSG-: Bundesdatenschutzgesetz: Kommentar. Beck, Mnchen, 8. berarbeitete und ergnzte auflage edition (2005)
5. Hardjono, T.: User-managed access (uma) profile of oauth 2.0, December 2015. https://docs.kantarainitiative.org/uma/draft-uma-core.html
6. Jones, M., Bradley, J., Sakimura, N.: Json web token (jwt). RFC 7519, RFC Editor, May 2015. http://www.rfc-editor.org/rfc/rfc7519.txt
7. Jones, M., Hardt, D.: The oauth 2.0 authorization framework: Bearer token usage. RFC 6750, RFC Editor, October 2012. http://www.rfc-editor.org/rfc/rfc6750.txt
8. Lowe, G.: Casper: A compiler for the analysis of security protocols. J. Comput. Secur. 6(1,2), 53–84 (1998)
9. Rivest, R.L., Lampson, B.: Sdsi-a simple distributed security infrastructure. In: Crypto (1996)
10. Sakimura, N., Bradley, J., Jones, M., de Medeiros, B., Mortimore, C.: OpenID Connect Core 1.0 incorporating errata set 1. Technical report, November 2014
11. Wachs, M., Schanzenbach, M., Grothoff, C.: A censorship-resistant, privacy-enhancing and fully decentralized name system. In: Gritzalis, D., Kiayias, A., Askoxylakis, I. (eds.) CANS 2014. LNCS, vol. 8813, pp. 127–142. Springer, Heidelberg (2014)
12. Wachs, M., Schanzenbach, M., Grothoff, C.: On the feasibility of a censorship resistant decentralized name system. In: Danger, J.-L., Debbabi, M., Marion, J.-Y., Garcia-Alfaro, J., Heywood, N.Z. (eds.) FPS 2013. LNCS, vol. 8352, pp. 19–30. Springer, Heidelberg (2014)

PRIAM: A Privacy Risk Analysis Methodology

Sourya Joyee De[(✉)] and Daniel Le Métayer

INRIA, Université de Lyon, Lyon, France
{sourya-joyee.de,daniel.le-metayer}@inria.fr

Abstract. Privacy Impact Assessments (PIA) are recognized as a key step to enhance privacy protection in new information systems and services. They will be required in Europe when the new General Data Protection Regulation becomes effective. From a technical perspective, the core of a PIA is a Privacy Risk Analysis (PRA), which has received relatively less attention than organizational and legal aspects of PIAs. In this work, we propose a rigorous and systematic PRA methodology. We illustrate it with a quantified self use-case in the extended paper [9].

Keywords: Privacy · Personal data · Privacy Impact Assessment · PIA · Privacy Risk Analysis · PRA · Risk · Harm

1 Introduction

Most new information systems and services deployed nowadays rely on the use of personal data. If appropriate measures are not taken, they can lead to various privacy breaches [12,14]. To ensure that such risks are properly understood and addressed, there is a growing recognition that a Privacy Impact Assessment (PIA) should be conducted before the design of a product processing personal data. Several countries like Canada, the USA and the UK [20] have played a leading role in this movement. Europe has also promoted PIAs in areas such as RFIDs [16] and smart grids [17] and is strongly emphasizing privacy and data protection risk analysis in its new General Data Protection Regulation [2]. Beyond legal requirements, conducting a PIA is in the interest of any company intending to deploy a potentially sensitive system or service. Indeed, too hasty deployments may trigger strong public opposition or loss of trust from users [4].

Relevant sources of information and recommendations are already available [1,6,7,19] to help experts define the objectives and overall organization of a PIA. However, they do not show precisely how the technical part of the PIA (henceforth referred to as Privacy Risk Analysis, or PRA) should be performed. The objective of this paper is to fill this gap and propose a detailed, rigorous and systematic PRA methodology. Great care has also been taken to keep this methodology, called PRIAM (Privacy RIsk Analysis Methodology), concrete, customizable and compatible with most existing PIA recommendations.

We believe that the two main challenges to conduct a PRA are (1) the consideration of all factors having an impact on privacy risks and (2) the appropriate

© Springer International Publishing AG 2016
G. Livraga et al. (Eds.): DPM and QASA 2016, LNCS 9963, pp. 221–229, 2016.
DOI: 10.1007/978-3-319-47072-6_15

assessment of these impacts and their contribution to the assessment of the overall risks. To address them, PRIAM revolves around seven *components*, each associated with a set of *attributes* to be defined and used for the computation of the risks. The *components* are: the *information system*, the *stakeholders* (both inputs of the analysis), the *personal data*, the *risk sources*, the *privacy weaknesses*, the *feared events* and the *privacy harms*. *Attributes* are used directly or indirectly for risk calculation. The *components* can be defined by the analyst in any order compatible with the dependencies among *attributes* (Table 1).

PRIAM consists of: (1) an *Information Gathering Phase* and (2) a *Risk Assessment Phase*. The goal of the first phase (Sect. 2) is to gather all relevant information to determine the values of the *attributes*. The second phase (Sect. 3) uses these values to compute the risk levels. PRIAM is illustrated with a quantified self use-case (fitness tracking system) in an extended version of this paper [9]. We discuss related works in Sect. 4 and conclude in Sect. 5.

2   PRIAM: Information Gathering Phase

In this section, we describe the *Information Gathering Phase* for the seven *components* of the PRIAM framework.

2.1   Definition of the Information System

The first step in PRIAM is the description of the *information system* in terms of the following *attributes*: (1) the *functional specification*; (2) the *interface* including all interactions with the external world, users and other systems; (3) the *data flows* (using a data flow diagram) providing the internal view of the system, including sub-systems, their locations, the data they process, access rights and the flows among sub-systems; (4) the *supporting assets*, which host or handle personal data, such as hardware, data stores or software; (5) the *actors* having access to the system or interacting with it, with their roles inside the organization of the data controller and 6) the *controls* consisting of technical measures (e.g., anonymization techniques, encryption tools, etc.), organizational measures (e.g., incident management, audit procedures, awareness programs, etc.) and legal measures (e.g., privacy statements, contracts, Binding Corporate Rules, etc.).

2.2   Definition of the Stakeholders

Stakeholders are described using the following *attributes*: (1) the *communication view* describing all communications among *stakeholders* and (2) the *stakeholder relationships* describing the dependencies among *stakeholders* (e.g., economic, hierarchical). Dependencies need to be taken into account because power imbalances may create difficult situations for the weaker party even if he is a victim of illegal or unfair practices.

2.3   Definition of the Personal Data

Each type of *personal data* (e.g., health, contact data) is described by the following *attributes*: (1) *form* (e.g., raw, encrypted, noisy); (2) *precision* depending on the data type (e.g., street, city for location data); (3) *volume* or number of data items collected per time period (e.g., every 15 min for electricity consumption); (4) *purpose* or the reason for processing the data, to be defined precisely according to European regulation; (5) *retention* or the time period after which the data is deleted; (6) *visibility* or the set of actors, *stakeholders* or external entities with access to the data and (7) *intervenability* (inspired by [21]) describing possibilities for the data subject to exercise his rights (e.g., access, update).

2.4   Definition of the Risk Sources

The sources of risks are the entities whose actions can lead to a privacy breach. Theses entities are often referred to as "adversaries" or "attackers" in the security literature but we prefer to use the term *"risk source"* here as it is less security connotated and not limited to malicious actors. We define a *risk source* as follows:

Definition 1 (Risk source). *A risk source is any entity (individual or organization) which may process (legally or illegally) data belonging to a data subject and whose actions may directly or indirectly, intentionally or unintentionally lead to privacy harms.*

Potential sources of risk should be considered in a systematic way including the data controller, processors, data subject and its acquaintances and malicious third parties [9]. Each *risk source* is described by the following *attributes*: (1) *insider/outsider* (w.r.t. the data controller organization); (2) *individual/organization*; (3) *relationships* between *risk sources* and data subjects (e.g., friend, employee); (4) *background information* describing additional information about the data subjects available to the *risk source* that may help it to carry out a privacy breach (e.g., re-identification); (5) *access rights* to the data processed by the system (e.g., a system administrator may have access to all data) and (6) *technical resources*, including tools, skills and computation power.

2.5   Definition of the Privacy Weaknesses

We define *privacy weaknesses* as follows:

Definition 2 (Privacy weakness). *A privacy weakness is a weakness in the data protection mechanisms (technical, organizational or legal) of a system or a lack thereof that can ultimately result in privacy harms.*

The term "vulnerability" is often used with a close meaning in the area of computer security but we choose the expression *"privacy weakness"* here because in some cases *privacy harms* (Sect. 2.7) can stem from the functionality of the system itself (e.g., in the case of video-surveillance systems), which would probably not be considered as a vulnerability in the usual sense of the word. Each *privacy weakness* is associated with the *attribute exploitability*, which characterizes the conditions to be able to exploit it. *Exploitability* refers to resources such as *background information* or *technical resources* comparable to *risk source attributes* (e.g., a *privacy weakness* could be exploited only by *risk sources* having substantial *background information* on a data subject).

2.6   Definition of the Feared Events

For a privacy risk analysis, it is necessary to make a distinction between *feared events*, which are "technical events" of the system, and *privacy harms* (Sect. 2.7) which correspond to the impact of *feared events* on people. Potential *feared events* should be considered in a systematic way including unauthorized access to data, use of data for unauthorized purposes, disclosure of data to unauthorized parties etc. [9].

Definition 3 (Feared Event). *A feared event is an event of the system that occurs as a result of the exploitation of one or more privacy weaknesses and may lead to privacy harms.*

Each *feared event* is characterized by the following *attributes*: (1) *motivation* (may be different for different *risk sources*) of the *risk sources* to cause the *feared event*, taking into account both incentives and disincentives (e.g., the fear of losing customer trust, being subject to legal proceedings); (2) *scale* measuring the number of potential individuals whose personal data is concerned by a *feared event* and (3) *irreversibility* denoting the difficulty with which a *feared event* can be cancelled out (e.g., the disclosure of personal information on a widely used social network may be irreversible in practice).

2.7   Definition of the Privacy Harms

Privacy harm assessment is the ultimate goal of the analysis. The notion has been exclusively studied by lawyers [5,18] but has received less attention from computer scientists. We use the following definition:

Definition 4 (Privacy Harms). *A privacy harm is the negative impact of the use of the information system on a data subject, or a group of data subjects, or society as a whole, from the standpoint of physical, mental, or financial well-being or reputation, dignity, or any fundamental right.*

The categories of *harms* [5,18] to be considered in a PRA are: (1) *physical harms* like physical ailments, death, or injury; (2) *economic harms* such as loss of benefits or robbery; (3) *mental or psychological harms* such as fear of misuse of personal data, fear of being treated unfairly, anxiety, or mental distress; (4) *harms to dignity, reputation* such as embarrassment or humiliation and (5) *societal harms* like chilling effect due to surveillance. Potential *harms* should be considered in a systematic way, for example, based on existing classifications [7].

Table 1. Dependencies among the main *attributes*

	Components	Attributes	Influencing Attributes
Affected *attributes*	Privacy Weakness	Exploitability	Controls
	Risk Sources	Access Rights	Visibility, Insider/Outsider
		Technical Resources	Insider/Outsider, Individual/Organization
		Background Information	Insider/Outsider, Relationship
	Feared Events	Irreversibility	Intervenability
	Harms	Victims	Scale
		Intensity	Irreversibility, Stakeholder Relationship, External Factors
Risk Level		Severity	Victims, Intensity
		Likelihood	Exploitability, Motivation, Technical Resources, Background Information, Access Rights

Each *harm* is described by the following *attributes*: (1) the *victims* who may be individuals, groups of people or society as a whole and (2) the *intensity* of the *harm*, which depends mostly on the magnitude of the *harm* and the difficulty for the victims to overcome it [6,7].

To conclude this section, we summarize in Table 1 the dependencies among the main *attributes* of the PRIAM *components*. The *Information Gathering Phase* can be conducted in any order compatible with these dependencies.

3   PRIAM: Risk Assessment Phase

When the *Information Gathering Phase* is completed, the analyst has all the ingredients to conduct the second phase which is the *Risk Assessment Phase* itself. The *risk level* is expressed as a pair: (*severity, likelihood*) for each *privacy harm*. In order to evaluate this *risk level* it is necessary to consider the *attributes* discussed in Sect. 2 and the dependencies among *harms, feared events, privacy weaknesses* and *risk sources*. We first describe these dependencies before discussing the evaluation of the *severity* and the *likelihood* of the *harms*.

Harm Trees. A *privacy harm* results from one or more *feared events*. Similarly, a *feared event* results from the exploitation of one or more *privacy weaknesses* by one or more *risk sources* (colluding or not). For example, a *risk source* may get access to *personal data* if it is stored or communicated without encryption, or if it is supposed to be anonymized but the *risk source* has sufficient *background information* to de-anonymize it. The exploitation of a given *privacy weakness* may lead to multiple *feared events*. For example, if a data controller does not enforce sufficient system audit, then it will be easier (because it is likely to remain undetected) to use data for unauthorized purposes and/or disclose it to third parties. These relationships are expressed through *harm trees*, akin to attack trees in computer security [13]. The root node denotes a *privacy harm*. Leaf nodes denote *privacy weaknesses* exploited by the most likely *risk source* and are represented by pairs (*privacy weakness, risk source*). Intermediate nodes (apart from AND and OR nodes) denote feared events. Child nodes are connected by an AND node if all of them are necessary to give rise to the parent node and by an OR node if any one of them is sufficient. In the context of a fitness tracking system [9], Fig. 1 shows that the harm "increased health insurance premium" occurs as the service provider (A.1) performs excessive inference (e.g., deriving health risk profiles) from fitness data (FE.3) and sells this derived data to health insurance providers (FE.4) and the insurance company (A.7) re-identifies it (FE.5). Insufficient system audit (V.5) and excessive data collection (V.27) exploited by A.1 causes FE.3. The lack of legal *control* (V.22) preventing A.7 from re-identification facilitates FE.5.

Computation of Severity. Among the factors to be considered to assess the *severity* of a *privacy harm*, a high weight should be assigned to *intensity*. For example, when a fitness tracker service causes undesirable disclosure of intimate personal habits to the public [12], the *intensity* of the potential psychological *harm* must be considered significant because, once such data is disclosed, the *feared event* is practically *irreversible* and it may be very difficult for the data subject to recover from the *harm*. The analyst can refer to existing proposals (e.g., CNIL guidelines [6,7]) which consider these factors for *severity* level evaluation. *Severity* is by essence rather subjective and its classifications would be very general. Thus, it should ideally be assessed in collaboration with all *stakeholders* (including representatives of the data subjects) in the context of a PIA [19].

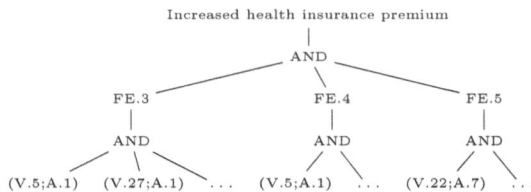

Fig. 1. Example of a harm tree

Computation of Likelihood. The likelihood of a *harm* is computed from the likelihoods of the corresponding *feared events* derived from the *likelihoods of exploitation* of the *privacy weaknesses*. The likelihood of exploitation depends on two factors: the *motivation* of the *risk sources* (for the *feared event* to which the exploitation would lead) and their *capacity* to exploit the *privacy weaknesses*. This *capacity* is determined by the relationship between the *attributes* of the *risk source* (*background information, access rights* and *technical resources*) and the *exploitability* of the *privacy weaknesses*. For example, if the exploitation of a *privacy weakness* requires substantial *background information* on data subjects then only *risk sources* having this *background information* and strong *motivation* have high *likelihood of exploitation*. The computation of the *likelihood of a harm* is the application of the following rules to the *harm tree*, where P_i is the likelihood of the ith child node: [R1.] AND node with independent children: $P = \prod_i P_i$. [R2.] AND node with potentially dependent children[1]: $P = Min_i(P_i)$. [R3.] OR node with independent children: $P = 1 - \prod_i (1 - P_i)$. [R4.] OR node with dependent children[2]: $P = Min_i(1, \Sigma_i P_i)$.

4   Related Works

The existing literature on PIA consists of (1) proposals focusing mostly on organizational and management level tasks with few details about the PRA phase [19]; (2) proposals [1,6,7,10,11,15] focusing almost entirely on the PRA phase and (3) proposals [16,17] covering all PIA steps (including the PRA phase) in some detail. Wright [19] reviews various existing PIAs and explains PIA phases such as team formation, preparation of a PIA plan, agreement on a budget, etc. It also includes more technically oriented tasks like information flow analysis, privacy impact assessment and risk identification, but does not discuss methods to conduct the risk assessment itself. Since we focus on the PRA phase in this paper, we discuss previous works only in categories 2 and 3 above.

Different PRA methodologies use different terminologies and definitions for PRA *components*. For example, some [6,7,17] use the term "prejudicial effect" rather than *"privacy harm"*. Some works [1,15,16] consider the impacts for data controllers. However, the interests of the data subjects and the data controllers are generally different (and even conflicting) and it is better to separate the issues. The term *feared events* has rarely been used in the sense of our definition (the main exceptions being [6,7]). Deng et al. [10] discuss a number of privacy threats and identify events (*privacy weaknesses* here) that lead to privacy threats. According to Oetzel and Spiekermann [15], threats prevent reaching a privacy target to be achieved for privacy protection. The concept of privacy target is also used in the BSI framework [16]. In [11], threat sources lead to threat events that affect privacy assets. The authors do not differentiate between threats and *feared events* and focus on one specific threat, the disclosure of assets. In the LINDDUN framework [10], threat trees link what the framework defines as threats to vulnerabilities. Similarly, Friginal et al. [11] describe attack trees to link what they define as adverse impacts to attack scenarios. However, they do not link *harms* and *privacy weaknesses*. In [1], risk is computed as a product of likelihood and impact. Others use a risk map [6,7,17] to plot estimated risks.

In this work, we provide a taxonomy of all information required for a PRA and identify various interdependencies among *attributes*, not discussed in previous works. The extended version [9] of this paper presents, in full details, both PRIAM and its application to fitness tracking system. Only some concepts discussed here (but not the PRIAM methodology) are used in [8].

---

[1] In order to err on the safe side in terms of privacy protection, we consider dependent nodes such that one node may potentially imply all other nodes.

[2] In order to err on the safe side in terms of privacy protection, we consider dependent nodes such that each node may exclude all other nodes. Hence the use of the sum.

5   Conclusion

PRIAM helps to conduct a PRA systematically and traceably. The *components* and their *attributes* reduce the risk of overlooking or under-estimating key factors for privacy risk evaluation. PRIAM is customizable and open-ended and the lists of *components* and their *attributes* can be completed case by case. For example, the domains chosen for the *component attributes* and *risk levels* can be adapted based on the context and the preferences of the analyst and the decision makers. So, PRIAM can accommodate both quantitative and qualitative analyses. Based on the PRA results, one can select counter-measures that bring the *risk level* of all *harms* below an acceptable level while minimizing implementation costs. A study of all *harm trees* whose *risk levels* are above the acceptable threshold reveals the *privacy weaknesses* having the strongest impact on the *harms*. This can help prioritize counter-measures. In general, it would be useful to integrate in the same framework a PRA methodology like PRIAM and a privacy by design methodology [3] to ensure that all design choices are justified and documented by the risk analysis, thereby achieving strong accountability objectives.

Acknowledgements. This work has been partially funded by the French ANR-12-INSE-0013 project BIOPRIV and Inria Project Lab CAPPRIS.

References

1. Privacy Risk Management for Federal Information Systems (2015). http://csrc.nist.gov/publications/drafts/nistir-8062/nistir-8062-draft.pdf
2. European Commission. General Data Protection Regulation (2016)
3. Antignac, T., Le Métayer, D.: Trust driven strategies for privacy by design. In: Damsgaard Jensen, C., Marsh, S., Dimitrakos, T., Murayama, Y. (eds.) IFIPTM 2015. IFIP AICT, vol. 454, pp. 60–75. Springer, Heidelberg (2015)
4. Baringer, F.: New Electricity Meters Stir Fear (2011). www.nytimes.com
5. Calo, R.: The Boundaries of Privacy Harm. Ind. LJ **86**, 1131 (2011)
6. CNIL. Privacy Impact Assessment (PIA) Methodology (2015)
7. CNIL. Privacy Impact Assessment (PIA) Tools (2015)
8. De, S.J., Le Métayer, D.: Privacy harm analysis: a case study on smart grids. In: International Workshop on Privacy Engineering, IEEE (2016)
9. De, S.J., Le Métayer, D.: PRIAM: A Privacy Risk Analysis Methodology. INRIA Research Report, (RR-8876), July 2016
10. Deng, M., Wuyts, K., Scandariato, R., Preneel, B., Joosen, W.: A privacy threat analysis framework: supporting the elicitation and fulfilment of privacy requirements. Requirements Eng. **16**(1), 3–32 (2011)
11. Friginal, J., Guiochet, J., Killijian, M.-O.: Towards a privacy risk assessment methodology for location-based systems. In: Stojmenovic, I., Cheng, Z., Guo, S. (eds.) MindCare 2014. LNICSSITE, vol. 131, pp. 748–753. Springer, Heidelberg (2014). doi:10.1007/978-3-319-11569-6_65
12. Hill, K.: Fitbit moves quickly after users' sex stats exposed. Forbes **26**, 515–519 (2011)
13. Kordy, B., Mauw, S., Radomirović, S., Schweitzer, P.: Attack-defense trees. J. Logic Comput. **24**(1), 55–87 (2014)

14. Lisovich, M., Mulligan, D.K., Wicker, S.B., et al.: Inferring personal information from demand-response systems. Secur. Priv. IEEE **8**(1), 11–20 (2010)
15. Oetzel, M.C., Spiekermann, S.: A systematic methodology for privacy impact assessments: a design science approach. Eur. J. Inf. Syst. **23**(2), 126–150 (2014)
16. Oetzel, M.C., Spiekermann, S., Grüning, I., Kelter, H., Mull, S.: Privacy Impact Assessment Guideline for RFID Applications (2011). www.bsi.bund.de
17. SGTF. Data Protection Impact Assessment Template for Smart Grid and Smart Metering Systems (2014). http://ec.europa.eu/
18. Solove, D.J.: A taxonomy of privacy. U. Pa. L. Rev. **154**, 477–564 (2006)
19. Wright, D.: Making privacy impact assessment more effective. Inf. Soc. **29**(5), 307–315 (2013)
20. Wright, D., Finn, R., Rodrigues, R.: A comparative analysis of privacy impact assessment in six countries. J. Contemp. Eur. Res. **9**(1), 160–180 (2013)
21. Zwingelberg, H., Hansen, M.: Privacy protection goals and their implications for eID systems. In: Camenisch, J., Crispo, B., Fischer-Hübner, S., Leenes, R., Russello, G. (eds.) Privacy and Identity Management for Life. IFIP AICT, vol. 375, pp. 245–260. Springer, Heidelberg (2012)

A Study from the Data Anonymization Competition *Pwscup 2015*

Hiroaki Kikuchi[1]([✉]), Takayasu Yamaguchi[2], Koki Hamada[3], Yuji Yamaoka[4], Hidenobu Oguri[5], and Jun Sakuma[6]

[1] Meiji University, 4-21-1 Nakano, Nakano Ku, Tokyo 164-8525, Japan
`kikn@meiji.ac.jp`
[2] NTT DOCOMO, Inc., Yokusuka, Kanagawa, Japan
[3] NTT Secure Platform Laboratories, Musashino, Tokyo, Japan
[4] Fujitsu Laboratories Ltd., Kawasaki, Kanagawa, Japan
[5] NIFTY Corporation, Shinjuku-ku, Tokyo, Japan
[6] University of Tsukuba, Tsukuba, Ibaraki, Japan

Abstract. Data anonymization is required before a big-data business can run effectively without compromising the privacy of the personal information it uses. It is not trivial to choose the best algorithm to anonymize some given data securely for a given purpose. In accurately assessing the risk of data being compromised, there should be a balance between utility and security. Therefore, using common pseudo microdata, we proposed a competition for the best anonymization and re-identification algorithms. This paper reports the results of the competition and the analysis of the effectiveness of the anonymization techniques. The competition results show that there is a trade-off between utility and security, and 20.9 % of records were reidentified on average.

1 Introduction

Many business organizations collect our personal data with the aims of sharing this data with partners and using data-mining algorithms to extract useful knowledge related to the behavior of customers and their preferences for goods. To prevent data from being re-identified, many anonymization algorithms have been proposed, aiming to retain the utility of data that have been *anonymized*. It is not trivial to anonymize data so that the risk of re-identification is eliminated because there is a trade-off between utility and security. If we alter the data sufficiently, the data can be secure against re-identification. However, excessive anonymization also sacrifices accuracy. Hence, we must carefully determine the best algorithm for data anonymization to ensure security against re-identification risk without loss of data utility.

Our Approach. To address the issues in anonymization, we proposed a data anonymization and re-identification competition using a common dataset [3] in 2015. We adopted the educational dataset "pseudo microdata," which was synthesized by a governmental agency, Japan's National Statistics Center (NSTAC).

© Springer International Publishing AG 2016
G. Livraga et al. (Eds.): DPM and QASA 2016, LNCS 9963, pp. 230–237, 2016.
DOI: 10.1007/978-3-319-47072-6_16

This is based on real statistics about income and expenditure for Japanese households. To simplify our analysis, we assume there is a maximum-knowledge adversary who can access the original dataset before anonymization. This assumption makes our competition clear and simple. We have defined some utility measures, combined with some security measures in [3].

In this paper, we report the results of our competition from utility and security perspectives and examine the submitted anonymized data to find the best strategy for making data secure against re-identification. Our analysis includes the relationship the utility measures and the effect of k-anonymization. The results of the competition provide useful knowledge related to data anonymization as well as evaluation of re-identification risk.

2   Anonymization

2.1   Outline of the Competition

On October 21st, 2015, we held the first competition for data anonymization and re-identification, PWSCUP (Privacy Workshop CUP) 2015 "Ice and Fire"[1], in Nagasaki, Japan. It was organized by the Special Interest Group (SIG) for Computer Security (CSEC) of the Information Processing Society of Japan (IPSJ).

A total of 17 teams (more than 80 people in total) participated in the competition. Most participants were privacy-technologies researchers from universities and industrial laboratories.

2.2   Fundamental Definitions

A *dataset* X consists of n *records*, $x_1, \ldots, x_n$, of the form $x_i = (x_i^1, \ldots, x_i^m)$, defined in terms of m attributes, $X^1, \ldots, X^m$. Let I^X be a *record index sequence* for database X. For example, $I^X = (1, \ldots, n)$ is the identity. We treat a dataset as containing *personal data* if some attributes are related to personal information such as name or postal address and are expressive enough to identify a particular subject.

A set of attributes is known as *Quasi Identifier* (QI) if they link the records generated by a single user [2]. Various properties to reduce the risk of re-identification from an anonymized dataset have been studied such as k-anonymity [5] and ℓ-diversity [4]. Dynamic attributes are often referred to as *Sensitive Attributes* (SAs) because they may contain critical information that the user may wish to hide.

2.3   Anonymization

Many anonymization algorithms have been proposed to preserve privacy, while retaining the utility of the data that have been *anonymized*. In this paper, we use anonymization as a general process, possibly implemented by multiple algorithms, rather than by a particular algorithm.

---

[1] "Ice" and "fire" refer to anonymization and re-identification attempts, respectively.

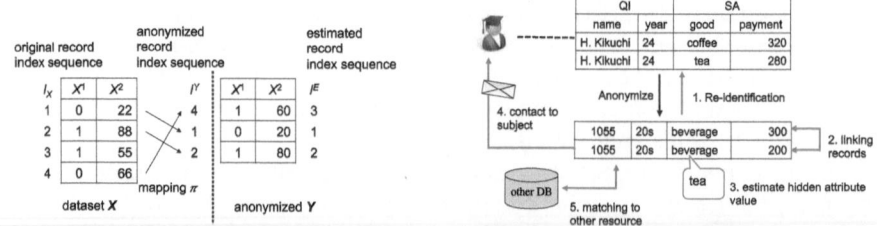

Fig. 1. Original, anonymized and estimated record index sequences

Fig. 2. Privacy threads and re-identification

Definition 21. Let Y be an *anonymized dataset* generated from a dataset X. The anonymized dataset Y contains n' ($n' \leq n$) records, $y_1, \ldots, y_{n'}$, of tuples of m'($m' \leq m$) attributes chosen from $\{X^1, \ldots, X^m\}$ of X. A record $y_j = (y_j^1, \ldots, y_j^{m'})$ of Y is de-identified from the corresponding record x_i of X such that $j = \pi(i)$, where π is a mapping $\pi : \{1, \ldots, n\} \rightarrow \{1, \ldots, n'\}$. The anonymizing processes such as sampling, record swapping, or record shuffling are represented by means of an *anonymized record index sequence* $I^Y = (i_1^Y, \ldots, i_{n'}^Y) = (\pi^{-1}(1), \ldots, \pi^{-1}(n'))$.

Figure 1 illustrates a sample anonymized dataset. The figure shows how an anonymized process is specified by means of anonymized record index sequences I^Y. In the example, $I^Y = (4, 1, 2)$ where $\pi(4) = 1, \pi(1) = 2$, and the third record x_3 has been dropped for some reason.

2.4 Re-Identification

In this paper, a *re-identification* is a process that attempts to identify the record subject x_i from the anonymized record y_j based on some features of the original record. However, the term "re-identification" is ambiguous because some possible meanings must be interpreted in context.

Consider the examples of privacy threads in the data anonymization in Fig. 2. The dataset X of two records with four attributes, "name," "year," "good," and "payment," are anonymized as the lower table Y, where names are replaced by pseudonyms, values are rounded, and the values "coffee" and "tea" are unified as a general "beverage."

Definition 22 (Re-identification). Given an anonymized dataset Y, an adversary estimates the record index sequence $I^E = (i_1^E, \ldots, i_{n'}^E) \cong I^Y$ by employing an algorithm E.

2.5 Common Dataset

Attributes in a dataset X are partitioned into three subsets: (1) a direct identifier such as a name and social security number (2) a QI subset comprising a

Table 1. Statistics for the NSTAC pseudo microdata [1]

Dataset	# records	# QIs	# SAs	
			Expenditure	Income
	n	m		
Full	59,400	14	149	34
Simple	8,333	14	11	N/A

combination of attributes, such as sex and age identifies unique individual, and (3) other attributes that contain SAs, such as disease and religion.

The NSTAC "pseudo microdata"[2] is a dataset of family income and expenditure in Japan, which was synthesized in 2012 by NSTAC for educational purposes in schools [1]. The dataset consists of 59,400 records, each representing the income and expenditure for a family (including 5,002 single-person households), in 2004. The statistical features of the real data were preserved in the NSTAC pseudo microdata under the assumption that the values in all continuous attributes are (logarithmic) normally distributed. Table 1 shows some fundamental statistics for the NSTAC pseudo microdata.

Our competition involves the following tasks.

1. Data anonymization.
   Given an original X (of NSTAC pseudo micro-data), perform data anonymization and submit the anonymized data Y and the corresponding record index I^Y. A player is allowed to submit at most three different anonymized datasets for the original data X. The player whose anonymized data is the most useful and the most secure against any re-identification attacks will be the winner for this task.

2. Re-identification.
   Given some anonymized data Y, estimate the process of data anonymization and submit the estimated record index I^E. An adversary is allowed to submit only one estimated record index I^E for each Y. The adversary who performs the most accurate re-identification with the highest ratio will be the winner for this task.

2.6 Security: *Re-Id*

Let Y and $I^Y = (i_1^Y, \ldots, i_{n'}^Y)$ be some anonymized data and their corresponding anonymized record index sequence. Let $I^E = (i_1^E, \ldots, i_{n'}^E)$ be the estimated record index sequence of Y using re-identification algorithm E. The *re-identification ratio* of E is defined as

$$\text{re-id}^E(I^Y, I^E) = \frac{\left| \{ j \in \{1, \ldots, n'\} | i_j^Y = i_j^E \} \right|}{n'}.$$

---

[2]   http://www.nstac.go.jp/services/ippan-microdata.html (in Japanese) and http://www.nstac.go.jp/en/services/public.html.

2.7 Definition of Utility and Security

Table 2 shows the list of measures in terms of utility $(U_1 \ldots, U_5)$ and security $(S_1, S_2, E_1, \ldots, E_4)$, defined in [3]. We show the general meanings of theses measures with the target attribute (SA or QI).

Table 2. Measures of utility $(U_1, \ldots, U_6)$ and of security $S_1, S_2, E_1, \ldots, E_4$

No	Measures	Meaning	Target
U_1	meanMAE	Error of means for all SAs	SA
U_2	crossMean	Error of mean of some SAs for some QIs	QI
U_3	crossCnt	Error of record counts for some QIs	QI
U_4	corMAE	Error of correlations of all pairs of SAs	SA
U_5	IL	Error of all values of all records	QI, SA
U_6	nrow	Number of records	N/A
S_1	k-anony	k-anonymity (minimum k)	QI
S_2	k-anonyMean	k-anonymity (mean k)	QI
E_1	IdRand	re-id by a random guess in a subset of records with QIs	Qi
E_2	IdSA	re-id by searching in a subset of records with QIs	QI, SA
E_3	Sort	re-id by sorting for sum of values of SAs	SA
E_4	SA21	re-id by searching all records for 21th SA	SA

3   Results and Evaluation

3.1 Competition Results

Table 3 shows the top 10 anonymized data for the competition involving the measures $U_1, \ldots, U_6$ for utility, S_1, S_2 for k-anonymity, and $E_1, \ldots, E_4, E_{AYA}$ for re-identification ratios.

The anonymized data are ranked by the sum of utilities and the security against all re-identification techniques. For example, the 5th-ranked data preserves higher utilities, while the security is not so good, i.e., most records were re-identified with re-id of 40.92. However, some anonymized data e.g., the 4th, 6th and 7th-ranked focused on its security rather than utilities. The first and the second data, submitted by the same team (02), balanced both scores very well and succeeded that most records were not identified by $E_1, \ldots, E_4$ as the values are almost zero.

Note that score S_1 indicates whether the data are altered so that k-anonymity is satisfied. For instance, the 4th, 6th, and 10th-ranked data guarantee that there are at least $k = 3$ records for any combinations of QIs. The 7th-ranked satisfies the $k = 5$ degree of anonymity.

Table 3. Utilities and re-id scores of the top 10 anonymized data Y

Rank	Team	U_1	U_2	U_3	U_4	U_5	U_6	S_1	S_2	E_1	E_2	E_3	E_4	E_{AYA}	Max E_i
1	02	0.00	0.00	0.00	0.09	0.01	0.00	1.00	13.71	0.00	0.00	0.00	0.00	0.03	0.03
2	02	0.00	0.00	0.00	0.09	0.01	0.00	1.00	13.68	0.00	0.00	0.00	0.00	0.08	0.08
3	01	0.00	0.00	0.00	0.07	0.02	0.00	1.00	36.07	0.00	0.02	0.00	0.00	0.36	0.36
4	02	0.00	4321.75	1.54	0.03	0.01	0.00	3.00	36.07	0.00	0.02	0.01	0.00	0.21	0.30
5	10	0.00	0.00	0.00	0.00	0.03	0.00	1.00	36.07	0.00	0.08	0.08	0.01	0.92	0.92
6	15	0.00	31,400.95	0.99	0.00	0.02	0.00	3.00	4.86	0.19	0.24	0.25	0.05	0.57	0.57
7	07	0.00	46,944.41	2.16	0.00	0.02	0.00	5.00	89.60	0.00	0.00	0.00	0.00	0.63	0.63
8	10	0.00	0.00	0.00	0.00	0.03	0.00	1.00	36.07	0.00	0.07	0.07	0.01	0.93	0.93
9	10	0.00	0.00	0.00	0.00	0.03	0.00	1.00	36.07	0.00	0.07	0.07	0.01	0.93	0.93
10	15	0.00	31,572.91	1.01	0.00	0.02	0.00	3.00	4.91	0.20	0.24	0.25	0.05	0.63	0.63

3.2 Evaluation of Utility Measures

Several strategies for anonymization were used. From the observation of Fig. 3, where utility measures U_1, U_3, U_5 are plotted in the order of increasing U_5, we find four large peaks. At the first one (left), we think that only QI attributes were altered without changing any SA because measure U_3 of QI is high. In contrast, the third peak (around ID 16) shows the evidence that SAs were altered well without changing any QI because measure U_1 of SA is high. In this way, we see that a variety of data anonymization strategies were attempted in the competition.

3.3 Trade-Off Between Utility and Security

We can observe a trade-off between utility and security for the set of anonymized data in Fig. 4, where the 24 submitted data are scattered over the space of the maximum re-id ratio (Y axis) and the representative utility measure U_5 (Y axis).

Security against re-identification is maximized at the cost of utility loss. For example, the cluster of anonymized data plotted at the bottom right has high security and low utility. However, the top-left cluster of anonymized data

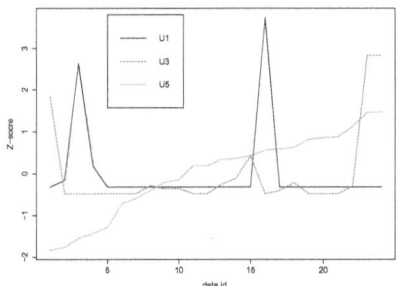

Fig. 3. Distribution of utilities U_1, U_3, U_5

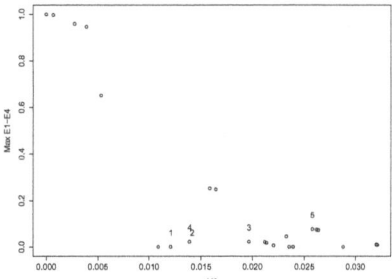

Fig. 4. Relationship between utility and security

preserve the property of the original data X accurately, but they are vulnerable against any re-identification attempt. We indicate the top five anonymized data with their ranks, which are plotted slightly lower than the trade-off between utility and security. The secret techniques might be applied to the top data to optimize processing for both security and utility perspectives.

3.4   Evaulation of Re-Identifications Technique

In the competition, the players were allowed to submit the estimated record index once per anonymized data and they were not required to estimate all data. Hence, some teams carefully chose their victim data that looked easy to re-identify. For example, the 5th-ranked team achieved the highest re-id ratio, 51.4%, by attempting only eight anonymized datasets. The first-ranked team tried to re-identify as many records as they could and won the highest score of 51,628 out of 174,993 records. The re-id ratio of 29.9% is smaller than that of the 5th team.

We also note that the average re-identification ratio for the teams was 20.9%. Even though the data were carefully altered by several smart algorithms, it is almost impossible to perfectly prevent data from being re-identified. There is no perfect algorithm for data anonymization. The competition results showed the limitations of anonymization techniques.

3.5   Effect of k-anonymity

We found that some data were processed so that k-anonymity was satisfied for some $k > 1$. However, the k-anonymized data did not always improve the security against re-identification.

To see the effect of k-anonymity, we show the maximum re-identification ratio of anonymized data with respect to the average measures of k (S_2) in Fig. 5. Most anonymized data with $k = 1$ (no attempt for k-anonymity) have the maximum re-identification ratio distributed from 0 to 1.0, shown at the left edge in the figure. In the figure, the highest k is at $S_2 = 107$ and its re-identification is

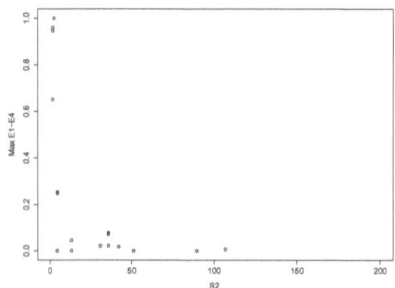

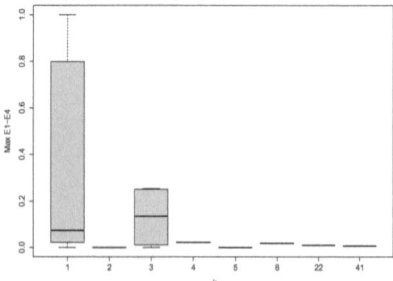

Fig. 5. Re-identification ratio with respect to mean k-anonymity (S_2)

Fig. 6. Bar-plot of re-identification ratio with respect to k

almost zero. Generally, higher S_2 data are more secure against re-identification than the data without k-anonymity. However, there are some exceptions around S_2 of 30.

Figure 6 illustrates the bar-plot of re-identification ratio for each of minimum k (S_1). The mean re-identification for $k > 1$ is 0.013, which is smaller than that of $k = 1$. Note the mean of data for $k = 3$ is worse than that of $k = 1$. Hence, a naive processing for k-anonymity is not necessarily significant for security.

4   Conclusions

We have studied reasonable methods for evaluating the quality of data anonymization by mounting a competition. We have designed the measures for anonymized data in terms of data utility and security against the threat of re-identification. We have developed a competition platform that enables players to participate from remote sites.

As far as we know, this is the first ever data-anonymization competition. We believe that it is a significant undertaking because the competition style is attractive to many engineers and the techniques are evaluated in a common environment. Therefore, methodologies for useful and secure data anonymization are sure to be improved via the competition. We now plan to analyze the results of our competition to identify the most significant elements in anonymization.

References

1. Akiyama, H., Yamaguchi, K., Ito, S., Hoshino, N., Goto, T.: Usage and development of educational pseudo micro-data -sampled from national survey of family income and expenditure in 2004. Techn. Report Nat. Stat. Cent. (NSTAC) **16**, 1–43 (2012). (in Japanese)
2. El Emam, K., Arbuckle, L.: Anonymizing Health Data Case Studies and Methods to Get You Started. O'Reilly, CA, USA (2013)
3. Kikuchi, H., Yamaguchi, T., Hamada, K., Yamaoka, Y., Oguri, H., Sakuma, J., Ice, F.: Quantifying the Risk of Re-identification and Utility in Data Anonymization. In: Proceedings of the IEEE 30th International Conference on Advanced Information Networking and Applications (AINA), pp. 1035–1042 (2016)
4. Machanavajjhala, A., Kifer, D., Gehrke, J., Venkitasubramaniam, M.: L-diversity: Privacy beyond k-anonymity. ACM Trans. Knowl. Discov. Data **1**, 1 (2007). Article 3
5. Sweeny, L.: k-anonymity. Int. J. Uncertainty Fuzziness Knowl. Based Syst. **10**, 571–588 (2002)

Refactoring Preserves Security

Florian Kammüller[(✉)]

Department of Computer Science, Middlesex University London, London, UK
f.kammueller@mdx.ac.uk

Abstract. Refactoring allows changing a program without changing its behaviour from an observer's point of view. To what extent does this invariant of behaviour also preserve security? We show that a program remains secure under refactoring. As a foundation, we use the Decentralized Label Model (DLM) for specifying secure information flows of programs and transition system models for their observable behaviour. On this basis, we provide a bisimulation based formal definition of refactoring and show its correspondence to the formal notion of information flow security (noninterference). This permits us to show security of refactoring patterns that have already been practically explored.

1 Introduction

In distributed systems, we are interested in specifying and verifying security[1] of data values. Usually, values are labelled to indicate their confidentiality level. The labels express the owners and the readers of a value. However, a value in itself is not security critical: everyone may know the value 42 but in association with a specific usage it can become a secret, for example, if 42 is the PIN code of an online banking account. Security models, like the decentralized label model (DLM) [10] we use for the presentation of our framework, assign security labels to the input and output variables (or channels) of a computer program. This enables the analysis of flows of values through this program judging whether certain computations violate the specified secure information flows. This analysis is called Information Flow Control (IFC) [2]. Besides the easy to spot direct flows, e.g., by assignment or parameter passing, there are more subtle cases where "the information flow is disguised as control flow" [1], like in the classical if-then-else example, where the control flow copies the confidential bit x_H to the public y_L.

$$\text{if } x_H = 1 \text{ then } y_L := 1 \text{ else } y_L := 0 \text{ end}$$

Refactoring [4,9] is a technique that is applied in order to improve the internal structure of a software artifact to enhance readability of the code, make it more amenable to extensions, and thus support its maintainability. Integrated Development Environments (IDE) like Eclipse support refactoring.

Our contribution is a correspondence theorem between a formal characterisation of refactoring and a formal characterization of noninterference of a program. Assuming that a program is initially correctly labeled, i.e., permits only

---

[1] For simplicity we concentrate on confidentiality in this paper.

© Springer International Publishing AG 2016
G. Livraga et al. (Eds.): DPM and QASA 2016, LNCS 9963, pp. 238–245, 2016.
DOI: 10.1007/978-3-319-47072-6_17

the labeled information flows, then our theorem can be applied to show that a (proper) refactoring of the program code preserves the security of that program. Thereby, this paper provides a formal basis of what has been introduced by examples [5].

In this paper, we first review the concepts of the decentralized label model (DLM) [10] (Sect. 2). Then, we provide a formal definition of refactoring and information flow security, relating the two by a security preservation theorem (Sect. 3). As a proof of concept, we finally show how our theoretical framework can be applied. The refactoring mechanism "Extract method" for Java Information Flow (Jif) [5] can now be shown to be security preserving by a simple application of our theoretical framework (Sect. 4).

2   Decentralized Label Model — DLM

A value in the DLM model [10] always carries the label of the variable it resides in. Values become labeled when they are read from input variables by that variable's label. If the program *writes* this variable, then the old label of the value assigned to this variable is forgotten and the value becomes reassigned with the new label of the destination. This process is called *relabeling*. To preserve security, information may only flow up: the relabeling must respect the security levels in that a value that has label L_0 can be relabeled with label L_1 iff $L_0 \sqsubseteq L_1$. Writing includes assignment of a value to a variable or passing a value as a parameter to a method call but also implicit flows as described in the if-then-else example above.

2.1   Labels

Every value used or computed in a program execution has an associated label which stands for a set of allowed *flows (owner, reader)* from a principal *owner* to a a principal *reader*. There may be a range of permitted flows for a variable, therefore we accumulate all possible flows into labels. A label is a set of *label components* that summarise the allowed flows for a single owner o, i.e., a component (o, R_K) specifies that the owner o permits all readers $r \in R_K$. A label can have a list of label components. The allowed flows of a label are given as the union of all flows of all components of L and all flows (o, r) for all o for which there is *no* component (o, R_K) with $r \in R_K$ in L. The meaning of this addition to the explicitly stated components in a label is: if a principal o is *not* an owner in the label L, then L describes flows (o, r) for every principal r.

To summarise, a label $L = \{o_0 : R_0; \ldots; o_n : R_n\}$, where $O_L \overset{\text{def}}{=} \{o_i \mid i \in 0..n\}$, denotes the set of flows

$$[\![L]\!] \overset{\text{def}}{=} \{(o_i, r) \mid o_i \in O_L \wedge r \in R_i\} \cup \{(o, r) \mid o \notin O_L\}.$$

For example, for the label $L_{ex} \overset{\text{def}}{=} \{\text{al} : \{\text{eve}\}; \text{bob} : \{\text{al}\}\}$ we have

$$[\![L_{ex}]\!] = \{(\text{al}, \text{al}), (\text{al}, \text{eve}), (\text{bob}, \text{bob}), (\text{bob}, \text{al}), (\text{eve}, \text{eve}), (\text{eve}, \text{al}), (\text{eve}, \text{bob})\}.$$

assuming that al, bob, and eve are all possible principals.

2.2   Label Lattice and Relabeling

Given this interpretation of labels as sets of allowed flows (o, r), the set of labels forms a complete lattice together with the following partial order on labels.

$$L_0 \sqsubseteq L_1 \overset{\text{def}}{=} [\![L_0]\!] \supseteq [\![L_1]\!]$$

The lattice operations join $\sqcup$ and meet $\sqcap$ are defined as follows.

$$L_0 \sqcup L_1 \overset{\text{def}}{=} [\![L_0]\!] \cap [\![L_1]\!]$$
$$L_0 \sqcap L_1 \overset{\text{def}}{=} [\![L_0]\!] \cup [\![L_1]\!]$$

When values flow from one variable with label L_0 to another with label L_1 we call this a relabeling as discussed above; it is allowed if L_1 is equally or more restrictive than L_0, i.e., $L_0 \sqsubseteq L_1$.

The lattice operations *join* ($\sqcup$) and *meet* ($\sqcap$) allow combining labels thus supporting inference of labels for compound expressions.

$$owners(L_1 \sqcup L_2) \quad = owners(L_1) \cup owners(L_2)$$
$$readers(L_1 \sqcup L_2, O) = readers(L_1, O) \cap readers(L_2, O)$$

The dual equations hold for the operation meet ($\sqcap$).

In the following, we assume that all program variables are labelled correctly, i.e., the labels correspond to the actual flows in the programs. In practice, this assumption is enforced by a process of (static) checking.

2.3   Observation and State Transition Model

In the decentralised label model, an observation happens when values are written to output channels (variables) which have a set of readers associated to it. These are the principals who will be able to observe values written to that destination (a channel or variable). The owners assigned to an input variable are the principals whose data was observed in order to obtain that value.

For the system model we follow the classical state transition model mainly used for security modeling, e.g., [6–8]. A system is described by its traces of events. Since we consider a programming system, the events are changes of state variables according to inputs, outputs, and computation steps. Each step in the state transition corresponds to a step in the operational semantics of the programming language. We consider deterministic programming languages with no real parallelism, i.e., events happening in different steps lead to traces where "parallel" events are resolved using interleaving. A system trace in our model is a possibly infinite sequence $s_0 \to s_1 \to s_2 \to \dots$ of maps $s_i : Var \mapsto Val$ from program variables $Var \overset{\text{def}}{=} \{v_0, \dots, v_n\}$ to their values $Val \overset{\text{def}}{=} \{a_0, \dots, a_n\}$. In our system model, we assume that each state is reachable from some initial state s_{init}, i.e., $s_{init} \to^* s_0$. Each variable v_i in the program has a DLM label assigned to it and the transition relation respects the labeling.

3   Security of Refactoring

Let $Var \stackrel{\text{def}}{=} \{v_0, \ldots, v_n\}$ denote the labeled state variables of program P and Q.[2]

We define a map $\mathcal{L}$ that assigns to each variable its label, i.e., set of components.

$$\mathcal{L} : v_i \mapsto \{(o_j, R_j) \mid o_j \in \mathcal{P} \wedge R_j \subseteq \mathcal{P}\}, j \in 0..m, i \in 0..n$$

The indistinguishability relation $\sim_\alpha$ describes that from an observation point α (which is a label) two states $s_0, s_1 : Var \mapsto Val$ look the same, i.e., variables that are at or below α appear equal in s_0, s_1.

$$s_0 \sim_\alpha s_1 \stackrel{\text{def}}{=} \text{dom}(s_0) = \text{dom}(s_1) \wedge \forall v \in Var. \, \mathcal{L}(v) \sqsubseteq \alpha \Rightarrow s_0(v) = s_1(v).$$

Indistinguishability is often called "low-equivalence": only variables that are above α may differ in states that are related. Thus an attacker at level α cannot perceive a difference in different program runs that are due to variables labeled with a more restrictive label (higher in the order $\sqsubseteq$).

We use the highest observation point seeing all variables (in terms of $\sqsubseteq$) to express the program equality that defines a refactoring.

Definition 1 (Refactoring). *Let s_0, t_0 be states in P and Q respectively. Let*

$$Obs \stackrel{\text{def}}{=} \bigsqcup_{i \in 0..n} \mathcal{L}(v_i).$$

Q is a refactoring of P iff
$s_0 \sim_{Obs} t_0$ and $s_0 \rightarrow s_0'$ implies $t_0 \rightarrow^* t_0'$ and $s_0' \sim_{Obs} t_0'$ for some t_0'.

For an attacker we can specify a viewpoint in order to quantify his attack powers. For the sake of the generality of the exposition, we assume a very powerful attacker that is a principal $a \in \mathcal{P}$ with observation point $Att \stackrel{\text{def}}{=} \bigsqcup_{i \in 0..m} (o_i, \{a, o_i\})$. The attacker a is a reader for any owner o_i, i.e., can see data of all owners. The following observation holds for this attacker and for any other choice of an attacker, since we have chosen Obs to be the least upper bound of the label lattice.

Lemma 1

$$Att \sqsubseteq Obs$$

Lemma 2

$$s_0 \sim_{Obs} t_0 \Rightarrow s_0 \sim_{Att} t_0$$

Definition 2 (Security (Noninterference)). *Program P is secure for attacker a with viewpoint Att iff $s_0 \sim_{Att} s_1$ and $s_0 \rightarrow s_0'$ implies $s_1 \rightarrow^* s_1'$ and $s_0' \sim_{Att} s_1'$ for some s_1'.*

---

[2] We should consider differently named bijective sets of variables for P and Q since renaming is also a refactoring but for the sake of simplicity we omit it here.

Lemma 3. *The relations $\sim_\alpha$ and 'P refactors to Q' are equivalence relations, i.e., are reflexive, transitive, and symmetric.*

Lemma 4. *Security and refactoring are defined for the one step transition $s_0 \to s_0'$ but they naturally extend to the reflexive transitive closure $s_0 \to^* s_0'$.*

1. *Let P be secure for α. If $s_0 \sim_\alpha s_1$ and $s_0 \to^* s_0'$, then there exists s_1' such that $s_1 \to^* s_1'$ and $s_0' \sim_\alpha s_1'$.*
2. *Let P refactors to Q. If $s_0 \sim_{Obs} t_0$ and $s_0 \to^* s_0'$, then there exists t_0' such that $t_0 \to^* t_0'$ and $s_0' \sim_{Obs} t_0'$.*

Lemma 5. *Let Q be a refactoring of P. For any state s_0 in Q, there is a state t_0 in P with $s_0 \sim_{Obs} t_0$.*

Theorem 1 (Refactoring is secure). *Let Q be a refactoring of P and let P be secure for a. Then Q is also secure for a.*

Proof. Let P be a program that refactors to Q for Obs and let P be secure for attacker a, i.e., the observation point Att. We need to show that for any s_0, s_1 in Q with $s_0 \sim_{Att} s_1$, if $s_0 \to s_0'$ (see arrow (1) in Fig. 1) then $s_1 \to^* s_1'$ for some s_1' (see arrow (4) in Fig. 1) such that $s_0' \sim_{Att} s_1'$ (d). Lemma 5 shows that, because P refactors to Q, we have t_0 and t_1 in P such that $s_0 \sim_{Obs} t_0$ (i) and $s_1 \sim_{Obs} t_1$ (ii). Lemma 2 immediately implies that then also these states are indistinguishable from the observation point of attacker a, i.e., $s_0 \sim_{Att} t_0$ and $s_1 \sim_{Att} t_1$. (see the left of Fig. 1). Since indistinguishability is symmetric and transitive according to Lemma 3, we can deduce that $t_0 \sim_{Att} t_1$ (iii).

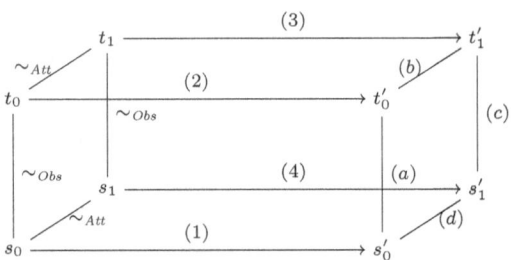

Fig. 1. Proof structure for Theorem 1

Since $s_0 \sim_{Obs} t_0$ and $s_0 \to s_0'$, there exists t_0' such that $t_0 \to^* t_0'$ in P and $t_0' \sim_{Obs} s_0'$ because P refactors to Q ((1), (2) and (a) in Fig. 1).

Since P is secure according to assumption and $t_0 \sim_{Att} t_1$ (iii), we obtain a t_1' with Lemma 4.1 such that $t_1 \to^* t_1'$ and $t_0' \sim_{Att} t_1'$ ((2), (3), and (b) in Fig. 1).

Since P refactors to Q and we have that $t_1 \sim_{Obs} s_1$ (symmetry of $\sim_{Obs}$ and (i)) we obtain a s_1' such that $s_1 \to^* s_1'$ (iv) and $t_1' \sim_{Obs} s_1'$ ((3), (4), and (c) in Fig. 1).

Summarizing we get $s_0' \sim_{Obs} t_0'$, $t_0' \sim_{Att} t_1'$, and $t_1' \sim_{Obs} s_1'$ ((a), (b), and (c) in Fig. 1), hence with Lemmas 2 and 3, we get $s_0' \sim_{Att} s_1'$ ((d) in Fig. 1) and $s_1 \to^* s_1'$ (iv) which finishes the proof.

4 Example

We can show now with our framework that a major refactoring pattern, the "Extract method" refactoring is secure. We first motivate and explain this refactoring and the resulting labeling on an example. With this preparation, we show that the labeling we propose for the refactoring is bisimilar hence secure.

The example is depicted in Fig. 2 showing how Refactoring extracts shared code and puts it into a new method. The labels in the example indicate that the symmetric key skey is owned by bob but can be read also by alice: {B, {A, B}}. The entry and exit levels of the method send and receive are bounds for the entry and exit level of the *program counter (pc)*. A *pc* is a common technique in information flow control originating in Fenton's Data Mark Machine [3]. The *pc* encodes the highest security level that has been reached in all possible control flows leading to the current control state. The program counter *pc* is derived from the labels of the state variables in the static analysis process. This derivation depends on the static analysis rules of a concrete IFC language, like Jif [10].

```
public class secure_node {
  List<<byte>> {B, {A,B}} skey
  public Integer {B, {A,B}}
    send(Integer m; R r):
      {B, {A,B}}{
┌─────────────────────────────────────┐
│ k = skey.subList(0,4);               │
│ s = k^m;                             │
│ skey = skey.subList(0,4).clear();    │
└─────────────────────────────────────┘
    r.put(s);
    }
  public Integer {B, {A,B}}
    receive(Integer c):
      {B, {A,B}}{
┌─────────────────────────────────────┐
│ k = skey.subList(0,4);               │
│ s = k^c;                             │
│ skey = skey.subList(0,4).clear();    │
└─────────────────────────────────────┘
    return s;
    }
}
```

```
public class secure_node {
  List<<byte>> {B, {A,B}} skey
  public Integer {B,{A,B}}
    send(Integer m; R r):
      {B,{A,B}}{
┌─────────────────────────────────────┐
│ s = crypt(m);                        │
└─────────────────────────────────────┘
    r.put(s);
    }
  public Integer {B, {A,B}}
    receive(Integer c):
      {B, {A,B}}{
┌─────────────────────────────────────┐
│ s = crypt(c);                        │
└─────────────────────────────────────┘
    return s;
    }
╔═════════════════════════════════════╗
║ public Integer {B, {A,B}}           ║
║   crypt(Integer t):                 ║
║     {B, {A,B}}{                     ║
║     k = skey.subList(0,4);          ║
║     s = k^t;                        ║
║     skey =                          ║
║       skey.subList(0,4).clear();    ║
║     return s;                       ║
║     }                               ║
╚═════════════════════════════════════╝
}
```

Fig. 2. Symmetric key encrypted messages can be sent by methods send and receive in the Java class secure_node on the left. Symmetric key encryption and decryption is implemented using exclusive or (^) on a code block of size Integer (4 Bytes). Used key-bits are eliminated with clear(). The class can be used for instances to principals Alice and Bob for shared key encryption. Labels are abbreviated for brevity in the code by A for alice and B for bob. Refactoring allows to extract shared code block ("xor"ing an integer and eliminating used key-bits) into new method crypt. Labels are transferred consistently.

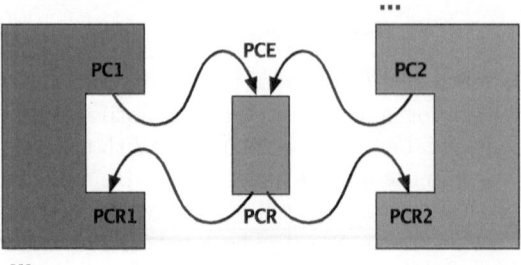

Fig. 3. Refactored program Q with extracted method

Generalising from the example, we need to compare the traces of the program P and the refactored program Q where a common code block has been extracted as depicted in Fig. 3. The markers in the figure show the program counters (pc) at the exit and entry points between two parts of the original program and the extracted code block. In the practical application of refactoring to Jif programs [5] we provided the following rule for determining the correct labels for refactoring a Jif program by extracting a common code block into a new method illustrated in Fig. 3. We chose the entry and exit level of the extracted method such that the entry level is an upper bound to the entry levels of the origin and the exit level is the lower bound of the extracted code [5].

$$\text{PCE} \stackrel{\text{def}}{=} \text{PC1} \sqcup \text{PC2}$$
$$\text{PCR} \stackrel{\text{def}}{=} \text{PCR1} \sqcap \text{PCR2}$$

The labels in the example in Fig. 2 are trivially consistent with the above rule since

$$\{A, \{A, B\}\} \sqcap \{A, \{A, B\}\} = \{A, \{A, B\}\} = \{A, \{A, B\}\} \sqcup \{A, \{A, B\}\}.$$

To justify the security of this rule now in the current framework, we compare the traces of program P with those of the refactored program Q. Let t_P be a trace of P and s_P be a state in that trace corresponding to the program point before the code block to be extracted. Then there is a trace t_Q of Q with an indistinguishable state s_Q before the call to the extracted method, i.e., $s_P \sim_{Obs} s_Q$. Let, in t_P the next state be s'_P, i.e., $t_P = \langle \ldots s_P \to s'_P \ldots \rangle$. The entry level of the extracted code in Q is PCE = PC1 $\sqcup$ PC2 and the pc in the current state s_Q of t_Q is PCi $\sqsubseteq$ PCE for $i \in 1, 2$. Therefore, the execution of Q can proceed and $s_Q \to^* s'_Q$ with $s'_P \sim_{Obs} s'_Q$ (possibly more than one step is necessary due to the method call of the extracted method). The important point is that the choice of the entry levels permits the same execution paths in both programs P and Q. A similar argument shows that the same execution paths are permitted for P and Q at the exit point of the extracted method. Therefore, the programs P and Q are bisimilar with the chosen definition of PCE and PCR, i.e., according to Definition 1 they are a refactoring.

Using Theorem 1, we can thus immediately conclude that the program Q, that is refactored from P by Extract method, is secure if P is.

5   Conclusions

Refactoring [4,9] is a technique of much practical value to software engineering increasing the quality of program code while preserving properties. Therefore, different techniques to improve the quality can be applied and good features preserved.

Security is a difficult property to deal with. Information Flow Control with DLM is a technique operating at the program code level that enables giving precise specification of security. However, DLM is difficult to use for the common programmer. We propose a process of security refactoring, in which program code labelled according to a security policy by a team of programmers and security experts can then subsequently be improved by common programmers *without changing the specified security properties*.

In this paper, we have provided the theoretical foundation for this process.

References

1. Boudol, G., Castellani, I.: Noninterference for concurrent programs. In: Orejas, F., Spirakis, P.G., Leeuwen, J. (eds.) ICALP 2001. LNCS, vol. 2076, pp. 382–395. Springer, Heidelberg (2001). doi:10.1007/3-540-48224-5_32
2. Denning, D.E., Denning, P.J.: Certification of programs for secure information flow. Commun. ACM **20**(7), 504–513 (1977)
3. Fenton, J.S.: Information protection systems. Ph.D. thesis, Univ. Cambridge (1973)
4. Fowler, M.: Refactoring: Improving the Design of Existing Code. Addison Wesley, Boston (2004)
5. Helke, S., Kammüller, F., Probst, C.W.: Secure refactoring with java information flow. In: Garcia-Alfaro, J., Navarro-Arribas, G., Aldini, A., Martinelli, F., Suri, N. (eds.) DPM/QASA -2015. LNCS, vol. 9481, pp. 264–272. Springer, Heidelberg (2016). doi:10.1007/978-3-319-29883-2_19
6. Mantel, H.: On the Composition of Secure Systems. Security and Privacy, Oakland (2002)
7. Mantel, H., Sands, D., Sudbrock, H.: Assumptions and guarantees for compositional noninterference. In: IEEE CSF (2011)
8. Mclean, J.: A general theory of composition for trace sets closed under selective interleaving functions. In: Security and Privacy (1994)
9. Mens, T., Tourvé, T.: A survey of software refactoring. IEEE Trans. Softw. Eng. **30**(2), 126–139 (2004)
10. Myers, A.C., Liskov, B.: A decentralized model for information flow control. In: ACM Symposium on Operating Systems Principles, SOSP 1997 (1997)

Author Index